Robert Schwandl

METROS IN B

GLASGOW Subway
150

Tyne and Wear Metro
136

MANCHESTER
Metrolink
118

BLACKPOOL
Tramway
134

SHEFFIELD
Supertram
112

LIVERPOOL
Merseyrail
126

NOTTINGHAM
Express Transit
106

BIRMINGHAM
Midland Metro
100

DOCKLANDS
Light Railway
86

LONDON
Underground
4

U-Bahnen & Stadtbahnen in Großbritannien
Underground & Light Rail Networks in the U.K.

CROYDON Tramlink
94

Berlin
2006

Robert Schwandl

METROS IN BRITAIN

U-Bahnen & Stadtbahnen in Großbritannien
Underground & Light Rail Networks in the U.K.

U-Bahnen in Europa - Band 2
Metros in Europe - Vol. 2

for Mark & Dean

My sincere thanks are due to:

Thomas Bowman, Peter Courtenay, Iain D.O. Frew, Stuart Neyton, Norbert Reulke, Thomas Schunk, Alexander Seefeldt, Anthony Steer, Olaf Wenke, and especially to Felix Thoma and Brian Hardy.

Robert Schwandl Verlag
Hektorstraße 3
D-10711 Berlin

Tel. 030 - 3759 1284 (0049 - 30 - 3759 1284)
Fax 030 - 3759 1285 (0049 - 30 - 3759 1285)

www.robert-schwandl.de
info@robert-schwandl.de

1. Auflage, 2006

Text © Robert Schwandl
Fotos © Robert Schwandl (wenn nicht anders angegeben | *unless otherwise stated*)

Satz: Robert Schwandl
Druck: Ruksaldruck, Berlin

ISBN 3-936573-12-3

VORWORT

Der zweite Band der Reihe über U-Bahnen in Europa führt uns nach Großbritannien. Hier haben wir den Begriff ‚Metro' sehr weit gefasst und alle in England und Schottland derzeit vorhandenen städtischen Schienenverkehrsmittel mit aufgenommen.

Nachdem in den fünfziger und sechziger Jahren sämtliche Straßenbahnen aus britischen Städten verschwunden waren, gab es in den Neunzigern eine hoffnungsvolle Wiedergeburt. In wenigen Jahren entstanden mehrere moderne Stadtbahnnetze, die in vielen Fällen bestehende Bahntrassen nutzten und somit günstiger zu bauen waren.

Derzeit sieht die Zukunft britischer Stadtbahnen allerdings wieder sehr traurig aus, da die Regierung in London keine Geldmittel für *Light Rail*, geschweige denn für U-Bahnen zur Verfügung stellt. Baufertige Planungen für neue Stadtbahnnetze gibt es für Leeds, Liverpool und South Hampshire (Portsmouth), Erweiterungen der bestehenden Netze sind in Birmingham, Nottingham und Manchester vorgesehen. Durch eine gewisse politische Unabhängigkeit Schottlands werden in den nächsten Jahren einzig der Stadtbahn in Edinburgh Chancen auf Verwirklichung eingeräumt. Bei Redaktionsschluss dieses Buchs sind in Großbritannien im Bereich des städtischen Schienennahverkehrs lediglich die Verlängerung der Docklands Light Railway von King George V bis Woolwich Arsenal und der Abzweig der Piccadilly Line zum Terminal 5 am Flughafen Heathrow in Bau.

In Großbritannien wird der Begriff ‚Metro' inzwischen für alle möglichen Arten von Bahnen verwendet, angefangen von der Stadtbahn in Birmingham bis hin zu den s-bahn-artigen Vorortbahnen in London. Aber am besten ist es, Sie entdecken die Bahnen selbst, wir liefern Ihnen dazu die wichtigsten Eckdaten und zahlreiche Bilder.

Ich wünsche Ihnen eine gute Fahrt!

Robert Schwandl
Berlin, im Februar 2006

ERLÄUTERUNGEN | *EXPLANATORY NOTES*

{22-08-1856 [Stratford –] Leyton – Loughton}	....	Streckeneröffnung vor Übernahme durch die London Underground
		Line opening prior to London Underground service
30-07-1900	Shepherd's Bush – Bank	.... Streckeneröffnung	*Line opening*
24-09-1900	+ Bond Street	.... Neuer Bahnhof auf bestehender Strecke	*New station on existing route*

Es werden nur Strecken aufgelistet, die derzeit in Betrieb sind. | *Only routes in service are listed.*

FOREWORD

This second volume of the 'Metros in Europe' series takes us to Britain, where we have used the term 'metro' in a very wide sense. The book includes all urban railway networks, from the well-known London Underground to the Blackpool Tramway. With almost all tramway systems having disappeared from British cities in the 1950s and 1960s, there was a true renaissance during the 1990s with many modern light rail systems being built. Many of these made use of abandoned railway routes, thus reducing the cost of their construction. At present the future of urban rail in Britain does not look very bright, with no funds being made available by the central government in London. Detailed planning for light rail schemes has been concluded in Leeds, Liverpool and South Hampshire (Portsmouth), and expansion of existing networks has long been planned for Birmingham, Manchester and Nottingham. Due to Scotland being autonomous to a certain extent, the tram project in Edinburgh is the only one with some chance of getting the final go-ahead in the next few years. At the time of writing, the only urban rail projects in Britain currently under construction are the Docklands Light Railway extension from King George V to Woolwich Arsenal, and the Piccadilly Line extension to Heathrow Terminal 5.

In Britain we can see clearly, that the term 'Metro' can be used for any kind of urban railway, from the tramway-like system of Birmingham to high-frequency suburban railways of the London overground network.

We would like to take you for a ride on every urban railway in the U.K. and provide you with the basic details and a large number of photographs.

Have a pleasant journey!

Robert Schwandl
Berlin, February 2006

Inhalt Contents

LONDON

Underground	4
Subsurface Lines	8
Circle Line	10
Hammersmith & City Line	18
Metropolitan Line	20
District Line	26
East London Line	34
Tube Lines	38
Northern Line	40
Central Line	48
Waterloo & City Line	57
Bakerloo Line	58
Piccadilly Line	64
Victoria Line	72
Jubilee Line	78
Docklands Light Railway	86
Croydon Tramlink	94

BIRMINGHAM Midland Metro	100
NOTTINGHAM Express Transit	106
SHEFFIELD Supertram	112
MANCHESTER Metrolink	118
LIVERPOOL Merseyrail	126
BLACKPOOL Tramway	134
NEWCASTLE Tyne & Wear Metro	136
GLASGOW Subway	150

LONDON

London ist die Hauptstadt Großbritanniens und mit ca. 7,4 Mill. Einwohnern in der Region *Greater London* (1579 km²) nach Istanbul, Moskau und Paris die viertgrößte Stadt Europas.

London war die erste Stadt der Welt, in der unterirdische Bahnstrecken gebaut wurden. Die ersten Abschnitte des heutigen *Subsurface*-Netzes mit der *Metropolitan Railway* wurden bereits 1863 in Betrieb genommen, auch wenn diese Linien bis 1905 mit Dampf betrieben wurden. London war aber auch Pionier im Bereich der elektrischen Untergrundbahnen, denn die 1890 eröffnete *City & South London Railway* kann man als erste richtige Metrolinie der Welt betrachten. Der Großteil der heutigen Strecken durch die Innenstadt wurde im ersten Jahrzehnt des 20. Jahrhunderts gebaut, nur die Victoria und die Jubilee Line entstanden später. Ab 1908 wurde für die meisten Linien, obwohl sie von verschiedenen Privatgesellschaften betrieben wurden, der Begriff ‚**UndergrounD**' an den Stationseingängen verwendet. 1933 wurden alle Linien verstaatlicht und als ‚London Underground' Teil von *London Passenger Transport Board*, oder kurz *London Transport*. Im Jahr 2002 wurde die Infrastruktur der U-Bahn nach dem Modell der *Public Private Partnership* an Privatfirmen übergeben, für den Betrieb ist weiterhin *London Underground Ltd* zuständig. Bis 2032 ist das Konsortium *Tube Lines* für die Unterhaltung und die Erneuerung der Jubilee, Northern und Piccadilly Line verantwortlich, die übrigen Linien gingen an *Metronet*. Die East London Line soll 2010 an die staatliche

London is the capital of the United Kingdom of Great Britain and Northern Ireland, and with a population of 7.4 million in what is known as Greater London (1579 sq km), it is Europe's fourth largest city, after Istanbul, Moscow and Paris.

London was the first city in the world to build urban underground railways. The first sections of the present subsurface network, including the original Metropolitan Railway, were brought into service in as early as 1863, although steam locomotives remained in service on these lines until 1905. London was also, however, the pioneer in building electric underground lines, with the 'City & South London Railway' opening in 1890, the first real metro line in the world. Most of the present lines in the central area were built in the first decade of the 20th century, with only the Victoria and the Jubilee Lines having been added later. From 1908, most lines, although operated by various privately owned companies, started adopting the term 'UndergrounD' to be displayed at station entrances. In 1933, all lines were integrated into the newly formed public 'London Passenger Transport Board', or simply 'London Transport'. In 2002, the Underground infrastructure was transferred to two private companies under the Public Private Partnership scheme, although operation of the lines remains with London Underground Ltd. Until 2032, 'Tube Lines' will maintain, renew and upgrade the Jubilee, Northern and Piccadilly Lines, including trains and stations, whereas 'Metronet' will be responsible for the rest of the lines. In 2010, the East London Line is planned to be transferred to Network Rail, the public company in charge of mainline infrastructure around Britain.

The official Underground map shows the network in an extremely distorted form. The design of this diagram is an idea of Harry Beck's from 1931 which ignores the significant differences in distance between stations in the central area and in the suburbs. In the area confined by the Circle Line, the average distance between stations is 780 m (the shortest being between Leicester Square and Covent Garden at 260 m). Outside this area the average is 1440 m between stations (the longest being between Chalfont & Latimer and Chesham at 6.2 km).

LONDON Underground

421 km (181 km unterirdisch | *underground*), 328 Bahnhöfe | *Stations*

Von mehreren Linien befahrene Strecken wurden einmal berechnet, gleichnamige Bahnhöfe auf getrennten Strecken wurden mehrfach gezählt.
Routes shared by different lines were counted once, and stations of the same name on separate routes were counted multiple.

Bahninfrastrukturgesellschaft Network Rail übergeben werden. Auf dem offiziellen Netzplan der Londoner U-Bahn ist das Netz stark verzerrt dargestellt. Den ersten Plan dieser Art schuf Harry Beck im Jahre 1931, dabei bleiben die teils enormen Unterschiede bei den Stationsabständen im Zentralbereich im Vergleich zu den Vororten unberücksichtigt. Innerhalb des von der Circle Line begrenzten Bereichs liegen die Stationen durchschnittlich 780 m voneinander entfernt (der kürzeste Abstand liegt mit 260 m zwischen Leicester Square und Covent Garden). Im äußeren Bereich hingegen ist der mittlere Abstand 1440 m (der längste ist mit 6,2 km zwischen Chalfont & Latimer und Chesham).

Während sich der Großteil des U-Bahnnetzes auf der Nordseite der Themse erstreckt, wird die Südseite von einem dichten Netz von Vorortbahnen erschlossen, was neben den schwierigeren Bodenverhältnissen ein Grund war, warum die U-Bahn kaum in die südlichen Bezirke vorgedrungen ist. Innerhalb des Zentralbereichs, jetzt auch als ‚Zone 1' im 6-Tarifzonen-System bekannt, ist die U-Bahn häufig stark überlastet. Das liegt einerseits an starken Pendlerströmen in bzw. aus der Innenstadt, andererseits aber auch am Mangel an durchgebundenen Vorortlinien, wodurch Millionen Fahrgäste gezwungen sind, an den zahlreichen Kopfbahnhöfen zur U-Bahn umzusteigen, und nicht etwa wie bei einer S-Bahn oder dem Pariser RER direkt in die Innenstadt gebracht werden. Für die erste Strecke dieser Art, die sog. CrossRail zwischen den Bahnhöfen Liverpool Street und Paddington, liegen seit Jahrzehnten detaillierte Pläne vor, doch bislang ist nichts geschehen. Die einzige durchgehende Vorortbahn ist Thameslink, die innerhalb der Zone 1 entlang ihrer Nord-Süd-Strecke sechs Bahnhöfe hat. Derzeit befördert die Londoner U-Bahn, die meist einfach als ‚The Tube' [die Röhre] bezeichnet wird, täglich mehr als drei Millionen Fahrgäste, wobei Victoria der am meisten frequentierte U-Bahnhof ist.

Most of the Underground network lies north of the River Thames, the southern side being dominated by suburban railways. More complicated ground conditions were another reason why no further plans have been made to extend the Underground to the southern boroughs.

The Underground gets very busy in the central area, labelled Zone 1 among six fare zones. This is partly due to heavy peak-hour traffic to and from the centre, but is mostly because of a lack of direct cross-city routes served by suburban railways in an RER or S-Bahn manner. Millions of passengers are forced to change from suburban trains at a number of termini to continue their journey into the centre proper on one of the Tube lines. The first of several such links, aptly branded CrossRail, to link Paddington and Liverpool Street mainline stations has been in the pipeline for decades, but nothing has of yet come of it. The only suburban route through the central area is Thameslink, with six stations within Zone 1 along its through-running north-south routes.

At present, the London Underground, or simply ‘the Tube', carries over 3 million passengers a day, with Victoria being the busiest of all Underground stations.

(Photos top left and bottom right by Thomas Schunk)

London Underground	
Service Update	
Time: 10:58 Date: 20 September 2005	
Bakerloo line	Good Service
Central line	Good Service
Circle line	**MINOR DELAYS**
District line	Good Service
East London line	Good Service
Hammersmith and City line	**PART SUSPENDED**
Jubilee line	Good Service
Metropolitan line	Good Service
Northern line	**MINOR DELAYS**
Piccadilly line	Good Service
Victoria line	Good Service
Waterloo and City line	Good Service

) the clockwise service owing to a faulty train ; H&C line - P

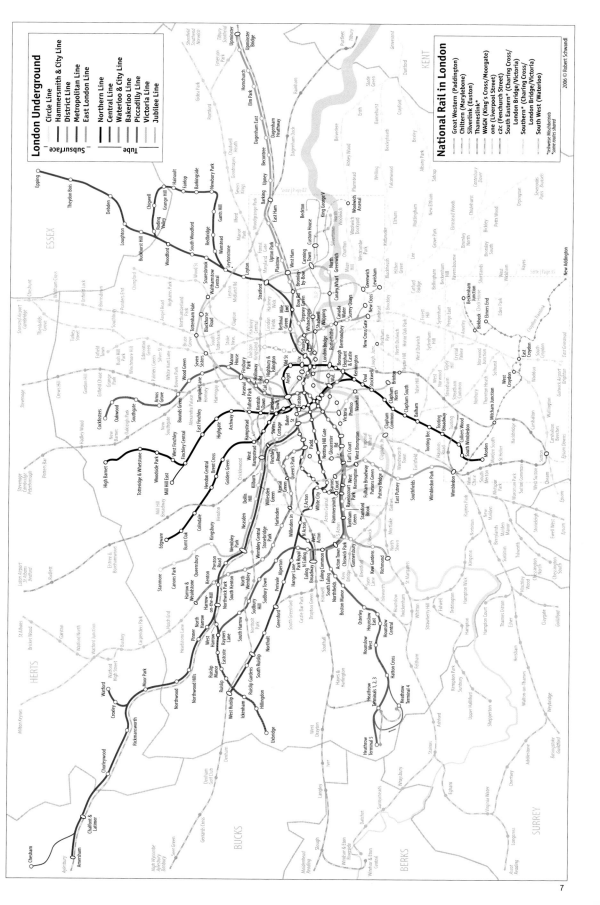

The oldest lines of the present London Underground network were built at low depth (about 5-10 m) by the cut-and-cover method and are therefore referred to as the 'subsurface lines'. In this method a trench is first dug from the surface, then the tunnel floor and walls are built, before finally the route is covered and the surface reinstated. This method is mostly used for tunnels running under major roads, although for the first underground routes through London many properties had to be demolished, and after completion of the tunnel, reconstructed. This method, though cheaper, has become less popular worldwide as it causes long disruptions at the surface.

The following lines constitute the London Underground subsurface network:

- Circle Line
- Hammersmith & City Line
- Metropolitan Line
- District Line
- East London Line

Die ältesten Untergrundbahnstrecken wurden in London in geringer Tiefe (ca. 5-10 m) in offener Bauweise gebaut, sie werden deshalb als *Subsurface Lines* (Unterpflasterbahnen), im Gegensatz zu den *Tube Lines* (Röhrenbahnen), bezeichnet. Dabei wird erst ein Graben geöffnet, dann die Tunnelsohle und die Seitenwände errichtet, das Ganze abgedeckt und schließlich die Oberfläche wieder hergestellt. Diese Bauweise ist gut für Strecken entlang breiter Straßen geeignet (und wurde in abgewandelter Form meist bei der Berliner U-Bahn angewandt), allerdings mussten bei der Londoner U-Bahn auch sehr viele Gebäude abgerissen und nach Fertigstellung des Tunnels wieder aufgebaut werden. Obwohl diese Bauweise etwas billiger ist, wird sie heute weltweit immer weniger angewandt, weil die Beeinträchtigungen an der Oberfläche zu groß sind.

Zu den Londoner *Subsurface Lines* gehören die folgenden Linien:

- Circle Line
- Hammersmith & City Line
- Metropolitan Line
- District Line
- East London Line

Außer der East London Line sind alle andere *Subsurface*-Lines miteinander verbunden und fahren auf der Circle Line, der Ringlinie, auf denselben Gleisen. Das Tunnelprofil ist ähnlich wie bei einer richtigen Eisenbahn, wodurch auch wesentlich geräumigere Fahrzeuge als auf den *Tube Lines* eingesetzt werden können.

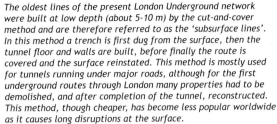

① C-Zug | *C-Stock* (Wimbledon – Edgware Road)
② D-Zug | *D-Stock* (Turnham Green > Gunnersbury)
③ A-Zug | *A-Stock* (Hillingdon)

Except for the East London Line, the subsurface lines are interlaced, sharing the same tracks particularly along the Circle Line, the centrepiece of the system. The tunnel profile is similar to that of mainline railways and the rolling stock used is notably larger than that of tube lines. Cars of A stock (Metropolitan Line) are 2.95 m wide, 16.17 m long and 3.69 m high, those of C stock (Circle and Hammersmith & City Lines) are 2.92 m wide, 16.03 m long (trailers 14.94 m) and 3.69 m high, and cars of D stock (District Line) are 2.85 m wide, 18.37 m long and 3.62 m high. In comparison, the average tube stock is only 2.63 m wide, 16.09-17.77 m long and 2.88 m high, and thus travelling on subsurface lines is certainly more comfortable. For further details about London Underground rolling stock refer to Brian Hardy's publication listed on page 158.

Both subsurface and tube stock is largely compatible outside tunnels, and shared service is provided on the Rayners Lane - Uxbridge section as well as on a short stretch around Ealing Common. With the floor height of subsurface trains being 980 mm, and that of tube trains only 610 mm, a compromise platform height had to be chosen at shared stations.

Die A-Züge auf der Metropolitan Line sind 2,95 m breit, 16,17 m lang und 3,69 m hoch, die C-Züge auf der Circle und Hammersmith & City Line sind 2,92 m breit, 16,03 m lang (Beiwagen 14,94 m) und 3,69 m hoch, und die D-Züge der District Line sind 2,85 m breit, 18,37 m lang und 3,62 m hoch. Im Gegensatz dazu sind die *Tube*-Züge nur 2,63 m breit, 16,09-17,77 m lang und 2,88 m hoch, so dass man sich vorstellen kann, dass eine Fahrt auf einer *Subsurface Line* bequemer ist. Für weitere Details zum Wagenpark der Londoner U-Bahn empfehlen wir das umfangreiche Werk von Brian Hardy (siehe Literaturverzeichnis Seite 158).

Außerhalb der Tunnelstrecken sind die Fahrzeuge beider Profile miteinander kompatibel, so dass auf einigen Strecken auch ein Mischbetrieb stattfindet (Rayners Lane - Uxbridge, und bei Ealing Common). Da die Fußbodenhöhe der *Subsurface*-Züge bei 980 mm, die der *Tube*-Züge aber nur bei 610 mm liegt, musste an gemeinsam bedienten Bahnhöfen eine mittlere Bahnsteighöhe gewählt werden.

Beide Teilnetze haben eine Spurweite von 1435 mm. Die Stromzufuhr mit 630 V Gleichstrom erfolgt über ein 2-Stromschienen-System, eine außenliegende Stromschiene als Hinleiter (+) und eine zwischen den Gleisen liegende als Rückleiter (–).

Mit einer Länge von 147 km (davon sind nur etwa 20% unterirdisch) stellt das *Subsurface*-Netz etwa ein Drittel des gesamten Londoner U-Bahnnetzes dar.

Bis 2010 soll die East London Line sowohl im Süden als auch im Norden verlängert (siehe S. 34) und danach an Network Rail übergeben werden. Auf der Metropolitan Line ist eine kurze Verbindung zwischen Croxley und Watford Junction größtenteils entlang bestehender Eisenbahnstrecken geplant.

① C-Zug | *C-Stock* (Wimbledon – Edgware Road)
② Innenraum eines D-Zugs vor der Modernisierung |
Inside D-Stock before refurbishment

(Photo Thomas Schunk)

Both systems have 1435 mm standard gauge and use two power rails, the positive rail lying on the outside and the negative between the tracks; traction voltage is 630 V dc.

With a total length of 147 km, the subsurface network makes up about one third of the entire Underground network, although only about 20 % of the routes served by these lines are actually underground (mostly the Circle Line plus short sections of some branches).

At present, there are plans to extend the East London Line in both directions (see p. 34) and transfer it to Network Rail in 2010. On the Metropolitan Line, a link from Croxley to Watford Junction is planned, running mostly along the existing mainline tracks.

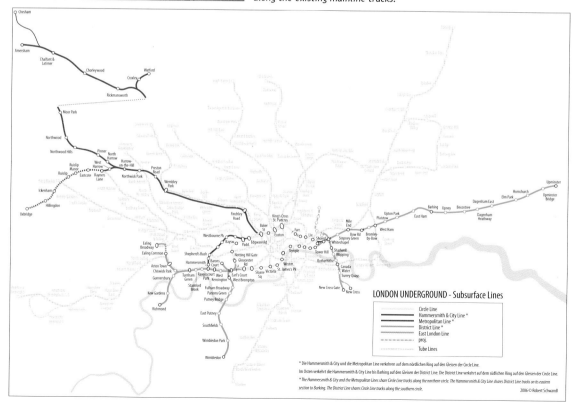

LONDON UNDERGROUND - Subsurface Lines

— Circle Line
— Hammersmith & City Line *
— Metropolitan Line *
— District Line *
— East London Line
‑ ‑ proj.
······· Tube Lines

* Die Hammersmith & City und die Metropolitan Line verkehren auf dem nördlichen Ring auf den Gleisen der Circle Line.
Im Osten verkehrt der Hammersmith & City Line bis Barking auf den Gleisen der District Line. Die District Line verkehrt auf dem südlichen Ring auf den Gleisen der Circle Line.
* *The Hammersmith & City and the Metropolitan Lines share Circle Line tracks along the northern circle. The Hammersmith & City Lines shares District Line tracks on its eastern section to Barking. The District Line shares Circle Line tracks along the southern circle.*

2006 © Robert Schwandl

Die Circle Line (Ringlinie) erschien als solche erst 1949 auf dem Netzplan der Londoner U-Bahn, obwohl sie durch die ältesten U-Bahn-Tunnel der Welt fährt. Der nördliche Teil der Ringstrecke wurde bereits 1863 eröffnet. Damals fuhren Dampfzüge von Paddington im Westen bis nach Farringdon in der City. Die als *Metropolitan Railway* bezeichnete Strecke wurde bald an beiden Enden verlängert und bekam mehrere Äste. Wenig später begann die *Metropolitan District Railway* mit dem Bau einer Strecke zwischen South Kensington und Westminster, und von dort entlang der Themse weiter in Richtung City. Beide Bahngesellschaften sollten sich bald darauf zusammenschließen, stattdessen wurden sie immer mehr zu Konkurrenten, vor allem nachdem 1884 der gemeinsame Betrieb auf der Ringstrecke begonnen hatte.
Die Circle Line ist bis auf kurze Abschnitte südlich vom Bahnhof High Street Kensington und im Bereich von Farringdon fast völlig unterirdisch. Mehrere Stationen, wie z.B. Paddington, Sloane

The Circle Line as such only appeared on the London Underground map in 1949, although the route it serves includes the first underground sections ever built. The northern part of the circular route dates back to 1863, when the first steam-powered trains began running under London roads from Paddington in the west to Farringdon in the City. This route became known as the 'Metropolitan Railway', and was subsequently extended at each end, with several branches. Soon after, the 'Metropolitan District Railway' began building its first route, which ran from South Kensington to Westminster and then along the north shore of the River Thames. Both companies were to be merged soon after, but this never happened. Instead, they were actually competing when shared operation along the full circle began in 1884.
The Circle Line is mostly underground, except for short stretches south of High Street Kensington station and in the Farringdon area. Several stations lie in a partly open cutting (e.g. Padding-

LONDON Underground - Circle Line

20.5 km (~ 19 km unterirdisch | underground), 27 Bahnhöfe | Stations

Datum	Strecke
10-01-1863	Edgware Road - Farringdon
23-12-1865	Farringdon - Moorgate
01-10-1868	Edgware Road - Gloucester Road
24-12-1868	Gloucester Road - Westminster
30-05-1870	Westminster - Blackfriars
03-07-1871	Blackfriars - Mansion House
12-07-1875	Moorgate - Liverpool Street
18-11-1876	Liverpool Street - Aldgate
25-09-1882	Aldgate - Tower Hill
06-10-1884	Tower Hill - Mansion House

1905 elektrischer Betrieb | electric service

Square oder South Kensington, liegen in einem offenen Einschnitt. Entlang der Strecke gibt es außerdem bis heute zahlreiche Öffnungen, die ursprünglich zum Dampfablassen nötig waren. Während die Circle Line im Norden hauptsächlich unter breiten Straßenzügen und im Südosten entlang der Themse verläuft, ist die Streckenführung an anderen Abschnitten weniger leicht nachvollziehbar, da die Trasse an vielen Stellen überbaut wurde.

Gegenwärtig wird die Circle Line gemeinsam mit der Hammersmith & City Line betrieben. Auf beiden Linien werden C-Züge eingesetzt, die 1969 bzw. 1977 von Metro-Cammell in Birmingham geliefert wurden. Diese Fahrzeuge sind 2,92 m breit, 16 m lang (Beiwagen sind 15 m lang) und 3,69 m hoch. Die 6-Wagen-Züge wurden von 1991 bis 1994 modernisiert. Der Betriebshof für die 46 C-Züge (davon elf von der District Line) befindet sich in Hammersmith.

Tagsüber verkehrt die Circle Line alle 8 Minuten. Fast die gesamte Strecke der Circle Line wird von anderen Linien mitbenutzt, im Norden von der Hammersmith & City Line und von der Metropolitan Line, und im Süden und Westen von der District Line, so dass an jedem Bahnhof alle paar Minuten ein Zug fährt. Alle sechs Verzweigungen entlang der Ringstrecke sind niveaugleich, so dass es bei vier ineinander verflochtenen Linien immer wieder zu Behinderungen und Verspätungen kommen kann.

Die Circle Line verbindet alle wichtigen Fernbahnhöfe, außer Waterloo und London Bridge, die auf der Südseite der Themse liegen. Eine Fahrt auf dem gesamten Ring dauert etwa eine Stunde.

ton, Sloane Square and South Kensington). There are still numerous openings along the route, these initially being necessary to allow the steam produced by the locomotives to escape. Whereas the northern part of the Circle runs along major roads, and the southeastern along the River Thames, other parts were later built over and the alignment is not clearly visible from the surface.

At present, the Circle Line is operated together with the Hammersmith & City Line. Both lines share the C stock, which was manufactured by Metro-Cammell in Birmingham and delivered in two batches in 1969 and 1977. They are 2.92 m wide, 3.69 m high and 16 m long (trailers 15 m). These 6-car trains were refurbished between 1991 and 1994. The depot for the 46 trains (including 11 for the District) is located at Hammersmith.

During the day, Circle Line trains operate every 8 minutes. Almost the entire Circle Line route is shared by other lines, the Metropolitan and the Hammersmith & City Lines on the northern side and the District Line on the southern and western sides, with trains every few minutes at all stations. All six junctions along the circle are level, which inevitably makes operation of four interlaced lines very complicated and often causes delays.

The Circle Line links all mainline termini spread around Central London, except Waterloo and London Bridge, which lie on the south bank of the River Thames. A trip around the full circle takes about one hour.

Barbican (Photo Brian Hardy)

At **Baker Street** ①②, the Circle and Hammersmith & City Lines use the original station opened in 1863 on the world's first urban underground line, while the Metropolitan Line has a separate 4-track station at the northern side, lying partly in the open. All lines converge just east of Baker Street station at a flat junction. Although later extended, **Great Portland Street** station ③ is preserved in its original style. The following stations along the first underground route have been extensively rebuilt during the last 140 years. **Euston Square** station ④ lies some 400 m from Euston mainline station, and transfer to the tube lines is easier at **King's Cross St. Pancras**. **Farringdon** ⑤⑥, located in a partly open cutting, was originally the terminus of the 1863 line, but was resited in 1865. Thameslink trains stop here at parallel platforms at a slightly lower level.

Am U-Bahnhof **Baker Street** ①② benutzen die Circle und die Hammersmith & City Line den originalen Bahnhof von 1863. Die Metropolitan Line hält in einem eigenen, teilweise nach oben offenen viergleisigen Bahnhof auf der Nordseite. Östlich von Baker Street laufen alle Strecken niveaugleich zusammen. Bis auf eine spätere Bahnsteigverlängerung ist der Bahnhof **Great Portland Street** ③ noch weitgehend in seinem Ursprungszustand zu sehen, die folgenden Stationen wurden jedoch im Laufe der letzten 140 Jahre mehrmals umgebaut. **Euston Square** ④ liegt ca. 400 m vom Fernbahnhof Euston, das Umsteigen zu den anderen U-Bahn-Linien kann am Bahnhof **King's Cross St. Pancras** bequemer erfolgen. Die im Einschnitt liegende Station **Farringdon** ⑤⑥ war 1863 der östliche Endpunkt der ersten U-Bahnstrecke. An den parallelen Bahnsteigen halten die Züge der Thameslink.

Die Circle Line verbindet fast alle Kopfbahnhöfe, darunter auch **Moorgate** ① und **Liverpool Street** ②. Zwischen Liverpool Street und Tower Hill befindet sich ein Gleisdreieck mit niveaugleichen Kreuzungen, auf dem westlichen Schenkel liegt die viergleisige Station **Aldgate** ③. Die Circle Line benutzt hier die äußeren Gleise, während die Metropolitan Line auf den inneren wenden kann. Die Station **Tower Hill** ④ wurde 1967 nach Osten verschoben und liegt wieder an der Stelle der früheren Station ‚Tower of London', die aber nur von 1882 bis 1884 auf der *Metropolitan Railway* in Betrieb war. Der U-Bahnhof **Monument** ⑤⑥ wurde in den neunziger Jahren renoviert. Er ist über Rolltreppen und Fußgängertunnel mit dem U-Bahnhof Bank verbunden, so dass man zu vier weiteren Linien, darunter die Docklands Light Railway, umsteigen kann.

The Circle Line links almost all mainline railway termini, including **Moorgate** ① and **Liverpool Street** ②. Between the latter and Tower Hill there is a track triangle with flat junctions, with the 4-track *Aldgate* station ③ being squeezed in on the western side of it. Circle Line trains use the outer platforms, while Metropolitan Line trains reverse on the inner tracks. The present **Tower Hill** station ④ replaced the former station in 1967, which lay a little further west. The present location coincides with an early station named The Tower of London, which was in service on the Metropolitan Railway from 1882 until 1884. **Monument** station ⑤⑥ was refurbished during the 1990s. It is linked by escalators and pedestrian tunnels to Bank station, thus providing transfer to four different lines, including the DLR.

(Photo ① Brian Hardy)

Cannon Street station is only about 300 m west of Monument and open only during daytime hours on Mondays to Saturdays. Another 300 m further west is the 3-track **Mansion House** station, available as a terminus for some services.
As at Farringdon, interchange to London's only cross-city mainline service, Thameslink, is provided at **Blackfriars** ①. From here the route continues along the north bank of the River Thames to Westminster, passing through the well-preserved **Temple** ②③ station. **Westminster** station ④ was totally rebuilt during the 1990s in conjunction with the Jubilee Line extension and now boasts a concrete-stainless steel-glass design. The London Underground's head office is located above **St. James's Park** station ⑤. **Victoria** ⑥ is one of the busiest stations along the Circle and District Lines.

Der U-Bahnhof **Cannon Street** liegt nur ca. 300 m westlich von Monument und ist nur tagsüber Montag bis Samstag geöffnet. Weitere 300 m westlich befindet sich die Station **Mansion House**, wo ein drittes Gleis für außerplanmäßiges Kehren zur Verfügung steht. Am U-Bahnhof **Blackfriars** ① kann man zur Thameslink, Londons einziger s-bahn-artiger Vorortbahn, umsteigen.
Die U-Bahnstrecke führt von hier weiter am Nordufer der Themse entlang. Auf diesem Abschnitt liegt der gut erhaltene Bahnhof **Temple** ②③. Der U-Bahnhof **Westminster** ④ wurde im Zuge der Bauarbeiten für die Verlängerung der Jubilee Line in den neunziger Jahren fast vollständig im Beton-Glas-Edelstahl-Stil neu gebaut. Das Hauptverwaltungsgebäude der U-Bahn befindet sich über dem U-Bahnhof **St. James's Park** ⑤. **Victoria** ⑥ gehört zu den am meisten frequentierten Stationen der Circle Line.

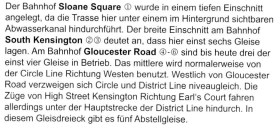

Der Bahnhof **Sloane Square** ① wurde in einem tiefen Einschnitt angelegt, da die Trasse hier unter einem im Hintergrund sichtbaren Abwasserkanal hindurchführt. Der breite Einschnitt am Bahnhof **South Kensington** ②③ deutet an, dass hier einst sechs Gleise lagen. Am Bahnhof **Gloucester Road** ④-⑥ sind bis heute drei der einst vier Gleise in Betrieb. Das mittlere wird normalerweise von der Circle Line Richtung Westen benutzt. Westlich von Gloucester Road verzweigen sich Circle und District Line niveaugleich. Die Züge von High Street Kensington Richtung Earl's Court fahren allerdings unter der Hauptstrecke der District Line hindurch. In diesem Gleisdreieck gibt es fünf Abstellgleise.

Sloane Square station ① was built in a deep open cutting to cross under the Ranelagh Sewer, which now flows inside a bridge-like culvert visible in the background. *South Kensington* station ②③ lies in a wide cutting, which originally had six tracks. At *Gloucester Road* station ④-⑥, three of the four original tracks are still in use today, the central track normally being used by westbound Circle Line trains only. West of Gloucester Road station, eastbound District Line trains converge on a flat junction. Trains from High Street Kensington to Earl's Court dive under the main District Line tracks. Five sidings are located within the triangular junction.

High Street Kensington station ①-③ *lies within a shopping mall, with about two thirds of the platforms' length in the open. There are four platform faces, the two western terminating tracks normally being used by the shuttle trains operating from here to Kensington Olympia.*
Notting Hill Gate station ④, *where interchange with the Central Line is provided, is preserved in almost its original form, including the overall vaulted glass roof, once a feature of many stations on the early Metropolitan Railway.*
North of Notting Hill Gate the Circle Line turns east and runs parallel to the Central Line for a short stretch. **Bayswater** ⑤⑥ *station lies only about 200 m from Queensway station on the Central Line.*

Der Bahnhof **High Street Kensington** ①-③ ist in einem älteren Einkaufszentrum integriert. Etwa zwei Drittel der Bahnsteiglänge liegen im Freien. Von den vier Gleisen enden die beiden westlichen stumpf und dienen vor allem den Shuttle-Zügen nach Kensington Olympia.
Notting Hill Gate ④, wo man zur Central Line umsteigen kann, ist noch weitgehend im Ursprungszustand erhalten. Dazu gehört ein Glasdach auf voller Länge, wie es anfangs an vielen Bahnhöfen der *Metropolitan Railway* zu sehen war.
Nördlich von Notting Hill Gate biegt die Circle Line Richtung Osten ab und fährt ein Stück parallel zur Central Line. Der Bahnhof **Bayswater** ⑤⑥ liegt nur etwa 200 m vom U-Bahnhof Queensway an der Central Line entfernt.

Die Station **Paddington** ①-③ an der Circle Line liegt parallel zur Praed Street vor dem Fernbahnhof, während sich die gleichnamige Station an der Hammersmith & City Line nördlich neben den Fernbahngleisen befindet. Beide Strecken vereinigen sich niveaugleich westlich des Bahnhofs **Edgware Road** ④⑤. Diese viergleisige Station liegt im Einschnitt und hat zwei Abstellgleise. Hier endet die District Line von Wimbledon kommend. Diese Teillinie der District Line wird mit C-Zügen der Circle bzw. Hammersmith & City Line befahren.

*Paddington station ①-③ on the Circle Line is located in front of the mainline station, parallel to Praed Street, whereas the other Paddington station on the Hammersmith & City Line lies at the northern side and parallel to the mainline tracks. Both routes merge at a flat junction west of **Edgware Road** station ④⑤. Edgware Road is a 4-track station in an open cutting, with two sidings. This station is the terminus for District Line services from Wimbledon, which are actually operated with Circle Line / Hammersmith & City Line C stock.*

Up until 1990, the Hammersmith & City Line was shown on maps as part of the Metropolitan Line. It is now operated together with the Circle Line and the only section not shared with other lines is from Edgware Road to Hammersmith. The original 'Hammersmith & City Railway', which was totally built on the surface, dates back to 1864. As with the first tunnel section between Paddington and Farringdon, the western extension was built to standard and broad gauge to allow through service on the broad-gauge Great Western Railway. When opened there were only two intermediate stations, Ladbroke Grove and Shepherd's Bush (which was relocated further north in 1914). Until 1940 there was a link from Latimer Road to Kensington Olympia (formerly Addison Road) on the West London Railway. At Hammersmith, the original terminus was located slightly to the north of the present station

Barking

Bis 1990 wurde die Hammersmith & City Line auf den Netzplänen als Teil der Metropolitan Line dargestellt. Die Linie wird heute gemeinsam mit der Circle Line betrieben. Der einzige nur von dieser Linie befahrene Abschnitt liegt zwischen Edgware Road und Hammersmith. Die ursprüngliche, völlig an der Oberfläche errichtete *Hammersmith & City Railway* wurde 1864 eröffnet. Wie auf den ersten Tunnelstrecken zwischen Paddington und Farringdon lag hier damals ein 3-Schienen-Gleis, um durchgehenden Verkehr auf der früher breitspurigen *Great Western Railway* zu ermöglichen. Bei Inbetriebnahme gab es auf dieser Strecke nur zwei Zwischenbahnhöfe, nämlich Ladbroke Grove und Shepherd's Bush (letzterer wurde 1914 weiter nördlich neu gebaut und ein weiterer Bahnhof Goldhawk Road eingefügt). Bis 1940 gab es eine Verbindung von Latimer Road nach Kensington Olympia (vormals Addison Road) an der West London Railway. In Hammersmith wurde der ursprüngliche Endbahnhof 1868 etwas nach Süden verschoben, als eine Verbindungskurve zwischen Addison Road und Richmond in Betrieb genommen wurde, die eine Haltestelle Hammersmith Grove Road unmittelbar westlich des heutigen Endbahnhofs hatte (mehr über den Richmond-Ast unter District Line).

Derzeit fährt die Hammersmith & City Line in Hammersmith alle 8 Minuten Richtung Barking ab, wobei jeder zweite Zug entweder in Whitechapel (tagsüber) oder Plaistow (in Spitzenzeiten) endet. Sonntags verkehren alle Zügen nur bis Whitechapel.
Von 1908 bis 1959 gab es in der Nähe der Station White City (vormals Wood Lane) auf der Central Line eine gleichnamige Station auf der Hammersmith & City Line, die allerdings von 1914 bis 1920 geschlossen war. Da das Gebiet zwischen den beiden Shepherd's Bush-Bahnhöfen und White City derzeit neu bebaut wird, soll 2007 auch an der Hammersmith & City Line wieder ein Halt entstehen.

LONDON Underground - Hammersmith & City Lin
25.4 km (~ 12 km unterirdisch | *underground*), 28 Bahnhöfe | *Stations*
19.4 km gemeinsam mit | *shared with* Circle/Metropolitan and District Lines

{31-03-1858	Bromley-by-Bow – Barking}
10-01-1863	Paddington – Farringdon
13-06-1864	Paddington – Hammersmith
23-12-1865	Farringdon – Moorgate
01-02-1866	+ Westbourne Park
16-12-1868	+ Latimer Road
30-10-1871	+ Royal Oak
12-07-1875	Moorgate – Liverpool Street
18-11-1876	Liverpool Street – Aldgate
06-10-1884	Liverpool Street – Whitechapel
02-06-1902	Whitechapel – Bromley-by-Bow – Barking
11-06-1902	+ Bow Road
23-06-1902	+ Stepney Green
01-04-1914	+ Goldhawk Road
.... 2007	+ White City

1905/06 elektrischer Betrieb | *electric service*

until 1868, when a link between Addison Road on the West London Railway and Richmond was opened, with Hammersmith Grove Road station just to the west of the present station (see District Line for Richmond branch).
At present, Hammersmith & City Line trains leave Hammersmith every 8 minutes for Whitechapel (off-peak) or Plaistow (peak), with every other train continuing to Barking. On Sundays all trains terminate at Whitechapel.
From 1908 until 1959, though closed from 1914 until 1920, there was a station at White City, located near the present station on the Central Line. As the area between the two Shepherd's Bush stations and White City is currently under full redevelopment a new station is expected to open here in 2007.

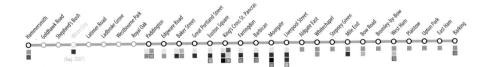

The western leg of the Hammersmith & City Line diverges from the Circle Line at Praed Street junction, which lies between **Edgware Road** and **Paddington** ①. The latter is located at the northern side of the mainline station. From here the route continues along the northern side of the Great Western Mainline. After serving **Royal Oak**, trains dive under the mainline tracks to reach **Westbourne Park** ②. **Shepherd's Bush** ③ station is located some 500 m from the station of the same name on the Central Line.

The terminus **Hammersmith** ④-⑥ lies at the northern side of the busy Hammersmith Broadway, which transferring passengers have to cross to get to the Hammersmith station on the District and Piccadilly Lines. The depot for the C stock can be seen to the east of the line just north of Hammersmith.

Der westliche Ast der Hammersmith & City Line zweigt von der Circle Line an der Praed Street zwischen den Bahnhöfen **Edgware Road** und **Paddington** ① ab. Letzterer liegt an der Nordseite des Fernbahnhofs. Die Strecke führt erst an der Nordseite der Fernbahngleise Richtung Westen. Nach dem Bahnhof **Royal Oak** tauchen die Züge der Hammersmith & City Line unter der Fernbahn hindurch und erreichen **Westbourne Park** ②. Der Bahnhof **Shepherd's Bush** ③ liegt etwa 500 m vom gleichnamigen Bahnhof auf der Central Line entfernt. Der Endbahnhof **Hammersmith** ④-⑥ befindet sich auf der Nordseite des stark befahrenen Hammersmith Broadway, welchen die Fahrgäste überqueren müssen, um in die District oder Piccadilly Line umzusteigen. Der Betriebshof für die C-Züge ist östlich der Trasse nördlich von Hammersmith zu sehen.

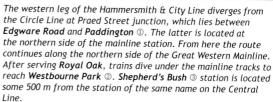

Croxley

The present Metropolitan Line covers most services formerly provided by the Metropolitan Railway, which began operating along the world's first urban underground route between Paddington and Farringdon in 1863 (see Circle Line).

The original Metropolitan Railway began to grow in all directions (see tables on page 10 and 18 for details about routes shared with the Circle and Hammersmith & City Lines in the central area). The first stretch now exclusively used by the Metropolitan Line was opened between Baker Street and Swiss Cottage in 1868, with intermediate stations at St. John's Wood Road and Marlborough Road. This branch was initially only single-track, with passing loops at stations. It was doubled during the 1870s, when the Metropolitan Railway was extended as a surface railway towards the northwest, running mainly through still sparsely populated areas. By 1889 it had reached Chesham, and in 1892

Die heutige Metropolitan Line umfasst den Großteil der Strecken, die einst von der *Metropolitan Railway* befahren wurden. Darunter war die erste städtische Untergrundbahn der Welt (1863) zwischen Paddington und Farringdon (siehe Circle Line).

Die *Metropolitan Railway* wurde schnell in alle Richtungen verlängert (siehe S. 10 und 18 für die Abschnitte, die gemeinsam mit der Circle und der Hammersmith & City Line befahren werden). Der älteste Abschnitt, der heute ausschließlich von der Metropolitan Line benutzt wird, wurde 1868 von Baker Street bis Swiss Cottage eröffnet. Auf dieser anfangs nur eingleisigen Strecke gab es zwei Zwischenstationen, St. John's Wood Road und Marlborough Road, an denen jeweils auch ein Ausweichgleis vorhanden war. Die Strecke wurde in den siebziger Jahren des 19. Jahrhunderts zweigleisig ausgebaut, als die *Metropolitan Railway* Richtung Nordwesten verlängert wurde, damals größtenteils durch unbebautes Gebiet. Bereits 1889 fuhren die Züge bis Chesham und 1892 bis Aylesbury (ca. 60 km von Baker Street). In Aylesbury trafen sie auf die Züge der *Manchester, Sheffield and Lincolnshire Railway*, welche ab 1899, jetzt als *Great Central Railway*, zum neuen Kopfbahnhof Marylebone in der Nähe von Baker Street fuhren. Das Gebiet entlang der *Metropolitan Railway* wurde bald als ‚Metroland' bekannt, denn viele Siedlungsprojekte wurden direkt von der Bahngesellschaft vorangetrieben. Bis 1935/36 fuhren die Züge der *Metropolitan Railway* zu weit entfernten Zielen wie Brill oder Verney Junction, beide etwa 20 km westlich von Aylesbury.

Aylesbury (about 60 km from Baker Street), where it was linked to the 'Manchester, Sheffield and Lincolnshire Railway' from 1899, which from then on, now as the 'Great Central Railway', started mainline services to the newly built Marylebone terminus near Baker Street station. The area along the Metropolitan Railway soon became known as Metro-Land, with many housing estates being promoted directly by the railway company. Until 1935/36, Metropolitan steam trains served such remote destinations as Brill and Verney Junction, each about 20 km west of Aylesbury.

In 1904 an 11 km branch was opened from Harrow to Uxbridge, with several stations being added at a later date as the population grew in the area. This branch was actually promoted by the District Railway as an extension of their line from Ealing (now served by the Piccadilly Line); from 1910 it was served by both companies. In 1905 electric service began on both the original underground line and the surface route to Uxbridge. Whereas EMUs with saloon stock cars began operating to Uxbridge, destinations northwest of Harrow were served by loco-hauled trains with compartment carriages, the electric locomotives being swapped for steam at Harrow.

As service frequencies increased it became necessary to quadruple the tracks between Finchley Road and Wembley Park, which was done in 1913/15; widening the tunnel section down to Baker Street was still considered not financially viable. During the 1920s electric operation was extended to Rickmansworth and a 3 km branch opened to Watford, though with a terminus located at the western edge of that town. Soon after, another pair of tracks was added to the

Uxbridge

1904 wurde ein 11 km langer Abzweig von Harrow nach Uxbridge eröffnet. Mehrere Stationen wurden erst später eingefügt, nachdem die Bebauung dichter geworden war. Diese Strecke war eigentlich ein Projekt der *District Railway*, als Teil des Astes von Ealing, der jetzt von der Piccadilly Line befahren wird. Ab 1910 fuhren Züge beider Gesellschaften nach Uxbridge. Der elektrische Betrieb begann auf der innerstädtischen Tunnelstrecke und oberirdisch bis nach Uxbridge im Jahr 1905. Während auf diesem Ast elektrische Triebwagen eingesetzt wurden, verkehrten Richtung Aylesbury weiterhin lokbespannte Züge mit Abteilwagen, bis Harrow nun allerdings mit Elektrolokomotiven.

Da das Passagieraufkommen immer mehr stieg, musste die Strecke von Finchley Road bis Wembley Park 1913-15 viergleisig ausgebaut werden. Der Ausbau der unterirdischen Strecke von Finchley Road bis Baker Street schien zu jener Zeit noch nicht machbar. Während der zwanziger Jahre wurde die *Metropolitan Railway* bis Rickmansworth elektrifiziert und ein 3 km langer Abschnitt nach Watford, wo der Endbahnhof am westlichen Rand der Stadt lag, in Betrieb genommen. Kurz darauf erfolgte der viergleisige Ausbau bis nach Harrow. 1932 erhielt die *Metropolitan Railway* schließlich noch einen weiteren Ast von Wembley Park nach Stanmore, durch ein Gebiet, in welchem die Bautätigkeit gerade erst begann. Ein Jahr später ging die Bahngesellschaft im öffentlichen Betrieb *London Transport* auf und wurde fortan als Metropolitan Line bezeichnet. Bald darauf wurde der Betrieb westlich von Aylesbury eingestellt, 1935 nach Brill und 1936 nach Verney Junction. Gleichzeitig musste eine Lösung für den Engpass zwischen Finchley Road und Baker Street gefunden werden. Schließlich wurden zwei weitere Röhrentunnel gebaut und der Ast nach Stanmore sowie zwei der vier Gleise zwischen Finchley Road und Wembley Park 1939 am U-Bahnhof Baker Street an die Bakerloo Line angeschlossen (siehe Jubilee Line). Die Metropolitan Line wurde erst 1960 bis Amersham und Chesham elektrifiziert, der Betrieb auf dem Abschnitt Amersham - Aylesbury wurde an British Railways übergeben. Bis 1962 wurde die Strecke bis zum Abzweig Watford South viergleisig ausgebaut. Zwischen Harrow und diesem Abzweig werden die Express-Gleise nun auch von den halbstündlichen Dieselzügen der Chiltern Line von/nach Marylebone benutzt.

Außerhalb der Hauptverkehrszeiten werden auf der Metropolitan Line folgende Linienführungen angeboten:
1) Aldgate - Uxbridge: alle 10 Minuten, mit Halt an allen Stationen
2) Baker Street - Watford: alle 10 Minuten, mit Halt an allen Stationen
3) Baker Street/Aldgate - Amersham: 4 Züge pro Stunde (ergänzt durch 2 Chiltern Line-Züge), ohne Halt von Wembley Park bis Harrow-on-the-Hill, und von dort bis Moor Park;
4) Chalfont & Latimer - Chesham: alle 30 Minuten

Die Metropolitan Line wird mit 8-Wagen-Zügen (2,95 m breit, 16,17 m lang und 3,69 m hoch) betrieben. Diese als A-Züge bezeichneten Fahrzeuge wurden von Cravens in Sheffield hergestellt und in zwei Serien 1960 bzw. 1962 geliefert. Die eingleisige Strecke nach Chesham wird von einem 4-Wagen-Zug im Pendelverkehr bedient.

Wembley Park - Harrow section. In 1932 yet another branch was built from Wembley Park to Stanmore, mainly through open countryside to serve future housing estates. One year later, in 1933, the Metropolitan Railway became part of a unified public transport system - the London Passenger Transport Board, which became more commonly known as 'London Transport', and the Metropolitan Railway became the Metropolitan Line. As a consequence, services beyond Aylesbury were withdrawn soon after: to Brill in 1935, and to Verney Junction in 1936. A solution had to be found for the capacity constraints on the 2-track underground section between Finchley Road and Baker Street. Eventually two tube tunnels were excavated and the Stanmore branch plus the 'slow' tracks between Wembley Park and Finchley Road were linked to the Bakerloo Line at Baker Street in 1939 (see Jubilee Line). The Metropolitan Line was eventually electrified from Rickmansworth to Amersham and Chesham in 1960, and services beyond Amersham were transferred to British Railways. By 1962 the route had become 4-track up to the Watford South Junction. Between Harrow-on-the-Hill and Amersham, tracks are shared with half-hourly Chiltern Line diesel services from Marylebone. At present, the Metropolitan Line consists of the following basic off-peak services (with extra trains during peak hours):
1) Aldgate - Uxbridge: every 10 minutes, calling at all stations;
2) Baker Street - Watford: every 10 minutes, calling at all stations;
3) Baker Street/Aldgate - Amersham: 4 trains per hour (complemented by 2 Chiltern services), skipping stations between Wembley Park and Harrow-on-the-Hill, and between Harrow-on-the-Hill and Moor Park;
4) Chalfont & Latimer - Chesham: every 30 minutes

The Metropolitan Line is operated with 8-car trains of A stock (2.95 m wide, 16.17 m long, 3.69 m high), manufactured by Cravens of Sheffield in two batches between 1960 and 1962. The single-track Chesham branch is served by a 4-car shuttle train.

LONDON Underground - Metropolitan Line

65.3 km (~ 9.5 km unterirdisch | *underground*), 34 Bahnhöfe | *Stations*

6.4 km gemeinsam mit | *shared with* Circle and Hammersmith & City Lines
8.6 km gemeinsam mit | *shared with* Piccadilly Line

10-01-1863	Baker Street – Farringdon
23-12-1865	Farringdon – Moorgate
13-04-1868	Baker Street – Swiss Cottage
12-07-1875	Moorgate – Liverpool Street
18-11-1876	Liverpool Street – Aldgate
30-06-1879	Swiss Cottage – West Hampstead
24-11-1879	West Hampstead – Willesden Green
02-08-1880	Willesden Green – Harrow-on-the-Hill
25-05-1885	Harrow-on-the-Hill – Pinner
01-09-1887	Pinner – Rickmansworth
08-07-1889	Rickmansworth – Chesham
01-09-1892	Chalfont & Latimer – Amersham (– Aylesbury)

14-10-1893	+ Wembley Park
04-07-1904	Harrow-on-the-Hill – Uxbridge
25-09-1905	+ Ickenham
26-05-1906	+ Rayners Lane, Eastcote
21-05-1908	+ Preston Road
09-05-1910	+ Moor Park
05-08-1912	+ Ruislip Manor
17-11-1913	+ West Harrow
22-03-1915	+ North Harrow
28-06-1923	+ Northwick Park
10-12-1923	+ Hillingdon
02-11-1925	Moor Park – Watford
13-11-1933	+ Northwood Hills

Elektrischer Betrieb | *Electric service:*

1905	Aldgate – Uxbridge
1925	Harrow-on-the-Hill – Rickmansworth
1960	Rickmansworth – Amersham / Chesham

Aldgate ①-③ *is the regular terminus for Metropolitan Line trains from Uxbridge. Services from other branches are extended here during peak hours. The 'Met' uses the inner tracks, the outer tracks being used by the Circle Line. From Aldgate up to the junction east of Baker Street, tracks are shared with the Circle and Hammersmith & City Lines.*

At **Baker Street** ④-⑥*, the Metropolitan Line has a separate 4-track station to the north of the original 1863 Circle Line station. Initially, there was only a single-track link to the Circle Line, but when the station was rebuilt with four tracks in 1912, both inner tracks were connected to the Circle Line, although the flat junction was maintained. The present building on top of the station complex dates from the late 1920s (see p.12).*

Aldgate ①-③ ist der fahrplanmäßige Endpunkt der Züge aus Uxbridge. Züge von anderen Strecken werden in der Hauptverkehrszeit hierher durchgebunden. Die ‚Met' benutzt die beiden mittleren Gleise, während die äußeren von der Circle Line befahren werden. Von Aldgate bis zum niveaugleichen Abzweig östlich von Baker Street benutzt die Metropolitan Line dieselben Gleise wie die Circle bzw. Hammersmith & City Line.

Am Bahnhof **Baker Street** ④-⑥ gibt es für die Metropolitan Line eine eigene viergleisige Station nördlich der im Jahr 1863 eröffneten Anlage an der Circle Line. Die anfangs eingleisige Verbindung zur Circle Line wurde beim viergleisigen Ausbau 1912 zweigleisig ausgeführt. Das heutige Eingangsgebäude stammt aus den zwanziger Jahren (siehe S. 12).

Nach Inbetriebnahme der Entlastungsstrecke von Baker Street bis
Finchley Road als Teil eines neuen Astes der Bakerloo Line 1939
wurden die Zwischenstationen auf der Metropolitan Line geschlossen. An den Bahnhöfen **Finchley Road** ① und **Wembley Park** ②③
kann man heute am selben Bahnsteig zur Jubilee Line, welche auf
den mittleren Gleisen hält, umsteigen.

Der Halt **Northwick Park** ④ wurde 1923 eingefügt und die Strecke
1931 bis Harrow viergleisig ausgebaut. Die ‚langsamen' Gleise
befinden sich in der Mitte. Links im Bild kann man außerdem die
separaten Gleise der Chiltern Line sehen.

Westlich von **Harrow-on-the-Hill** ⑤⑥ fädelt der Ast nach Uxbridge
niveaufrei aus. Die bis Moor Park auch von der Chiltern Line
benutzten Express-Gleise liegen ab hier an der Südseite.

After the relief tunnels had opened for the Bakerloo Line in 1939,
the intermediate stations on the Metropolitan Line between
Baker Street and Finchley Road were closed. At **Finchley Road** ①
and **Wembley Park** ②③ cross-platform interchange between the
Metropolitan and Jubilee Lines is now provided, with the Jubilee
Line using the centre pair of tracks.

Northwick Park station ④ was added in 1923, and in 1931 the
line was quadrupled up to Harrow-on-the-Hill. The 'slow' tracks
are in the middle, and on the far left, the separate Chiltern Line
tracks can be seen.

West of **Harrow-on-the-Hill** ⑤⑥ the Uxbridge branch diverges in
a burrowing junction, and the 'fast' tracks to Moor Park (shared
by Chiltern Line trains) get aligned on the southern side.

At **Rayners Lane** ① the Metropolitan Line was joined by the District Line in 1910, and tracks have been shared with the Piccadilly Line since 1933, making a compromise platform height necessary. When the Uxbridge branch opened in 1904, there was only one intermediate station, located at **Ruislip** ②. By 1913 several very basic 'halts' had been established, which were later rebuilt into proper stations. **Hillingdon** station ③ was totally rebuilt slightly further west in 1992 to make way for a highway construction scheme.

The original **Uxbridge** terminus was abandoned in 1938 when a new station ④-⑥ opened right in the town centre. The 3-track station is covered with a massive concrete roof, similar to that found at Cockfosters (see p. 71).

Am Bahnhof **Rayners Lane** ① mündete ab 1910 die District Line in die Metropolitan Line, die Strecke bis Uxbridge wurde daraufhin gemeinsam betrieben. Seit 1933 wird dieser Ast auch von der Piccadilly Line befahren, so dass an den Bahnsteigen eine mittlere Einstiegshöhe gewählt werden musste. Bei Eröffnung der Strecke 1904 gab es nur die Zwischenstation **Ruislip** ②, bis 1913 wurden dann mehrere einfache Haltestellen eingerichtet, die später zu richtigen Bahnhöfen umgebaut wurden. **Hillingdon** ③ wurde 1992 etwas weiter westlich neu gebaut, um Platz für eine Straßenerweiterung zu schaffen. Der ursprüngliche Endbahnhof **Uxbridge** ④-⑥ wurde 1938 zugunsten einer zentraleren Lage aufgegeben. Die heutige dreigleisige Station ähnelt mit ihrem Betondach dem Bahnhof Cockfosters auf der Piccadilly Line (siehe S. 71).

Von **Harrow-on-the-Hill** geht die viergleisige Strecke weiter bis zum Abzweig Richtung Watford. Die Express-Gleise liegen nun an der Südseite und werden von den Chiltern Line-Zügen mitbenutzt. Während der Bahnhof **Pinner** ① bereits seit 1885 existiert, wurde **Northwood Hills** ② erst 1933 eingefügt.
In **Watford** ③ endet die Metropolitan Line zu weit westlich vom Stadtzentrum, weshalb eine neue Verbindungsstrecke von **Croxley** über Watford High Street bis Watford Junction seit langem geplant ist. Dafür können größtenteils bestehende Gleisanlagen genutzt werden.

Von **Chalfont & Latimer** ④-⑥ besteht ein halb-stündlicher Pendelverkehr auf der eingleisigen Strecke nach **Chesham**. Die Stationen zwischen **Rickmansworth** und **Amersham** ⑦ werden auch von den Zügen der Chiltern Line bedient, die von London-Marylebone nach Aylesbury verkehren, so dass von diesen Stationen tagsüber ein 10-Minuten-Takt Richtung Londoner Innenstadt besteht.

From **Harrow-on-the-Hill** the 4-track route continues to Watford South Junction, the 'fast' tracks now on the southern side and shared by Chiltern Line diesel services. Whereas a station has existed at **Pinner** ① since 1885, **Northwood Hills** ② is the latest addition to the present Metropolitan Line (1933).
At **Watford** ③, the Metropolitan Line terminates too far west of the town centre, and therefore a new link from **Croxley** to Watford Junction via Watford High Street has been planned for a long time.
From **Chalfont & Latimer** ④-⑥, a half-hourly shuttle service is provided on the single-track line to **Chesham**.
Stations from **Rickmansworth** to **Amersham** ⑦ are also served by half-hourly Chiltern Line trains from Marylebone to Aylesbury, thus providing a 10-minute service to central London.

Southfields

The 'Metropolitan District Railway' was founded soon after the opening of the first underground route in 1863 from Paddington to Farringdon in order to build a line from Kensington to the City, which would then form a circular line with the Metropolitan Railway's routes. The southern side of the circle was developed together with the Victoria Embankment along the River Thames. Instead of being merged, as was initially planned, the Metropolitan and the District Railway became direct competitors on the jointly operated ring line. The District Railway expanded mainly towards the west, to West Brompton in 1869, and to Hammersmith in 1874. The latter route was then linked to the existing railway from Kensington Addison Road (now Olympia) to Richmond via Hammersmith Grove Road, which was owned by the L&SWR (London & South Western Railway). Through service from Mansion House to Richmond started in 1877. It only took two years before a branch to Ealing Broadway was added to the District network. As with the Metropolitan Railway, the building of new railways brought about a rapid increase in housing development in the newly served areas. Between 1883 and 1885, District steam trains continued over Great Western tracks from Ealing to Windsor. In 1880 the short branch to West Brompton was extended to Putney Bridge, which also attracted leisure traffic at the Thames riverside. The next branch to follow was in 1883 from Acton Town to Hounslow (now part of the Piccadilly Line). The extension across the River Thames from Putney Bridge to Wimbledon was actually built by the L&SWR (1889), but the District Railway was granted running powers on it. The District's expansion into the western suburbs continued, with a branch to South Harrow opening in 1903 after it had been used in extensive tests for electric operation. A further planned extension to Uxbridge was then built by the Metropolitan Railway and opened in 1904. The District also started operating to Uxbridge from 1910. The Ealing Common - Uxbridge section was transferred to the Piccadilly Line in 1932/33. The District's western network was completed in 1905 with a short branch from Acton Town to South Acton. This service was withdrawn in 1959. With four District branches and several mainline trains sharing tracks between Hammersmith and Turnham Green, it became necessary to quadruple this stretch, and the District Railway got its own pair of tracks in 1911.

While the District Railway expanded rapidly towards the west, things were less dynamic at the eastern end. Completion of the missing section of the Circle Line was not achieved until 1884,

Die Metropolitan District Railway wurde kurz nach Eröffnung der ersten Untergrundbahn von Paddington nach Farringdon gegründet. Die neue Gesellschaft wollte von Kensington in die City eine eigene Strecke bauen, die dann gemeinsam mit der Metropolitan Railway eine Ringlinie bilden sollte. Die Strecke entlang der Themse wurde zusammen mit dem Victoria Embankment, einer Uferpromenade, errichtet. Statt sich später, wie ursprünglich geplant, zusammenzuschließen, wurden die beiden Bahngesellschaften auf der gemeinsam betriebenen Ringstrecke immer mehr zu Konkurrenten. Die District Railway wurde im Laufe der folgenden Jahre vor allem Richtung Westen verlängert, 1869 bis West Brompton und 1874 bis Hammersmith, von dort dann weiter über die bereits bestehende Strecke der L&SWR (London & South Western Railway) von Kensington Addison Road (jetzt Olympia) über Hammersmith Grove Road nach Richmond. Der durchgehende Betrieb von Richmond bis Mansion House begann 1877. Zwei Jahre später wurde der Ast nach Ealing Broadway fertig gestellt. Wie bei der Metropolitan Railway brachten auch die neuen District-Strecken eine rege Bautätigkeit entlang der Bahn mit sich. Zwischen 1883 und 1885 fuhren die Dampfzüge der District über die Gleise der Great Western von Ealing weiter bis Windsor. 1880 wurde der kurze Abzweig nach West Brompton bis Putney Bridge verlängert, so dass auch Ausflügler ans Themse-Ufer gebracht werden konnten. Als nächstes folgte 1883 der Ast von Acton Town nach Hounslow (heute Teil der Piccadilly Line).

Die Verlängerung über die Themse von Putney Bridge bis Wimbledon wurde eigentlich von der L&SWR gebaut, aber die District bekam 1889 die Genehmigung für den Passagierverkehr auf dieser Strecke. Anfang des 20. Jahrhunderts ging der Netzausbau im Westen Londons weiter. Der Ast nach South Harrow wurde 1903 eröffnet, nachdem er einige Zeit als Teststrecke für den elektrischen Betrieb benutzt worden war. Eine weitere Verlängerung nach Uxbridge wurde schließlich von der Metropolitan Railway gebaut

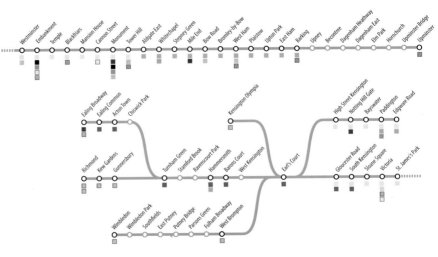

und 1904 in Betrieb genommen, jedoch ab 1910 auch von der District mitbenutzt (der Abschnitt Ealing Common - Uxbridge wurde 1932/33 an die Piccadilly Line abgegeben). Die letzte westliche Strecke der District war 1905 ein Ast zwischen Acton Town und South Acton, der Betrieb auf dieser kurzen Linie wurde allerdings 1959 ganz eingestellt. Auf dem Abschnitt zwischen Hammersmith und Turnham Green fuhr die District also in vier verschiedene Richtungen, dazu kamen einige Regionalzüge. Um einen reibungslosen Verkehr zu gewährleisten, wurde auf dieser Strecke 1911 ein zweites Gleispaar nur für die District in Betrieb genommen. Während die *District Railway* den Westen Londons eroberte, ging die Verlängerung am östlichen Ende langsamer voran. Gleichzeitig mit der Vollendung der Ringlinie 1884 wurde auch eine Verlängerung nach Whitechapel mit einem Verbindungstunnel zur East London Line in Betrieb genommen. Bis 1905 gab es durchgehenden Verkehr von der District nach New Cross Gate. Kurz vor der Jahrhundertwende begann die District mit dem Bau einer weiteren 3 km langen unterirdischen Strecke, um in Bromley-by-Bow einen Anschluss an die LT&SR (*London, Tilbury & Southend Railway*) zu schaffen, über deren Gleise sie dann weiter Richtung Barking und Upminster fahren konnte.

Während des letzten Jahrzehnts des 19. Jahrhunderts, als die ersten elektrischen Röhrenbahnen ihren Betrieb aufnahmen, war es immer deutlicher geworden, dass sowohl die District als auch die Metropolitan etwas tun mussten, um den Komfort für die Fahrgäste vor allem auf den mit Rauch verschmutzten unterirdischen Strecken zu verbessern. Die Metropolitan hätte erst einen Wechselstrombetrieb mit Oberleitung bevorzugt, doch schließlich einigte man sich darauf, das gesamte Netz mit 630 V Gleichstrom mit zwei Stromschienen zu elektrifizieren, wie es auch bei der Bakerloo, Piccadilly und Hampstead (jetzt Teil der Northern) Line geschehen sollte, die damals im Bau waren. Der Elektrifizierung der District-Strecken war 1905 abgeschlossen und brachte erhebliche Fahrzeitverkürzungen mit sich.

Bis 1932 bekam die District auch eigene Gleise zwischen Barking und Upminster. Gleichzeitig übernahm die Piccadilly Line einige Fahrten vom Hounslow-Ast (die District fuhr dort noch bis 1964), der Ast nach Uxbridge wurde 1933 völlig von der District auf die Piccadilly Line übertragen.

Während der Abschnitt von Putney Bridge bis Wimbledon 1994 schließlich ins Eigentum von London Underground überging, untersteht der Ast nach Richmond bis heute der staatlichen Bahnbehörde Network Rail. Dieser Abschnitt wird gemeinsam mit Silverlinks North London Line befahren.

Außerhalb der Hauptverkehrszeiten gibt es auf der District Line folgende Linienführungen:

    Richmond – Upminster: alle 10 Minuten
    Ealing Broadway – Tower Hill: alle 10 Minuten
    Wimbledon – Upminster: alle 10 Minuten
    Wimbledon – Edgware Road: alle 10 Minuten
    Kensington Olympia – High Street Kensington: alle 15 Minuten

Außer auf der Strecke Edgware Road – Wimbledon, wo C-Züge eingesetzt werden, fahren auf allen District-Strecken D-Züge (2,92 m breit, 18,3 m lang und 3,62 m hoch), die zwischen 1979 und 1983 geliefert wurden und derzeit modernisiert werden.

when an extension to Whitechapel with a link to the East London Railway was also opened. Through running of District trains to New Cross Gate was withdrawn in 1905. Just before the turn of the century the District began to construct another 3 km underground route to link its own lines to the LT&SR (London Tilbury & Southend Railway) west of Bromley-by-Bow and share tracks from there onwards to Barking and Upminster.

During the last decade of the 19th century, when the first electrically operated tube lines were brought into service, it became evident that the District as well as the Metropolitan Railway had to do something to improve travel conditions for passengers, especially in the still smoke-filled tunnel stretches. Although the Metropolitan Railway had preferred an AC system with overhead wires, the entire network was eventually electrified at 630 V dc with two conductor rails, the same as that provided for the Bakerloo, Piccadilly and Hampstead (now part of the Northern Line) tube lines then under construction. The electrification of most District routes was completed by late 1905 and led to a considerable reduction in travel times.

By 1932 two separate tracks had been laid for the District Railway between Barking and Upminster. At the same time, some services on the Hounslow branch were transferred to the Piccadilly Line, the District having been totally withdrawn from that route in 1964. In 1933 the Uxbridge branch also became part of the Piccadilly Line in lieu of the District.

Whereas ownership of the Putney Bridge to Wimbledon section was eventually taken over by London Underground in 1994, Network Rail is still responsible for the Richmond branch, which is also served by the Silverlink Metro North London Line.

At present, the District Line operates the following basic off-peak services (with extra trains and destinations during peak hours):

    Richmond - Upminster: every 10 minutes
    Ealing Broadway - Tower Hill: every 10 minutes
    Wimbledon - Upminster: every 10 minutes
    Wimbledon - Edgware Road: : every 10 minutes
    Kensington Olympia - High Street Kensington: every 15 min

Except for the Edgware Road to Wimbledon service, which shares the C stock used on the Circle and Hammersmith & City Lines, all other District routes are served by D stock trains (2.92 m wide, 18.3 m long and 3.62 m high), which entered service between 1979 and 1983 and are currently undergoing refurbishment.

LONDON Underground - District Line

64.5 km (~ 14 km unterirdisch | *underground*), 60 Bahnhöfe | *Stations*
  20.8 km gemeinsam mit | *shared with* Circle and Hammersmith & City Lines
  1.5 km gemeinsam mit | *shared with* Piccadilly Line

{31-03-1858	Bromley-by-Bow – Barking}
01-10-1868	Edgware Road – Gloucester Road
24-12-1868	Gloucester Road – Westminster
{01-01-1869	Hammersmith Grove Rd – Richmond}
12-04-1869	Gloucester Road – West Brompton
30-05-1870	Westminster – Blackfriars
03-07-1871	Blackfriars – Mansion House
30-10-1871	+ Earl's Court
{01-02-1872	Earl's Court – Kensington Olympia}
{01-04-1873	+ Ravenscourt Park}
09-09-1874	Earl's Court – Hammersmith
01-06-1877	Hammersmith – Richmond
01-07-1879	Turnham Green – Ealing Broadway

01-03-1880	West Brompton – Putney Bridge
06-10-1884	Mansion House – Whitechapel
{01-05-1885	Barking – Upminster}
03-06-1889	Putney Bridge – Wimbledon
02-06-1902	Whitechapel – Bromley-by-Bow (– Upminster)
11-06-1902	+ Bow Road
23-06-1902	+ Stepney Green
09-10-1905	+ Barons Court
01-02-1912	+ Stamford Brook
17-12-1934	+ Upminster Bridge
13-05-1935	+ Elm Park
07-04-1986	Earl's Court – Kensington Olympia
	(regelmäßiger Betrieb | *regular service*)

1905 elektrischer Betrieb außer | *electric service except*
1908 East Ham – Barking
1932 Barking – Upminster
1946 Earl's Court – Kensington Olympia

All District Line services pass through the 4-track **Earl's Court** station ①②. The present station dates from 1878, when the diveunder from High Street Kensington was also built. At the western side a diveunder for the Hammersmith-bound track was added in 1914.

Between **West Kensington** and **Barons Court** ③④ the Piccadilly Line surfaces from its tube tunnels between the District Line tracks, thus allowing cross-platform interchange at Barons Court and **Hammersmith** ⑤⑥. At the latter, interchange is also provided to the Hammersmith & City Line (see p. 19), although passengers have to walk across a busy road junction. In 1877, District trains began running through from Mansion House to Richmond over the existing L&SWR tracks.

Alle Strecken der District Line führen durch den viergleisigen Bahnhof **Earl's Court** ①②. Die heutige Station stammt von 1878, als auch eine kreuzungsfreie Einfädelung des Gleises von High Street Kensington gebaut wurde. Am westlichen Ende wurde die Strecke Richtung Hammersmith 1914 niveaufrei angelegt. Zwischen **West Kensington** und **Barons Court** ③④ tauchen die Gleise der Piccadilly Line zwischen denen der District Line auf, so dass man sowohl in Barons Court als auch in Hammersmith am selben Bahnsteig umsteigen kann. In **Hammersmith** ⑤⑥ besteht auch eine Umsteigemöglichkeit zur Hammersmith & City Line (s. S. 19), allerdings muss man dafür eine stark befahrene Kreuzung überqueren. Ab 1877 fuhren die Züge der District von Mansion House über Hammersmith weiter auf den Gleisen der L&SWR nach Richmond.

Die Piccadilly Line fährt zwischen den Gleisen der District Line weiter bis Acton Town. Sie durchfährt im Normalbetrieb die folgenden drei Stationen ohne Halt, auch wenn ihr in **Ravenscourt Park** ① und **Turnham Green** ② zwei und in **Stamford Brook** eine Bahnsteigkante (Richtung Westen) zur Verfügung stehen. In Turnham Green hält die Piccadilly Line früh morgens und spät abends. **Chiswick Park** ③ wurde 1933 umgebaut und besitzt seither ein typisches Eingangsgebäude von Charles Holden. Nördlich von **Acton Town** laufen die Gleise der Piccadilly (Uxbridge-Ast) und der District Line zusammen, so dass am Bahnhof **Ealing Common** ④ dieselben Bahnsteige benutzt werden müssen. Etwa 500 m weiter nördlich, nach Überqueren der Central Line, biegt die District Line niveaugleich nach Westen ab und endet auf der Nordseite des Bahnhofs **Ealing Broadway** ⑤.

*Between Barons Court and Acton Town the Piccadilly tracks continue between the District tracks. There are two platform faces for the Piccadilly Line at **Ravenscourt Park** ① and **Turnham Green** ②, but only a westbound platform at **Stamford Brook**. Piccadilly trains do not normally stop at these stations, except for Turnham Green, where they stop during early mornings and late evenings only. **Chiswick Park** ③ was rebuilt in 1933, and boasts one of Charles Holden's typical red-brick entrance buildings.*

*North of **Acton Town**, the District and the Piccadilly Uxbridge branch converge into a single pair of tracks through **Ealing Common** ④ station. About 500 m further north and after crossing over the Central Line, the District Line diverges at a flat junction to terminate at the northern side at **Ealing Broadway** ⑤.*

The branch to Richmond was opened in as early as 1869 by the L&SWR. East of Ravenscourt Park station it was originally linked to the Hammersmith & City Line and, via a curve, to the West London Line at Addison Road (now Kensington Olympia) station. The section between **Gunnersbury** ① and **Richmond** ②③ is shared with North London Line services operated by Silverlink Metro. Although the link between **Earl's Court** and **Kensington Olympia** ④⑤ (originally Addison Road) had already been opened by the District Railway in 1872, it was initially only used by the LNWR to operate an 'Outer Circle' from Mansion House to Broad Street (next to Liverpool Street station) via Kensington, Willesden Junction and the North London Railway. Until 1986, District Line service on this short branch was only during exhibitions at Olympia. At present, a shuttle service is provided every 15 minutes between Kensington Olympia and High Street Kensington via Earl's Court.

Der Ast nach Richmond wurde bereits 1869 von der L&SWR eröffnet. Die Strecke war ursprünglich östlich von Ravenscourt Park mit der Hammersmith & City Line verbunden, über eine Kurve erreichte sie dann die West London Line am Bahnhof Addison Road (jetzt Kensington Olympia). Der Abschnitt zwischen **Gunnersbury** ① und **Richmond** ②③ wird auch von der North London Line, die von Silverlink Metro betrieben wird, benutzt.

Auch wenn der Ast von Earl's Court nach **Kensington Olympia** ④⑤ (vormals Addison Road) von der *District Railway* bereits 1872 gebaut worden war, wurde er vorerst nur von der LNWR als Teil einer äußeren Ringlinie von Mansion House nach Broad Street (neben dem Bahnhof Liverpool Street) über Kensington, Willesden Junction und die *North London Railway* befahren. Derzeit wird dieser Ast alle 15 Minuten von High Street Kensington über Earl's Court im Pendelverkehr bedient.

Die erste Verlängerung der District führte 1869 nach **West Brompton** ①, wo der Bahnhof aus jener Zeit gut erhalten ist. Diese Strecke wurde 1880 über **Fulham Broadway** ② bis **Putney Bridge** ③ verlängert. Die südliche Abschnitt über die Themse, von der L&SWR gebaut und erst 1994 an die London Underground übergeben, ging 1889 in Betrieb. An den Bahnhöfen **Southfields** ④ und **Wimbledon Park** ⑤ sind noch viele Details dieser Zeit zu erkennen. Am Endbahnhof **Wimbledon** ⑥ kann man zu den Vorortbahnen von/nach Waterloo sowie zur Croydon Tramlink (siehe S. 94) umsteigen. Von Wimbledon fahren die District-Züge abwechselnd nach Edgware Road und nach Upminster (oder enden je nach Tageszeit auf einem Zwischenbahnhof dieser Strecke).

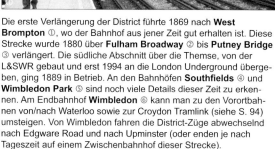

The District Railway's first western extension reached **West Brompton** ① in 1869. This station preserves many features from that period. The line was subsequently extended to **Putney Bridge** ③ via **Fulham Broadway** ② in 1880. The southern stretch south of the River Thames followed in 1889. This section was built by the L&SWR and was only handed over to London Underground in 1994. **Southfields** ④ and **Wimbledon Park** ⑤ are well-preserved 19th century stations. At the **Wimbledon** terminus ⑥ interchange is provided to mainline services to and from Waterloo, as well as to the Croydon Tramlink (see p. 94). District Line trains from Wimbledon run alternately to Edgware Road and to Upminster (or any intermediate terminus depending on the time of day).

In the east of London the District Line has only one leg, which diverges from the Circle Line east of **Tower Hill** station. **Aldgate East** station ① was relocated further east in 1938, and the following station St. Mary's was then closed. The Hammersmith & City Line shares the District's eastern route to Barking, although some of its services terminate at **Whitechapel** ②. The double-track curve between the District and East London Lines still exists but has not been used in regular service since 1941.

The District's underground route continues through **Stepney Green** ③, **Mile End** ④ (where cross-platform interchange to the Central Line is provided) and **Bow Road** ⑤ before joining the surface railway alignment from Fenchurch Street to Southend and Tilbury. **West Ham** station ⑥ was rebuilt in the 1990s in connection with the Jubilee Line extension to Stratford.

Der östliche Ast der District Line zweigt von der Circle Line östlich der Station **Tower Hill** niveaugleich ab. Der U-Bahnhof **Aldgate East** ① wurde 1938 nach Osten verschoben und die nächste Station St. Mary's gleichzeitig geschlossen. Bis Barking wird die Strecke auch von der Hammersmith & City Line benutzt. Manche Züge dieser Linie enden auch in **Whitechapel** ②. Die zweigleisige Verbindungskurve zur East London Line wird seit 1941 nicht mehr im Regelbetrieb befahren. Der unterirdische Abschnitt der District Line führt weiter über **Stepney Green** ③, **Mile End** ④ (wo man am selben Bahnsteig zur Central Line umsteigen kann) bis **Bow Road** ⑤. Anschließend fährt sie an der Oberfläche parallel zur Bahnstrecke von Fenchurch Street nach Southend und Tilbury weiter. Der Bahnhof **West Ham** ⑥ wurde in den neunziger Jahren in Zusammenhang mit der Verlängerung der Jubilee Line erneuert.

Der Betrieb auf der oberirdischen Strecke von Bromley-by-Bow nach Barking und Upminster wurde anfangs auf den Gleisen der 1858 eröffneten *London, Tilbury & Southend Railway* abgewickelt. An manchen Stationen, wie **Plaistow** ①② oder **East Ham** ③, sind Eingangsgebäude und Bahnsteigdächer aus dieser Zeit erhalten. **Barking** ④⑤ ist der östliche Endpunkt der Hammersmith & City Line. Das Bahnhofsgebäude im Beton-Glas-Stil stammt von 1961. Der Abschnitt von Barking bis Upminster wurde erst 1932 von der Fernbahn getrennt und elektrifiziert. Damals wurden die Bahnhöfe **Upney** und **Dagenham Heathway** neu gebaut und die 1926 eingerichtete Haltestelle **Becontree** umgebaut. **Elm Park** und **Upminster Bridge** ⑥ folgten wenige Jahre später. **Upminster** ⑦ wurde zu jener Zeit umgebaut und präsentiert sich heute mit einem ganz einfachen Bahnsteigdach.

Service from Bromley-by-Bow to Barking and Upminster was initially provided over the mainline rail tracks of the 'London, Tilbury & Southend Railway', which opened in 1858. Some stations, like Plaistow ①② and East Ham ③, preserve pleasant canopies and station buildings from that period.

Barking ④⑤ is the eastern terminus of the Hammersmith & City Line. The station building, a Network Rail station now leased to 'c2c', was rebuilt in 1961 in concrete/glass style.

The section between Barking and Upminster was only separated from mainline services and electrified in 1932, when Upney and Dagenham Heathway opened, and Becontree, opened in 1926, was rebuilt. Elm Park and Upminster Bridge ⑥ were added in the following years. The terminus Upminster ⑦ was modified at that time and now shows a rather simple platform roof.

The East London Line's origins go back to the early 19th century, when the first attempts were being made to dig a tunnel under the River Thames. After many technical problems had been solved, the engineer Marc Brunel completed the first underwater tunnel in 1843 with the help of a primitive tunnelling shield. What was meant to become a road tunnel eventually opened as an 11.6 m wide pedestrian tunnel with a dividing wall, as no money was left to build the necessary access ramps. 22 years later the tunnel was acquired by the 'East London Railway', which was founded to create a mainline railway link between the 'London, Brighton and South Coast Railway' (at New Cross Gate) and the 'South Eastern Railway' (at New Cross) on the south bank, and the 'Great Eastern Railway' at Liverpool Street on the north bank of the River Thames. After the route had been completed to Liverpool Street in 1876, several companies used the tunnel to reach various southern destinations, such as Croydon or Brighton.

Shoreditch

When the Circle Line was completed in 1884 together with a branch to Whitechapel, the East London Railway was linked to the District and Metropolitan Railways via a curve east of the now closed St. Mary's station. Both companies began direct services through the Thames tunnel. The District Railway ceased serving the East London Railway in 1905, when the rest of its lines were electrified. The Metropolitan services were withdrawn one year later, but resumed following electrification in 1913 to operate from Shoreditch and New Cross and New Cross Gate. Direct services from Hammersmith via the northern Circle Line finally ceased in 1941. To the mainline companies the cross-river link had always been of more importance for freight traffic, which continued until 1962. The track link between Shoreditch and Liverpool Street was cut in 1966.

Die Ursprünge der East London Line gehen zurück auf das frühe 19. Jahrhundert, als die ersten Versuche für einen Tunnel unter der Themse unternommen wurden. Nach vielen technischen Problemen konnte der Ingenieur Marc Brunel 1843 den ersten Unterwassertunnel mit Hilfe eines einfachen Schilds vollenden. Was eigentlich als Straßentunnel geplant war, wurde schließlich ein 11,6 m breiter Fußgängertunnel mit einer Trennwand, denn das Geld für die notwendigen Rampen für Fuhrwerke fehlte. 22 Jahre später erwarb die East London Railway diesen Tunnel und machte daraus eine Eisenbahnverbindung, die ab 1876 den Bahnhof Liverpool Street auf der Nordseite der Themse mit der London, Brighton and South Coast Railway (in New Cross Gate) und der South Eastern Railway (in New Cross) auf der Südseite verknüpfte. Verschiedene Gesellschaften befuhren den Tunnel auf

When the Metropolitan Railway was integrated into London Transport in 1933, the East London Railway become part of the Metropolitan Line. From the early 1970s the 'East London Section' of the Metropolitan Line was shown separately on maps, in purple with a centred white stripe. The name 'East London Line' appeared on maps for the first time in 1984, the present line colour having been used since 1990.

In conjunction with the Jubilee Line extension, the East London Line was closed completely in 1995 to allow for the construction of the Canada Water interchange station, the sealing of the original underwater tunnels and total line refurbishment. The East London Line is operated with six 4-car trains belonging to the same A stock, which is used on the Metropolitan Line and was refurbished between 1994 and 1998.

At present, trains depart from Whitechapel every 6 minutes, and run alternately to New Cross and New Cross Gate. Shoreditch station is only served during peak hours and on Sunday mornings.

After many years of isolated existence the East London Line will finally be extended at both ends. The northern extension will diverge from the existing line between Whitechapel and Shoreditch (the latter is to be closed in June 2006) and climb from the cutting to a new viaduct to reach the first station Shoreditch High Street, which will lie several hundred metres west of the present

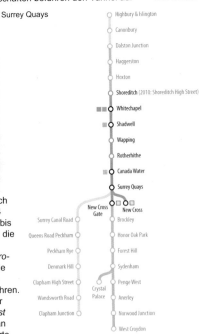

Surrey Quays

ihrem Weg nach Süden, z.B. nach Croydon oder Brighton. Als 1884 die Circle Line und der Abzweig bis Whitechapel fertig waren, wurde die East London Railway mit der District Railway und mit der Metropolitan Railway verbunden. Beide Bahnen begannen direkte Züge durch den Themse-Tunnel zu führen. Die District verkehrte bis zu ihrer Elektrifizierung 1905 auf der East London Railway, die Metropolitan noch ein Jahr länger. Diese kehrte

Highbury & Islington
Canonbury
Dalston Junction
Haggerston
Hoxton
Shoreditch (2010: Shoreditch High Street)
Whitechapel
Shadwell
Wapping
Rotherhithe
Canada Water
Surrey Quays

New Cross Gate — New Cross
Surrey Canal Road — Brockley
Queens Road Peckham — Honor Oak Park
Peckham Rye — Forest Hill
Denmark Hill — Sydenham
Clapham High Street — Penge West
Wandsworth Road — Crystal Palace — Anerley
Clapham Junction — Norwood Junction
West Croydon

allerdings 1913 wieder zurück, um zwischen Shoreditch und New Cross bzw. New Cross Gate Personenverkehr anzubieten. Bis 1941 gab es von Hammersmith über die nördliche Circle Line direkte Züge zur *East London Railway*. Für andere Bahngesellschaften war die Verbindung unter der Themse nur für den Güterverkehr von Bedeutung, der aber schließlich 1962 endete. 1966 wurde die Gleisverbindung zum Bahnhof Liverpool Street unterbrochen.

Als die Metropolitan 1933 zu *London Transport* kam, wurde die *East London Railway* ein Teil der Metropolitan Line. Ab den frühen siebziger Jahren wurde ihre *East London Section* auf den Netzplänen als violette Linie mit einem weißen Streifen in der Mitte dargestellt. Der Name ‚East London Line' erschien dann erstmals 1984, und seit 1990 ist sie nun auch farblich klar als eigenständige Linie zu erkennen.

In Zusammenhang mit der Verlängerung der Jubilee Line wurde die East London Line 1995-1998 komplett geschlossen, um den Turmbahnhof Canada Water einzubauen und gleichzeitig die alten Tunnel unter der Themse abzudichten und alle Stationen zu sanieren.

Die East London Line wird mit sechs zwischen 1994 und 1998 modernisierten A-Zügen, wie sie sonst auf der Metropolitan Line eingesetzt werden, betrieben.

Derzeit fahren die Züge alle sechs Minuten von Whitechapel abwechselnd nach New Cross und New Cross Gate. Der Bahnhof Shoreditch wird nur während der Hauptverkehrszeiten und Sonntag morgens bedient.

Nach vielen Jahren etwas im Abseits soll die East London Line in den nächsten Jahren an beiden Enden verlängert werden. Im Norden wird die neue Strecke nördlich von Whitechapel die bestehende Trasse verlassen (der derzeitige Endpunkt Shoreditch wird im Sommer 2006 endgültig geschlossen) und über eine Rampe aus dem Einschnitt in Hochlage geführt. Die erste Station Shoreditch High Street wird mehrere Hundert Meter westlich der heutigen Endstation auf einem Viadukt liegen. Im Anschluss daran geht die Trasse auf das brachliegende Kingsland Viadukt über, auf dem von 1865 bis 1986 die Züge der *North London Railway* zum Bahnhof Broad Street, der direkt neben dem Bahnhof Liverpool Street lag, fuhren. In einer ersten Phase sollen die Züge bis Dalston Junction, später dann bis Highbury & Islington fahren.

Im Süden ist geplant, die East London Line in New Cross Gate mit der Bahnstrecke nach Brighton zu verbinden und Züge bis Crystal Palace bzw. West Croydon zu führen. Später soll eine weitere Verbindung südlich von Surrey Quays Richtung Queens Road Peckham (die es bereits zwischen 1871 und 1911 gab), mit einer neuen Zwischenstation Surrey Canal Road, gebaut werden. Diese Strecke würde erst bis Clapham Junction führen, längerfristig könnte daraus eine Ringlinie (*Orbirail*) über Willesden Junction und die West London und North London Line werden.

Die Verlängerung bis Dalston Junction wird von *Transport for London* mit der Absicht gebaut, die East London Line 2010 an die staatliche Infrastrukturgesellschaft Network Rail zu übergeben. Auf der neuen Strecke soll dann ein metro-ähnlicher Vorortverkehr angeboten werden: alle 5 Minuten soll ein Zug von Dalston Junction abwechselnd nach New Cross, Crystal Palace und West Croydon fahren.

station. Just west of the new station the route will join the disused Kingsland Viaduct in Hackney, which from 1865 until 1986 took trains from the North London Railway to Broad Street station, once located next to Liverpool Street station. In a first phase, the northern terminus will be Dalston Junction, and in a second phase, the link to the North London Line will be rebuilt so that East London Line trains can terminate at Highbury & Islington.

In the south, the East London Line will be linked from New Cross Gate to the Brighton Line and terminate at Crystal Palace and West Croydon, sharing tracks with suburban services from London Bridge. Later, another link will be built between Surrey Quays and Queens Road Peckham (a link that also existed from 1871 until 1911), with a new intermediate station at Surrey Canal Road. This link would allow a branch to Clapham Junction, which may be the first step towards an envisaged outer circular route via Willesden Junction along the West London and North London Lines, already branded 'Orbirail'. The northern extension from Whitechapel to Dalston Junction is being carried out by Transport for London, and when completed in 2010 the East London Line will be transferred to Network Rail to become a 'metro-style' National Rail service, providing 12 trains per hour from Dalston Junction, with four trains each to New Cross, Crystal Palace and West Croydon.

Canada Water

New Cross Gate

LONDON Underground - East London Line

7.3 km (~ 3 km unterirdisch | *underground*), 9 Bahnhöfe | *Stations*

{07-12-1869 Wapping – New Cross Gate}
{10-04-1876 Wapping – Liverpool Street}
{01-07-1876 Surrey Quays – New Cross}
06-10-1884 (Aldgate East –) Shadwell – New Cross / New Cross Gate
 [District + Metropolitan Railways]
31-03-1913 Shoreditch – Shadwell [Metropolitan Railway]
19-08-1999 + Canada Water

1913 elektrischer Betrieb | *electric service*

For many decades **Shoreditch** ①② station has only been served during peak hours. It will be closed in summer 2006 to allow for the extension of the East London Line towards Dalston Junction along the disused Kingsland Viaduct. The future Shoreditch High Street station will be located further west.

At **Whitechapel** ③④, interchange with the District and Hammersmith & City Lines is provided, and at **Shadwell** ⑤, where a new entrance building opened in 1983, the Docklands Light Railway station is within a short walk. The East London Line is underground from just south of Whitechapel up to a point north of Surrey Quays. As on the Circle Line, there are several openings, mostly next to stations, and originally built in to allow steam to escape, such as this one at the northern end of **Wapping** station ⑥.

Seit vielen Jahrzehnten wird der Bahnhof **Shoreditch** ①② nur während der Hauptverkehrszeiten angefahren. Er wird im Sommer 2006 endgültig geschlossen, damit die East London Line nach Norden über das Kingsland Viaduct bis Dalston Junction verlängert werden kann. Die zukünftige Station Shoreditch High Street wird weiter westlich liegen.

In **Whitechapel** ③④ besteht Anschluss an die District und die Hammersmith & City Line, und in **Shadwell** ⑤, wo 1983 ein neues Eingangsgebäude errichtet wurde, an die Docklands Light Railway. Die East London Line ist von Whitechapel bis kurz vor Surrey Quays unterirdisch. Wie auf der Circle Line gibt es mehrere Tunnelöffnungen, durch die einst der Dampf abgelassen werden konnte, wie in Bild ⑥ am nördlichen Ende der Station **Wapping** zu sehen.

Während die gesamte Linie von 1995 bis 1998 zur Sanierung geschlossen war, wurden die Bahnsteigwände mit Emailplatten verkleidet, die Motive der Umgebung oder, wie in **Wapping** ①-③, die Geschichte des ersten Unterwassertunnels zeigen. Wegen der engen Bahnsteige überlegte man, Wapping und **Rotherhithe** nach Verlängerung der East London Line überhaupt zu schließen, aber nun werden sie doch erhalten bleiben. Der Turmbahnhof **Canada Water** ④ wurde 1999 zwischen Rotherhithe und Surrey Quays gebaut, so dass man bequem zur Jubilee Line umsteigen kann. Südlich von **Surrey Quays** ⑤ spaltet sich die Linie in zwei Äste, einen geradeaus nach Süden bis **New Cross Gate** ⑥, sowie einen nach Osten, teils eingleisig, nach **New Cross**. An beiden Endstationen, die etwa 600 m voneinander entfernt liegen, kann man zu Vorortbahnen von/nach London Bridge umsteigen.

When the line was closed from 1995 until 1998 for refurbishment, the station walls were clad with enamelled panels displaying themes from the area, or as at **Wapping** ①-③, the history of the first underwater tunnel. Due to their narrow and short platforms, Wapping and **Rotherhithe** were once in danger of being closed permanently after the extension of the East London Line, but they will now remain in service.

Canada Water station ④ was added in 1999 between Rotherhithe and Surrey Quays to provide interchange with the Jubilee Line. The line splits into two branches south of **Surrey Quays** ⑤, with one branch continuing straight south to **New Cross Gate** ⑥ and the other turning east to terminate at **New Cross**. Both termini provide interchange with suburban services from London Bridge, and lie some 600 m apart.

Central Line > Lancaster Gate

Once most of the subsurface underground routes for steam-powered trains had been built during the 1860s and 1870s, it became clear that the cut-and-cover method could not be used for lines penetrating the central area of the city, as this method of construction had caused too much disruption at the surface. The first deep-level tunnel under the River Thames had already opened in 1843 and was later incorporated into the East London Railway (see p. 34). The lack of ventilation on longer deep-level sections, however, made this option unviable for the time being. In 1869, James Henry Greathead began to build the 'Tower Subway', a 400 m tunnel under the River Thames excavated with the help of a circular, 2 m diameter iron shield to protect his workers, who manually cut the earth away. The tiny cable-hauled 'Tower Subway' opened in 1870, but operated only for a few months, although the tunnel remained in use until 1896 for pedestrians. Once electric traction became available Greathead's method was further developed, resulting in the first electric 'tube' line, opened in 1890 to link the City to Stockwell (see p. 40). It gained immediate popularity and during the follow-

Nachdem die *Subsurface*-Strecken (Unterpflasterbahnen) für dampfbetriebene Züge während der sechziger und siebziger Jahre des 19. Jahrhunderts in offener Bauweise gebaut worden waren, wurde klar, dass diese Bauweise in der Innenstadt nicht angewandt werden kann, da die Beeinträchtigungen an der Oberfläche zu erheblich wären. Der erste tief liegende Tunnel wurde unter der Themse bereits 1843 errichtet und später in die *East London Railway* integriert (siehe S. 34). Die Unmöglichkeit, den Rauch aus so tiefen Tunneln abzulassen, schloss diese Bauweise vorerst für weitere Tunnelstrecken aus. 1869 begann James Henry Greathead mit dem Bau der *Tower Subway*, einem 400 m langen Tunnel unter der Themse, welcher mit Hilfe eines runden Eisenschilds mit 2 m Durchmesser gegraben wurde, der den Bauarbeitern Schutz bot, während sie das Erdreich manuell abtrugen. Die winzige *Tower Subway* wurde von einem Kabel gezogen und war ab 1870 nur wenige Monate in Betrieb. Der Tunnel blieb noch bis 1896 für Fußgänger geöffnet. Die Greathead-Methode wurde weiterentwickelt, und mit Erfindung des elektrischen Antriebs entstand die erste elektrische ‚Röhrenbahn' (*Tube*). Sie führte ab 1890 von der City bis Stockwell (siehe S. 40) und erfreute sich großer Beliebtheit, so dass im Laufe des folgenden Jahrzehnts zahlreiche Pläne für weitere *Tube*-Linien kreuz und quer durch die Innenstadt erarbeitet wurden. Sowohl Tunnel als auch Stationen wurden von vertikalen

Northern Line > Burnt Oak (Photo Thomas Schunk)

ing decade many similar lines were designed all across central London. Tunnels as well as stations were excavated from shafts, thus causing as little disturbance as possible at the surface. Diameters of running tunnels were eventually fixed at approximately 3.55 m (the modern standard for single-track bored tunnels being 5-6 m), with station tunnels at 6.5 m. The tube tunnels run at an average depth of 20 m mostly through clay, ideal for subterranean excavation.

Although the term 'Tube' is now loosely used for any line forming part of the London Underground network, the proper tube network comprises the following lines:

- Northern Line
- Central Line
- Bakerloo Line
- Piccadilly Line
- Victoria Line
- Jubilee Line
- Waterloo & City Line

Due to the small profile of the running tunnels, rolling stock used on these lines is also of limited size. Depending on the type of stock used, trains are 2.62-2.64 m wide, 15.98-17.77 m long, and 2.87-2.88 m high (the subsurface stock being 800 mm higher). The floor height is approximately 600 mm above the top of the rails,

Bakerloo Line > Edgware Road

Schächten aus gegraben, so dass an der Oberfläche von den Bauarbeiten wenig zu merken war. Der Durchmesser der Streckentunnel wurde mit 3,55 m festgelegt (der heutige Standard bei eingleisigen Röhrentunneln liegt bei 5-6 m), und in den Stationen mit 6,5 m. Die Strecken verlaufen in einer durchschnittlichen Tiefe von 20 m meist durch eine Tonschicht, welche sich besonders gut für solche unterirdische Bauarbeiten eignet.

Auch wenn der Begriff *Tube* heute für die U-Bahn als solches sogar offiziell benutzt wird, besteht das eigentliche *Tube*-Netz aus folgenden Linien:

- Northern Line
- Central Line
- Bakerloo Line
- Piccadilly Line
- Victoria Line
- Jubilee Line
- Waterloo & City Line

Aufgrund des stark eingeschränkten Tunnelprofils ist auch der Wagenpark dementsprechend beengt. Je nach Baureihe sind die Fahrzeuge zwar 2,62-2,64 m breit, 15,98-17,77 m lang, aber nur 2,87-2,88 m hoch (die *Subsurface*-Züge sind 80 cm höher). Die Fußbodenhöhe liegt bei 60 cm über Schienenoberkante, einen stufenlosen Einstieg gibt es aber nur an den neueren Stationen der Jubilee Line. An Bahnsteigen, die sowohl von *Tube*- als auch von *Subsurface*- (im Fall der Piccadilly Line) bzw. Vorortbahnzügen (im Fall der Bakerloo Line) benutzt werden, muss man etwa 15 cm hintersteigen, an den meisten anderen Bahnhöfen muss man etwa gleich weit hinaufsteigen. Für weitere Details zum Wagenpark der Londoner U-Bahn empfehlen wir das umfangreiche Werk von Brian Hardy (siehe Literaturverzeichnis Seite 158).

Mit einer Länge von 261 km (+ 21 km gemeinsam mit anderen Strecken) stellen die *Tube*-Linien etwa zwei Drittel des Gesamtnetzes der Londoner U-Bahn dar. Davon sind etwa 152 km unterirdisch. Außer der 3 km langen Verlängerung der Piccadilly Line zum Terminal 5 am Flughafen Heathrow, die bis 2008 fertig gestellt sein soll, gibt es derzeit keine konkreten Pläne zur Erweiterung des *Tube*-Netzes.

level access into the cars being provided only at the new Jubilee Line stations. At stations served by both tube and subsurface stock (as on the Piccadilly Line) or by tube and mainline stock (as on the Bakerloo Line) an approximately 150 mm step down is required, at most standard tube stations an equally high step upwards is necessary. For further details about London Underground rolling stock refer to Brian Hardy's publication listed on page 158.

Piccadilly Line > Cockfosters

With a total length of 261 km (+ 21 km of shared routes), the tube lines represent about two thirds of the entire London Underground network, with approximately 152 km lying actually underground.
Except for the 3 km Piccadilly Line extension to Terminal 5 at Heathrow Airport, scheduled to open in 2008, there are currently no plans to extend any of the tube lines.

LONDON UNDERGROUND - Tube Lines

	Bakerloo Line
	Central Line
	Jubilee Line
	Northern Line
	Piccadilly Line
	Victoria Line
	Waterloo & City Line
	Subsurface Lines

2006 © Robert Schwandl

Burnt Oak (Photo Thomas Schunk)

Although the Northern Line only appeared on the London Underground map with this name in 1937, its origins go back to 1890, when the first electrically powered underground line opened in London between King William Street (near the present Monument station) and Stockwell - the 'City & South London Railway'. Today's Northern Line is a complex system of routes, with three termini in the north, and one in the south. What makes this line different from any other in the world is the existence of two alternative routes through the city centre, the Bank or City branch and the Charing Cross or West End branch. Both branches are served by trains from all northern termini, which is made possible by a complex grade-separated junction immediately south of Camden Town station.

The original City & South London Railway ran through tube tunnels with a diameter of only 3.1-3.2 m. Although initially planned to be hauled by a cable (like the Glasgow Subway opened six years later), it eventually became the first electric metro line in the world, with carriages then being hauled by electric locomotives. The 5.6 km line had intermediate stations at Borough, Elephant & Castle, Kennington and Oval, all with 61 m long platforms. With the initial success of the line an extension north was soon under consideration. The original northern terminus was to be given up and new 3.5 m diameter tunnels under the river were to be built to replace the steep gradients, barely manageable by the locomotives. The new route also provided a station at London Bridge, a major railway station on the south bank. Within 10 years of opening, King William Street had become London's first abandoned underground station.

Auch wenn die Northern Line unter diesem Namen erst im Jahre 1937 auf dem Netzplan der Londoner U-Bahn erschien, so gehen ihre Anfänge auf das Jahr 1890 zurück, als Londons erste elektrische Untergrundbahn, die *City & South London Railway*, von King William Street (in der Nähe der heutigen Station Monument) und Stockwell in Betrieb ging. Die heutige Northern Line ist eigentlich ein Netz für sich. Sie hat im Norden drei verschiedene Endpunkte und im Süden einen. Was sie allerdings weltweit einzigartig macht, sind die beiden Streckenführungen durch die Innenstadt, einmal über das West End bzw. Charing Cross, und einmal über die City bzw. Bank. Beide Strecken sind mit allen nördlichen Ästen über eine komplizierte niveaufreie Kreuzung südlich des U-Bahnhofs Camden Town verbunden.

Die originale *City & South London Railway* hatte einen Tunneldurchmesser von nur 3,1-3,2 m. Sie sollte anfangs, so wie sechs Jahre später die Subway in Glasgow, mit Kabelantrieb funktionieren, schließlich wurde daraus doch die erste elektrisch betriebene U-Bahn bzw. Metro der Welt, auch wenn in den ersten Jahren die Wagons von Elektrolokomotiven gezogen wurden. Die 5,6 km lange Strecke hatte vier Zwischenstationen (Borough, Elephant & Castle, Kennington und Oval) mit 61 m langen Bahnsteigen. Aufgrund des großen Erfolgs wurde eine Verlängerung Richtung Norden bald in Erwägung gezogen. Die nördliche Endstation sollte aufgegeben werden und die Streckentunnel unter der Themse mit 3,5 m Durchmesser neu gebaut werden, da die Lokomotiven die starken Steigungen der ursprünglichen Strecke kaum überwinden konnten. Auf der neuen Strecke sollte auch eine Station London Bridge entstehen, um einen der wichtigsten Vorortbahnhöfe anzuschließen. Nur 10 Jahre nach seiner Eröffnung wurde der Bahnhof King William Street geschlossen. Gleichzeitig wurde die Verlängerung nach Norden bis Moorgate und nach Süden bis Clapham Common, wo man noch heute am besten den Stil der Bahnhöfe jener Zeit bewundern kann, eröffnet. Die *City & South London Railway* erreichte schließlich 1901 Angel und 1907 Euston.

Clapham Common

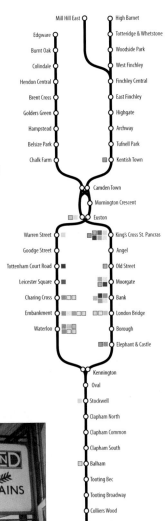

In der Zwischenzeit hatte ein regelrechter U-Bahn-Bauboom in ganz London eingesetzt, unter anderem wurde 1907 die *Charing Cross, Euston & Hampstead Railway*, später einfach als *Hampstead Tube* bezeichnet, von Charing Cross bis Golders Green mit einem Abzweig bis Archway in Betrieb genommen. Diese Strecke war eine von mehreren, die unter der Führung des Amerikaners Charles Tyson Yerkes gebaut wurden. Der Durchmesser der Streckentunnel war fortan 3,55 m und der Stationen 6,5 m, die Bahnsteige wurden 107 m lang gebaut.

Während der zwanziger Jahre wurde die *Hampstead Tube* im Norden Richtung Edgware durch größtenteils unbebautes Gebiet verlängert. Die *Underground Group* von Yerkes hatte mittlerweile auch die *City & South London Railway* aufgekauft, mit dem Ziel, diese mit der *Hampstead Tube* zu einer Linie zu verknüpfen. Dazu mussten auf der älteren Strecke das Tunnelprofil erweitert und die Bahnsteige verlängert werden. Nach dem Umbau wurde die Strecke nach Süden bis Morden verlängert und schließlich das Bindeglied zwischen Kennington und Embankment gebaut, womit 1926 die heutige Linienführung in der Innenstadt geschaffen war.

Die letzte große Erweiterung der Northern Line fand in den dreißiger Jahren statt, nachdem 1933 alle U-Bahnstrecken von *London Transport* übernommen worden waren. Die Verlängerung von Archway Richtung Norden sollte hauptsächlich über bestehende Vorortbahnstrecken erfolgen, nämlich nach Edgware über Mill Hill East und nach High Barnet. Das weitreichende Projekt umfasste außerdem einen Ast von Highgate nach Alexandra Palace und eine neue Strecke von Edgware nach Bushey Heath. Die 1904 eröffnete Großprofil-Röhrenbahn (4,9 m Durchmesser) der *Great Northern & City Railway* von Finsbury Park nach Moorgate sollte in dieses Projekt integriert werden [Die *Northern City Line*, wie sie heute heißt, wurde 1914 Teil der Metropolitan Line und gehörte ab 1933 zur Northern Line; sie wurde schließlich 1975 an British Rail übergeben und Teil des Vorortbahnnetzes]. Die Bauarbeiten begannen an all diesen Abschnitten, sie wurden jedoch durch den 2. Weltkrieg unterbrochen und an manchen Strecken nie wieder fortgesetzt.

Auf der Northern Line sind seit 1998 106 von Alstom gebaute 6-Wagen-Züge der Baureihe 1995 im Einsatz (2,63 m breit, 17,77 m lang und 2,88 m hoch). Die Betriebshöfe befinden sich in Golders Green und Morden, weitere Abstellgleise gibt es in Edgware, Highgate und High Barnet.

Das Betriebsschema der Northern Line ist nur schwer darzustellen. Nördlich von Camden Town fährt auf jedem Ast alle 3½-4 Minuten ein Zug, ab Camden Town fahren diese abwechselnd über Charing Cross und Bank Richtung Süden. Manche Züge der Charing Cross-Strecke enden in Kennington. Zwischen Kennington und Morden verkehrt alle 3 Minuten ein Zug. Von Finchley Central fährt jeder vierte Zug nach Mill Hill East.

Constructed at the same time as the northern extension to Moorgate, two more stations were added at the southern end, Clapham North and Clapham Common, both of which have preserved much of their original appearance. The City & South London Railway eventually reached Angel in 1901 and Euston in 1907.

In the meantime, a real construction boom for further tube lines had begun all over London, and the 'Charing Cross, Euston & Hampstead Railway', later simply referred to as the 'Hampstead Tube', opened in 1907 from Charing Cross to Golders Green and Archway, one of several tube lines promoted by the American businessman Charles Tyson Yerkes. Diameters of 3.55 m had become the standard for tube tunnels, with stations 6.5 m in diameter and having 107 m long platforms.

During the 1920s, the Hampstead Tube was extended north to Edgware through mostly undeveloped areas, thus encouraging the building of new housing estates along the line. Meanwhile, the City & South London Railway had been acquired by Yerkes' Underground Group in 1913, and the decision was taken that both railways should be linked, making platform extensions and tunnel widening on the older route necessary. Once reconstruction had been completed the line was extended south to Morden in 1926, and a link between Kennington and Embankment was added to create the layout in the central area as we know it today.

The last major expansion of the Northern Line took place during the 1930s, once all Underground lines had been taken over by London Transport in 1933. Extensions north of Archway were mainly to be built over existing railways, running to Edgware via Mill Hill East and to High Barnet. Another branch from Highgate to Alexandra Palace, with a link between Finsbury Park and Highgate, as well as an extension from Edgware to Bushey Heath, were also included in the ambitious project, which was to have incorporated the 'Great Northern & City Railway' opened in 1904 between Moorgate and Finsbury Park, a 4.9 m diameter tube railway built to take mainline trains [The 'Northern City Line', as it is now known, had become part of the Metropolitan Railway network in 1914 and was transferred to the Northern Line in 1933; it was eventually handed over to British Rail in 1975 and is now part of the National Rail suburban network]. Work began on all the above-mentioned branches but the outbreak of World War II interrupted the expansion project, and the conversion of some railway routes has never materialised.

Since 1998, the Northern Line has been operated by a fleet of 106 six-car trains of 1995 stock built by Alstom (2.63 m wide, 17.77 m long and 2.88 m high). The line's main depots are located at Golders Green and Morden, with additional smaller stabling facilities at Edgware, Highgate and High Barnet.

The timetable operated on the Northern Line is difficult to summarize, but basically the main daily off-peak service comprises a train every 3½-4 minutes on either branch north of Camden Town, running south from there alternately via one of the central routes (at the same service interval), with some services on the Charing Cross branch terminating at Kennington. On the Finchley branch every fourth train goes to Mill Hill East, while between Kennington and Morden there is a train every 3 minutes.

LONDON Underground - Northern Line

59.1 km (~ 40.4 km unterirdisch | *underground*), 52 Bahnhöfe | *Stations*

{22-08-1867	[Finsbury Park –] East Finchley – Mill Hill East [– Edgware]}
{01-04-1872	Finchley Central – High Barnet}
18-12-1890	Stockwell – King William Street
24-02-1900	[X] Borough – King William Street
25-02-1900	Borough – Moorgate
03-06-1900	Stockwell – Clapham Common
17-11-1901	Moorgate – Angel
{14-02-1904	Moorgate – Finsbury Park} [Great Northern & City Line]
12-05-1907	Angel – Euston
22-06-1907	Charing Cross – Archway
22-06-1907	Camden Town – Golders Green
06-04-1914	Charing Cross – Embankment
19-11-1923	Golders Green – Hendon Central
20-04-1924	Euston (Bank branch) – Camden Town
18-08-1924	Hendon Central – Edgware
27-10-1924	+ Burnt Oak
13-09-1926	Embankment – Kennington
13-09-1926	Clapham Common – Morden
06-12-1926	+ Balham
{01-03-1933	+ West Finchley}
03-07-1939	Archway – East Finchley
14-04-1940	East Finchley – High Barnet
19-01-1941	+ Highgate
18-05-1941	Finchley Central – Mill Hill East

*The extension of the Northern Line from Golders Green to Edgware opened in two stages from 1923 to 1924. The rebuilding of the **Edgware** terminus ①② began in the late 1930s for a further extension to Bushey Heath, which was later abandoned. The entire route is on the surface except for a 1 km tunnel between **Colindale** and **Hendon Central** ③. Most stations boast a similar entrance building in neo-Georgian style with doric pillars like that at **Brent Cross** ④. **Golders Green** ⑤ was one of the original northern termini of the Hampstead Tube, located near the tunnel mouth. From **Hampstead** to Mornington Crescent, all stations, though refurbished, preserve the original Yerkes style, as seen at **Chalk Farm** ⑥.*

Die Verlängerung der Northern Line von Golders Green nach Edgware wurde in zwei Stufen 1923/24 in Betrieb genommen. Der Umbau des Endbahnhofs **Edgware** ①② begann in den späten dreißiger Jahren, in Vorbereitung einer Verlängerung nach Bushey Heath, die dann aber nie vollendet wurde. Bis auf einen 1 km langen Tunnel zwischen **Colindale** und **Hendon Central** ③ ist der gesamte nördliche Abschnitt oberirdisch. Die meisten Stationen haben ein ähnliches Eingangsgebäude im neo-georgischen Stil mit dorischen Säulen, wie das in **Brent Cross** ④. **Golders Green** ⑤ war eine der ursprünglichen Endstationen der Hampstead-Linie und liegt westlich des Tunnelportals. Von Hampstead bis Mornington Crescent sind alle Röhrenbahnhöfe weitgehend im originalen Stil zu sehen, auch wenn sie zwischenzeitlich neu verfliest wurden, wie am U-Bahnhof **Chalk Farm** ⑥.

Die eingleisige Strecke nach **Mill Hill East** ①② war die letzte Erweiterung der Northern Line. Wie der Ast nach **High Barnet** ③ wurde die Strecke von der *London & North Eastern Railway* im Zuge eines noch viel weitreichenderen Projekts übernommen. Beide Strecken laufen im Bahnhof **Finchley Central** ④ zusammen, von wo alle 3½-4 Minuten ein Zug Richtung Innenstadt fährt. **Tufnell Park** ⑤ liegt auf der 1907 eröffneten Strecke und zeigt sich bis heute im typischen Yerkes-Stil, auch wenn die heutigen Fliesen von einer Renovierung vor wenigen Jahren stammen. Die Verzweigung südlich des viergleisigen U-Bahnhofs **Camden Town** ⑥ wurde 1924 so umgebaut, dass die Züge jetzt kreuzungsfrei von beiden nördlichen Ästen über beide innerstädtischen Strecken Richtung Kennington fahren können.

The single-track **Mill Hill East** branch ①② was the last addition to the Northern Line. Along with the **High Barnet** branch ③ it was taken over in the early 1940s from the 'London & North Eastern Railway' as part of a much larger expansion scheme which did not come to fruition. Both branches converge at **Finchley Central** ④, from where a train runs into central London every 3½-4 minutes. **Tufnell Park** ⑤ is one of the original stations opened in 1907; the platforms have been refurbished recently in mock original style. The junction south of the 4-track **Camden Town** station ⑥ was rebuilt in 1924, and allows grade-separated operation from both northern branches to either the Bank branch or the route to Kennington via Charing Cross.

Mornington Crescent ①, one of the original stations on the Hampstead Tube was closed for refurbishment from 1992 until 1998. At *Euston*, each branch of the Northern Line has a separate station. The one on the Bank branch was rebuilt in the 1960s to provide interchange with the then new Victoria Line on the same level, but in opposite directions. Transfer from the Charing Cross branch to the Victoria Line is possible both at Euston ② and at *Warren Street*. At *Goodge Street* ③④, one of the typical entrance buildings designed by Leslie Green for the Yerkes tube lines, with its ox-blood red faience façade, has been preserved. Many stations in the central area were refurbished during the 1980s and 1990s, some like *Tottenham Court Road* ⑤ with additional tiling, others like *Leicester Square* ⑥ with enamelled panels showing abstract themes.

Mornington Crescent ①, einer der originalen U-Bahnhöfe der Hampstead-Linie, blieb von 1992 bis 1998 wegen einer Generalsanierung geschlossen. In **Euston** hat jede der beiden Northern Line-Strecken einen eigenen Bahnhof, wobei der auf der BankStrecke in den sechziger Jahren grundlegend umgebaut wurde, um bahnsteiggleiches Umsteigen zur Victoria Line in gegengesetzter Richtung zu ermöglichen. Zur Charing Cross-Strecke kann man sowohl in Euston ② als auch an der **Warren Street** umsteigen. Am Bahnhof **Goodge Street** ③④ ist eines der typischen, von Leslie Green für die Yerkes-Linien entworfenen Eingangsgebäude mit roter Fayence-Fassade zu sehen. Viele der U-Bahnhöfe in der Innenstadt wurden in den achtziger und neunziger Jahren umgestaltet, wie z.B. **Tottenham Court Road** ⑤ mit einem Fliesenmosaik oder **Leicester Square** ⑥ mit Emailplatten.

Am U-Bahnhof **Charing Cross** ①② wurde die Schalterebene in typischen Farben der siebziger Jahre gestaltet, die Bahnsteigebene zeigt die Entstehungsgeschichte des originalen Eleanor-Kreuzes, das einst vor dem Bahnhof Charing Cross stand. Der heutige Bahnsteig Richtung Norden im U-Bahnhof **Embankment** ③ stammt von 1914, als die Northern Line in einer Schleife von Charing Cross nach Süden verlängert wurde, um die Umsteigebeziehung zur *District Railway* zu verbessern. **Waterloo** ④ ist die einzige Zwischenstation auf dem 1926 eröffneten, 2,6 km langen Verbindungsstück zwischen Embankment und Kennington. In **Kennington** ⑤⑥, wo beide Innenstadtstrecken in einer viergleisigen Station zusammenlaufen, steht das einzige erhaltene Eingangsgebäude von 1890. Die Züge von Charing Cross können hier in einer Schleife unter den älteren Gleisen wenden.

At **Charing Cross** ①②, the ticket hall boasts typical 1970s colours, while the platform level was refurbished with David Gentleman's mural illustrating the making of the original 'Eleanor Cross'. The present northbound platform at **Embankment** ③ opened in 1914, when a short extension in the form of a single-track loop was completed south from Charing Cross to improve transfer to the District Railway. The appearance of the station is now similar to those on the other lines passing through. **Waterloo** ④ is the only station to have been built on the 2.6 km link between Embankment and Kennington opened in 1926. At **Kennington** ⑤⑥, where both central branches converge in a 4-platform station, the only remaining 1890 entrance pavilion has been preserved. Trains from the Charing Cross branch can terminate here in a loop under the original tracks.

From **Euston**, the eastern branch of the Northern Line runs via Bank, the heart of the City of London. At **King's Cross St. Pancras** ① transfer is provided to five other lines. Until 1992, the busy **Angel** station ② had a narrow island platform similar to those at Clapham North and Clapham Common. For northbound trains a new platform was then built in a separate tunnel and the southbound platform ③ widened by covering the former northbound trackbed. **Old Street** station ④ was refurbished in the mid-1970s with a sound-deadening vault. The former northbound platform at **London Bridge** ⑤ was converted into a central corridor in conjunction with the Jubilee Line extension, and northbound trains were diverted through a new tunnel. **Borough** station ⑥ was part of the original City & South London Railway, although nothing is preserved from that period.

Von **Euston** führt die östliche Strecke der Northern Line über Bank in der City nach Süden. In **King's Cross St. Pancras** ① kann man zu fünf anderen Linien umsteigen. Bis 1992 hatte **Angel** ② einen engen Mittelbahnsteig, wie er heute noch in Clapham North und Clapham Common zu sehen ist. Richtung Norden wurde damals eine neue Bahnsteigröhre gebaut und der Bahnsteig Richtung Süden ③ verbreitert, indem das zweite Gleis überdeckt wurde. **Old Street** ④ wurde in den siebziger Jahren mit einer lärmschluckenden Decke ausgestattet. Im U-Bahnhof **London Bridge** ⑤ wurde der frühere Bahnsteig Richtung Norden im Zuge der Verlängerung der Jubilee Line zu einem Verteilertunnel umgebaut und parallel dazu eine neue Bahnsteigröhre errichtet. Die Station **Borough** ⑥ war schon auf der originalen *City & South London Railway* zu finden, wenn auch aus dieser Zeit nichts erhalten ist.

Auf dem Südast der Northern Line sind an den Bahnhöfen
Clapham North ① und **Clapham Common** ② noch zwei der nur
3,4 m breiten Mittelbahnsteige mit nur einem Ausgang zu sehen.
Die übrigen Stationen bis South Wimbledon sind weitgehend
einheitlich gestaltet, wie z.B. **Clapham South** ③ oder **Tooting
Broadway** ⑤. Die meisten haben auch ein ähnliches Empfangsge-
bäude, in **Balham** ④ gibt es sogar zwei davon, wobei eines direkt
mit dem Vorortbahnhof verbunden ist. Der südliche Endbahnhof der
Northern Line, **Morden** ⑥, liegt in einem teils offenen Einschnitt.
Südlich der Station befindet sich einer der Betriebshöfe der Linie.
Die Gleise reichen bis zum Vorortbahnhof Morden South. Auf
halber Strecke zwischen South Wimbledon und Morden quert die
Croydon Tramlink, aber es gibt keine Umsteigemöglichkeit.

Along the southern leg of the Northern Line, *Clapham North*
① and *Clapham Common* ② preserve a single, only 3.4 m wide
island platform with exits only at one end. The rest of the
stations south to *South Wimbledon* are of identical design, like
Clapham South ③ or *Tooting Broadway* ⑤. Most have a very
similar entrance building to the two seen at *Balham* ④, one of
them being linked directly to the mainline railway station. The
southern terminus of the Northern Line at *Morden* ⑥ lies in a
cutting, though partly covered. One of the Northern Line's depots
is located south of the station, with tracks reaching close to the
Morden South railway station. Halfway between South Wimbledon and Morden the Northern Line is crossed by the Croydon
Tramlink, but no transfer is provided.

47

East Acton *(Photo Brian Hardy)*

The Central Line is London's most important east-west link and serves both the shopping area around Oxford Street as well as the business district in the City. On its central underground section it is a typical tube line, whereas on outer stretches its appearance is similar to that of a suburban, though high-frequency railway.

Construction of the 'Central London Railway' began in 1896. Tunnels were excavated with a diameter of 3.5 m and station length was fixed at 99 m. Soon after it opened from Shepherd's Bush to Bank (9.3 km) on 30 July 1900 (only 11 days after the first Métro line had opened in Paris), it was nicknamed the 'Twopenny Tube' for its flat fare. For the first three years electric locomotives hauled the passenger carriages, until they were replaced by motorized cars in 1903 due to excessive vibration caused by the locos.

Although the 'Central London Railway' was an immediate success, extensions at either end followed rather slowly. In 1908, the access lines to the depot at Wood Lane west of Shepherd's Bush were rebuilt in the form of a loop (operated in an anti-clockwise direction), and the surface-level station Wood Lane was added to improve access to the 'Franco-Brit-ish Exhibition' held there that year. At the eastern end a short extension to Liverpool Street opened in 1912 to provide a link to the mainline rail services towards the eastern suburbs. Liverpool Street remained the line's eastern terminus for the following 34 years.

In 1917, the 'Great Western Railway' completed a new link between Ealing and Wood Lane, and the Central London Railway began to provide electric passenger service on it from 1920. To allow for this extension the loop arrangement at Wood Lane had

Die Central Line ist Londons wichtigste Ost-West-Verbindung, welche sowohl die Einkaufsstraße Oxford Street als auch das Bankenviertel in der City erschließt. Auf ihrem mittleren, unterirdischen Abschnitt stellt sie eine typische *Tube*-Linie dar, während sie auf äußeren Strecken eher einer S-Bahn mit dichtem Takt gleicht. Der Bau der *Central London Railway* begann 1896. Die Streckentunnel wurden mit einem Durchmesser von 3,5 m und die Stationen mit 99 m langen Bahnsteigen errichtet. Bald nach Inbetriebnahme der 9,3 km langen Strecke von Shepherd's Bush bis Bank am 30. Juli 1900 (nur 11 Tage nach Eröffnung der Pariser Métro), bekam sie den Beinamen ‚Twopenny Tube', die 2-Pfennig-Linie, weil auf der Linie ein Einheitstarif galt. Während der ersten drei Jahre wurden die Wagons von elektrischen Lokomotiven gezogen, aber bereits 1903 wurden diese durch Triebwagen ersetzt, da sie zu starke Vibrationen verursacht hatten.

Trotz des unmittelbaren Erfolgs ließen Verlängerungen an beiden Enden auf sich warten. 1908 wurden die Zufahrtsgleise zum Betriebshof westlich der Endstation Shepherd's Bush zu einer gegen den Uhrzeigersinn befahrenen eingleisigen Schleife umgebaut und die oberirdische Station Wood Lane errichtet. Dadurch wurde das Ausstellungsgelände der in jenem Jahr abgehaltenen ‚Franco-British Exhibition' besser erschlossen. Am östlichen Ende kam 1912 ein kurzer Abschnitt bis zum Fernbahnhof Liverpool Street dazu; hier endete die Central Line 34 Jahre lang.

1917 baute die *Great Western Railway* eine Verbindungsbahn zwischen Ealing und Wood Lane, auf der die *Central London Railway* ab 1920 den Personenverkehr übernahm. Dazu musste die Schleife am Bahnhof Wood Lane umgebaut und zwei zusätzliche Bahnsteige errichtet werden.

Bank - "Mind the Gap"

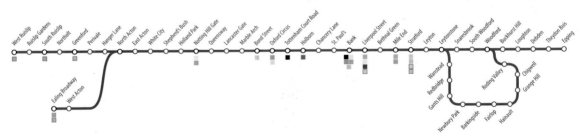

1913 kam auch die *Central London Railway* unter die Kontrolle der Yerkes-Gruppe und wurde schließlich 1933 in *London Transport* integriert. 1935 wurden weitreichende Pläne für Verlängerungen an beiden Enden, meist durch Übernahme bestehender Vorortbahnen, angekündigt. Von Liverpool Street wurde eine unterirdische Strecke bis Stratford

Ealing Broadway *(Photo Thomas Schunk)*

und weiter bis Leyton gebaut. Von dort sollte es nach Ongar auf den Gleisen der *Great Eastern* gehen. Ab Leytonstone kam eine weitere unterirdische Strecke entlang der Eastern Avenue dazu, die im Osten an den Fairlop-Ring, der von derselben Bahngesellschaft betrieben wurde, anschließen sollte. Im Westen wurden entlang der *Great Western*-Strecke nach High Wycombe bis West Ruislip zwei separate Gleise für die Central Line verlegt. All diese Erweiterungen waren bis 1949 abgeschlossen, bis auf die 9,7 km lange Strecke Epping - Ongar, welche erst 1957 von der Central Line übernommen und 1994 endgültig geschlossen wurde.

Während der neunziger Jahre wurde die Central Line grundlegend erneuert und mit neuen Signalanlagen für den automatischen Betrieb ausgerüstet. Die Aufgaben des Fahrers beschränken sich seither darauf, die Türen zu schließen und den Zug in Bewegung zu setzen. Zwischen 1993 und 1995 wurden 85 8-Wagen-Züge der Baureihe 1992 von Alstom geliefert (2,62 m breit, 16,25 m lang und 2,87 m hoch). Die Betriebshöfe der Central Line liegen in Ruislip und Hainault, außerdem gibt es Abstellmöglichkeiten in White City, Woodford und Loughton.

Die Central Line verkehrt außerhalb der Hauptverkehrszeiten alle 6½-7 Minuten nach West Ruislip, Ealing Broadway, Loughton und Hainault, sowie alle 10 Minuten bis Epping. Dazu kommen weitere Züge auf dem Abschnitt zwischen White City und Newbury Park. Von Hainault fahren Züge alle 20 Minuten, allerdings nur bis 20:15 Uhr, bis Woodford weiter.

LONDON Underground - Central Line

73.3 km (~ 26 km unterirdisch | *underground*), 50 Bahnhöfe | *Stations*

{22-08-1856	[Stratford –] Leyton – Loughton}
{24-04-1865	Loughton – Epping [– Ongar]}
30-07-1900	Shepherd's Bush – Bank
24-09-1900	+ Bond Street
{01-05-1903	[Ilford –] Newbury Park – Woodford}
{15-06-1903	North Acton – Greenford East Junction}
{01-10-1904	Greenford East Junction – Greenford}
{02-04-1906	Greenford – West Ruislip}
14-05-1908	Shepherd's Bush – Wood Lane (> White City)
28-07-1912	Bank – Liverpool Street
03-08-1920	Wood Lane – Ealing Broadway
05-11-1923	+ North Acton, West Acton
04-12-1946	Liverpool Street – Stratford
05-05-1947	Stratford – Leytonstone
30-06-1947	North Acton – Greenford
14-12-1947	Leytonstone – Woodford
14-12-1947	Leytonstone – Newbury Park
31-05-1948	Newbury Park – Hainault
21-11-1948	Greenford – West Ruislip
21-11-1948	Woodford – Loughton
21-11-1948	Woodford – Hainault
25-09-1949	Loughton – Epping

to be rebuilt and two additional platforms were added.

In 1913, the 'Central London Railway' was absorbed by the Yerkes Underground Group, and remained part of it until 1933, when it was integrated into London Transport. In 1935, ambitious plans to extend the Central Line at both ends mainly along existing railway corridors were announced. From Liverpool Street an underground extension was built to Stratford and Leyton, from where the line was to continue on the Great Eastern line to Ongar. From Leytonstone an underground branch along Eastern Avenue was added, which at its eastern end was linked to the Fairlop loop, until then operated by the same railway company as the Ongar line. In the west, two additional tracks were laid as far as West Ruislip along the Great Western route to High Wycombe. All these extensions were completed by 1949, when the Central Line reached its present form, except for the 9.7 km Epping - Ongar section, which was electrified in 1957 and closed permanently in 1994.

During the 1990s, the Central Line underwent full modernisation, including a totally new signalling system which allows automatic operation, the driver's duties being reduced to closing the doors, starting the train and observing the line ahead. 85 new eight-car trains known as '1992 stock' were delivered by Adtranz in Derby, entering service between 1993 and 1995 (2.62 m wide, 16.25 m long and 2.87 m high). The Central Line has major depots at Ruislip and Hainault, with further siding facilities at White City, Woodford and Loughton.

The main Central Line Monday to Saturday off-peak service comprises a train every 6½-7 minutes to West Ruislip, Ealing Broadway, Loughton and Hainault, and every 10 minutes to Epping. There are additional trains between White City and Newbury Park. The service between Hainault and Woodford operates every 20 minutes until 20:15 by extending trains from Hainault.

The Central Line was extended in two stages in 1947/48 from North Acton to **West Ruislip** ①, running parallel to the mainline railway to High Wycombe. A further planned extension to Denham was abandoned due to Green Belt regulations. At **Greenford** ②, a bay track is located between the Central Line tracks, this being used by half-hourly suburban trains from Ealing or Paddington. East of **Hanger Lane** ③ a new station may be built in the future to provide interchange with the Piccadilly Line at Park Royal. The shorter branch to **Ealing Broadway** ④ terminates between mainline and District Line tracks. Both western Central Line branches converge at **North Acton** ⑤, where some trains from the east also terminate. **East Acton** station ⑥ preserves its original appearance from when it opened as a simple 'halt' in 1920.

Die Central Line wurde 1947/48 in zwei Stufen von North Acton nach **West Ruislip** ① parallel zur Bahnstrecke nach High Wycombe verlängert. Ein weiteres Teilstück bis Denham wurde schließlich wegen der Grüngürtel-Gesetze nicht mehr verwirklicht. Am Bahnhof **Greenford** ② gibt es zwischen den Gleisen der Central Line ein stumpfes Gleis für die halbstündlichen Vorortzüge von Ealing bzw. Paddington. Östlich von **Hanger Lane** ③ soll eine weitere Station eingerichtet werden, um das Umsteigen zur Piccadilly Line am Bahnhof Park Royal zu ermöglichen. Der kürzere Ast nach **Ealing Broadway** ④ endet zwischen der Fernbahn und der District Line. Die beiden westlichen Äste vereinigen sich in **North Acton** ⑤, wo auch manche Züge aus Richtung Osten enden. **East Acton** ⑥ ist weitgehend in der Form der ursprünglichen Haltestellen der zwanziger Jahre erhalten.

1947 wurde die frühere Station Wood Lane etwa 300 m weiter nördlich durch die Station **White City** ersetzt. Die ursprüngliche Endstation **Shepherd's Bush** ①② wurde in den Achtzigern neu gestaltet. Bei einer Bahnsteigverlängerung kurz vor dem 2. Weltkrieg entstand an einem Ende eine Säulenreihe statt der sonst üblichen Trennwand, weil die beiden Gleise zu nahe aneinander lagen. Während **Holland Park** ③ mit unauffälligen beigefarbenen Fliesen verkleidet ist, zeigt sich der U-Bahnhof **Lancaster Gate** ④ noch als einziger mit weißen Originalfliesen, wie sie 1900 an allen Bahnhöfen der *Central London Railway* zu sehen waren. Die Station **Marble Arch** ⑤ wurde mit verschiedenen, aus Emailplatten hergestellten Bögen verziert. Am U-Bahnhof **Bond Street** ⑥ sollen die Fliesenbänder an der Decke wegen der unmittelbaren Nähe zu großen Kaufhäusern Geschenkpapier andeuten.

In 1947, Wood Lane station (terminus from 1908 until 1920) was replaced by *White City* station some 300 m further north. The original western terminus was *Shepherd's Bush* ①②, clad with new tiling during the 1980s, when most stations in the central area were redecorated. When the platforms were lengthened just before World War II, pillars were built at one end instead of a full dividing wall as the running tunnels were too close. *Holland Park* station ③ displays inconspicuous beige tiles, whereas *Lancaster Gate* ④ is the only station that preserves the original white tiling, once typical for all stations along the 'Central London Railway'. Several arches, all in a different style made of enamelled panels, now decorate the platforms at *Marble Arch* ⑤. At *Bond Street* ⑥ the additional tiling insinuates wrapping paper, a reference to the shopping facilities in the neighbourhood.

Oxford Circus station ①, currently under refurbishment at platform level, boasts a typical Leslie Green station building, although this one (now exit only) was actually built for the Bakerloo Line in 1906. At *Tottenham Court Road* ②-④ the exit area was redecorated in the 1980s with colourful mosaics. In 1933, the former British Museum station was closed and replaced by a new station called *Holborn* ⑤ further east to improve interchange with the Piccadilly Line. The station design now makes reference to the nearby museum. As at Notting Hill Gate and St. Paul's, the platforms at *Chancery Lane* ⑥⑦ were built above each other so as not to intrude on private properties. Between 1958 and 2005 this station was closed on Sundays, but it is now open daily.

Am U-Bahnhof **Oxford Circus** ①, dessen Bahnsteigebene derzeit renoviert wird, ist ein typisches Eingangsgebäude von Leslie Green zu sehen, auch wenn dieses 1906 für die Bakerloo Line errichtet wurde und heute nur als Ausgang dient. Am U-Bahnhof **Tottenham Court Road** ②-④ wurden Bahnsteige und Ausgänge in den achtziger Jahren mit bunten Mosaiken verkleidet. 1933 wurde der frühere Bahnhof British Museum geschlossen und weiter östlich durch **Holborn** ⑤ ersetzt, um das Umsteigen zur Piccadilly Line zu verbessern. Heute zieren Motive aus jenem Museum die Bahnsteigwände. Wie in Notting Hill Gate und St. Paul's liegen die Bahnsteige im U-Bahnhof **Chancery Lane** ⑥⑦ übereinander angeordnet, so musste kein Privatgrundstück in Anspruch genommen werden. Von 1958 bis 2005 war dieser Bahnhof sonntags geschlossen.

Bank ①② war der ursprüngliche Endbahnhof am östlichen Ende der *Central London Railway*. Wie in Tottenham Court Road gab es hier nie ein Eingangsgebäude, stattdessen diente die unterirdische Schalterhalle von Anfang an als Unterführung unter der verkehrsreichen Straßenkreuzung. Das bekannte ‚Mind the Gap!' (Achten Sie auf den Spalt!) konnte erstmals an den gekrümmten Bahnsteigen der Central Line vernommen werden. An der Station Bank kann man zur Waterloo & City Line, zur Northern Line, zur Docklands Light Railway und sogar zur Circle bzw. District Line am Bahnhof Monument, der über Gänge und Rolltreppen mit dem U-Bahnhof Bank verbunden ist, umsteigen.

Die Verlängerung bis **Liverpool Street** ③④ erfolgte 1912. Sie war erst möglich, als die *Central London Railway* auf eine weitere Verlängerung Richtung Osten verzichtet hatte, sonst hätte die *Great Eastern Railway* den Bau des U-Bahnhofs auf ihrem Gelände nicht gestattet. Neben dem Fern- und Vorortbahnhof Liverpool Street bot diese Verlängerung auch einen Anschluss an die Vorortzüge im Bahnhof Broad Street, der bis 1986 gleich westlich des Bahnhofs Liverpool Street lag. Die Zugänge zu den Bahnsteigen der Central Line wurden zwischen 1986 und 1992 umgebaut und die Bahnsteigwände mit neuen weißen Fliesen versehen. Die Decken wurden mit weißen Metallplatten verkleidet.

Bank station ①② was the original eastern terminus of the Central London Railway, and as at Tottenham Court Road no surface station building was built here, the subsurface ticket hall was instead meant to serve as a pedestrian subway under the road crossing. The 'Mind the Gap'- announcement was first heard on the curved Central Line platforms. At Bank, transfer is provided to the Waterloo & City Line, the Northern Line, the Docklands Light Railway and even to the District and Circle Lines at Monument station.

The extension to *Liverpool Street* ③④ in 1912, built to provide access to Liverpool Street and Broad Street mainline stations (the latter no longer existing), was only possible once the Central London Railway had given up plans for further expansion east, otherwise the Great Eastern Railway would not have granted permission to build a station under their property. Accesses to the Central Line platforms were improved from 1986 to 1992, and the platform walls were retiled in white, although the ceiling is now covered with white panels.

(Photo ② Thomas Schunk)

From Liverpool Street the route continues underground to Stratford, with only two intermediate stations along a 7 km stretch. **Bethnal Green** ① station lies some 500 m from the mainline station of the same name. At **Mile End** ②, the Central Line climbs to the surface to provide easy cross-platform interchange with the District Line. The massive columns were retiled in the late 1980s. The trains continue east under the mainline tracks, emerging from the tunnel just before arriving at the elevated **Stratford** station ③, where cross-platform interchange is provided with trains to and from Shenfield. Just east of Stratford the Central Line disappears into another 1.2 km tunnel before joining the former railway alignment south of **Leyton** station ④⑤. The Central Line splits just north of **Leytonstone** ⑥, with the Hainault branch immediately diving into another tunnel.

Von Liverpool Street geht die unterirdische Strecke bis Stratford weiter. Auf dem 7 km langen Abschnitt gibt es nur zwei Zwischenstationen. **Bethnal Green** ① liegt etwa 500 m vom gleichnamigen Vorortbahnhof entfernt. Vor **Mile End** ② steigt die Central Line nach oben, um an diesem Bahnhof ein bequemes Umsteigen zur District Line am selben Bahnsteig zu ermöglichen. Die wuchtigen Säulen wurden in den späten achtziger Jahren neu verfliest. Die Strecke führt weiter unter den Gleisen der Hauptbahn und kommt kurz vor **Stratford** ③ an die Oberfläche. Hier besteht bahnsteiggleicher Anschluss an die Vorortzüge von und nach Shenfield. Sofort nach Stratford beginnt ein 1,2 km langer Tunnel, bis südlich von **Leyton** ④⑤ dann die alte Bahntrasse erreicht wird. Unmittelbar nördlich des Bahnhofs **Leytonstone** ⑥ spaltet sich die Central Line, wobei der Ast nach Hainault im Tunnel verschwindet.

Entlang der Eastern Avenue wurden drei unterirdische Stationen gebaut: **Wanstead** als typischer Röhrenbahnhof, **Redbridge** ① in geringer Tiefe und nur über Treppen zugänglich, und **Gants Hill** ②③ in Anlehnung an die Moskauer Metro mit einem langen Mittelschiff. Nach einer längeren Kurve erreicht die Central Line südlich von **Newbury Park** die ehemalige Bahnstrecke der *Great Eastern* von Ilford nach Woodford. **Hainault** ④⑤ ist der planmäßige Zielbahnhof für die Züge aus Ealing, auch wenn manche bereits in Newbury Park enden. Der Abschnitt von Hainault bis Woodford, der durch die Grafschaft Essex führt, wird alle 20 Minuten bedient. Der Bahnhof **Roding Valley** ⑥ wurde 1936 auf der 1903 eröffneten Strecke eingefügt, sein heutiges Aussehen stammt von 1949.

Three underground stations were built along the Eastern Avenue route: *Wanstead* as a typical tube station, *Redbridge* ① as a subsurface station accessible only via stairs, and the deep-level *Gants Hill* station ②③ imitating a Moscow-style platform level with a large central concourse. After a long curve, the Central Line joins the former Great Eastern Railway alignment from Ilford to Woodford just south of *Newbury Park* station. *Hainault* ④⑤ is the regular terminus for trains from Ealing Broadway, although certain trains terminate at Newbury Park. The section of the Hainault loop between Hainault and Woodford, which passes through Essex, is served every 20 minutes. Opened in 1936, *Roding Valley* station ⑥ was a late addition to a railway line in service since 1903, and it was rebuilt in its present form in 1949.   (Photo ⑥ Brian Hardy)

From Leytonstone the Epping branch continues north on the surface, with most stations, like **Snaresbrook** ①, preserving many features from the pre-Underground period. **Woodford** ② is the terminus for trains from Hainault. Just where the Hainault loop branches off, the Central Line leaves the Greater London area for Essex. Steam trains had served this line from as early as 1856 up to Loughton, and on to Epping from 1865. **Loughton** station ④ had been rebuilt in 1940 before the route was taken over by London Underground in 1948, but other stations like **Buckhurst Hill** ③ or the terminus **Epping** ⑥ preserve station buildings dating back to the late 19th century. Leaving **Debden**, the panorama along the line becomes more and more rural ⑤. Epping station lies 31 km from Tottenham Court Road.

Von Leytonstone führt der Epping-Ast weiter oberirdisch Richtung Norden. Die meisten Bahnhofsgebäude und Bahnsteigdächer dieser Strecke, wie in **Snaresbrook** ①, stammen aus der Zeit vor dem U-Bahn-Betrieb. In **Woodford** ② enden die alle 20 Minuten von Hainault weitergeführten Züge. Da, wo der Hainault-Ring abzweigt, verlässt die U-Bahn das Gebiet von Greater London, der äußere Abschnitt liegt in der Grafschaft Essex. Dampfzüge fuhren auf dieser Strecke bis Loughton ab 1856 und bis Epping ab 1865. Der Bahnhof **Loughton** ④ wurde 1940 umgebaut, bevor die Strecke 1948 an London Underground übergeben wurde. In **Buckhurst Hill** ③ oder an der Endstation **Epping** ⑥ hingegen ist das Eingangsgebäude aus dem 19. Jahrhundert erhalten. Ab **Debden** wird die Gegend entlang der U-Bahnstrecke immer ländlicher ⑤, schließlich liegt Epping 31 km von Tottenham Court Road entfernt.

Die Waterloo & City Line entstand 1898 als eine der ersten elektrischen U-Bahnen der Welt. Sie wurde von der *London & South Western Railway* gebaut, um deren Kopfbahnhof Waterloo mit der City zu verbinden, und erst 1994 an London Underground übergeben.

Londons kürzeste U-Bahn-Linie wird mit 4-Wagen-Zügen ④ betrieben, die weitgehend baugleich mit den ab 1993 für die Central Line gelieferten Zügen sind. Diese Wagen waren bislang in den Farben des ehemaligen *Network SouthEast* zu sehen, sie werden jedoch im Frühjahr 2006 im Zuge einer Generalsanierung der Strecke umgestrichen. Die völlig unterirdische Strecke hat keine Gleisverbindung zum übrigen Netz, so dass die Fahrzeuge mit einem Kran in die nach oben offene Abstellanlage gehoben werden mussten.

Während es sich bei der Station **Bank** (bis 1940 ‚City') ①② um einen Röhrenbahnhof handelt, liegt die Station **Waterloo** ③ in geringer Tiefe unter den Gleisen des Fernbahnhofs. Die älteste erhaltene Röhrenbahn bekam den Spitznamen ‚The Drain' - das Abwasserrohr. Die Strecke führt von Waterloo erst nach Norden, unter der Themse hindurch und schwenkt westlich des U-Bahnhofs Blackfriars nach Osten. Sie endet schließlich stumpf westlich des U-Bahnhofs Bank der Central Line. Hier besteht außerdem eine Umsteigemöglichkeit zur Northern Line, zur Docklands Light Railway sowie zur Station Monument an der Circle/District Line.

Die Waterloo & City Line verkehrt montags bis freitags nur von 6:15 bis 21:45 und samstags von 8:00 bis 18:30 alle 3-5 Minuten. Sonntags ist die Verbindung geschlossen.

LONDON Underground - Waterloo & City Line

2.4 km (völlig unterirdisch | *completely underground*)
2 Bahnhöfe | *Stations*
{08-08-1898   Waterloo – Bank}
05-04-1994   Waterloo – Bank [London Underground]

When opened in 1898, the Waterloo & City Line was among the first electric metro lines in the world. Its construction was promoted by the 'London & South Western Railway' to link their terminus at Waterloo to the City of London. It was only handed over to London Underground in 1994.

London's shortest tube line is operated with 4-car trains ④, which are almost identical to the 1992 stock acquired for the Central Line. Up to now these cars have carried the blue & white livery of the former Network SouthEast, although they are being repainted in spring 2006 when the line closes for an extensive refurbishment.

The totally underground route is not linked physically to any other line, so cars had to be lifted into the sidings with a crane. While **Bank** station ①② (until 1940 called City) is a typical tube station, the **Waterloo** terminus ③ lies at low depth under the mainline tracks. The tube line nicknamed 'the drain', runs north from Waterloo, crossing under the river before turning east near Blackfriars station; it terminates west of the Central Line station at Bank. Here interchange is also provided with the Northern Line, the Docklands Light Railway, as well as the Circle and District Lines via their Monument station. The Waterloo & City Line only operates from 06:15 until 21:45 on Mondays to Fridays, and from 08:00 until 18:30 on Saturdays. There is no service on Sundays.

Piccadilly Circus *(Photo Thomas Schunk)*

The Bakerloo Line can be divided into two sections: 1) the proper tube line from Elephant & Castle to Queen's Park (10.9 km), and 2) the shared surface section running over Network Rail tracks from Queen's Park to Harrow & Wealdstone (12.7 km).

The 'Baker Street & Waterloo Railway' was one of several underground lines proposed in the last decade of the 19th century, after the 'City & South London Railway' (see p. 40) had began electric operation through tube tunnels in 1890. Construction began in 1898, and before its completion, extensions to Marylebone and Paddington mainline stations in the north and to Elephant & Castle in the south were authorised. In 1901, however, when construction was already well-advanced, the company came into financial trouble, and was eventually rescued by the American Charles Tyson Yerkes, who also acquired the District Railway, as well as the 'Piccadilly Tube' (see p. 64) and the 'Hampstead Tube' (see p. 41) then under construction, all of which were then built to the same standards. The line finally opened in March 1906 and soon became known popularly as the 'Bakerloo Tube'. Most access buildings were designed by Leslie Green in red faience, and have become one of the distinctive features of the London Underground system. At platform level, walls were covered with tiles showing a different pattern at each station. The remaining sections to Elephant & Castle and Edgware Road opened soon after; the section from Edgware Road to Paddington, however, was still awaiting construction, as it was not clear in which direction the line might eventually continue from there.

In 1909, the 'London & North Western Railway' (LNWR) began to lay two additional tracks to its four existing ones along what is now the West Coast Mainline from Euston to Watford. An agreement was reached between the LNWR and the Bakerloo Line to build a tube link between Queen's Park and Paddington instead of an envisaged underground route to Euston mainline station, and share operation along the new electrified surface route to Watford. The originally planned route from Edgware Road to Paddington had to be changed accordingly so that it projected northwards. Once completed, some Bakerloo Line trains began operating over LNWR tracks as far as Willesden Junction in 1915, before being extended all the way to Watford Junction two years later. In order to use standard tube stock on the Watford line,

Die Bakerloo Line kann in zwei Abschnitte unterteilt werden: 1) die eigentliche *Tube* von Elephant & Castle bis Queen's Park (10,9 km), und 2) die oberirdische Verlängerung auf den Network Rail-Gleisen von Queen's Park bis Harrow & Wealdstone (12,7 km). Die *Baker* Street & Water*loo* Railway war eines von vielen U-Bahn-Projekten des letzten Jahrzehnts des 19. Jahrhunderts, nachdem 1890 die *City & South London Railway* (siehe S. 40) als erste elektrische Röhrenbahn in Betrieb genommen worden war. Der Bau begann 1898 und noch vor Fertigstellung des ersten Abschnitts wurden bereits Verlängerungen im Norden zu den Fernbahnhöfen Marylebone und Paddington, und im Süden bis Elephant & Castle genehmigt. 1901, als die Arbeiten schon weit fortgeschritten waren, geriet die Bahngesellschaft in finanzielle Schwierigkeiten, doch das Projekt wurde schließlich durch Charles Tyson Yerkes gerettet. Dieser Amerikaner hatte bereits die *District Railway* erworben und finanzierte den Bau der Piccadilly Line (siehe S. 64) und der *Hampstead Tube* (siehe S. 41). Bei allen drei *Tube*-Linien wurden somit dieselben Parameter angewandt. Die *Baker Street & Waterloo Railway* wurde schließlich 1906 eröffnet und bekam bald den einfacheren Namen *Bakerloo Tube*. Die meisten Eingangsgebäude wurden von Leslie Green im roten Fayence-Stil errichtet, sie sind heute eines der wesentlichen Erkennungsmerkmale der Londoner U-Bahn. Die Bahnsteigwände wurden mit jeweils unterschiedlichen Fliesenmustern gestaltet.

Die ersten Verlängerungen bis Elephant & Castle und bis Edgware Road wurden wenig später in Betrieb genommen, das letzte Teilstück bis Paddington verzögerte sich aber deshalb, weil noch nicht klar war, in welche Richtung die Linie später gehen sollte.

1909 begann die *London & North Western Railway* (LNWR) entlang der heutigen *West Coast Mainline* von Euston bis Watford ein separates Paar Vorortgleise zu verlegen. Daraufhin vereinbarte die LNWR mit der *Bakerloo Tube*, eine unterirdische Verbindung zwischen Paddington und Queen's Park anstatt einer unterirdischen Strecke nach Euston zu bauen. Der Betrieb auf den neuen elektrifizierten Gleisen nach Watford sollte gemischt abgewickelt werden. Die ursprünglich geplante Strecke von Edgware Road bis Paddington musste nun so umgeplant werden, dass eine Weiterführung Richtung Norden möglich war. Die Bakerloo-

Wembley Central

Züge begannen 1915 bis Willesden Junction zu fahren, zwei Jahre später erreichten sie Watford Junction. In den dreißiger Jahren mussten die Bahnsteige umgebaut werden, so dass normale *Tube*-Züge halten konnten. Wegen der höheren Vorortbahnzüge, muss man in die *Tube*-Züge bis heute hinuntersteigen.

Eine Verlängerung der Bakerloo Line Richtung Süden nach Camberwell und weiter erschien immer wieder in den Planungen (um 1950 sogar auf den Netzplänen als ‚im Bau‘), daraus wurde aber bis heute nichts. Im Norden hingegen kam ein zweiter Ast hinzu, nachdem für die Metropolitan Line zwischen Baker Street und Finchley Road eine Entlastungsstrecke gebaut worden war. Diese Strecke zusammen mit den ‚langsamen‘ Gleisen von Finchley Road bis Wembley Park und dem Ast nach Stanmore wurden 1939 in die Bakerloo Line eingegliedert. 1979 wurde daraus die neue Jubilee Line (siehe S. 78).

1982 wurde der Betrieb auf der Watford-Strecke bis Stonebridge Park verkürzt, ab 1984 fuhren die Züge in den Hauptverkehrszeiten weiter bis Harrow & Wealdstone. Ab 1988 fuhren die Bakerloo-Züge wieder ganztags von Montag bis Samstag bis Harrow & Wealdstone, seit 1989 nun auch sonntags.

Auf der Bakerloo Line sind 36 7-Wagen-Züge der Baureihe 1972 im Einsatz (2,64 m breit, 16 m lang und 2,88 m hoch). Diese wurden von Metro-Cammell in Birmingham hergestellt und zwischen 1990 und 1995 modernisiert. Der Betriebshof der Bakerloo Line liegt in Stonebridge Park, weitere Abstellanlagen gibt es in Queen's Park und London Road (bei Lambeth North).

Außerhalb der Hauptverkehrszeiten fahren die Bakerloo-Züge an allen Tagen von Elephant & Castle alle 3-3½ Minuten ab, sechs Züge pro Stunde fahren bis Harrow & Wealdstone durch (dazu kommen ab Queen's Park stündlich drei weitere der Silverlink Metro), andere Zielbahnhöfe sind Queen's Park oder Willesden Junction (in diesem Fall dient der Betriebshof Stonebridge Park zum Wenden).

the platforms along the surface stretch were rebuilt during the 1930s to a compromise height for both tube and mainline rolling stock, resulting in a step down into the tube trains up to the present day.

While an extension south from Elephant & Castle to Camberwell and beyond reappeared on the table again and again (and around 1950 was even shown on official network maps as under construction), a branch was added to the Bakerloo Line in the north by building two relief tunnels for the Metropolitan Line between Baker Street and Finchley Road and transferring the 'slow' tracks to Wembley Park and the Stanmore branch to the Bakerloo Line in 1939. The Baker Street - Stanmore branch remained with the Bakerloo Line until it became part of the new Jubilee Line in 1979 (see p. 78).

In 1982, services to Watford were curtailed to Stonebridge Park. Peak-hour trains were extended to Harrow & Wealdstone again from 1984, but in 1988 through service to Harrow was resumed during all operating hours on Mondays to Saturdays and also on Sundays from 1989.

The Bakerloo Line is operated by a fleet of 36 trains of 1972 stock, with each train made up of seven cars. They were manufactured by Metro-Cammell in Birmingham and refurbished between 1990 and 1995 (2.64 m wide, 16 m long and 2.88 m high). The line's depot is located at Stonebridge Park, with additional smaller stabling facilities at Queen's Park and London Road (near Lambeth North).

During off-peak hours daily Bakerloo trains depart from Elephant & Castle every 3-3½ minutes, with 6 trains per hour serving Harrow & Wealdstone (with three additional Silverlink Metro trains per hour from Queen's Park). Other regular destinations are Queen's Park and Willesden Junction, where from the latter, trains run empty to Stonebridge Park depot to reverse.

Warwick Avenue

LONDON Underground - Bakerloo Line

23.6 km (~ 10.6 km unterirdisch | *underground*), 25 Bahnhöfe | *Stations*

12.7 km gemeinsam mit | *shared with* Silverlink Metro

{20-07-1837	[Euston –] Queen's Park – Harrow & Wealdstone [– Watford]}
10-03-1906	Baker Street – Lambeth North
05-08-1906	Lambeth North – Elephant & Castle
27-03-1907	Baker Street – Marylebone
15-06-1907	Marylebone – Edgware Road
01-12-1913	Edgware Road – Paddington
31-01-1915	Paddington – Kilburn Park
11-02-1915	Kilburn Park – Queen's Park
10-05-1915	Queen's Park – Willesden Junction
06-06-1915	+ Maida Vale
01-10-1916	+ Kensal Green
16-04-1917	Willesden Junction – Harrow & Wealdstone [– Watford Jctn]
01-08-1917	+ Stonebridge Park
03-07-1933	+ South Kenton

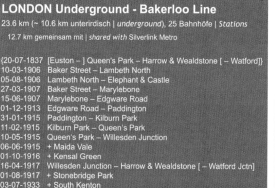

Harrow & Wealdstone ①② *is the present northwestern terminus of the Bakerloo Line, although from 1917 until 1982 tube trains continued to Watford Junction. Tracks between Queen's Park and Harrow & Wealdstone are owned by Network Rail and shared by Silverlink Metro services to and from Euston. Among the busiest stations on the surface section is* **Wembley Central** ③, *located in a cutting and built over in the mid-1960s.* **Willesden Junction** ④ *provides transfer to the North London Line and is the terminus for some Bakerloo trains, which then run empty to Stonebridge Park depot to reverse. Like* **North Wembley**, **Kensal Green** *station* ⑤ *preserves platform canopies from 1916. West of the 4-track* **Queen's Park** *station* ⑥, *the Bakerloo Line diverges from the mainline, stopping at the inner platform faces before diving into the tunnel just east of the station.*   *(Photo* ⑤ *Brian Hardy)*

Harrow & Wealdstone ①② ist der derzeitige Endbahnhof der Bakerloo Line. Von 1917 bis 1982 fuhren die *Tube*-Züge weiter bis Watford Junction. Die Gleise zwischen Queen's Park und Harrow sind Eigentum von Network Rail und werden auch von der Silverlink Metro von/nach Euston benutzt. Zu den wichtigsten Bahnhöfen auf dem oberirdischen Abschnitt zählt **Wembley Central** ③. Diese Station liegt im Einschnitt und wurde 1966 überbaut. **Willesden Junction** ④ ist Kreuzungspunkt mir der North London Line und Endstation für manche Bakerloo-Züge, die aber erst im Betriebshof Stonebridge Park wenden können. Wie in **North Wembley** sind auch in **Kensal Green** ⑤ Bahnsteigdächer von 1916 erhalten. Westlich von Queen's Park beginnen die eigenen Gleise der Bakerloo Line. Die Züge halten in **Queen's Park** ⑥ auf den mittleren Gleisen, um anschließend im Tunnel zu verschwinden.

1915 wurde die Bakerloo Line von Paddington bis Queen's Park verlängert, von wo der Mischbetrieb auf den Vorortgleisen begann. Die drei U-Bahnhöfe dieses Abschnitts, **Kilburn Park**, **Maida Vale** ①② und **Warwick Avenue** (s. S. 59) sind ähnlich gestaltet und weisen eine weniger interessante Fliesenstruktur auf als die älteren Stationen der Yerkes-Linien. **Paddington** ③④ wurde in den späten achtziger Jahren umgestaltet und zeigt nun Motive aus dem Tunnelbaubereich. Die Umgestaltung des Bahnhofs **Baker Street** ⑤⑥ wurde 1982 abgeschlossen, nachdem die Jubilee Line 1979 den Ast nach Stanmore übernommen hatte. Zwischen beiden Linien kann man hier auf derselben Ebene umsteigen. Die Bahnsteigwände ziert ein Bild von Sherlock Holmes, denn der legendäre Detektiv soll in der Nähe gelebt haben. Die Stationsschilder sind geschickt an einem Kabelkanal angebracht.

In 1915, the Bakerloo Line was extended from Paddington to Queen's Park, where a link was created for through-running on mainline tracks. The three underground stations on this extension, Kilburn Park, Maida Vale ①② and Warwick Avenue (see p. 59), have a similar design, all with less elaborate tiling than the earlier stations on the Yerkes tube lines. Paddington station ③④ was refurbished in the late 1980s with themes illustrating the construction of tube tunnels with the help of shields. The refurbishment of Baker Street station ⑤⑥ was completed in 1982, after the Stanmore branch had become part of the new Jubilee Line in 1979. Cross-platform interchange is provided between both lines. The platform walls display the head of Sherlock Holmes, the legendary detective who lived nearby. The brown conduit bearing the station name hides all necessary cables.

Regent's Park station ①② had not been included in the original proposal for the 'Baker Street & Waterloo Railway', but it was opened along with the initial section because of major delays in the construction of the line. It is actually located beneath the 1863 Metropolitan Railway tunnel. *Oxford Circus* station ③ has been rebuilt several times since 1906, most notably when cross-platform interchange with the Victoria Line was created in the mid-1960s. The labyrinth of walkways depicted on the walls reflects perfectly the situation in many interchange stations. The original access building, now shared with the other lines, is shown on page 52. The entire station complex at *Piccadilly Circus* ④-⑥ was refurbished in 1989, with the subsurface ticket hall having been restored in a 1920s-style (though with modern ticket machines).

Der Bahnhof **Regent's Park** ①② war im ursprünglichen Projekt der *Baker Street & Waterloo Railway* nicht enthalten. Wegen der Verzögerungen beim Bau konnte er aber gleichzeitig mit dem ersten Abschnitt in Betrieb genommen werden. Er liegt direkt unter dem Tunnel der 1863 eröffneten *Metropolitan Railway*. Der U-Bahnhof **Oxford Circus** ③ wurde seit 1906 mehrmals umgebaut, am wesentlichsten, als die Victoria Line auf derselben Ebene Mitte der sechziger Jahre gebaut wurde. Das an den Bahnsteigwänden angebrachte Labyrinth gibt sehr gut die tatsächliche Situation in vielen Umsteigebahnhöfen wieder. Das originale Bahnhofsgebäude, das nun allen Linien dient, ist auf Seite 52 zu sehen. Der gesamte Stationskomplex am **Piccadilly Circus** ④-⑥ wurde 1989 umgestaltet, die Schalterhalle wurde dabei im Stil der zwanziger Jahre restauriert (allerdings mit modernen Fahrscheinautomaten).

Der U-Bahnhof **Charing Cross** ①② wurde 1983 mit Tafeln verkleidet, die Gemälde aus der benachbarten National Gallery zeigen. Auf diese Weise wurde das Erscheinungsbild der Bahnsteige auf der Bakerloo und der Northern Line der moderneren Jubilee Line, die von 1979 bis 1999 hier endete, angepasst. Am Fernbahnhof **Waterloo** ③ hält die Bakerloo Line an einem stark gekrümmten Bahnsteig, so dass die Durchsage ‚Mind the Gap' unerlässlich ist. In **Lambeth North** ④⑤ ist das Empfangsgebäude von Leslie Green erhalten. Über den meist zweistöckigen Gebäuden sollten eigentlich Büros oder Wohnungen errichtet werden, viele blieben aber seit 100 Jahren unvollendet. Die Bahnsteigebene wurde in den frühen neunziger Jahren im alten Stil, jedoch mit neuen Fliesen restauriert. Der Endbahnhof **Elephant & Castle** ⑥ wird zusammen mit dem gleichnamigen Bahnhof auf der Northern Line derzeit renoviert.

Charing Cross station ①② was redecorated in 1983 with melamine panels depicting paintings from the nearby National Gallery. This was done in order to improve the Bakerloo and Northern Line platform areas, with the Jubilee Line having reached Charing Cross in 1979. At *Waterloo* ③, the Bakerloo Line stops at a sharply curved platform, making the 'Mind the Gap' announcement inevitable. At *Lambeth North* ④⑤, the original access building designed by Leslie Green has been preserved. The 2-storey buildings were meant to have offices and flats on top, but many have remained isolated buildings for the last 100 years. The platform level at Lambeth North was refurbished in the early 1990s in mock original style. The terminus *Elephant & Castle* ⑥ is currently undergoing modernisation along with the Northern Line platforms.

The Piccadilly Line opened in 1906 as one of three tube lines built under the direction of Charles Tyson Yerkes, who had also taken over the District Railway in 1901. Initially called the 'Great Northern, Piccadilly & Brompton Railway', the new underground line was a result of the merging of three separate projects:
1) a deep-level tube line under the District Line between Earl's Court and Mansion House to relieve the subsurface route;
2) a tube line from South Kensington to Piccadilly Circus;
3) a tube line under the Great Northern mainline tracks from Finsbury Park to King's Cross and further south to Holborn and Strand.
Construction of the Piccadilly Line began in 1902 following the same standards applied on the other Yerkes lines, with running tunnels being driven from vertical shafts through the clay stratum. The shafts were later used for lifts or spiral staircases to access the platforms. At the western end, a short surface section to Hammersmith along the District Line was later included in the project. The entire 14 km route from Finsbury Park to Hammersmith began revenue service on 15 December 1906, although some intermediate stations had not yet been completed. A short branch from Holborn to Strand (later renamed Aldwych) without any intermediate station was added on 30 November 1907. The branch operated as a shuttle until it closed permanently in 1994, although a through 'theatre train' from Strand to Finsbury Park operated for a year from opening. In 1965 parliamentary powers had been obtained for an extension to Waterloo, but this never happened.
By 1907, the Finsbury Park - Hammersmith section had 21 stations, three of which were permanently closed in the course of the past century - Down Street and York Road in 1932, and Brompton Road in 1934. The Piccadilly Line still includes the shortest distance between two neighbouring stations, the 260 m from Covent Garden to Leicester Square.
The Piccadilly Line's layout remained unaltered until expansion began in the early 1930s. The 12 km northern extension was built on a totally new alignment, in tube tunnels to Arnos Grove and then on the surface except

Northfields

for a short tunnel at Southgate. In 1933 it reached Cockfosters, virtually on the edge of the built-up area. The western extensions, however, were realised by relieving the District Line of some of the traffic converging at Earl's Court. Through the years the District Line had expanded into the western suburbs, and by 1910 had several different termini west of Earl's Court: South Harrow (and from there to Uxbridge), Ealing Broadway, Hounslow West, Richmond and Wimbledon. The Piccadilly Line was now to take over the route to South Harrow and some services to

Die Piccadilly Line wurde 1906 als eine von drei *Tube*-Linien der Yerkes-Gruppe, zu der seit 1901 außerdem noch die *District Railway* gehörte, eröffnet. Die ursprüngliche Bezeichnung *Great Northern, Piccadilly & Brompton Railway* deuten darauf hin, dass hier mehrere Projekte zusammengeschlossen wurden:
1) eine tief liegende Entlastungsstrecke unter der District Line von Earl's Court bis Mansion House,
2) eine *Tube*-Linie von South Kensington bis Piccadilly Circus,
3) eine *Tube*-Linie unter den Ferngleisen der *Great Northern* von Finsbury Park bis King's Cross und weiter nach Süden bis Holborn und Strand.
Der Bau der Piccadilly Line begann 1902 nach denselben Parametern, wie sie auf den anderen Yerkes-Linien angewandt wurden. Die Streckentunnel wurden von vertikalen Schächten aus durch Tonschichten vorgetrieben. Diese Schächte wurden anschließend für Aufzüge oder Wendeltreppen genutzt. Am westlichen Ende wurde später ein kurzer oberirdischer Abschnitt bis Hammersmith entlang der *District Railway* in das Projekt aufgenommen. Die gesamte, 14 km lange Strecke von Finsbury Park bis Hammersmith wurde am 15. Dezember 1906 in Betrieb genommen, obwohl einige Zwischenstationen noch nicht vollendet waren. Eine kurze Zweiglinie von Holborn bis Strand (später in Aldwych umbenannt) kam am 30. November 1907 hinzu. Im ersten Jahr gab es zwar einen ‚Theaterzug' von Strand nach Finsbury Park, sonst wurde die kurze Zweigstrecke bis zu endgültigen Schließung 1994 nur im Pendelverkehr von Holborn aus bedient. Dabei hatte das Parlament 1965 eine Verlängerung nach Waterloo genehmigt, aber daraus wurde nichts.
1907 hatte die Strecke von Finsbury Park bis Hammersmith 21 Stationen, drei davon wurden später wieder geschlossen: Down Street und York Road 1932 und Brompton Road 1934. Auf der Piccadilly Line findet man bis heute den kürzesten Abstand zwischen zwei benachbarten Bahnhöfen, nämlich 260 m zwischen Covent Garden und Leicester Square. Bis in die frühen dreißiger Jahre blieb die Linienführung der Piccadilly Line unverändert. Dann wurde eine 12 km lange Verlängerung nach Norden gebaut - bis Arnos Grove in tiefen Röhrentunneln und der Rest, bis auf einen kurzen Tunnel in Southgate, an der Oberfläche.

LONDON Underground - Piccadilly Line

65.6 km (~ 32 km unterirdisch | *underground*), 52 Bahnhöfe | *Stations*

8.6 km gemeinsam mit | *shared with* Metropolitan Line
1.5 km gemeinsam mit | *shared with* District Line

{01-06-1877	Hammersmith – Turnham Green} [District Railway]
{01-07-1879	Turnham Green – Ealing Broadway} [District Railway]
{01-05-1883	Acton Town – Hounslow Town} [District Railway]
{21-07-1884	Osterley – Hounslow West} [District Railway]
{01-04-1886	+ Hounslow Central} [District Railway]
{23-06-1903	Ealing Common – South Harrow} [District Railway]
{04-07-1904	Rayners Lane – Uxbridge} [Metropolitan Railway]
{25-09-1905	+ Ickenham} [Metropolitan Railway]
{26-05-1906	+ Rayners Lane, Eastcote} [Metropolitan Railway]
15-12-1906	Hammersmith – Finsbury Park
08-01-1907	+ South Kensington
11-04-1907	+ Covent Garden
{16-04-1908	+ Northfields} [District Railway]
{01-03-1910	South Harrow – Rayners Lane – Uxbridge} [District Railway]
{05-08-1912	+ Ruislip Manor} [Metropolitan/District Railway]
{10-12-1923	+ Hillingdon} [Metropolitan/District Railway]
04-07-1932	Hammersmith – South Harrow
19-09-1932	Finsbury Park – Arnos Grove
09-01-1933	Acton Town – Northfields
13-03-1933	Northfields – Hounslow West
13-03-1933	Arnos Grove – Oakwood
31-07-1933	Oakwood – Cockfosters
23-10-1933	South Harrow – Uxbridge
19-07-1975	Hounslow West – Hatton Cross
16-12-1977	Hatton Cross – Heathrow Terminals 1, 2, 3
12-04-1986	Hatton Cross – Heathrow Terminal 4
	– Heathrow Terminals 1, 2, 3
.... 2008	Heathrow Terminals 1, 2, 3 – Heathrow Terminal 5

Seit 1933 endet die Piccadilly Line in Cockfosters praktisch am Rand des bebauten Gebiets.

Im Westen hingegen wuchs die Piccadilly Line auf Kosten der District Line, indem sie zwei Strecken von dieser übernahm. Im Laufe der Jahre erschloss die District große Teile des Londoner Westens und hatte 1910 mehrere Zielbahnhöfe westlich von Earl's Court: South Harrow (bzw. Uxbridge), Ealing Broadway, Hounslow West, Richmond und Wimbledon. Die Piccadilly Line sollte nun die Strecke nach South Harrow sowie einzelne Fahrten nach Hounslow übernehmen. Der Abschnitt von Hammersmith bis Turnham Green war bereits viergleisig (die Strecke war bis 1950 Eigentum der *Southern Railway*), er musste aber umgebaut werden, da die Piccadilly Line bisher in Hammersmith an der Nordseite endete, nun aber die mittleren Gleise übernehmen und an den Bahnhöfen Ravenscourt Park und Stamford Brook ohne Halt durchfahren sollte. Von Acton Town bis Northfields wurden für die Piccadilly zwei eigene Gleise verlegt. Auf der Strecke von Northfields bis Hounslow West, die 1884 von der *District Railway* eröffnet worden war, sollten die Piccadilly und die District Line auf denselben Gleisen verkehren, was von 1933 bis 1964 auch geschah. Bereits 1932 hatte die Piccadilly den Ast nach South Harrow übernommen, welcher 1903 von der District eröffnet und anfangs für Probefahrten mit Elektroantrieb genutzt worden war. Die Verbindung von South Harrow bis Rayners Lane und die anschließende Strecke bis Uxbridge der *Metropolitan Railway*, die seit 1910 auch von der *District Railway* bedient worden war, ging 1933 auf die Piccadilly Line über. Der Abschnitt zwischen Acton Town und dem niveaugleichen Abzweig Richtung Ealing Broadway ist bis heute nur zweigleisig, so dass hier die Piccadilly und die District Line auf denselben Gleisen fahren.

Nach dieser großen Erweiterung, die abgeschlossen war, als auch die Piccadilly Line unter die Kontrolle von *London Transport* kam, veränderte sich die Streckenführung erst wieder 1975, als eine unterirdische Verlängerung von Hounslow West bis Hatton Cross, und 1977 weiter zum Flughafen Heathrow fertig gestellt war. 1986 wurde auch der Terminal 4 über eine 6 km lange eingleisige Schleife angeschlossen. 2008 kommt noch ein 2 km langer Abzweig vom Bahnhof Heathrow Terminal 1, 2, 3 zum Terminal 5 hinzu.

Auf der Piccadilly Line sind 86 Züge der Baureihe 1973 im Einsatz (2,63 m breit, 17,48 m lang und 2,88 m hoch). Diese 6-Wagen-Züge wurden von Metro-Cammell in Birmingham gebaut und in den späten neunziger Jahren von Bombardier Porail modernisiert. Die Betriebshöfe befinden sich in Northfields und Cockfosters, weitere Abstellanlagen gibt es in Arnos Grove und South Harrow. Außerhalb der Hauptverkehrszeiten fahren die Piccadilly-Züge alle fünf Minuten vom Flughafen Heathrow, der Ast nach Rayners Lane wird alle 10 Minuten bedient, wobei jeder zweite Zug nach Uxbridge weiterfährt. Auf der östlichen Strecke fahren die Züge im Abstand von wenigen Minuten bis Cockfosters, manche enden auch in Arnos Grove.

Hounslow. The section from Hammersmith to Turnham Green had already been equipped with four tracks (all of which had been owned by the 'Southern Railway' until 1950), but extending the Piccadilly Line over two of them required some rebuilding, as this line had terminated at the northern side of Hammersmith station but was now meant to use the centre tracks on its way west without stopping at Ravenscourt Park and Stamford Brook. From Acton Town to a resited station at Northfields, a second pair of tracks was laid for the Piccadilly Line. From Northfields to Hounslow West, a route opened by the District Railway in 1884, the Piccadilly was to share tracks with the District Line from 1933, a situation which continued until 1964. Piccadilly services had already begun in 1932 on the branch to South Harrow, a line opened by the District Railway in 1903 and initially used for tests with electric traction. District services ceased on this route when the Piccadilly Line took over. The link between South Harrow and Rayners Lane, and the shared service with the Metropolitan Line from there to Uxbridge, which had been provided by the District Line since 1910, was transferred to the Piccadilly Line in 1933. The section from Acton Town to Hanger Lane Junction where the District Line turns west towards Ealing Broadway has remained with only two tracks, which are shared by both lines.

After this massive expansion, completed just in time for the integration of the Piccadilly Line into London Transport, the line's layout was not modified until it was extended underground for 5 km from Hounslow West to Hatton Cross (1975) and Heathrow Airport (1977). In 1986, a 6 km single-track loop was added to serve the new Terminal 4, and a 2 km branch is at present under construction to link the future Terminal 5 to the Terminals 1, 2, 3 station, scheduled to open in 2008.

The Piccadilly Line is operated with a fleet of 86 trains of 1973 tube stock, manufactured by Metro-Cammell in Birmingham, with each train made up of six cars (2.63 m wide, 17.48 m long and 2.88 m high). These trains were refurbished by Bombardier Porail during the late 1990s. The Piccadilly Line has depots at Northfields and Cockfosters, with stabling sidings at Arnos Grove and South Harrow.

During off-peak hours, the Piccadilly Line runs to Heathrow Airport every five minutes, whereas the route to Rayners Lane is served every 10 minutes (every other train continues to Uxbridge). At the eastern end there is a train every few minutes to Cockfosters, with some services terminating at Arnos Grove.

*nur früh morgens und spät abends
only early mornings and late evenings*

Der nordwestliche Abschnitt von **Uxbridge** ① bis Rayners Lane wird sowohl von der Piccadilly (in den Hauptverkehrszeiten alle 15, sonst alle 20 Minuten) als auch von der Metropolitan Line befahren (siehe S. 24). Der Bahnhof **Rayners Lane** ② wurde 1938 von R.H. Uren im Stil von Charles Holden umgebaut. Der Abschnitt von Ealing Common bis Rayners Lane über **South Harrow** ging 1932/33 von der District auf die Piccadilly Line über, damals wurden die meisten Bahnhöfe umgebaut. **Sudbury Hill** ③ und **Sudbury Town** ④ sind zwei frühe Werke von Charles Holden. Dieser Architekt war in den dreißiger Jahren maßgeblich für den Stil der U-Bahn-Bauwerke verantwortlich. Viele seiner Bauten stehen unter Denkmalschutz. Die beiden Bahnsteige in Sudbury Town sind nur durch eine öffentliche Fußgängerbrücke miteinander verbunden. Die heutige Station **Park Royal** ⑤ wurde 1936 von Felix Lander im Holden-Stil vollendet. Sie ersetzte eine frühere Station nördlich der heutigen Central Line. Die Möglichkeit einer zusätzlichen Station auf der Central Line mit Umsteigemöglichkeit am Bahnhof Park Royal ist nicht ausgeschlossen.

*The northwestern section between **Uxbridge** ① and **Rayners Lane** ② is shared with the Metropolitan Line (see p. 24), with Piccadilly trains running through to Uxbridge every 20 minutes during off-peak hours and every 15 minutes during peak hours. Rayners Lane station was rebuilt in 1938 by R.H. Uren in Holden style. The section from Ealing Common to Rayners Lane via **South Harrow** was transferred from the District Line to the Piccadilly Line in 1932/33, when most stations were rebuilt. **Sudbury Hill** ③ and **Sudbury Town** ④ are two of Charles Holden's early works. During the 1930s, this architect created a new emblematic design for station buildings on the Underground, and many of his works are now listed buildings. At Sudbury Town, both platforms are only linked by a public footbridge. The present **Park Royal** station ⑤ was completed in 1936, designed by the architect Felix Lander following the Holden tradition; it replaced an earlier station located to the north of the present Central Line. Studies have been carried out for an additional station on the Central Line to provide interchange between the two lines.*

Der U-Bahnhof **Heathrow Terminal 4** ① wurde 1986 entlang einer eingleisigen Schleife eröffnet. Der Bahnhof **Heathrow Terminal 1, 2, 3** ② wurde in offener Bauweise in einem riesigen Kasten errichtet. Alle Flughafen-Terminals werden von Paddington aus ebenso durch den Heathrow Express bedient, der auch jeweils an unterirdischen Bahnhöfen hält. Bis 2008 werden beide Bahnen unabhängig voneinander zum Terminal 5 verlängert. Für den Abschnitt von **Hatton Cross** ③ bis Heathrow T123 wurden unter den Startbahnen Tunnelröhren mit 3,7 m Durchmesser aufgefahren, die Strecke von Hatton Cross bis **Hounslow West** ④ hingegen wurde in offener Bauweise errichtet. Ein kurzes Stück führt im Freien über den Fluss Crane. In **Hounslow Central** ⑤ ist ein Empfangsgebäude von 1912 erhalten, während **Hounslow East** ⑥ vor wenigen Jahren vollständig umgebaut wurde.

Heathrow Terminal 4 station ① is the latest addition to the Piccadilly Line. It opened along a single-track loop in 1986. Heathrow Terminals 1, 2, 3 station ② was built from the surface in a large box. All terminals at Heathrow are also served by the Heathrow Express from Paddington, which stops underground at both Terminals 1, 2, 3 as well as Terminal 4. By 2008, both Tube and Heathrow Express will have been extended on separate routes to Terminal 5. The section from Hatton Cross ③ to Heathrow T123 was built in 3.7 m diameter tube tunnels lying under runways, whereas the section from Hatton Cross to Hounslow West ④ runs through a cut-and-cover tunnel, with a short open air section across the River Crane. Hounslow Central ⑤ preserves a small station building from 1912, while Hounslow East ⑥ has recently been totally rebuilt. (Photo ① Brian Hardy)

Northfields station ①② was resited a year before Piccadilly service started in 1933, and boasts another of Charles Holden's rectangular entrance buildings. North of **Acton Town** ③ the Piccadilly Heathrow branch merges with the branch from Rayners Lane, which shares tracks with the District Line up to the junction north of Ealing Common station. From Acton Town, Piccadilly trains normally run non-stop to Hammersmith, serving **Turnham Green** only during early morning and late evening hours. *Hammersmith* station ④ was rebuilt in 1993, the new ticket hall displaying elements of the original western terminus of the line. The Piccadilly continues east between the District tracks, providing cross-platform interchange at **Barons Court** ⑤ before entering the tunnel east of this station. **Earl's Court** tube station ⑥ is located beneath the surface District station.

Der Bahnhof **Northfields** ①② wurde 1932, kurz vor Ankunft der Piccadilly Line, verschoben. Hier ist ein weiteres, rechteckiges Gebäude von Charles Holden zu sehen. Nördlich von **Acton Town** ③ trifft der Heathrow-Ast auf den Ast von Rayners Lane, der sich hier auf einem kurzen Stück die Gleise mit der District Line teilt. Von Acton Town fahren die Piccadilly-Züge normalerweise ohne Halt bis Hammersmith, nur früh morgens und spät abends halten sie in **Turnham Green**. Der Bahnhof **Hammersmith** ④ wurde 1993 umgebaut, dabei wurden Teile der ursprünglichen Endstation in die neue Schalterhalle integriert. Auch am Bahnhof **Barons Court** ⑤ kann man von der Piccadilly zur District Line auf demselben Bahnsteig umsteigen, östlich davon verschwindet die Piccadilly Line im Tunnel. Die *Tube*-Station in **Earl's Court** ⑥ liegt direkt unter dem oberirdischen Bahnhof der District Line.

Die meisten Stationen der Piccadilly Line im Stadtzentrum wurden in den achtziger Jahren umgestaltet. **South Kensington** ① nimmt Bezug auf das benachbarte Naturhistorische Museum, indem auf einem Bahnsteig lebende und auf dem anderen ausgestorbene Tiere gezeigt werden. Nachdem in **Knightsbridge** ②③ 1934 ein zweiter Zugang eröffnet worden war, wurde die westlich davon liegende Station Brompton Road geschlossen. Knightsbridge wurde 2005 mit Metallplatten verkleidet, der U-Bahnhof **Hyde Park Corner** ④ hingegen ist weitgehend im Originalstil erhalten. Während sich **Green Park** ⑤ seit 1985 im späten Flower-Power-Stil präsentiert, wurde der Bahnhof **Piccadilly Circus** ⑥ gemeinsam mit dem der Bakerloo Line 1986-89 neu gestaltet. Der in Linienfarbe gehaltene Kabelkanal mit dem Stationsnamen kam in jener Zeit in vielen innerstädtischen Stationen zur Anwendung.

Most stations along the central section of the Piccadilly Line were refurbished during the 1980s. **South Kensington** (1989) ① makes a reference to the nearby National History Museum, with extinct animals shown on the westbound platform, and living ones on the eastbound. When a second entrance was opened at **Knightsbridge** ②③ in 1934, the adjacent station Brompton Road was closed. The platforms were refurbished in 2005 and introduced a totally new style to the Underground. **Hyde Park Corner** station ④, however, largely preserves its original appearance in typical Yerkes style. **Green Park** ⑤ was redecorated in 1985 in post-flower power fashion, and **Piccadilly Circus** ⑥ was retiled together with the Bakerloo Line station in 1986-89. The conduit in line colour and bearing the station name was used in many central stations at that time to hide all necessary cables.

At only 260 m, the distance between **Leicester Square** ① and **Covent Garden** ②-④ stations is the shortest on the entire Underground network. Whereas the first has been redecorated with enamelled panels, the latter still preserves the original 1906 style. Both stations become very busy with tourists, who are now encouraged to walk the short distance to avoid overcrowding. The interchange station at **King's Cross St Pancras** ⑤ was redesigned in 1987, with the tiling pattern inspired by the letters K and X. A much larger ticket hall is currently under construction for all lines serving what are two of the busiest mainline stations. There has been a 2 km gap between King's Cross and **Caledonian Road**, ever since the early closure of York Road station in 1932. At **Holloway Road** ⑥⑦, both the original Leslie Green station building as well as the 1906 platform areas are largely intact.

Die Entfernung zwischen den Bahnhöfen **Leicester Square** ① und **Covent Garden** ②-④ beträgt nur 260 m, die kürzeste des ganzen U-Bahnnetzes. Während der erstere mit Emailplatten neu gestaltet wurde, ist der letztere im Stil von 1906 erhalten. Touristen werden jetzt aufgefordert, den Weg zwischen diesen beiden Stationen lieber zu Fuß zurückzulegen, um das Gedränge zu vermeiden. **King's Cross St. Pancras** ⑤ wurde 1987 umgestaltet, wobei die bunten Fliesen die Buchstaben K und X (für Kreuz) andeuten sollen. Derzeit wird für alle hier verkehrenden Linien eine neue Eingangshalle gebaut. Zwischen King's Cross und **Caledonian Road** beträgt der Abstand 2 km, nachdem die Zwischenstation York Road bereits 1932 geschlossen wurde. Am U-Bahnhof **Holloway Road** ⑥⑦ ist sowohl das Eingangsgebäude von Leslie Green sowie das typische Bahnsteigdesign von 1906 erhalten.

Finsbury Park ①② war anfangs der nördliche Endpunkt der Piccadilly Line. Er hatte schon damals vier unterirdische Bahnsteige, zwei für die Piccadilly und zwei für die *Great Northern & City Railway* nach Moorgate. Als die Victoria Line in den sechziger Jahren gebaut wurde, übernahm sie zwei dieser Bahnsteige. Um bequemes Umsteigen auf derselben Ebene zu ermöglichen, musste das stadteinwärtige Gleis der Piccadilly Line in den stadtauswärts führenden Tunnel der GN&CR umgeleitet werden. Die Ballons stammen von 1985. Das runde Empfangsgebäude in **Arnos Grove** ③ ist wahrscheinlich das bekannteste von Charles Holden. Ein niedrigeres ist in **Southgate** ④⑤ zu sehen. Dieser Bahnhof liegt auf einem kurzen Tunnelstück. Am Endbahnhof **Cockfosters** ⑥ gibt es über dem nördlichen Teil der Bahnsteige ein Betondach und ein kleines Eingangsgebäude.

Finsbury Park ①②, the line's original northern terminus, had four platforms from the beginning, two for the Piccadilly Line and two for the Great Northern & City Railway to Moorgate. When the Victoria Line was built in the 1960s, it took over two of the existing station tunnels, but to allow same-level interchange, the westbound Piccadilly Line was diverted into the former northbound GN&CR tunnel. The Piccadilly platforms were redecorated with balloons in mosaics in 1985. The surface station *Arnos Grove* ③ is an intermediate terminus for some services, and boasts probably the most emblematic of Charles Holden's station buildings. A lower structure can be seen at *Southgate* ④⑤, located on a short underground section. The terminus *Cockfosters* ⑥ has a concrete roof over the northern part of the platforms, and only a small entrance building.

Die Victoria Line war 1969 die erste neue U-Bahnlinie durch die Londoner Innenstadt seit dem Bauboom Anfang des 20. Jahrhunderts. Die Linie entstand aus einer Idee für eine Express-U-Bahn von Finsbury Park bis Victoria, die andere Linien entlasten sollte. Im Norden sollte sie auf zu elektrifizierende Vorortbahnstrecken übergehen (z.B. Richtung Bowes Park, Chingford oder Enfield Town), ähnlich wie es bei der Erweiterung der Central Line Richtung Osten in den vierziger Jahren verwirklicht worden war. Im Süden strebte man über Brixton, Streatham und Norbury den Endpunkt East Croydon an. Auch wenn man anfangs überlegte, die Tunnel mit einem größeren Durchmesser zu bauen, entschied man sich schließlich aus Kostengründen für Standard-Röhrentunnel. Die endgültige Streckenführung lag bereits 1951 weitgehend fest, nachdem von einer Verlängerung auf Vorortbahnstrecken doch abgesehen wurde. Der nördliche Endpunkt sollte nun der Bahnhof Wood Street (eine Station östlich des heutigen Endpunkts) sein, wo man am selben Bahnsteig Richtung Chingford umsteigen können sollte. Die Victoria Line sollte Anschluss an so viele Bahnstrecken wie möglich bieten, sowohl Vorortlinien als auch Underground. Wo es technisch machbar wäre, sollte man sogar auf derselben Ebene umsteigen können, was schließlich an fünf Bahnhöfen auch umgesetzt wurde, nämlich Finsbury Park, Highbury & Islington, Euston (Bank-Strecke), Oxford Circus und Stockwell. Der Bau der Victoria Line wurde zwar 1955 genehmigt, aber die Finanzierung ließ noch einige Jahre auf sich warten. 1960 wurde nördlich von Finsbury Park ein 1,6 km langer Probetunnel gebaut, um neue Schildvortriebsmaschinen und Betontübbings zu testen. Schließlich konnte

In 1969, the Victoria Line became the first underground line to have been opened across central London since the tube construction boom of the first decade of the 20th century. The line was conceived as an express tube line between Finsbury Park and Victoria that was to relieve other overcrowded lines. At its northern end it was to continue over electrified suburban railway routes (e.g. to Bowes Park, Chingford or Enfield Town), similar to the eastern expansion of the Central Line carried out during the 1940s. In the south, East Croydon was envisaged as a possible terminus, with a route via Brixton, Streatham and Norbury. Although a larger tunnel diameter had initially been considered, a standard tube tunnel was eventually decided on to reduce costs. The final alignment had been defined in as early as 1951, when through-running on suburban railways had eventually been discarded. The northern terminus was to be at Wood Street (one station east of the present terminus), where cross-platform interchange was to be provided with the Chingford line. The Victoria Line was to provide interchange with a maximum of other rail services, both Underground and suburban. Same-level interchange was considered, where possible, and eventually realised at five stations, Finsbury Park, Highbury & Islington, Euston (Bank branch), Oxford Circus and Stockwell. The construction of the new line was authorised in 1955, but financing remained a problem for several years. In 1960, a 1.6 km trial tunnel was built north of Finsbury Park to test new tunnelling machines with rotating cutters as well as a pre-cast concrete lining, two factors which would reduce construction costs. Finally, in 1962, construction on the line was given permission to proceed, although the northernmost section from Walthamstow Central to Wood Street had been dropped in 1961. Instead, the originally planned Hoe Street station was modified to intersect with the Chingford line and was renamed Walthamstow Central.

The Victoria Line was designed to be operated automatically from its opening day. Tests were carried out on the District Line between Stamford Brook and Ravenscourt Park in 1963, followed by more extensive trials on the Central Line shuttle between Hainault and Woodford from 1964.

LONDON Underground - Victoria Line

21.3 km (völlig unterirdisch | *totally underground*), 16 Bahnhöfe | *Stations*

01-09-1968	Walthamstow Central – Highbury & Islington
01-12-1968	Highbury & Islington – Warren Street
07-03-1969	Warren Street – Victoria
23-07-1971	Victoria – Brixton
14-09-1972	+ Pimlico

1962 mit dem Bau begonnen werden, nachdem ein Jahr vorher der letzte Abschnitt bis Wood Street aus den Plänen gestrichen worden war. Stattdessen wurde die Station Hoe Street (jetzt Walthamstow Central) so umgeplant, dass das Umsteigen zur Chingford-Linie nun hier möglich ist.

Die Victoria Line wurde von Anfang an für den automatischen Betrieb ausgelegt. Dazu wurden bereits 1963 Tests auf der District Line zwischen Stamford Brook und Ravenscourt Park, ab 1964 dann auf der Pendelstrecke der Central Line zwischen Hainault und Woodford ausgeführt.

Die Victoria Line wurde in drei Stufen in Betrieb genommen, die offizielle Eröffnung fand aber erst statt, nachdem der gesamte Abschnitt von Walthamstow Central bis Victoria fertig gestellt war. Die Stationen wurden eher einfach gestaltet. Das einzig Besondere ist ein in jeder Station unterschiedliches Fliesenmosaik, das in den Nischen über den Sitzbänken angebracht ist und Bezug auf die Umgebung oder den Namen der Station nimmt. In den meisten Stationen war die Decke anfangs mit weißen Melaminplatten verkleidet, was die Helligkeit der Bahnsteigebene erhöhte. Diese Kunststoffplatten wurden nach dem katastrophalen Brand im U-Bahnhof King's Cross 1987 durch Metallverkleidungen ersetzt.

Bevor die Grundstrecke der Victoria Line vollendet worden war, begann 1967 der Bau einer Verlängerung nach Süden, wobei die Strecke südlich von Brixton nicht mehr in den Planungen enthalten war, da sie zu wenige Fahrgäste gebracht hätte. Wegen der schwierigeren Bodenverhältnisse wurde diese Strecke wie in früheren Zeiten manuell mit Hilfe eines Greathead-Schilds gebaut. Die südliche Verlängerung ging 1971 in Betrieb und bot in Stockwell wiederum eine bequeme Umsteigemöglichkeit auf derselben Ebene zu einer anderen Linie. Hier konnten die Tunnel der Victoria Line parallel zu den bestehenden der Northern Line errichtet werden. Der U-Bahnhof Pimlico wurde erst 1968 beschlossen und deshalb auch erst 1972 eröffnet.

In den vergangenen Jahren wurde ein Abzweig von Seven Sisters bis Northumberland Park in Erwägung gezogen, denn dazu könnten größtenteils die Zufahrtsgleise zum Betriebshof genutzt werden. Im Süden wurde vorgeschlagen, eine eingleisige Schleife zum Bahnhof Herne Hill zu bauen.

Die Victoria Line hat einen Wagenpark mit 43 8-Wagen-Zügen, der größtenteils aus eigens für diese Linie gebauten Fahrzeugen der Baureihe 1967 (2,64 m breit, 16 m lang, 2,88 m hoch) von Metro-Cammell in Birmingham besteht. Darunter sind außerdem 31 Wagen der Baureihe 1972, die in den späten achtziger Jahren von der Northern Line übernommen wurden. Alle Wagen wurden zu dieser Zeit modernisiert. Derzeit baut Bombardier für die Victoria Line 47 neue 8-Wagen-Züge, die zwischen 2009 und 2012 im Fahrgasteinsatz sein sollen. Der Betriebshof der Victoria Line liegt in Northumberland Park und ist von der Station Seven Sisters aus erreichbar.

Die Victoria Line verkehrt alle 2-3 Minuten, wobei im Norden manche Züge in Seven Sisters enden.

① Baureihe 1967 Innenraum | *Inside 1967 Stock*
② Northumberland Park Depot *(Photo Brian Hardy)*
③ Neuer Zug | *new train © Bombardier*

Revenue service on the new line began in three stages, although the official opening ceremony was only held after the entire route between Walthamstow Central and Victoria had been completed.

The design of the stations was kept quite austere, with the only decorative elements being a special tiling pattern in the area in the seat recesses, different in each station and inspired by the station's name or its surroundings. At most stations the ceiling was covered with white melamine panels, which helped to increase illumination. These panels were replaced by metal ones after the disastrous fire at King's Cross in 1987.

Before the northern section of the cross-city route had been completed, work began on the southern stretch in 1967, although the section beyond Brixton was dropped as it would not have attracted enough traffic. Due to more difficult ground conditions this route was once again excavated by hand mining with Greathead shields, as had been done on the older tube lines. The southern section was opened in 1971 and included one more same-level interchange station at Stockwell, where the Victoria Line platforms were built on either side of the existing Northern Line station tunnels. Pimlico station was only added to the project in 1968, and therefore opened a year later.

A branch has been proposed in recent years from Seven Sisters to Northumberland Park over the access tracks to the depot, and a single-track loop from Brixton to Herne Hill has also been considered.

The Victoria Line has a fleet of 43 eight-car trains consisting of mostly purpose-built 1967 stock (manufactured by Metro-Cammell in Birmingham; 2.64 m wide, 16 m long, 2.88 m high), as well as 31 cars of 1972 stock taken over from the Northern Line in the late 1980s, when the entire fleet was refurbished and the car bodies painted. At present, 47 new 8-car trains are being built by Bombardier for delivery between 2009 and 2012. The Victoria Line's depot is located at Northumberland Park, which is linked to the line from Seven Sisters.

The Victoria Line runs every 2-3 minutes, with some trains terminating at Seven Sisters instead of Walthamstow Central.

Walthamstow Central
Blackhorse Road
Tottenham Hale
Seven Sisters
Finsbury Park
Highbury & Islington
King's Cross St. Pancras
Euston
Warren Street
Oxford Circus
Green Park
Victoria
Pimlico
Vauxhall
Stockwell
Brixton

The Victoria Line's northern terminus is **Walthamstow Central** ①-③, although the original idea was to extend it one station further north to Wood Street on the Chingford suburban line. At Walthamstow Central the tube station can only be accessed via the mainline platforms. **Blackhorse Road** ④ was the only station on the first section of the Victoria Line to have a proper surface building; a footbridge to the National Rail station on the other side of a major road was only built later. All stations from Euston to Walthamstow Central provide interchange with National Rail services. At **Tottenham Hale** ⑤, a shared ticket office was built to allow transfer to trains towards Stansted Airport and Cambridge. The **Seven Sisters** ⑥ were a group of seven trees which gave the area its name. This station has three tracks, the centre one leading to the Northumberland Park depot.

Der nördliche Endpunkt der Victoria Line ist **Walthamstow Central** ①-③, auch wenn die Strecke ursprünglich bis Wood Street an der Chingford-Linie weiterführen sollte. Die Bahnsteige der Endstation sind nur über die Bahnsteige des Vorortbahnhofs zugänglich. **Blackhorse Road** ④ war der einzige Bahnhof des ersten Abschnitts mit einem richtigen Eingangsgebäude; eine Fußgängerbrücke über eine Hauptstraße zum Vorortbahnhof kam erst später hinzu. An allen Stationen zwischen Walthamstow Central und Euston kann man zu einer Vorort- bzw. Fernbahnstrecke umsteigen. In **Tottenham Hale** ⑤ besteht Anschluss Richtung Flughafen Stansted und nach Cambridge. Bei den **Seven Sisters** ⑥ handelt es sich um eine Baumgruppe, die der Gegend ihren Namen gab. Das mittlere Gleis dieser dreigleisigen Station führt zum Betriebshof Northumberland Park.

Ein besonderes Merkmal der Victoria Line sind die guten Umsteige-
beziehungen zu anderen Linien auf derselben Ebene: in **Finsbury
Park** ① zur Piccadilly Line, nachdem die ehemaligen Bahnsteige
der Northern City Line umgebaut wurden; in **Highbury & Islington** ② zur Northern City Line (derzeit WAGN); in **Euston** ④ zur
Bank-Strecke der Northern Line; und am **Oxford Circus** ⑤⑥ zur
Bakerloo Line. In **King's Cross St. Pancras** ③ musste die Victoria
Line über der Piccadilly und Northern Line, aber unter dem Tunnel
der Thameslink hindurch geführt werden. Zwischen King's Cross
und **Warren Street** wurden die Tunnel der Victoria Line umgekehrt
angeordnet (Rechtsverkehr), um das Umsteigen in Euston in entge-
gengesetzter Richtung zu ermöglichen. Der enge Mittelbahnsteig
der Northern Line (Bank-Strecke) wurde gleichzeitig umgebaut und
durch eine zweite Bahnsteigröhre ergänzt.

*A special feature of the Victoria Line is its high number of same-
level interchanges with other lines: at **Finsbury Park** ① with the
Piccadilly Line by using the former Northern City Line platforms
in a re-arranged form, at **Highbury & Islington** ② with the
Northern City Line (now WAGN), at **Euston** ④ with the Northern
Line (Bank branch) in the opposite direction and at **Oxford Circus**
⑤⑥ with the Bakerloo Line. At **King's Cross St. Pancras** ③, the
new line had to find its way through an already busy interchange,
running above the Piccadilly and Northern Lines but below the
Thameslink tunnel. From north of King's Cross to south of **Warren
Street**, the Victoria Line tunnels were swapped to right-hand
running to allow for the special arrangement at Euston, where
the Northern Line (Bank branch) station was totally rebuilt to
eliminate the previously narrow island platform.*

At **Green Park** ① the tiling motif above the benches originally showed a stylized park seen from above. This was changed to simple leaves, similar to those used on the Jubilee Line (see p. 82). **Victoria** station ②-④ is the busiest on the line, as the line is heavily used to transfer passengers from the Victoria mainline station to one of the mainline stations at the northern side of the central area, namely Euston, St. Pancras or King's Cross. The original design of the line did not include a station between Victoria and Vauxhall, which lies on the southern side of the River Thames. Therefore **Pimlico** ⑤⑥, the only station along the line without any interchange facilities to other rail services, opened one year after the Brixton extension had been completed. Artworks decorating the station show the way to the nearby Tate Gallery (next page ①).   (Photo ② Thomas Schunk)

Im U-Bahnhof **Green Park** ① stellte das originale Fliesenmosaik einen abstrakten Park dar; mit Eröffnung der Jubilee Line (siehe S. 82) wurde es durch einfache Blätter ersetzt. Der U-Bahnhof **Victoria** ②-④ gehört zu den wichtigsten dieser Linie, denn er wird von vielen Fahrgästen benutzt, um vom Kopfbahnhof Victoria zu einem der Fernbahnhöfe am Nordrand der Innenstadt, nämlich Euston, St. Pancras oder King's Cross zu fahren. Ursprünglich war zwischen Victoria und Vauxhall keine Zwischenstation geplant. Deshalb wurde **Pimlico** ⑤⑥, die einzige Station der Victoria Line ohne Umsteigemöglichkeit zu anderen Bahnen, ein Jahr später als die Strecke nach Brixton eröffnet. Der Bahnhof liegt in der Nähe der Tate-Gallery, was als Motiv für die Bahnsteigebene, aber auch für die Ausgänge (nächste Seite ①) genutzt wurde.

Der Bahnhof **Vauxhall** ② liegt direkt am Südufer der Themse. Hier kann man zu den Vorortzügen von Waterloo Richtung Südwesten umsteigen. **Stockwell** ③ war 1890 der südliche Endpunkt von Londons erster elektrischer U-Bahn. Die Victoria Line hält hier parallel zur Northern Line, so dass man bequem auf derselben Ebene umsteigen kann. Seit 1971 ist **Brixton** ④-⑥ der südliche Endpunkt der Victoria Line, auch wenn ursprünglich eine Verlängerung bis Croydon geplant war. In den vergangenen Jahren entstand die Idee für eine eingleisige Schleife bis zum Bahnhof Herne Hill, denn so könnten die Engpässe in der Wendeanlage gelöst und Anschluss an eine weitere Vorortbahn geboten werden. Das Eingangsgebäude in Brixton wurde 2003 neu gebaut. Das Fliesenmosaik ist von ‚tons of bricks' (Tonnen von Ziegeln) inspiriert.

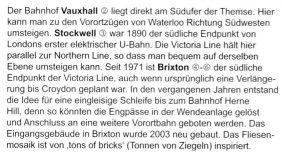

Vauxhall station ② *lies just across the river on the south bank of the Thames, and provides interchange with suburban services towards the southwest originating from Waterloo station. At* **Stockwell** ③, *the original southern terminus of London's first tube line opened in 1890, another same-level interchange was created by building the new station tunnels parallel to the existing ones on the Northern Line.* **Brixton** ④-⑥ *has been the southern terminus since 1971, although the early project included an extension south to Croydon. In recent years a single-track loop has been proposed from Brixton to Herne Hill, which would ease reversing at the southern end and provide an additional interchange with the southern suburban network. At Brixton, a new entrance building was completed in 2003. The tiling pattern on the station walls insinuates "tons of bricks".*

London Bridge

Die Jubilee Line ist auf dem Netzplan der Londoner U-Bahn erst seit 1979 zu sehen. Ihre Strecke kann man in fünf Abschnitte einteilen, die jeweils einen anderen geschichtlichen Hintergrund haben:
1) Der nördlichste Abschnitt von Wembley Park bis Stanmore wurde 1932 als ein weiterer Ast der *Metropolitan Railway* eröffnet. Er führte anfangs durch größtenteils unbebautes Gebiet, doch bald begann entlang der Strecke rege Bautätigkeit.
2) Der oberirdische Abschnitt von Finchley Road bis Wembley Park ist Teil der Verlängerung der ursprünglichen *Metropolitan Railway* nach Harrow-on-the-Hill, welche in drei Stufen von 1879 bis 1880 in Betrieb genommen wurde, auch wenn der Bahnhof Wembley Park erst 1894 hinzukam, um ein neues Ausstellungsgelände und Freizeitgebiet zu erschließen. Dieser Abschnitt wurde von 1913 bis 1915 viergleisig ausgebaut. Die Jubilee Line bedient nun alle Zwischenbahnhöfe, an denen die Metropolitan Line als Express-Metro ohne Halt durchfährt.
3) Der unterirdische Abschnitt Baker Street - Finchley Road entstand 1939 als Entlastungsstrecke für die hier nur zweigleisige Strecke der Metropolitan Line. Nachdem die beiden Streckentunnel fertig gestellt worden waren, wurde dieser Abschnitt zusammen mit den in 1) und 2) beschriebenen an die Bakerloo Line übergeben, so dass die Züge von Stanmore bis Elephant & Castle durchfuhren.
4) Nach Übernahme des Stanmore-Astes hatte die Bakerloo auf ihrem zentralen Abschnitt allmählich selbst mit Überlastung zu kämpfen. Deshalb wurde eine neue Entlastungsstrecke geplant,

The Jubilee Line only appeared on the London Underground map in 1979. Its present layout can be divided into 5 sections, each of which has a different history:
1) The northern section from Wembley Park to Stanmore opened in 1932 as one more of several branches built by the Metropolitan Railway. In its first years it ran mostly through open countryside but new housing development was soon attracted to these areas.
2) The surface Finchley Road - Wembley Park section is part of the original Metropolitan Railway extension to Harrow-on-the-Hill opened in three stages between 1879 and 1880, Wembley Park station only being added in 1894, however, to serve a new exhibition centre and leisure area. This section was quadrupled between 1913 and 1915, and the Jubilee Line now serves all intermediate stations, whereas the Metropolitan Line runs non-stop as an express metro line.
3) The underground Baker Street - Finchley Road section was opened in 1939 to relieve the 2-track bottleneck on the Metropolitan Line. Upon completion, the new stretch together with the sections described in 1) and 2) were transferred to the Bakerloo Line and operated as a branch, with through-running to Elephant & Castle.
4) After the Bakerloo Line had taken over the Stanmore branch it became heavily congested itself in the central area, necessitating the building of a new relief route. This was to become part of a new line called the Fleet Line, which was to run under

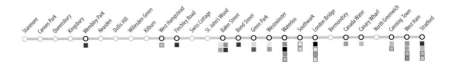

die Teil einer neuen Linie, der *Fleet Line*, werden sollte. Diese Linie sollte von Charing Cross unter der Fleet Street nach Osten zum Bahnhof Fenchurch Street führen. Anschließend sollte sie die Themse unterqueren und auf den südlichen Ästen der East London Line nach New Cross Gate und Lewisham fahren. Der Bau des zentralen Abschnitts von Baker Street bis Charing Cross begann 1972. Als Queen Elizabeth II im Jahr 1977 ihr 25-jähriges Kronjubiläum feierte, wurde die neue Linie in Jubilee Line umbenannt und bekam die Kennfarbe Silber. Von der Bakerloo Line wurde die Abschnitte 1) bis 3) übernommen, so dass 1979 der Betrieb von Charing Cross bis Stanmore aufgenommen werden konnte.

5) In den neunziger Jahren stellte die 16 km lange Verlängerung der Jubilee Line das größte Infrastrukturprojekt der Underground seit dem Bau der Victoria Line dar. Anstelle der früher geplanten Strecke auf der Nordseite der Themse sollten nun mehrere wichtige Punkte auf der Südseite sowie die schnell wachsende Stadtteil im früheren Hafen, den Docklands, erschlossen werden. Der neue Abschnitt zweigt südlich des U-Bahnhofs Green Park von der erst 1979 eröffneten Strecke ab und führt in tief liegenden Röhrentunneln mit einem Durchmesser von 4,35 m Richtung Osten. Die Tunnel wurden mit Schildvortriebsmaschinen meist durch Tonschichten aufgefahren. Anders als bisher wurden die Stationen und Verbindungsgänge so großzügig wie möglich angelegt, um auch bei steigendem Fahrgastaufkommen noch genügend Kapazität zu haben. Auch das moderne Design der Bahnhöfe vermittelt dem Fahrgast ein sehr unterschiedliches Bild zu den über 100 Jahre alten Röhrenbahnhöfen auf anderen Linien. Die unterirdischen Stationen wurden mit Bahnsteigtüren ausgestattet. Der östliche Abschnitt der Neubaustrecke verläuft von Canning Town bis Stratford an der Oberfläche, parallel zur North London Line. Die oberirdischen Stationen bekamen keine Bahnsteigtüren. Die Verlängerung der Jubilee Line wurde gerade rechtzeitig zu den Feierlichkeiten zum Beginn des neuen Jahrtausends vollendet.

Die 59 neu angeschafften 6-Wagen-Züge gehören zur Baureihe 1996 (2,63 m breit, 17,7 m lang, 2,88 m hoch). Im Dezember 2005 wurden alle Züge durch einen siebten Wagen erweitert. Der Betriebshof befindet sich südlich des Bahnhofs Stratford, außerdem gibt es in Stanmore eine große Abstellanlage. Einige Züge werden auch im Depot der Metropolitan Line in Neasden abgestellt. Trotz ihres sonst sehr modernen Erscheinungsbilds wird die Jubilee Line bislang manuell betrieben, auch wenn in Zukunft die Umrüstung auf automatischen Betrieb (ATO) wie bei der Central oder Victoria Line geplant ist.

Außerhalb der Hauptverkehrszeiten verlässt die Jubilee Line Stratford alle 3-4 Minuten. Etwa jeder zweite Zug fährt bis Stanmore, die anderen enden in Willesden Green oder Wembley Park.

Fleet Street from Charing Cross east to Ludgate Circus and Fenchurch Street. After diving under the River Thames it was to be connected to the southern branches of the East London Line and terminate at New Cross Gate and Lewisham. Construction on the central section from Baker Street to Charing Cross began in 1972. When Queen Elizabeth II celebrated her silver jubilee in 1977, the new line was renamed the Jubilee Line and the colour silver was adopted for it. It opened in 1979 from Charing Cross to Stanmore, and incorporated the Bakerloo Line section north of Baker Street.

5) The 16 km 'Jubilee Line Extension' from Green Park to Stratford in the 1990s was the biggest infrastructure project for the Underground since the opening of the Victoria Line. Instead of the originally planned route on the north bank of the River Thames, a new route was chosen to link several points on the south bank as well as the fast-growing Docklands area. The new route diverges from the 1979 alignment south of Green Park and runs eastwards in deep-level tube tunnels, these though having a larger diameter of 4.35 m, excavated mostly through clay by means of automated tunnel-boring machines. Stations and subterranean walkways were designed 'as large as possible' to cater for increased traffic in the future, which, along with a very modern station design, gives passengers a totally new image of what a modern metro line can look like, compared with the 100-year old tube stations accessible mostly via narrow labyrinths and endless flights of escalators. The new underground stations were equipped with platform screen doors. The eastern section of the extension runs on the surface from Canning Town to Stratford, paralleling the North London Line and these stations do not have platform screen doors. The Jubilee Line extension was completed just in time for the Millennium celebrations.

The initial 59 six-car trains, manufactured by Alstom, belong to the 1996 stock (2.63 m wide, 17.7 m long, 2.88 m high). A seventh car was added to each train in December 2005. The line's main depot is located south of Stratford station, with additional stabling sidings at Stanmore. Many Jubilee Line trains also stable at the Metropolitan Line's Neasden depot. Despite its overall modern design the Jubilee Line is currently driver-operated in manual mode, although ATO (Automatic Train Operation) is planned in the future.

During off-peak hours Mondays to Fridays, Jubilee Line trains leave Stratford every 3-4 minutes, with about every other train running through to Stanmore, and the rest terminating at Willesden Green or Wembley Park.

LONDON Underground - Jubilee Line

37.2 km (~ 19 km unterirdisch | *underground*), 27 Bahnhöfe | *Stations*

{30-06-1879 Finchley Road – West Hampstead} [Metropolitan]
{24-11-1879 West Hampstead – Willesden Green} [Metropolitan]
{02-08-1880 Willesden Green – Harrow-on-the-Hill} [Metropolitan]
{02-08-1880 + Neasden} [Metropolitan]
{12-05-1894 + Wembley Park} [Metropolitan]
{01-10-1909 + Dollis Hill} [Metropolitan]
{10-12-1932 Wembley Park – Stanmore} [Metropolitan]
{16-12-1934 + Queensbury} [Metropolitan]
{20-11-1939 Baker Street – Stanmore} [Bakerloo]
01-05-1979 (Charing Cross –) Green Park – Stanmore
14-05-1999 Stratford – North Greenwich
17-09-1999 North Greenwich – Bermondsey
24-09-1999 Bermondsey – Waterloo
07-10-1999 + London Bridge
20-11-1999 Waterloo – Green Park
20-11-1999 + Southwark
22-12-1999 + Westminster

The branch from Wembley Park to Stanmore opened in 1932 as part of the 'Metropolitan Railway', when the area was still mostly open countryside. **Stanmore** ① and **Kingsbury** have station buildings which adapt well with the typical suburban country house style, whereas at **Queensbury** a larger building with a row of shops was erected. **Canons Park** station ②③ lies on an embankment. West of Wembley Park station, the Jubilee Line gets aligned between the Metropolitan tracks to provide cross-platform interchange at the 6-track **Wembley Park** station ④, which has been rebuilt several times since its opening in 1894. **Neasden** ⑤ and **Willesden Green** ⑥ are two of the earliest stations on the Metropolitan Line, with their present platforms dating from 1914, when the line was widened with two additional 'fast' tracks.

Der Ast von Wembley Park bis Stanmore wurde 1932 als Teil der *Metropolitan Railway* durch weitgehend unbebautes Gebiet eröffnet. In **Stanmore** ① sowie in **Kingsbury** findet man ein im Landhausstil errichtetes Eingangsgebäude, in **Queensbury** hingegen wurde ein größeres Gebäude mit angrenzenden Geschäften gebaut. Der Bahnhof **Canons Park** ②③ liegt auf einem Damm. Westlich von Wembley Park fädelt die Jubilee Line zwischen den Gleisen der Metropolitan Line ein, so dass man am 6-gleisigen Bahnhof **Wembley Park** ④ am selben Bahnsteig umsteigen kann. Dieser Bahnhof wurde seit 1894 mehrmals umgebaut. **Neasden** ⑤ und **Willesden Green** ⑥ gehören zu den älteren Bahnhöfen der Metropolitan Line, das heutige Aussehen der Bahnsteige stammt von 1914, als die Strecke viergleisig ausgebaut wurde.

Bevor die Bakerloo Line 1939 den Stanmore-Ast von der Metropolitan Line übernehmen konnte, mussten die Gleise zwischen Finchley Road und Wembley Park neu geordnet werden. Die vorher auf der Nordseite liegenden Express-Gleise mussten nun außen liegen, damit man sowohl in Wembley Park als auch am Bahnhof **Finchley Road** ②③ bahnsteiggleich umsteigen konnte. In **Dollis Hill**, **Kilburn** und **West Hampstead** ① wurden im Rahmen dieser Arbeiten sehr ähnliche Bahnsteige errichtet. Die unterirdische Strecke von Finchley Road bis Baker Street wurde 1939 in Betrieb genommen, um die nur zweigleisige Strecke der Metropolitan Line zu entlasten. Es entstanden dabei zwei neue Bahnhöfe, **Swiss Cottage** und **St. John's Wood** ④⑤. Letzterer ersetzte sowohl

die Station Lords (anfangs St. John's Wood) als auch Marlborough Road auf der Metropolitan Line. Im U-Bahnhof **Baker Street** ⑥ der Bakerloo Line wurde 1979 ein vierter Bahnsteig, für die Jubilee Line Richtung Norden, eröffnet.

*Before the Stanmore branch could be transferred from the Metropolitan to the Bakerloo Line in 1939, the tracks on the Finchley Road - Wembley Park section had to be re-arranged, as the 'fast' tracks had previously been on the northern side, but were now to flank the 'slow' centre tracks to allow cross-platform interchange both at Wembley Park and **Finchley Road** ②③. At **Dollis Hill**, **Kilburn** and **West Hampstead** ① new platforms were built in a very similar style. The underground section from Finchley Road to Baker Street opened in 1939 to relieve the congested 2-track Metropolitan Line. Whereas a new station was also built at **Swiss Cottage**, the new **St. John's Wood** ④⑤ station was to replace two stations on the Metropolitan Line, Lords (originally St. John's Wood) and Marlborough Road. At **Baker Street** ⑥, an additional platform (northbound) for the Jubilee Line opened in 1979.*

In 1979, the new Jubilee Line opened from Stanmore to Charing Cross (the line's southern terminus until 1999). Although the three new stations are not much larger than those on the Victoria Line, they have a brighter and more pleasant appearance. As on the Victoria Line, a special motif was used to identify each station: a parcel at **Bond Street** ①②, as the station serves London's largest department stores on Oxford Street, and leaves at **Green Park** ③. At the latter, an additional deep-level subway was opened in 1999 to improve interchange with the Piccadilly Line ④. The new Jubilee Line route diverges from the 1979 alignment just south of Green Park station. Building a station at **Westminster** ⑤⑥, next to Big Ben and the Houses of Parliament and under the existing Circle/District Line, was the most complicated task on the 16 km route. (Photo ⑤ Thomas Schunk)

Die Jubilee Line wurde 1979 von Stanmore bis Charing Cross (südlicher Endpunkt bis 1999) eröffnet. Auch wenn die drei neuen Stationen kaum größer sind als die der Victoria Line, so vermitteln sie doch einen helleren und angenehmeren Eindruck. Ähnlich wie bei der Victoria Line wurde für jede Station ein Motiv gewählt: **Bond Street** ①② ziert ein Paket, ein Hinweis auf die großen Kaufhäuser in der Oxford Street, und Blätter schmücken den U-Bahnhof **Green Park** ③. Hier wurde 1999 ein neuer Verbindungstunnel ④ in tiefer Lage zur Piccadilly Line gebaut. Die neue Strecke der Jubilee Line zweigt südlich von Green Park von der älteren ab. Der Bau des U-Bahnhofs **Westminster** ⑤⑥, direkt neben dem Big Ben und dem Parlament und unter der Circle/District Line war die schwierigste Aufgabe auf der 16 km langen Neubaustrecke.

Der größte Unterschied zwischen der Victoria Line (1968-1971) und der neuen Strecke der Jubilee Line ist die Großzügigkeit der Stationen, vor allem die breiteren Zugänge und Verteilerebenen. In **Waterloo** ①-③ musste die neue Station in das bereits bestehende Labyrinth unter dem Fernbahnhof integriert werden. Der Bau eines internationalen Bahnhofs erleichterte diese Aufgabe. Der U-Bahnhof **Southwark** ④⑤ liegt nur 440 m von Waterloo entfernt und wurde erst später eingeplant. Er bietet eine direkte Umsteigemöglichkeit zum Vorortbahnhof Waterloo East und erschließt ein sonst mit keiner Bahn erreichbares Gebiet. Durch ein Glasdach fällt hier Tageslicht in die Zwischenebene. Am U-Bahnhof **London Bridge** ⑥ gibt es zwischen den Bahnsteigröhren eine riesige Zwischenröhre, so dass die Bahnsteige kaum überfüllt werden können. Die Bahnsteige der Northern Line wurde gleichzeitig umgebaut.

*The biggest difference between the Victoria Line opened between 1968 and 1971 and the Jubilee Line extension built during the 1990s is the spaciousness of the stations, in particular their larger access tunnels and distribution areas. At **Waterloo** ①-③, the new station had to be integrated into the labyrinth that already existed under the mainline station, whose expansion with an international terminal was carried out simultaneously. A late addition to the project, **Southwark** station ④⑤, only 440 m from Waterloo, was built to create a direct link to the Waterloo East mainline platforms and serve an area otherwise poorly served by rail lines. Through the glass roof, daylight falls into the impressive intermediate level. At **London Bridge** ⑥, a spacious central concourse prevents overcrowding on the platforms. The Northern Line platforms were rebuilt simultaneously.*

*Except for North Greenwich, **Bermondsey** is the only station
along the new Jubilee Line with no interchange to other rail services. **Canada Water** ①② serves an area under redevelopment, is
a major bus interchange, and above all, provides easy transfer
to the newly built station on the East London Line via only one
flight of escalators. To provide an additional link to the emerging
Docklands area was one of the main objectives of the Jubilee
Line extension. At **Canary Wharf** ③-⑥, the apparently oversized
station is the result of the drainage of a West India Docks basin,
which left a station box 280 m long, 32 m wide and 24 m deep.
The Docklands Light Railway passes elevated in front of the western exit, with Heron Quays station actually being closer and more
directly linked to the Jubilee Line station.*

Neben North Greenwich ist **Bermondsey** der einzige Bahnhof
der neuen Strecke der Jubilee Line ohne Umsteigemöglichkeit zu
einer anderen Bahnlinie. **Canada Water** ①② wurde in der Form
eines Turmbahnhofs errichtet, so dass man von der East London
Line über eine kurze Rolltreppe die Jubilee Line erreicht. Der
Bahnhof dient auch als Busumsteigeanlage und erschließt ein
Entwicklungsgebiet. Ein weiterer Schnellbahnanschluss für das
Docklands-Gebiet war ein wichtiger Faktor für die Entscheidung zur
Verlängerung der Jubilee Line. Der U-Bahnhof **Canary Wharf** ③-⑥
sieht trotz des hohen Passagieraufkommens etwas überdimensi-
oniert aus, was daher kommt, dass er in einem trockengelegten
Hafenbecken in Form eines 280 m langen, 32 m breiten und 24 m
tiefen Kastens errichtet wurde. Die Docklands Light Railway fährt
als Hochbahn vor dem Westausgang vorbei.

Der U-Bahnhof **North Greenwich** ①②, direkt neben der Veranstaltungshalle Millennium Dome gelegen, wurde mit Rücksicht auf einen möglichen Abzweig zu den Royal Docks, die heute mit der Docklands Light Railway erreicht werden können, dreigleisig gebaut. Unmittelbar südlich des Bahnhofs Canning Town kommt die Jubilee Line an die Oberfläche, nachdem sie die Themse viermal unterquert hat. In **Canning Town** ③ liegen die Bahnsteige der Docklands Light Railway direkt über denen der Jubilee Line, die der North London Line liegen daneben. In **West Ham** ④ wurde die sonst meist von Beton bestimmte Architektur mit Backstein in der Tradition von Charles Holden der späten zwanziger Jahre ergänzt. Die einfachen Bahnsteige in **Stratford** ⑤⑥ stehen in großem Kontrast zur riesigen Eingangshalle, die südlich der Bahnsteige der Central Line und der Vorortbahn errichtet wurde.

North Greenwich station ①②, which serves the Millennium Dome, was built with three tracks in provision for a future branch towards the Royal Docks, now served by two branches of the Docklands Light Railway. Just south of Canning Town, the Jubilee Line emerges from the tunnel after having crossed beneath the River Thames four times. At *Canning Town* ③, the DLR platforms were built above the Jubilee Line, with the North London Line platforms parallel to the latter. At *West Ham* ④, the otherwise concrete-dominated architecture was enhanced with red bricks, following a long tradition introduced on the Underground by Charles Holden during the late 1920s. The simple platforms at the terminus *Stratford* ⑤⑥ stand in contrast with the large new distribution hall built at the southern side of the Central Line and mainline station.

Die Idee für die **Docklands Light Railway** (DLR) wurde 1982 geboren. Sie sollte als Stadtbahn die City mit den Entwicklungsgebieten im ehemaligen Hafen, den Docklands, auf der Themse-Halbinsel Isle of Dogs verbinden. Der Bau des Grundnetzes von Tower Gateway bzw. Stratford bis Island Gardens (12 km, 15 Stationen) begann 1984 und wurde 1987 vollendet. Längere Abschnitte dieser Strecken konnten auf stillgelegten Bahntrassen errichtet werden. Bald nach Inbetriebnahme des Grundnetzes wurde mit dem Bau einer 1,6 km langen Tunnelstrecke zum Umsteigeknoten Bank direkt in der City begonnen. Außerdem mussten die anfangs nur 30 m langen Bahnsteige sofort verlängert werden, um ab 1991 2-Wagen-Züge einsetzen zu können.

Die ersten Entwürfe für diese Stadtbahn sahen auch die Möglichkeit von straßenbündigen Strecken zum U-Bahnhof Mile End vor. Schließlich entschied man sich aber für eine völlig unabhängige, fahrerlose, automatische Stadtbahn, die besser als ‚Leicht-Metro' bezeichnet werden sollte. Der Betrieb wird von der Leitzentrale am Bahnhof Poplar überwacht. Das SelTrac-Signalsystem von Alcatel arbeitet mit *Moving-Block*-Technologie.

Alle Züge sind allerdings mit sog. Passenger Service Agents besetzt, deren Aufgabe es einerseits ist, die Türen zu schließen, aber auch die Fahrscheine zu kontrollieren, da die DLR ohne Zugangssperren gebaut wurde. Die DLR war das erste Bahnsystem Großbritanniens, das barrierefrei zugänglich war. Derzeit wird die DLR von Serco Docklands Ltd betrieben und unterhalten. Im Rahmen der Olympia-Vorbereitung soll bis 2010 eine neue Strecke von Canning Town zum neuen Fernbahnhof Stratford International gebaut werden. Sie wird zwischen Canning Town und Stratford die bestehende Strecke der North London Line übernehmen, deren südlicher Abschnitt nach North Woolwich geschlossen werden soll. In den nächsten Jahren werden die Bahnsteige der Strecke Bank - Lewisham für den Einsatz von 3-Wagen-Zügen verlängert, wozu auch die Verstärkung einiger Viadukte und Brücken notwendig ist. Bis 2015 soll ein weiterer Ast von Gallions Reach bis Dagenham Dock mit vier Zwischenstationen gebaut werden.

The **'Docklands Light Railway'** (DLR) was conceived in 1982 as a low-capacity rail link from the City to the regeneration area in the former port on the Isle of Dogs peninsula. Construction started in 1984 on an initial network from Tower Gateway and Stratford to Island Gardens (12 km, 15 stations), which opened in 1987. Long sections of these routes were built on abandoned railway alignments. Soon after services started, work began on a 1.6 km underground extension to Bank and on lengthening the initially only 30 m long platforms, designed for single units, to allow operation with 2-car trainsets from 1991.

The first proposals for a rail link to the Docklands had included 'proper' light rail with some street-running to Mile End Underground station. The final decision was for a fully segregated, driverless automatic system which is better classified as a 'light metro'. It is monitored from the Control Centre located at Poplar. The signalling system is based on Alcatel's SelTrac system, which uses the 'moving block' technology. All trains are staffed, however, with Passenger Service Agents, who are responsible for door-closing and function as ticket inspectors, necessary as the system was built without access barriers. The DLR was the first fully accessible railway in the UK. Serco Docklands Ltd is in charge of operation and maintenance.

LONDON Docklands Light Railway

31.5 km (~ 3.2 km unterirdisch | *underground*), 38 Bahnhöfe | *Stations*

31-08-1987	Tower Gateway / Stratford – Island Gardens
29-07-1991	Bank – Shadwell
12-08-1991	+ Canary Wharf
28-03-1994	Poplar – Beckton
16-01-1996	+ Pudding Mill Lane
05-03-1998	+ Canning Town
20-11-1999	Island Gardens – Lewisham
03-12-1999	+ Cutty Sark
02-12-2005	Canning Town – King George V

Bei der DLR sind insgesamt 94 Fahrzeuge des Typs B92, die alle bis Ende 2006 renoviert werden, im Einsatz. Diese Gelenkwagen sind 28 m lang, 2,65 m breit und 3,51 m hoch. Bei einer Fußbodenhöhe von 1025 mm ermöglichen sie stufenloses Einsteigen. Die ursprünglichen Wagen des Typs P86 und P89 kann man heute bei der Stadtbahn in Essen sehen.

Die Stromversorgung der DLR erfolgt mit 750 V Gleichstrom über eine von unten bestrichene Stromschiene. Die beiden Enddrehgestelle sind angetrieben, das mittlere unter dem Gelenk nicht. Die Spurweite beträgt 1435 mm. Bei Bombardier werden derzeit 24 neue Fahrzeuge hergestellt, die ab 2009 ausgeliefert werden.

Auf der DLR gibt es vier Grundlinien, die außerhalb der Hauptverkehrszeiten alle 10 Minuten bedient werden (siehe rechts). Dazu kommen in den Spitzenzeiten Zusatzfahrten mit verkürzter Streckenführung.

As part of the Olympic bid, a new route from Canning Town to Stratford International, a new mainline station on the Channel Tunnel Rail Link, is very likely to become a reality by 2010. It will replace the existing North London Line service between Stratford and Canning Town, and the remaining section to North Woolwich will be abandoned. In the next few years platforms on the Bank - Lewisham route will be extended for 3-car operation, which will also require the strengthening of certain viaducts and bridges. Yet another branch, this time from Gallions Reach to Dagenham Dock with four intermediate stations, may be built by 2015.

The DLR is operated with a total of 94 vehicles (B92 stock), all currently being refurbished. The articulated vehicles are 28 m long, 2.65 m wide and 3.51 m high; with a floor height of 1025 mm the DLR provides level access into the vehicles. The original P86 and P89 stock can now be seen in service in Essen (Germany). The DLR is powered by 750 V dc via an aluminium third rail, with current being taken from the underside of the rail. The end bogies are motored, with a trailer bogie located under the articulation. Track gauge is standard 1435 mm. Bombardier is currently manufacturing 24 new vehicles for delivery from 2009.

The DLR operates four basic off-peak routes (each with trains every 10 minutes), with additional trains during peak hours:

(1) Bank – Lewisham (+ Bank – Canary Wharf, *Mon-Fri*)
(2) Bank – King George V
(3) Tower Gateway – Beckton
(4) Stratford – Lewisham

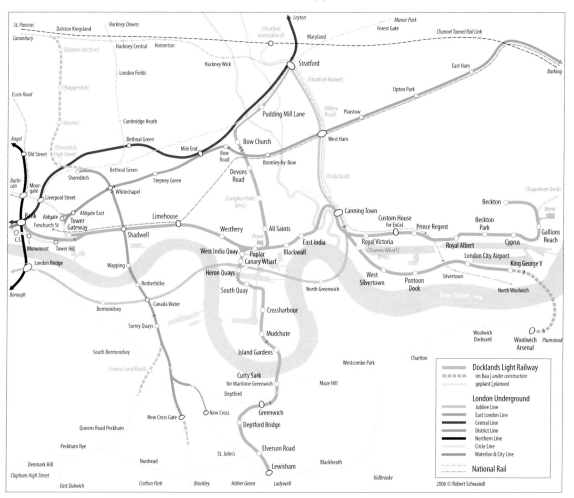

Der Bau der 1,6 km langen unterirdischen Strecke bis **Bank** ①
begann 1988. Die zweigleisige Station liegt in 42 m Tiefe unter der
King William Street. Die Streckentunnel haben einen Durchmesser
von 5 m und sind mit einem Notsteg ausgestattet. Bei Tower Hill gibt
es die Option für einen weiteren unterirdischen Bahnhof.
Die Station **Tower Gateway** ② liegt auf einem Betonviadukt. Beide
Äste treffen etwa 300 m östlich in einer niveaugleichen Kreuzung
aufeinander. Von hier führt die Strecke parallel zur Trasse der
Vorortbahn von/nach Fenchurch Street. In **Shadwell** ③ kann man
über einen kurzen Fußweg auf der Straße zur East London Line
umsteigen. Ab hier bis zur Kreuzung am West India Quay benutzt

die DLR ein Viadukt
der 1839 erbauten
und anfangs mit
Kabel gezogenen
*London & Blackwall
Railway*. Die Station
Limehouse ④, wo
man zu den Zügen
der *c2c* umsteigen
kann, ist seit 1999
auf voller Länge
überdacht. Auf dem
alten Viadukt erreicht
die DLR die Station
Westferry ⑤⑥.

*Work on the 1.6 km underground extension to Bank ① began
in 1988. The 2-track terminus lies 42 m beneath King William
Street. The running tunnels have a diameter of 5 m, and an
emergency walkway is provided. At Tower Hill, there is an option
for an additional underground station.*
*Tower Gateway ② sits on a reinforced concrete viaduct. Both
branches merge in a trailing junction some 300 m further east,
and continue alongside the mainline from Fenchurch Street
station. At Shadwell ③, transfer to the East London Line is via
street level. From there, the DLR uses a viaduct, built in 1839
for the initially cable-hauled 'London & Blackwall Railway', up to
the junction at West India Quay. At Limehouse ④, covered with a
full-length glass roof in 1999, interchange to c2c-trains is provided. The old viaduct takes the DLR to Westferry station ⑤⑥.*

Der ältere Betriebshof und die Leitzentrale der DLR liegen am viergleisigen Bahnhof **Poplar** ①. Östlich davon zweigt die Strecke nach Stratford in einer engen Kurve ab und führt weiter nach Norden auf einer ehemaligen Güterbahn, die Teil der North London Line war. Hier liegen die Stationen **All Saints** ②③ und **Devons Road**. Dazwischen ist bis 2008 die Station Langdon Park geplant. Ab **Bow Church** ④ ist die Strecke bis Stratford entlang der Hauptbahn eingleisig. In **Stratford** ⑤ kann man derzeit noch am selben Bahnsteig in die Vorortbahn und in die Central Line Richtung Liverpool Street umsteigen. Eine zweigleisige Endstation ist allerdings südlich der Central Line im Bau.

*The DLR control centre and original depot are located at the 4-track **Poplar** station ①. Just to the east, the Stratford route turns north in a tight curve and runs on a disused railway, once part of the North London Railway, to Bow Church, with intermediate stops at **All Saints** ②③ and **Devons Road**. A new station is planned at Langdon Park for 2008. From **Bow Church** ④, the line becomes single-track and runs alongside the Network Rail tracks to*

*Stratford, with a passing loop at **Pudding Mill Lane**. At **Stratford** ⑤, the bay platform provides transfer to suburban trains towards Liverpool Street and to westbound Central Line trains at the same level, but new platforms for a 2-track terminus are currently being built to the south of the westbound Central Line track.*

In 1994, an 8 km extension to Beckton through the Royal Docks area was added to the original DLR network. All stations have a similar design with emblematic red lift towers, like that at **East India** station ①. **Canning Town** station ② was completed four years later and lies above the Jubilee Line platforms. From Canning Town to **Custom House** ③ (ExCel - exhibition centre) the DLR runs parallel to the North London Line, which is to be abandoned soon. On a high viaduct between **Prince Regent** and **Royal Albert** stations, provisions have been made for a future Connaught station. The route then continues in the middle strip of the dual carriageway Royal Albert Way, with two almost identical stations at **Beckton Park** ④ and **Cyprus**, each within the central area of a roundabout. The main DLR depot is located north of **Gallions Reach** station ⑤ and accessible from both directions. From here, a branch may be built to Dagenham Dock to serve the Beckton Reach area. The unspectacular terminus **Beckton** ⑥ lies at grade and is accessible via stairs and a ramp.

1994 wurde die DLR um 8 km durch die Royal Docks bis Beckton verlängert. Alle Stationen wurden ähnlich gestaltet, als markantestes Element findet man die roten Aufzugtürme, wie an der Station **East India** ①. Der Bahnhof **Canning Town** ② wurde erst vier Jahre später in Betrieb genommen, er liegt über dem der Jubilee Line. Von Canning Town bis **Custom House** ③ (neben dem ExCel-Ausstellungszentrum) verläuft die Strecke parallel zur North London Line, welche auf diesem Abschnitt bald geschlossen werden soll.

Auf einem hohen Viadukt zwischen **Prince Regent** und **Royal Albert** gibt es die Möglichkeit, die Station Connaught zu bauen. Die Strecke führt weiter im Mittelstreifen des Royal Albert Way, wo zwei fast identische Stationen innerhalb eines Kreisverkehrs liegen, **Beckton Park** ④ und **Cyprus**. Der größere Betriebshof der DLR befindet sich östlich von **Gallions Reach** ⑤. Von hier ist ein Abzweig Richtung Dagenham Dock geplant. Die DLR endet an der einfachen Station **Beckton** ⑥, die über eine Rampe zugänglich ist.

Der fünfte Ast der Docklands Light Railway wurde im Dezember 2005 eröffnet. Er führt über **West Silvertown** ①, **Pontoon Dock** ②③ (wo man vom Bahnsteig einen wunderbaren Blick über den Millennium Dome und Canary Wharf genießen kann) zum **London City Airport** ④ und weiter bis **King George V** ⑤, von wo die Strecke unter der Themse bis Woolwich Arsenal verlängert wird. Bis auf den Endbahnhof liegt die Strecke meist auf einem Betonviadukt. Silvertown und North Woolwich werden auch von der North London Line bedient, die aber in Vorbereitung auf die Verlängerung der DLR von Canning Town nach Stratford bald geschlossen werden soll. Von King George V fahren die Züge in der Hauptverkehrszeit alle 7-8 Minuten ab (jeder zweite Zug endet dann in Canning Town), sonst alle 10 Minuten.

*The DLR's fifth leg was opened in December 2005. It includes stations at **West Silvertown** ①, **Pontoon Dock** ②③ (with a spectacular view of the Millennium Dome at North Greenwich with Canary Wharf in the background), **London City Airport** ④ and the terminus **King George V** ⑤. Except for the terminus, most of the route is on a concrete viaduct. Trains depart from King George V towards Bank every 10 minutes during off-peak, and every 7-8 minutes during peak hours, when every other train terminates at Canning Town. The area of Silvertown and North Woolwich is also served by the North London Line, but this service will soon be withdrawn in preparation for the DLR extension from Canning Town to Stratford.*

An extension from King George V under the River Thames to Woolwich Arsenal is currently under construction.

(Photos ①④ Brian Hardy)

The Stratford and Bank services converge at the 4-track **West India Quay** station ①②, which is only some 200 m from the impressive 3-track **Canary Wharf** station ③-⑤, though separated by the northern West India Dock. Trains continue south across the central West India Dock (which was partly drained for the Jubilee Line station) to **Heron Quays** ⑥, which was rebuilt in 2002, and since 2004 has provided a direct underground link to the Jubilee Line station at Canary Wharf.

Die Äste von Bank und Stratford laufen an der Station **West India Quay** ①② zusammen, welche nur ca. 200 m von der spektakulären dreigleisigen Station **Canary Wharf** ③-⑤ entfernt ist. Dazwischen liegt ein Hafenbecken. Über ein weiteres Hafenbecken (welches zum Teil für die Station der Jubilee Line trockengelegt wurde) geht es zur Station **Heron Quays** ⑥, die 2002 umgebaut und seit 2004 außerdem direkt mit dem Bahnhof Canary Wharf der Jubilee Line verbunden wurde.

Die Station **South Quay** ① soll weiter östlich neu gebaut werden, da ihre derzeitige Lage keine Bahnsteigverlängerung zulässt. An der Station **Crossharbour** gibt es ein Wendegleis für Verstärker- fahrten. Die Verlängerung nach Lewisham wurde 1999 eröffnet und verbindet Canary Wharf mit den Bezirken südlich der Themse. Die Station **Mudchute** musste tiefer gelegt werden, um die Einfahrt in den 1,65 km langen Röhrentunnel zu ermöglichen. Die ursprüngliche Endstation **Island Gardens** ② wurde geschlos- sen und unterirdisch in offener Bauweise neu gebaut. Auch der Bahnhof **Cutty Sark** ③④, im Zentrum von Greenwich, entstand in offener Bauweise. Am Bahnhof **Greenwich** ⑤ kann man am selben Bahnsteig von den DLR-Zügen Richtung Norden zu den Vorortzügen nach London Bridge umsteigen. Als Hochbahn führt die Trasse schließlich bis **Lewisham** ⑥, wo der Bahnsteig zwischen dem Bezirkszentrum und dem Vorortbahnhof liegt.

At **South Quay** ①, a new station is planned further east as the design of the present station does not allow for platform lengthen- ing. **Crossharbour** station serves the London Arena and has reversing sidings for special events and peak-hour serv- ices. The Lewisham extension opened in 1999 to provide a link between Canary Wharf and the south- ern side of the River Thames. The original **Mudchute** station had to be rebuilt at a lower level to allow the 1.65 km tube tunnel under the Thames to start just south of it. **Island Gardens** station ② was originally located on the surface and is now in a cut-and-cover box. Access to a pedestrian tunnel under the Thames, opened in 1902, is nearby. **Cutty Sark** station ③④ was also built from the surface; it serves the Greenwich town centre and the Maritime Museum. At **Greenwich** ⑤, same-level interchange is provided between northbound DLR trains and suburban services to London Bridge. The DLR route continues elevated to **Lewisham** ⑥, where the terminus is ideally located for the town centre and lies adjacent to the mainline station.

Beckenham Junction

Croydon (340.000 Einw.) ist der südlichste Londoner Bezirk, dessen Zentrum etwa 15 km südlich von Charing Cross liegt. Der Bezirk ist über mehrere Bahnstrecken an die Bahnhöfe Charing Cross bzw. London Bridge einerseits und Victoria andererseits angeschlossen, außerdem durch die Thameslink. Die Londoner U-Bahn hingegen wurde nie so weit nach Süden verlängert, auch wenn es in den fünfziger Jahren Planungen gab, die neue Victoria Line bis Croydon zu führen.

Die **Croydon Tramlink** ist ein typisches ‚Light Rail'- bzw. Stadtbahn-Netz britischer Bauart, da sie größtenteils auf bestehenden oder stillgelegten Bahntrassen errichtet wurde. Dazu kommen im Zentrum von Croydon straßenbündige Abschnitte, sowie eine Neubaustrecke auf eigenem Gleiskörper nach New Addington. Derzeit besteht das Netz aus drei Linien, darunter eine Durchmesserslinie und zwei Radiallinien. Alle Linien befahren im Zentrum im Uhrzeigersinn die eingleisige Schleife.

Der westliche Ast, der größtenteils durch angrenzende Bezirke führt, benutzt die Trasse der ehemaligen *Wimbledon to West Croydon Railway* von 1855. Auf dieser Strecke gibt es vier eingleisige Abschnitte, auch die Endstation Wimbledon ist eingleisig (Gleis 10). Westlich der Haltestelle Mitcham gibt es ein kurzes Stück mit verschlungenen Gleisen, wo die Strecke unter der A217 (London Road) durchführt. Der Eisenbahnbetrieb wurde erst im Mai 1997 für den Umbau eingestellt. Zu den wichtigsten Bauwerken an dieser Strecke zählen die Viadukte über Vorortbahnstrecken in Mitcham Junction sowie südlich von West Croydon, wo die Tram in Straßenlage geführt wird.

Am Bahnhof East Croydon verlässt die Tram das Zentrum und fährt bis kurz vor Sandilands auf der Straße. In Sandilands verzweigen sich die Linien, wobei in beiden Richtungen die Trasse

Croydon (340,000 inh.) is the southernmost borough of Greater London, lying about 15 km south of Charing Cross. The borough is served by several rail lines from Victoria and Charing Cross/ London Bridge, as well as by Thameslink, but the London Underground has never been extended that far south, although there had been plans in the 1950s for the new Victoria Line to also serve Croydon town centre.

The **Croydon Tramlink** is a typical modern light rail system, making using of former mainline railway routes, combined with some street-running sections in central Croydon and a new alignment to New Addington. The network is currently operated with three routes, with one route constituting a diameter line while the other two routes terminate in the town centre, running around a single-track loop in a clockwise direction.

The western leg, which runs mostly through neighbouring boroughs, makes use of the former 'Wimbledon to West Croydon Railway' (1855). Along this branch there are four single-track sections as well as the Wimbledon terminus, where only platform 10 is available. Just west of the Mitcham stop there is a short section of interlaced track that passes under the A217 London Road. The railway was closed for conversion in May 1997. Among the major infrastructural works carried out on this branch are the viaducts across the mainline at both Mitcham Junction

LONDON Croydon Tramlink

28 km (3 km im Straßenraum | *on-street*), 38 Haltestellen | *Stops*

10-05-2000 Route 3 Croydon Loop – New Addington
23-05-2000 Route 2 Croydon Loop – Beckenham Junction
30-05-2000 Route 1 Wimbledon – Elmers End
10-12-2005 + Centrale stop

der ehemaligen Bahn von Elmers End Richtung Sanderstead benutzt wird. Die Linien 1 und 2 fahren gemeinsam Richtung Norden bis Arena. Auf diesem Abschnitt befinden sich mehrere Bahnübergänge. Von Arena fährt die Linie 1 eingleisig bis Elmers End, die Endhaltestelle liegt an der Nordseite des Bahnhofs an der Strecke von Charing Cross nach Hayes. Die Linie 2 setzt ihre Fahrt auf einer Neubaustrecke am westlichen Rand des South Norwood Country Parks fort und erreicht in Birkbeck die Bahnstrecke von Crystal Palace nach Beckenham. Von dieser Bahnstrecke wurde ein Gleis für die Tramlink abgegeben. An der Haltestelle Avenue Road gibt es ein Ausweichgleis, Birkbeck und Beckenham Road hingegen haben nur eine Bahnsteigkante für beide Richtungen. Die Endhaltestelle der Linie 2 liegt auf der Südseite vor dem Bahnhof Beckenham Junction. Nach dem Abzweig östlich von Sandilands fährt die Linie 3 erst durch einen 500 m langen Tunnel und verlässt nach etwa 1 km die alte Bahntrasse. Die Strecke von Lloyd Park bis New Addington wurde für die Tramlink neu gebaut. Sie führt durchgehend auf eigenem Gleiskörper meist in Straßenrandlage und hat mehrere Bahnübergänge.

Bei der Tramlink sind 24 Stadtbahnwagen des Typs CR4000 (FLEXITY Swift) von Bombardier im Einsatz. Dieses Fahrzeug ist vom aus Köln bekannten K4000 (Niederflurstadtbahn) abgeleitet. Es ist 30,1 m lang und 2,65 m breit. Die Stromversorgung erfolgt mit 750 V Gleichstrom über Oberleitung. Die Fahrzeuge dürfen nur als Einzelwagen verkehren. Das erste gelieferte Fahrzeug bekam die Nummer 2530 und schließt somit an die alte Nummerierung der seit 1952 in London verschwundenen Straßenbahnen an.

and West Croydon, the latter taking the trams onto street-running sections through central Croydon.

From East Croydon, the trams leave the town centre on a street alignment up to Sandilands, where lines 1 and 2 diverge from line 3, with all three lines continuing along an out-of-service railway, which once linked Elmers End to Sanderstead. Lines 1 and 2 continue north along this route to Arena, with several level crossings on this section. From Arena, line 1 becomes single-track and terminates at the north side of Elmers End station on the Hayes - Charing Cross Line. Line 2 continues on a new alignment through the western side of the South Norwood Country Park before joining the Crystal Palace - Beckenham railway line at Birkbeck. The Birkbeck - Beckenham Junction section was reduced to single-track and the former westbound track converted for the Tramlink. Whereas Birkbeck and Beckenham Road have only one

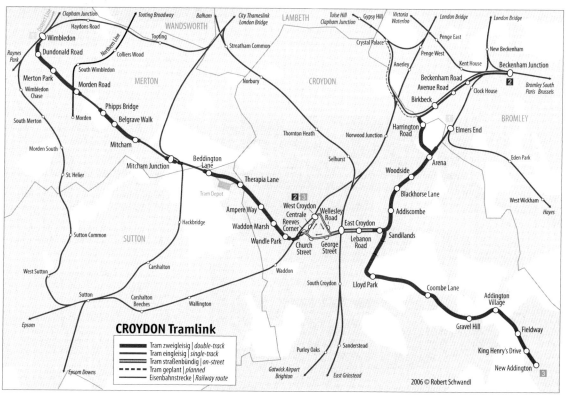

2006 © Robert Schwandl

platform for both directions, there is a passing loop with two side platforms at Avenue Road. Line 2 terminates at the south side of Beckenham Junction station, with two tracks lying outside the original station compound.

After branching off at Sandilands, line 3 runs south for 1 km along the former railway to Sanderstead, including a stretch through a 500 m tunnel. The route from the first stop Lloyd Park to the terminus at New Addington was purpose-built for the Tramlink and runs mostly alongside roads on reserved track with several level crossings.

Tramlink is operated with a fleet of 24 FLEXITY Swift CR4000 (2530-2553) trams, built by Bombardier in Vienna and based on the K4000 tram designed for the Cologne low-floor network. These vehicles are 30.1 m long and 2.65 m wide. They are powered with 750 V dc supplied by overhead wires. The trams are only allowed to operate as single units. The strange number assigned to the first tram delivered (2530) continues the traditional numbering system, the last trams having disap-

Die Tramlink ist Eigentum der *Tramtrack Croydon Ltd* (TCL) und wird von *Tram Operations Ltd* (TOL), einer Tochtergesellschaft der *First Group*, betrieben. Die Tramlink ist von 5:00 bis 1:15 Uhr in Betrieb. Tagsüber fahren die Linien 1 und 2 alle 10 Minuten und die Linie 3 alle 6-7 Minuten. Früh morgens und abends, sowie sonntags fahren alle Linien im 15-Minuten-Takt, wobei die Linie 2 dann auch nach Wimbledon durchgebunden wird. Das gesamte Netz ist barrierefrei zugänglich, dazu wurden in Wimbledon Aufzüge eingebaut. Die Tramlink ist in den Londoner Verkehrsverbund integriert, es gibt allerdings auch Fahrscheine, die nur für die Tramlink gelten. Fahrscheine müssen an Automaten an den Haltestellen gekauft werden, in den Fahrzeugen gibt es sporadische Kontrollen.

Derzeit ist eine Verlängerung bis Crystal Palace geplant. Dazu würde das zweite Gleis zwischen Beckenham Junction und Birkbeck übernommen und im Bereich Crystal Palace eine neue Strecke gebaut.

In London gibt es außerdem noch folgende Straßenbahnprojekte:
1) die West London Tram - von Shepherd's Bush über Acton und Ealing bis Uxbridge entlang der Uxbridge Road (A4020),
2) die Cross River Tram - von Euston nach Waterloo, mit Ästen an beiden Enden.

① Church Street ② Wimbledon ③ Arena

peared from London's streets in 1952.

Tramlink is owned by Tramtrack Croydon Ltd (TCL) and operated by Tram Operations Ltd (TOL), a subsidiary of the First Group. Tramlink operates between 05:00 and 01:15. During daytime service there is a tram every 10 minutes on lines 1 and 2, and every 6-7 minutes on line 3. At other times and on Sundays, all routes are served every 15 minutes, with line 2 being extended to Wimbledon. The entire system is fully accessible, with lifts having been installed at Wimbledon station. The network is integrated with the overall London fare system, although there are also cheap tram-only tickets. The Croydon Tramlink is an open system, and tickets have to be bought from ticket machines found on the platforms. There are sporadic inspections on the trams. At present, an extension to Crystal Palace is planned, which will be achieved by taking over the second track between Beckenham Junction and Birkbeck and adding a new alignment at the Crystal Palace end.

In London, other tram schemes in preparation include:
1) the West London Tram, linking Shepherd's Bush to Uxbridge along Uxbridge Road (A4020) through Acton and Ealing.
2) the Cross River Tram linking Euston to Waterloo, with several branches at both ends.

In **Wimbledon** ①② wurde das Gleis angehoben, um einen ebenen Einstieg in die Tramlink-Fahrzeuge zu schaffen. Hier kann man zu den Vorortbahnen von/nach Waterloo sowie zur District Line umsteigen. Östlich der Haltestelle **Mitcham Junction** ③ wurde ein eingleisiges Viadukt über die Thameslink-Ringstrecke nach Sutton gebaut. Obwohl einige Abschnitte der Strecke nach Wimbledon eingleisig sind, stehen an allen Haltestellen zwei Gleise für Zugbegegnungen zur Verfügung. An der Haltestelle **Reeves Corner** ④ halten die Bahnen nur Richtung Osten, wenige Meter weiter östlich beginnt die Ringstrecke rund um das Zentrum von Croydon ⑤ (hier von der Haltestelle **Church Street** aus gesehen). Im Dezember 2005 wurde in der Tamworth Road ein neuer Halt vor dem **Centrale**-Einkaufszentrum eingerichtet.

At **Wimbledon** ①②, the track was raised to allow level access into the low-floor vehicles. Transfer is possible here to National Rail services to and from Waterloo and to the District Line. At **Mitcham Junction** ③, a single-track flyover was built across the Thameslink Sutton loop. Although the Wimbledon branch is partly single-track, passing loops are available at all stops.

Reeves Corner ④ is a stop only for the inbound direction, and is loacted just before the start of the Croydon town centre loop ⑤ (here seen from **Church Street**). A new stop opened on Tamworth Road in December 2005 to provide access to the **Centrale** shopping mall.

All tram lines operate around the Croydon town centre loop in a clockwise direction. Both the **Church Street** ① and the **George Street** ③ stops lie in quite narrow streets. After serving **West Croydon** railway station, the trams return to the main route via **Wellesey Road** ②. **East Croydon** ④ is the main railway station in the Borough of Croydon, with connections to Gatwick Airport and the south coast. There are three tracks in front of the main station entrance, allowing trams to turn around in case of delays or disruptions. East of the **Sandilands** ⑤ stop, trams run down to meet the former railway alignment that once linked Elmers End to Sanderstead. Line 1 (Elmers End) and line 2 (Beckenham Junction) turn left here ⑥, whereas line 3 trams diverge towards the south to New Addington.

Alle Linien fahren im Zentrum von Croydon im Uhrzeigersinn auf der Ringstrecke. Die Haltestellen **Church Street** ① und **George Street** ③ liegen in engen Straßen. Nach dem Halt am Vorortbahnhof **West Croydon** kommen die Bahnen über die **Wellesey Road** ② auf die Hauptachse zurück. **East Croydon** ④ ist der Hauptbahnhof des Bezirks, hier kann man in die Züge zum Flughafen Gatwick oder an die Südküste umsteigen. Vor dem Bahnhof liegen drei Straßenbahngleise, so dass man hier im Fall von Störungen oder Verspätungen wenden kann. Östlich der Haltestelle **Sandilands** ⑤ fahren die Bahnen auf die alte Eisenbahntrasse von Elmers End Richtung Sanderstead hinunter ⑥. Die Linie 1 (Elmers End) und die Linie 2 (Beckenham Junction) biegen hier nach links und die Linie 3 (New Addington) nach rechts ab.

An der Haltestelle **Arena** ① trennen sich die Strecken der Linien 1 und 2. Die Linie 1 führt weiter eingleisig bis **Elmers End** und die Linie 2 fährt durch den South Norwood Country Park und dann eingleisig parallel zur Bahnstrecke von Crystal Palace nach **Beckenham Junction** ②. Die Endhaltestelle der Linie 2 befindet sich außerhalb des eigentlichen Bahnhofs. Die Linie 3 fährt erst entlang der ehemaligen Eisenbahnstrecke nach Sanderstead weiter nach Süden, bevor sie dann Richtung Südosten abbiegt und auf einer neuen Trasse, meist in Randlage oder durch offenes Feld, New Addington erreicht. Tram 2533 nähert sich hier ③ vom Westen der Haltestelle **Gravel Hill** ④. Östlich dieser Haltestelle ⑤ findet man einen von mehreren Bahnübergängen. Die Endhaltestelle **New Addington** ⑥ liegt in einem Wohngebiet, das zwischen 1930 und 1970 entstand.

At **Arena** ① lines 1 and 2 diverge, with line 1 becoming single-track for the route to Elmers End, and line 2 running on a new route through South Norwood Country Park and then single-track along the Crystal Palace - Beckenham Junction railway. Line 2 terminates at **Beckenham Junction** ② outside the original station compound.
Line 3 runs south through a tunnel along the former railway to Sanderstead, before turning southeast and continuing on a new route, mostly along roads or through open countryside. Tram 2533 ③ is here approaching the **Gravel Hill** stop ④ from the west. On this route there are several level crossings ⑤, like this one just east of the Gravel Hill stop. Line 3 terminates at **New Addington** ⑥, a housing estate developed between the 1930s and the 1960s.

BIRMINGHAM

Birmingham ist mit ca. 1 Mill. Einwohnern das Zentrum des Groß-raums West Midlands, zu dem außerdem die Kommunen Wolver-hampton, Walsall, Dudley, Sandwell und Solihull gehören. Hier leben etwa 2,3 Mill. Menschen.

Die **Midland Metro** ist eine moderne Stadtbahn, die aber eher mit den Straßenbahnen in Nottingham oder Sheffield als mit einer richti-gen Metro vergleichbar ist. Die Trasse verläuft zwar zu ca. 90% auf eigenem Gleiskörper, die Fahrgäste müssen allerdings die Gleise überqueren, um auf den gegenüberliegenden Bahnsteig oder zum Ausgang zu gelangen.

1984 wurde ein umfangreiches Netz mit mehreren vom Stadtzen-trum ausgehenden Linien geplant. Die erste Strecke sollte in die östlichen Vororte Hodge Hill und Chelmsley Wood gebaut werden, wozu einige Häuser abgerissen werden sollten. Das führte zu hefti-gen Protesten, so dass schließlich die am einfachsten zu bauende Strecke vorgezogen wurde. Diese führt von Birmingham über das ‚Black Country' nach Wolverhampton meist auf der Trasse einer stillgelegten Eisenbahn, so dass keine Häuser betroffen waren. Die ursprüngliche Eisenbahnstrecke von Snow Hill nach Wolverhampton (Low Level) wurde 1854 von der *Great Western Railway* eröffnet und auf ihr verkehrten in ihren besten Tagen Fernzüge von London Paddington nach Birkenhead. Der Fahrgastverkehr wurde 1972 eingestellt, da die Strecke weitgehend parallel zur Hauptbahn von Wolverhampton zum Bahnhof New Street in Birmingham verlief. Erst 1995 wurde die Strecke im südlichen Abschnitt bis zur neuen Station The Hawthorns (*Jewellery Line*) und von dort Richtung Kidderminster als Teil einer Durchmesserlinie wieder in Betrieb genommen.

Anders als etwa in Manchester oder Newcastle, findet man bei der Midland Metro, abgesehen vom Hill Top Tunnel, kaum Reste der ehemaligen Eisenbahn. Auf der ganzen Strecke wurden neue Gleise verlegt und einfache Haltestellen mit 35 cm hohen Bahnsteigen eingerichtet.

Bei der Midland Metro sind 16 Fahrzeuge vom italienischen Hersteller Ansaldo im Einsatz. Die T69 sind nur 24,4 m lang, 2,6 m breit und zu 60% niederflurig, so dass an allen drei Türen stufenlos eingestiegen werden kann. Die Endabschnitte haben eine Fußbo-denhöhe von 85 cm. Die Stromzufuhr erfolgt mit 750 V Gleichstrom über Oberleitung. Die Bahnen verkehren normalerweise als Einzel-

Birmingham (1 mill. inh.) is the centre of the metropolitan area of West Midlands, which also contains Wolverhampton, Walsall, Dudley, Sandwell, Solihull and Coventry. This conurbation, excluding Coventry, is home to some 2.3 million people.

The **Midland Metro** is a modern light rail system, closer to the tramways of Nottingham and Sheffield than a real metro. Although it runs segregated from other traffic along 90% of its length, passengers have to cross the tracks at most stops to get to the opposite platform or the exit.

The first of a number of routes proposed in 1984, most of which radiated from the Birmingham city centre, was to have been built to the eastern suburbs of Hodge Hill and Chelmsley Wood, which would have required the demolition of many homes. Due to strong opposition in those areas, the least controversial route was chosen instead. The line from Birmingham to Wolverhampton via the Black Country was to run mostly along a former railway alignment, so no private properties would be affected.

The original railway line from Snow Hill to Wolverhampton (Low Level) was opened in 1854 by the Great Western Railway and during its heyday it was used by long-distance trains from London Paddington to Birkenhead. Passenger service was eventually with-drawn in 1972 as the line paralleled the route from New Street Station. In 1995 a rail service was reintroduced between Snow Hill and a new station at The Hawthorns (Jewellery Line), and on to Kidderminster, forming part of a cross-city service.

Unlike Manchester or Newcastle, the Midland Metro does not preserve anything of the former railway line, except the Hill Top Tunnel. New track was laid along the entire route and simple uniform stops with 35 cm high platforms were established.

The Midland Metro is operated with a fleet of 16 trams, all built by Ansaldo in Italy. These T69 vehicles are only 24.4 m long, and 2.6 m wide. They are 60 % low-floor and provide level access at all 3 doors. The end sections are 85 cm above the rails. Power

BIRMINGHAM Midland Metro

20.4 km (2 km im Straßenraum | *on-street*), 23 Haltestellen | *Stops*

31-05-1999   Birmingham Snow Hill – Wolverhampton St. George's

wagen. Da man mit diesen Fahrzeugen nie wirklich zufrieden war, sollen sie durch neue ersetzt werden, sobald die ersten Streckenerweiterungen fertig gestellt sind.

Eine Verlängerung von Snow Hill durch das Stadtzentrum und weiter nach Südwesten bis Five Ways und Edgbaston (3,2 km) ist seit Jahren geplant. Auch eine unterirdische Lösung wurde mehrmals in Betracht gezogen, derzeit ist allerdings, wenn überhaupt, eine Streckenführung im Straßenraum durch die belebten Einkaufsstraßen die einzig machbare Variante. Die 11,7 km lange Strecke von Wednesbury über Dudley nach Brierley Hill wird jedoch größtenteils auf der Trasse der ehemaligen *South Staffordshire Line* verlaufen, nur im Zentrum von Dudley sind straßenbündige Abschnitte vorgesehen.

Die Midland Metro wird von *Travel Midland Metro* (ALTRAM) im Auftrag von *Centro*, der *West Midlands Passenger Transport Executive*, betrieben. Die Bahnen verkehren von 6:30 bis Mitternacht, tagsüber alle 6-8 Minuten und abends alle 12 Minuten, sonntags alle 10 Minuten. Fahrscheine werden in den Fahrzeugen von Schaffnern ausgegeben.

In Birmingham ist neben der Midland Metro noch die Cross-City Line erwähnenswert. Ähnlich einer S-Bahn verkehrt sie zwischen Four Oaks im Norden und Longbridge im Süden im 10-Minuten-Takt, allerdings werden die Gleise auf dem südlichen Abschnitt auch von Fernzügen benutzt.

is supplied at 750 V dc from an overhead wire. The trams usually operate as single units. As their performance has not been very satisfactory, they are planned to be replaced by new rolling stock when the next extensions are brought into service.

An extension from Snow Hill through the city centre and onwards to Five Ways and Edgbaston (3.2 km) has been proposed for many years. Again and again an underground solution for this route has been discussed, but with the present government's attitude towards urban railways, funding would never become available. Therefore, the street-running option along Bull Street, Corporation Street, Stephenson Street and Broad Street is more likely. The 11.7 km extension from Wednesbury to Dudley and Brierley Hill, however, will mostly be built along the abandoned South Staffordshire Line, with some street-running sections in the Dudley town centre.

The Midland Metro is operated by Travel Midland Metro (ALTRAM) on behalf of Centro, the West Midlands Passenger Transport Executive. Trams are in service between 06:30 and midnight, running at a frequency of 6-8 minutes during the day and 12 minutes in the evenings. On Sundays there is a tram every 10 minutes. Tickets are issued by conductors on the tram.

The Cross-City Line in Birmingham is also worth mentioning. This mainline service provides a train every 10 minutes between Four Oaks in the north and Longbridge in the south, though sharing tracks with other services along the southern leg.

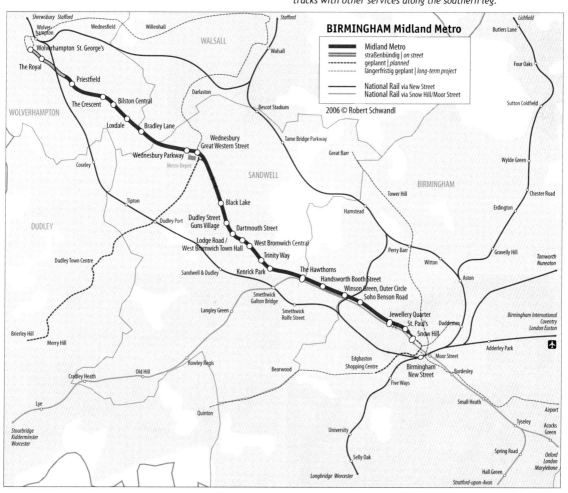

Der alte Bahnhof **Snow Hill** wurde 1976 abgerissen, 1987 startete dann vom heutigen Bahnhof aus der Vorortverkehr Richtung Süden. Erst 1995 gab es wieder durchgehenden Züge auf der Jewellery Line nach Stourbridge und Kidderminster. Der Bahnsteig 4 ①② wurde später als zweigleisige Endstation für die Midland Metro umgebaut. Von Snow Hill fährt die Midland Metro parallel zur Vorortbahn bis zur Station The Hawthorns. Der kurze Abschnitt bis **St. Paul's** ③ ist eingleisig. Nach mehreren kurzen Tunneln erreicht man die Station **Jewellery Quarter** ④⑤.

The old Snow Hill station was demolished in 1976, the present station opening in 1987 for services towards the south. In 1995, through-service on the rebuilt Jewellery Line to Stourbridge and Kidderminster followed. Platform 4 was later rebuilt for the 2-track tram terminus ①②.

From Snow Hill the Midland Metro runs parallel to the suburban tracks up to The Hawthorns. The short section between Snow Hill and St. Paul's ③ is single-track. After several short tunnels a joint station is found at Jewellery Quarter ④⑤.

Am Bahnhof **The Hawthorns** ①-③ trennt sich die mit Dieselzügen befahrene Jewellery Line von der Midland Metro, welche bis zur Haltestelle Priestfield auf der Trasse der ehemaligen *Great Western Railway* bleibt. An diese einst stark befahrene Bahn erinnern nur noch einzelne Straßenbrücken und der Hill Top-Tunnel.
In **West Bromwich** ④⑤, einem wichtigen Zentrum in der Industrieregion ‚Black Country', wurde neben der Haltestelle ein großer Busbahnhof eingerichtet.
Alle Haltestellen sind mit einfachen Unterständen ähnlich gestaltet. Meist müssen die Fahrgäste die Gleise überqueren, um zum gegenüberliegenden Bahnsteig zu kommen.

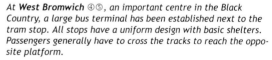

*At **The Hawthorns** ①-③, the diesel-operated Jewellery Line diverges from the Midland Metro, which continues along the former Great Western Railway alignment to Priestfield. Nothing except several road bridges and the Hill Top Tunnel remind us now of the once busy railway route.*

*At **West Bromwich** ④⑤, an important centre in the Black Country, a large bus terminal has been established next to the tram stop. All stops have a uniform design with basic shelters. Passengers generally have to cross the tracks to reach the opposite platform.*

103

Nach der Haltestelle **Wednesbury Parkway** (siehe S. 100), wo sich der Betriebshof und die Leitzentrale der Midland Metro befinden, folgt als nächster Halt Richtung Westen **Bradley Lane** ①②.
In **Bilston Central** ③-⑤ wurde die Lage des ehemaligen Bahnhofs nicht genutzt, sondern eine neue Haltestelle im Einschnitt direkt im Ortszentrum eingerichtet. Die versetzt angeordneten Bahnsteige sind von der Südseite, wo sich ein Busbahnhof befindet, auch per Aufzug zugänglich, neben Snow Hill der einzige Aufzug der Midland Metro.

*After passing the **Wednesbury Parkway** stop (see p. 100), adjacent to which the Metro Depot and Control Centre are located, the Midland Metro reaches **Bradley Lane** ①②.*
*At **Bilston Central** ③-⑤, the former station site was abandoned and a stop established further west in a cutting right in the centre of this town. The staggered platforms can be reached from a bus terminal located at the southern side via a lift, the only one on the line apart from that at Snow Hill.*

Nach dem Halt in **Priestfield** ①
verlassen die Bahnen der Midland
Metro die ehemalige Eisenbahntrasse
(die weiter zum Bahnhof Wolverhampton Low Level, östlich des heutigen
Bahnhofs, führte) und fahren mitten
im Autoverkehr weiter auf der Bilston
Road ②③ Richtung Wolverhampton
Zentrum. Auf dem langen Abschnitt
bis zur Haltestelle The Royal soll ein
zusätzlicher Halt New Inn entstehen.
Die Haltestelle **The Royal** ④ (benannt
nach einem 1997 geschlossenen
Krankenhaus) liegt wiederum in einem
vom Autoverkehr getrennten Bereich.
Vor Einfahrt in die Endhaltestelle
Wolverhampton St. George's ⑤
überqueren die Bahnen die 60 m lange
Wishbone-Brücke, welche über eine
abgesenkte Fußgängerebene innerhalb
eines großen Kreisverkehrs führt. Neben
einem 300 m langen Viadukt über ein
Güternebengleis bei Winson Green
stellt diese Brücke das wichtigste für die
Midland Metro errichtete Bauwerk dar.

*Just after serving **Priestfield** ① the trams leave the traditional
railway alignment (which went to Wolverhampton Low Level
station, located to the east of the present railway station) and
continue on Bilston Road ②③, sharing car lanes. A stop may be
added at New Inn, to fill the long gap between Priestfield and
The Royal. **The Royal** ④ stop (named after a hospital closed in
1997) lies in a reserved area.*

*Before entering the terminus at **Wolverhampton St. George's** ⑤,
the trams cross the 60 m Wishbone Bridge, purpose-built over
a sunken pedestrian island in the middle of a huge roundabout.
Together with a 300 m viaduct across a freight siding near Winson
Green, this is the Metro's most substantial new structure.*

Nottingham (274.000 Einw.) liegt in den East Midlands, etwa 180 km nördlich von London. Zusammen mit den angrenzenden Kommunen in der Grafschaft Nottinghamshire erreicht der Großraum eine Einwohnerzahl von ca. 500.000.

Die Straßenbahn von Nottingham wird offiziell als **Nottingham Express Transit** (NET) bezeichnet und ist die jüngste aller städtischen Schienenverkehrsmittel in Großbritannien. Die erste, 14 km lange Strecke wurde im März 2004 als Linie 1 eröffnet, eine Bezeichnung die auf weitere Strecken hoffen lässt. Etwa 10 km dieser Strecke verlaufen auf eigenem Gleiskörper, größtenteils parallel zur *Robin Hood Line*, einer lange ungenutzten Eisenbahnstrecke, die erst 1993-1998 stufenweise zwischen Nottingham und Worksop wieder in Betrieb genommen wurde.

Die Straßenbahn von Nottingham wird mit 15 Incentro-Fahrzeugen (201-215) betrieben, welche von Bombardier im Werk Derby gebaut wurden. Die Stromversorgung erfolgt mit 750 V Gleichstrom über Oberleitung. Jedes Fahrzeug ist 33 m lang und 2,4 m breit. Die 100%-niederflurigen, klimatisierten Bahnen werden, genauso wie die Haltestellen, mit Videokameras überwacht. Die Haltestellen werden sowohl über eine elektronische Anzeige als auch akustisch angekündigt. Das Zugpersonal ist abwechselnd als Fahrer und als Schaffner tätig. Jedes Fahrzeug trägt den Namen einer mit Nottingham in Beziehung stehenden Persönlichkeit, z.B. Lord Byron (205), D.H. Lawrence (202) und natürlich Robin Hood (211).

Die Straßenbahn von Nottingham wurde von *Arrow Light Rail Ltd.* gebaut und wird auch von diesem Konsortium betrieben.

Nottingham (274,000 inh.) lies in the East Midlands, about 180 km north of London. Together with the neighbouring towns in Nottinghamshire the conurbation is home to some 500,000 people.

The Nottingham tram system, officially called **Nottingham Express Transit** (NET), is the newest urban rail network in Britain. Since March 2004 there has been one 14 km line with a short spur, often referred to as Line One, thus insinuating that this is just the beginning of a more ambitious project. About 10 km of the route is on a segregated right-of-way, mainly running parallel to the Robin Hood Line, a long out-of-use railway line reopened in stages between Nottingham and Worksop between 1993 and 1998.

The Nottingham tram network is operated with a fleet of 15 5-section Incentro vehicles (201-215), built by Bombardier in Derby. The trams are powered by 750 V dc supplied via an overhead wire. Each unit is 33 m long and 2.4 m wide. The 100% low-floor air-conditioned trams, as well as all stops along the route, are equipped with CCTV cameras. The next stop is announced on an electronic display as well as acoustically. Train staff alternate between working as drivers and conductors. Each unit carries the name of a Nottingham-related personality, among them Lord Byron (205), D.H. Lawrence (202) and, of course, Robin Hood (211).

NET was built and is operated by Arrow Light Rail Ltd., a consortium including, among others, Transdev and Nottingham City

NOTTINGHAM Express Transit (NET)

14 km (4 km im Straßenraum | *on-street*), 23 Haltestellen | *Stops*

09-03-2004 Station Street - Hucknall / Phoenix Park

Daran beteiligt sind u.a. Transdev oder Nottingham City Transport, weshalb die Tram gut mit dem städtischen Busnetz verbunden ist. Die Schaffner verkaufen Fahrscheine, die entweder nur für die Straßenbahn oder für alle Verkehrsmittel gültig sind. Tagsüber verlassen die NET-Bahnen die Haltestelle Station Street alle sechs Minuten und fahren abwechselnd nach Hucknall oder Phoenix Park. Während der Hauptverkehrszeiten wird der Takt auf 5 Minuten verdichtet. Die Bahnen fahren von 6 Uhr morgens bis Mitternacht (sonntags 8:00 - 23:00). Entlang der Strecke wurden fünf Park & Ride-Plätze mit insgesamt 3000 Stellplätzen eingerichtet (an den Hst. Hucknall, Moor Bridge, Phoenix Park, Wilkinson Street und The Forest). An allen Haltestellen ist stufenloses Einsteigen gewährleistet. Neben einem Wartehäuschen verfügen die Haltestellen über eine elektronische Fahrzielanzeige. Die 2. Ausbaustufe der NET soll den Süden und Südwesten des Großraums erschließen: eine 7,6 km lange Strecke mit 13 Haltestellen soll nach Wilford und Clifton führen, wobei diese etwa zur Hälfte die ehemalige Trasse der *Great Central Railway* benutzen könnte; eine 9,8 km lange Strecke mit 15 Haltestellen soll das Entwicklungsgebiet ng2, das Queen's Medical Centre und die Universität erschließen, und dann weiter nach Beeston und Chilwell führen. Beide Strecken würden am Hauptbahnhof an die bestehende Strecke angeschlossen. Diese würde auf einer Brücke über den Gleisen des Hauptbahnhofs hinweg zu einer neuen Station an der Südseite verlängert, die derzeitige Endstation würde durch eine neue Zwischenstation am Broadmarsh Shopping Centre ersetzt. Keine der beiden südlichen Strecken wird wohl vor 2010 verwirklicht werden können.

Transport. The tram and city bus networks are well-integrated; NET-only or combined tickets are available from the conductors. During daytime service, trams leave Station Street every 6 minutes, running alternately to Hucknall and Phoenix Park. During peak hours intervals are reduced to 5 minutes. Tram service is provided from 06:00 until midnight (08:00-23:00 on Sundays). Along the route there are 5 park & ride sites for a total of 3,000 cars (Hucknall, Moor Bridge, Phoenix Park, Wilkinson Street and The Forest). All stops provide level access into the vehicles and have shelters. The waiting time for the next train is indicated electronically.

NET Phase 2 will take the trams to the south and southwest of the conurbation: a 7.6 km branch with 13 stops will serve Wilford and Clifton, with about half of the route following the former Great Central Railway; a 9.8 km branch with 15 stops will run through the redevelopment area ng2, then serve the Queen's Medical Centre and University of Nottingham before entering the neighbouring towns of Beeston and Chilwell. These extensions are to be linked to the existing line by a viaduct across the railway tracks and a new stop is to be built on the southern side of the station together with a bus terminal and extended station concourse. Between the new stop and Lace Market another stop is planned for Broadmarsh Shopping Centre. Neither of the southern branches is expected to be operating before 2010.

Station Street > Lace Market

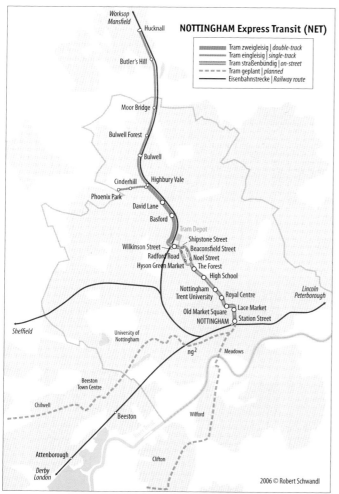

NOTTINGHAM Express Transit (NET)

Tram zweigleisig | double-track
Tram eingleisig | single-track
Tram straßenbündig | on-street
Tram geplant | planned
Eisenbahnstrecke | Railway route

2006 © Robert Schwandl

Die südliche Endhaltestelle **Station Street** ①② liegt erhöht an der Nordseite des Hauptbahnhofs auf der Trasse der ehemaligen *Great Central Railway*, die einst zur Victoria Station (heute ein Einkaufszentrum) führte. Im Stadtzentrum verläuft die NET-Strecke größtenteils im Straßenraum, mit einer engen Kurve direkt nach der Haltestelle **Lace Market**. Bahn Nr. 202 biegt hier ③ in die Victoria Street ein und erreicht wenig später die Haltestelle **Old Market Square** ④ am Rathaus. Die nächste Haltestelle **Royal Centre** ⑤ (und ① nächste Seite) liegt an der wichtigen Kreuzung mit der Parliament Street, neben den Theatre Royal.

The first NET line starts from an elevated stop, **Station Street** ① ②, on the northern side of Nottingham Station. This alignment was previously used by the Great Central Railway on its way into Victoria Station (now a shopping mall). The route through the city centre is mostly on-street, with a sharp curve after the **Lace** **Market** stop. ③ Tram 202 turns left into Victoria Street to reach **Old Market Square** ④, where a stop is located next to the Council House. Here trams turn right to climb up Market Street. The next stop **Royal Centre** ⑤ (① - p.107) is located at the crossroads with the busy Parliament Street, next to the Theatre Royal.

Im Stadtzentrum müssen die NET-Bahnen teils starke Steigungen überwinden, wie hier nahe der Haltestelle **Trent University** ②. Von der Haltestelle **The Forest** ③ führt das Gleis Richtung Norden geradeaus weiter entlang der **Noel Street**, während das Gleis Richtung Süden über die **Radford Road**, die Hauptstraße im Stadtteil Hyson Green, geleitet wird. Westlich der Haltestelle **Shipstone Street** ④ treffen beide Gleise vor der Haltestelle **Wilkinson Street** wieder aufeinander ⑤. Hier befindet sich auch der Betriebshof der NET. Wegen des allgemeinen Linksverkehrs kreuzen sich beide Gleise an jedem Ende der Hyson-Green-Schleife.

*Through the city centre the NET trams have to negotiate some serious gradients, such as here near the **Trent University** stop ②. From **The Forest** ③ the northbound track continues straight on along **Noel Street**, whereas the southbound is diverted along **Radford Road**, the main street in the Hyson Green area.*

*After serving **Shipstone Street** ④, both tracks rejoin before arriving at the **Wilkinson Street** stop ⑤, where the tram depot is located. Due to left-hand operation and the southbound track on the western route, the tracks cross each other at either end of the Hyson Green loop.*

An allen NET-Haltestellen ist stufenloses Einsteigen möglich, die Fahrzeuge sind 100% niederflurig.

Bei **Wilkinson Street** ① handelt es sich um eine typische Haltestelle mit Seitenbahnsteigen, einem kleinen Unterstand und elektronischer Fahrzielanzeige. Westlich dieser Haltestelle überquert die Straßenbahn erst die *Robin Hood Line* und biegt dann in einer großen Kurve ② nach Norden ab, bis sie ihre Trasse parallel zur Eisenbahn erreicht.

Bis **Highbury Vale**, wo für jeden Ast eigene Bahnsteige gebaut wurden, besteht ein 6-Minuten-Takt. Bis zu diesem Abzweig sind sowohl die NET als auch die *Robin Hood Line* zweigleisig. Der kurze Ast nach Phoenix Park ist eingleisig und benutzt die Trasse einer ehemaligen Bergwerksbahn. **Cinderhill** ③ ist die einzige Haltestelle mit nur einer Bahnsteigkante. An der Endhaltestelle **Phoenix Park** ④ wurde ein Parkplatz eingerichtet.

All stops along the NET route provide full accessibility to wheelchair users or people with prams. Trains are 100% low-floor.

Wilkinson Street ① *is a typical stop with side platforms, a shelter and electronic destination displays. West of this stop the trams cross the Robin Hood Line on a bridge before entering a curve* ② *towards the north to become aligned with this railway along the western side. Trams run every 6 minutes to Highbury Vale, where separate platforms were built for each branch. Up to this junction both the NET line as well as the Robin Hood Line are double-track.*

The short Phoenix Park branch is single-track and runs on a former railway formation which once served the long-gone Cinderhill Colliery. After stopping at Cinderhill ③*, the only bidirectional stop to have only one platform face, it terminates at Phoenix Park* ④*, where a park & ride site was established.*

An der Haltestelle **Bulwell** ①② kann man zur *Robin Hood Line* umsteigen. Diese verkehrt halbstündlich von Nottingham nach Mansfield und Worksop, hält aber in Bulwell nur stündlich. Nördlich von Highbury Vale sind sowohl die NET als auch die Eisenbahn eingleisig, der Straßenbahn stehen allerdings an allen Haltestellen zwei Gleise für Zugbegegnungen zur Verfügung.

Alle Haltestellen bis **Moor Bridge** ③ liegen innerhalb der Stadtgrenzen von Nottingham, der Einheitstarif gilt aber auch für die beiden außerhalb liegenden Haltestellen.

An der zweigleisigen Endhaltestelle **Hucknall** ④ kann man auch zur *Robin Hood Line* umsteigen. Neben der Haltestelle befindet sich ein großer Parkplatz für mehr als 400 Autos.

Anfangs wurde ein Straßenbahnbetrieb auf den Eisenbahngleisen nach dem Karlsruher Modell in Betracht gezogen, schließlich entschied man sich aber für einen völlig getrennten Betrieb auf eigenem Gleis.

At **Bulwell** ①② interchange is provided with the Robin Hood Line, which operates an half-hourly service between Nottingham and Mansfield, calling at Bulwell only once an hour.

North of Highbury Vale, tram and railway each become single-track, although the tram has a passing loop at each stop.

All stops up to **Moor Bridge** ③ lie within the Nottingham city boundaries, but the flat fares also cover the outer two stops.

Transfer to the Robin Hood Line is also possible at the 2-track terminus **Hucknall** ④. Next to the station there is a large car park for more than 400 cars. Initial plans considered track-sharing along the Robin Hood Line similar to the tram-train concept developed in Karlsruhe, but eventually the choice was for a totally segregated tram alignment.

SHEFFIELD

Sheffield (512.000 Einw.) liegt am südlichen Rand der historischen Grafschaft Yorkshire und gehört heute mit u.a. Doncaster, Rotherham und Barnsley (ca. 1,2 Mill. Einw.) zum Großraum South Yorkshire. Ähnlich wie Stuttgart erstreckt sich die Stadt über mehrere Hügel, wobei das Stadtzentrum in einem Talkessel liegt. Die letzte Straßenbahn der ersten Generation fuhr in Sheffield im Jahr 1960. 1994, also zwei Jahre nach Inbetriebnahme der hochflurigen Stadtbahn in Manchester, war die **Sheffield Supertram** die erste Niederflurstraßenbahn in Großbritannien. Anders als in Manchester wurden für die Supertram keine Eisenbahnstrecken direkt übernommen, weshalb die Entscheidung zugunsten der Niederflurtechnik auf der Hand lag. Das heutige Netz ist eine Mischung aus konventioneller Straßenbahn und etwa zur Hälfte auf eigenem Gleiskörper verlaufender Stadtbahn. Nur der 7 km lange Ast nach Meadowhall ist vollkommen vom Straßenverkehr getrennt, aber auch hier gibt es einige Bahnübergänge.

Die Supertram wird mit 25 von Siemens-Duewag in Düsseldorf gebauten Fahrzeugen betrieben. Die dreiteiligen Straßenbahnen sind 35 m lang und 2,65 m breit. Sie sind nur in den Endabschnitten im Türbereich niederflurig (42 cm), der Rest ist über zwei Stufen erreichbar. Die Stromzufuhr mit 750 V Gleichstrom erfolgt über Oberleitung. Die Haltestellen sind 26,5 m lang und ermöglichen einen stufenlosen Einstieg. Die Bahnsteigränder sind mit Blindenmarkierungen versehen. Alle Haltestellen sind gleich ausgestattet und verfügen über einen Unterstand, aber keine Fahrzielanzeiger. Die ursprünglich aufgestellten Fahrscheinautomaten wurden bereits 1996 wieder entfernt, heute werden die Fahrscheine von Schaffnern in der Bahn verkauft bzw. kontrolliert. Seit Anfang 2006 sind die ersten Fahrzeuge in neuem Anstrich zu sehen.

1997 wurde die *South Yorkshire Supertram Ltd* von der *Stagecoach Holding PLC* erworben, die derzeit das Netz unter der Bezeichnung Stagecoach Supertram betreibt.

Sheffield (512,000 inh.) lies at the southernmost tip of historical Yorkshire and is now part of the metropolitan county of South Yorkshire (incl. Doncaster, Rotherham and Barnsley - 1.2 mill. inh.). Sheffield is known for its hilly cityscape, with the city centre in the valley and the residential areas spreading out over seven hills. The last first-generation tramway closed in Sheffield in 1960.

The *Sheffield Supertram* was the first low-floor system in Britain when it opened in 1994, only two years after the Manchester Metrolink. As the Sheffield tram, however, does not use any former British Rail passenger lines, the choice of low-floor technology was obvious. The system is a mixture of conventional street-running tramway and segregated light rail. The share of reserved track is about 50%, with only the 7 km Meadowhall branch being totally segregated from road traffic, although with several level crossings.

The Sheffield tram system is operated with a fleet of 25 vehicles, all built by Siemens-Duewag in Düsseldorf. These 3-section trams are 35 m long and 2.65 m wide. The end sections are low-floor in

SHEFFIELD Supertram

29 km, 48 Haltestellen | Stops

21-03-1994	Fitzalan Square - Meadowhall ■
22-08-1994	Fitzalan Square - Spring Lane □■
05-12-1994	Spring Lane - Gleadless Townend ■□
18-02-1995	Fitzalan Square - Cathedral ■□
27-02-1995	Cathedral - Shalesmoor ■□
27-03-1995	Gleadless Townend - Halfway □■
03-04-1995	Gleadless Townend - Herdings Park ■
23-10-1995	Shalesmoor - Middlewood / Malin Bridge ■□
2001	+ Park Grange Croft □■

Nach anfänglichen Schwierigkeiten wegen des unkoordinierten parallelen Busverkehrs, ist die Supertram mittlerweile zu einem beliebten Transportmittel geworden. Eine gute Ampelvorrangschaltung ermöglicht einen reibungslosen Betrieb trotz des hohen Anteils an straßenbündigen Strecken.

Das Supertram-Netz besteht aus drei Linien, wobei die Blue Line (Malin Bridge - Halfway) und die Yellow Line (Middlewood - Meadowhall) tagsüber alle 10 Minuten verkehren, die Purple Line (Cathedral - Herdings Park) allerdings nur alle 30 Minuten. Von 9:00 bis 14:00 fahren die Bahnen der Purple Line als Yellow Line weiter nach Meadowhall. Abends und an Wochenenden verkehren alle Linien im 20-Minuten-Takt.

Netzerweiterungen (siehe Netzplan) werden in Erwägung gezogen, aber bislang gibt es dafür keinen genauen Zeitplan.

the door area (42 cm), whereas the rest is higher and accessible via steps. Power is supplied via an overhead wire at 750 V dc. Tram stops are 26.5 m long and provide level access into the vehicles. The platform edges are fitted with tactile markings for the blind. All stops show a standard design with shelters but no destination displays. The original ticket machines were withdrawn in as early as 1996, tickets now being inspected and sold on the tram by conductors. Since early 2006, the first trams have been seen in a new livery.

In 1997, South Yorkshire Supertram Ltd was acquired by Stagecoach Holding PLC, which now operates the system as Stagecoach Supertram. After initial difficulties due to parallel bus routes after bus deregulation, the Supertram has now become a very popular means of transport. Priority at traffic lights guarantees fast and reliable operation despite the high percentage of on-street running.

The Sheffield Supertram consists of three lines, with the Blue Line (Malin Bridge - Halfway) and the Yellow Line (Middlewood - Meadowhall) operating every 10 minutes during daytime service, and the Purple Line (Cathedral - Herdings Park) every 30 minutes. Between 09:00 and 14:30 Purple Line trams continue to Meadowhall displaying a yellow route sign. In the evenings and at weekends all three lines operate a 20-minute headway.

The possibility of a further expansion of the network has been examined (see map below), but no time frame for such work can as yet be given.

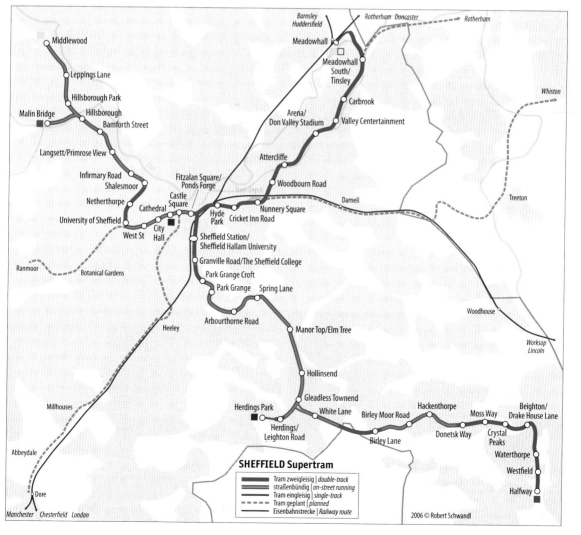

SHEFFIELD Supertram

Tram zweigleisig	double-track
straßenbündig	on-street running
Tram eingleisig	single-track
Tram geplant	planned
Eisenbahnstrecke	Railway route

2006 © Robert Schwandl

Im Stadtzentrum verkehrt die Supertram auf Straßenebene, teilweise auf einer abmarkierten Spur, entlang der High Street, Church Street und West Street. Hier befinden sich mehrere Haltestellen in kurzen Abständen. Vom Gleisdreieck am Park Square ① erreichen die Straßenbahnen über ein Viadukt den **Fitzalan Square** ② und fahren dann weiter hinauf zum **Castle Square** ③, einer wichtigen Kreuzung im Stadtzentrum. Die nächste Haltestelle befindet sich an der **Cathedral** ④, wo die von Herdings Park kommenden Bahnen (Purple Line) wenden und ihre Fahrt als Yellow Line Richtung Meadowhall fortsetzen. In Bild ⑤ ist Tram 116 nahe der Haltestelle **City Hall** auf der West Street mit Vollwerbung für das Einkaufszentrum Meadowhall zu sehen.

The route through the city centre runs on-street, though mostly separated from car traffic, along High Street, Church Street and West Street, with stops located close to each other. From the triangular junction at Park Square ① the trams cross a viaduct to reach **Fitzalan Square** ②, before climbing up to **Castle**

Square ③, a major crossroads in the city centre. The following stop is next to the **Cathedral** ④, where trams coming from Herdings Park (Purple Line) reverse to continue on the Yellow Line to Meadowhall. Tram 116 is seen here near the **City Hall** stop ⑤ on West Street, advertising the Meadowhall shopping mall.

Die Strecke nach Hillsborough wurde größtenteils als konventionelle Straßenbahn gebaut, bis auf den Abschnitt von University of Sheffield bis **Shalesmoor**, der im Mittelstreifen der Netherthorpe Road ③ liegt. Direkt westlich der Haltestelle **University** ① wurde zur Unterfahrung eines Kreisverkehrs ein kurzer Tunnel errichtet. Die Haltestelle **Netherthorpe** ② ist insofern einzigartig in Sheffield, als sie über einen Mittelbahnsteig verfügt, der von einer Unterführung aus über eine Rampe zugänglich ist. Nach der Haltestelle **Hillsborough** ④ biegt die Blue Line in die Holme Lane ein und endet an der Haltestelle **Malin Bridge**. Die Yellow Line fährt weiter durch den Stadtteil Hillsborough und endet am nordwestlichen Rand der **Middlewood** Road ⑤.

The route to Hillsborough is mainly an on-street tramway, except for the stretch between University of Sheffield and **Shalesmoor**, which runs in the middle strip of Netherthorpe Road ③. Just west of the **University** ① stop there is a short tunnel that dives under the Brook Hill roundabout. The **Netherthorpe** ② stop is unique in Sheffield in that it has an island platform, which is accessible from a pedestrian tunnel via a ramp. Just after the **Hillsborough** ④ stop, the Blue Line branches off to run down Holme Lane to its terminus at **Malin Bridge**. The Yellow Line continues through Hillsborough to terminate on the northeastern side of **Middlewood** Road ⑤.

Die Strecke nach Meadowhall beginnt am Gleisdreieck am Park Square ①. Sie verläuft durchgehend auf eigenem Gleiskörper, obwohl es einige Bahnübergänge gibt. Nach Überqueren des Sheffield & Tinsley-Kanals ② verläuft die Strecke ab der Haltestelle **Attercliffe** parallel zu einer Güterbahn. Die Supertram erschließt hier das Entwicklungsgebiet im Don-Tal und erreicht dann die Südseite des weitläufigen Einkaufszentrums Meadowhall. Nach wenigen 100 m im Schatten der hier aufgeständerten Autobahn M1 ③ trifft sie auf die Trasse der Fernbahn Richtung Doncaster, neber der sie die letzten 300 m ④ bis zur Endhaltestelle **Meadowhall** ⑤ eingleisig fährt.

The Meadowhall route starts from the triangular junction at Park Square ① and is totally separated from road traffic, although there are several level crossings. After crossing over the Sheffield & Tinsley Canal ② it gets aligned with a freight line just after the **Attercliffe** stop. It then serves the new development area in the Don Valley and reaches the southern side of the large Meadowhall Shopping Centre. After a few hundred metres running parallel with the elevated M1 motorway ③ the route gets aligned with the mainline to Doncaster. The last 300 m ④ before arriving at the **Meadowhall** interchange ⑤ is single-track.

Die Strecke nach Halfway bzw. Herdings ist gekennzeichnet durch starke Steigungen, hier klettern die Straßenbahnen von 69 m über N.N. im Stadtzentrum auf 212 m in Herdings, die Endhaltestelle Halfway liegt wiederum auf 69 m. Die Haltestelle **Sheffield Station** ① liegt an der Rückseite des Hauptbahnhofs, auf Höhe der Bahnsteigdächer an einem Abhang. Ab hier steigt die Strecke entlang der Park Grange Road (② zwischen den Haltestellen **Park Grange** und **Arbourthorne Road**, und ③ zwischen dieser und **Spring Lane**). Die Blue Line und die Purple Line trennen sich an der Haltestelle **Gleadless Townend**, von wo die Blue Line ihre Fahrt hinunter Richtung **Crystal Peaks** ④ und **Halfway** ⑤ fortsetzt.

*The route to Halfway/Herdings is characterised by its severe gradients, the trams climbing from 69 m above sea level in the city centre to 212 m at Herdings, the Halfway terminus being again at 69 m. The **Sheffield Station** stop ① lies at the back of the railway station, at roof level. From here the line continues uphill along Park Grange Road (② is between the **Park Grange** and **Arbourthorne Road** stops, and ③ between the latter and **Spring Lane**). The Blue and Purple Lines separate at **Gleadless Townend**, from where the Blue Line begins to run down to **Crystal Peaks** ④ before arriving at the **Halfway** terminus ⑤.*

Manchester hat ungefähr 430.000 Einwohner und bildet mit Wigan, Bolton, Bury, Rochdale, Oldham, Salford, Trafford, Stockport und Tameside den Großraum Greater Manchester im Nordwesten Englands. Manchester, Salford, Trafford und Stockport bilden ein geschlossen bebautes Gebiet mit 1,2 Millionen Einwohnern.

Die Stadtbahn von Manchester, die so genannte **Metrolink**, ist Eigentum der GMPTE (Greater Manchester Passenger Transport Executive) und wird von Serco Metrolink betrieben. Das heutige Netz erstreckt sich auf die Stadtgebiete von Manchester, Bury, Salford und Trafford. Metrolink war 1992 die erste moderne Stadtbahn Großbritanniens, es handelt sich dabei um die einzige britische Hochflurbahn, die auch im Straßenraum verkehrt.

Das heutige Netz umfasst zwei ehemalige British-Rail-Strecken, einen konventionellen Straßenbahnabschnitt durch das Stadtzentrum sowie eine Neubaustrecke teilweise auf eigenem Gleiskörper zu den Salford Quays und nach Eccles.

In den frühen siebziger Jahren entstand das sog. ‚Picc-Vic'-Projekt für eine unterirdische Verbindungsbahn zwischen den beiden Hauptbahnhöfen Piccadilly und Victoria. Ähnlich wie in Liverpool sollten U-Bahnhöfe an den beiden Hauptbahnhöfen sowie an der Whitworth Street, dem St. Peter's Square (genannt ‚Central') und am Royal Exchange mitten im Geschäftsviertel entstehen. 1977 wurde das Projekt wegen Geldmangels aufgegeben.

Die Bury-Linie, gebaut 1879, wurde 1916 mit 1200 V Gleichstrom über Stromschiene elektrifiziert. Als dieses System im Laufe der Jahre veraltet wurde, war ein Umbau zu einer Stadtbahn die beste Möglichkeit, diese Strecke weiterhin zu nutzen.

Die 1849 eröffnete Altrincham-Linie war 1931 mit 1500 V Gleichstrom elektrifiziert worden, 1971 wurde die Spannung jedoch auf 25 kV Wechselstrom umgestellt. Für den Stadtbahnbetrieb musste die Spannung dieser Linie auf 750 V Gleichstrom geändert werden,

Manchester (430,000 inh.) is part of the metropolitan county of Greater Manchester in the northwest of England, which also includes Wigan, Bolton, Bury, Rochdale, Oldham, Salford, Trafford, Stockport and Tameside. The continuously built-up area only covers Manchester, Salford, Trafford and Stockport, with a total population of 1.2 million.

*The Manchester light rail system is known as **Metrolink**. It is owned by GMPTE (Greater Manchester Passenger Transport Executive) and operated by Serco Metrolink. The present network serves parts of Manchester, Bury, Salford and Trafford. When opened in 1992 Metrolink was Britain's first new-generation tramway system, and it is still the only system that uses high-floor vehicles on street-running sections.*

The present Metrolink network consists of two former British Rail lines, a conventional on-street tramway route through the city centre and a partly segregated newly-built branch to the Salford Quays and to Eccles.

MANCHESTER Metrolink

36.6 km (3.4 km im Straßenraum | *on-street*), 37 Haltestellen | *Stops*

06-04-1992	Bury – Victoria	(15.9 km)
27-04-1992	Victoria – G-Mex	(3.1 km)
15-06-1992	G-Mex – Altrincham	(10.4 km)
20-07-1992	Market St/Mosley St – Piccadilly	(0.7 km)
06-12-1999	Cornbrook – Broadway	(3.0 km)
21-07-2000	Broadway – Eccles	(3.5 km)
31-03-2003	+ Shudehill	
02-09-2005	+ Cornbrook	

die Bury-Linie hingegen musste vollständig mit Oberleitung ausgerüstet werden. Alle Stationen beider Linien wurden behindertengerecht ausgebaut, entweder mit Rampen oder Aufzügen.

Wegen der bereits bestehenden Hochbahnsteige an der Bury- und der Altrincham-Linie entschied man sich bei der Metrolink für Hochflurfahrzeuge. Im Stadtzentrum beschränkte man den 91 cm hohen Abschnitt, außer an der Haltestelle Piccadilly Gardens, auf die beiden mittleren Türen, der restliche Teil wurde angerampt. Am Bahnhof Victoria wurde die Bury-Linie durch eine Öffnung in der südlichen Bahnhofsmauer mit dem straßenbündigen Abschnitt verbunden. Die Altrincham-Linie erreicht beim Ausstellungszentrum G-Mex (in der ehemaligen *Central Station*) über eine Rampe die Straßenebene. Der Metrolink-Bahnhof Piccadilly befindet sich zwischen den Bögen unter dem Fernbahnhof.

Nachdem das Grundnetz der Metrolink 1992 in Betrieb genommen worden war, wurde der Abzweig nach Eccles in zwei Stufen 1999 bzw. 2000 eröffnet. Diese Linie trennt sich von der Altrincham-Linie am Bahnhof Cornbrook und führt über den Manchester Ship Canal und dann durch das Sanierungsgebiet Salford Quays im ehemaligen Hafen. Cornbrook, ursprünglich nur eine Umsteigestation, bekam erst 2005 einen Ausgang zur Straße. Der westliche Abschnitt nach Eccles verläuft hauptsächlich im Straßenraum. Alle Haltestellen dieser Strecke hatten von Beginn an Hochbahnsteige für Doppeltraktionen.

Außerhalb der Hauptverkehrszeiten verlassen Metrolink-Züge die Bahnhöfe Bury und Altrincham alle sechs Minuten in Richtung Manchester. Die Bahnen fahren abwechselnd zum Bahnhof Piccadilly oder direkt weiter nach Bury bzw. Altrincham. Die Eccles-Strecke wird alle 12 Minuten von Piccadilly aus bedient. Alle Strecken werden am frühen Morgen sowie am Abend im 12-Minuten-Takt betrieben.

Anfangs wurden 26 Metrolink-Fahrzeuge von der italienischen Firma FIREMA (heute Ansaldo) erworben. Diese Gelenktriebwagen haben drei Drehgestelle, das mittlere ist nicht angetrieben. Die Fahrzeuge sind 29 m lang, 2,65 m breit und meistens in Einzeltraktion unterwegs. Wenn diese Züge in den Hauptverkehrszeiten in Doppeltraktion verkehren, ist es an einigen Haltestellen im

In the early 1970s, an underground scheme referred to as 'Picc-Vic' was proposed to link the city's major railway stations, Piccadilly and Victoria. The project was similar to the Liverpool city centre loop and included underground stations on Whitworth Street, at St. Peter's Square ('Central') and at Royal Exchange for the central shopping area, as well as under the respective railway terminals. In 1977 the project was abandoned due to a lack of funding.

The Bury line, opened in 1879, had already been electrified by as early as 1916 at 1200 V dc via a third rail. As this system had since become obsolete, conversion to light rail was considered the best option for this route.

The Altrincham line, opened in 1849, was electrified in 1931 using overhead wires and 1500 V dc, converted to 25 kV ac in 1971. For light rail operation, the tension on this line had to be switched to 750 V dc, whereas on the Bury line totally new overhead line equipment had to be installed. All stations along both lines were made accessible for mobility-impaired persons, either by ramps or by lifts.

MANCHESTER
Zentralbereich | Central Area

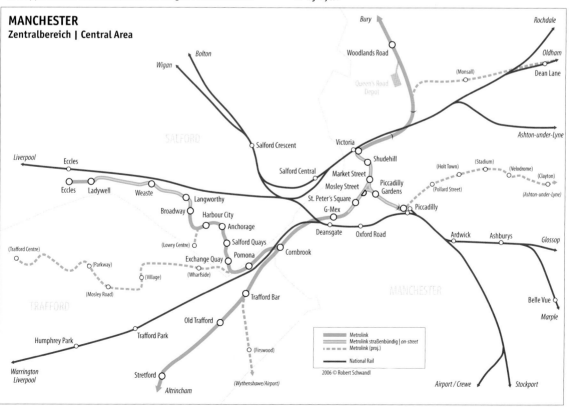

Metrolink
Metrolink straßenbündig | *on-street*
Metrolink (proj.)
National Rail

2006 © Robert Schwandl

Piccadilly

Stadtzentrum notwendig, am hinteren Wagen eine ausfahrbare Stufe zu benutzen.

Für die Erweiterung des Netzes mussten sechs neue Fahrzeuge (T68a, 2001-2006) von Ansaldo geliefert werden, bei denen die Kupplung und die Fahrgestelle abgedeckt sind. Mittlerweile wurden die Türen der meisten Fahrzeuge türkis gestrichen, um Sehbehinderten eine gesetzlich vorgeschriebene Kontrastfarbe zum sonst weißen Anstrich zu bieten.

Die Manchester Metrolink war 1992 ein sofortiger Erfolg, so dass es bald zu Kapazitätsproblemen kam. 2005 wurde endlich Geld für acht zusätzliche Fahrzeuge und eine notwendige Schienenerneuerung auf der Bury-Linie verfügbar gemacht. Während der neunziger Jahre wurden viele neue Strecken geplant und auch genehmigt, die bereits versprochenen Geldmittel wurden im Juli 2004 jedoch von der Regierung wieder zurückgezogen. Ende 2005 war noch kein Kompromiss gefunden worden, so dass man noch nicht sagen kann, wann die ehrgeizige Erweiterung stattfinden wird. Die Bauphase 3 umfasst die Umrüstung der Eisenbahnstrecke nach Oldham/ Rochdale auf Metrolink-Betrieb, eine vor allem auf der Straße verlaufende Strecke nach Ashton-under-Lyne, eine neue Linie auf einer ehemaligen Bahntrasse nach Wythenshawe und zum Flughafen, einen Abzweig ins Zentrum von Trafford und möglicherweise einen Ast nach Stockport über Didsbury. Falls alle diese Planungen realisiert werden, wird eine zweite Linie durch das Stadtzentrum, wohl entlang der Straße Deansgate, notwendig werden. In ferner Zukunft könnte ein Tunnel im Stadtzentrum wieder in Betracht gezogen werden.

The choice of high-floor vehicles was based on the existence of high platforms at all stations along the two railway lines. For the on-street section through the city centre a compromise was initially found for all stops except Piccadilly Gardens - the profiled platforms, which only had a short 91 cm high section matching the two central car doors, with the rest of the platform being formed by ramps.

At Victoria, the Bury line was linked to the city centre section via an opening cut into the station's southern wall. The Altrincham line was connected via a ramp next to the G-Mex exhibition centre (the former Central Station). At Piccadilly, the Metrolink station was built in the 'undercroft' of the railway station, between the arches supporting the mainline tracks.

With the initial network starting operation in 1992, an extension to Eccles was added in 1999/2000. This route diverges from the Altrincham line at Cornbrook and runs on a viaduct across the Manchester Ship Canal, and then at grade through the redeveloped areas of Salford Quays. Cornbrook, initially just an isolated transfer station, only became accessible from street level in 2005. The western section to Eccles runs mostly on-street. All stops along this extension were built with high platforms for double units from the beginning.

Metrolink trains leave Bury and Altrincham every six minutes during normal daytime service, and terminate alternately at Bury/Altrincham or at Piccadilly. The Eccles line is operated from Piccadilly every 12 minutes. All branches are served every 12 minutes in the early mornings and in the evenings.

Initially, 26 Metrolink vehicles (T68, 1001-1026) were acquired from the Italian firm FIREMA (now Ansaldo). These are articulated light rail vehicles mounted on 3 bogies, the central bogie being unmotored. The vehicles are 29 m long and 2.65 m wide and mostly operate as single units. When coupled in pairs for some peak-hour services the use of retractable steps is necessary at some city centre stops. For the Eccles extension another 6 vehicles (T68a, 2001-2006) were ordered from Ansaldo; these can be distinguished by their hidden couplers and bogies. Most trams of the first batch have since been repainted with turquoise doors, a colour that constrasts with the basic white livery in compliance with the Disability Discrimination Act.

The Manchester Metrolink was such an immediate success that capacity problems have occurred since it first opened. In 2005, funding for 8 additional vehicles and the urgent track renewal on the Bury line finally became available.

During the 1990s plans for new lines were developed and approved, but in July 2004 the already granted funds were withdrawn by the government. As of late 2005, a compromise has not yet been found, so it is too early to say when the 'big bang' will happen. The ambitious Phase 3 scheme includes conversion of the Oldham/Rochdale railway line to Metrolink standard, a mostly on-street route to Ashton-under-Lyne, a new route along a dismantled railway to Wythenshawe and the airport, a branch line to Trafford Centre, and possibly another branch to Stockport via Didsbury. If all these extensions are realised, a second cross-city link will probably be needed along Deansgate. One day in the future an underground route through the city centre might even once again be considered.

Piccadilly

G-Mex

In **Bury** ① wurde vor Umstellung auf Metrolink-Betrieb eine neue Station mit einem darüberliegenden Busbahnhof gebaut.

Einige Bahnhöfe auf der Bury-Linie, z.B. **Whitefield** ②, wurden für den Metrolink-Betrieb nur wenig umgebaut. Alle Bahnsteige sind entweder durch Rampen oder Aufzüge zugänglich, in **Crumpsall** ③ gibt es beides.

Nachdem die Züge am Mittelbahnsteig im Bahnhof **Victoria** ④ gehalten haben, verlassen sie das Bahngelände und fahren im Straßenraum durch das Stadtzentrum weiter. Eine Stadtbahn Richtung Bury nähert sich der Haltestelle **Market Street** ⑤, die Haupteinkaufsstraße im Herzen von Manchester.

A new station with a bus terminal on the surface was built at **Bury** ① prior to Metrolink operation. Some stations along the Bury line, like **Whitefield** ②, preserve most of their former appearance. All stations are fully accessible, either via ramps or lifts, or both as at **Crumpsall** ③.

After serving an island platform at **Victoria** ④, trams leave the railway alignment to continue on the roadway through the city centre. A Bury-bound tram approaches the **Market Street** ⑤ stop in the heart of the Manchester shopping area.

Der größte Teil der **Piccadilly Gardens** ① wurde in den letzten Jahren zur Fußgängerzone umgewandelt. Auf dem Gleis im Vordergrund fahren die Stadtbahnen von Bury nach Piccadilly. Die Haltestelle **Market Street** ② wurde 1998 mit einem Mittelbahnsteig, der zwei angerampte Einrichtungsbahnsteige an der High Street und der Market Street ersetzte, errichtet. Zwischen Victoria und Market Street entstand 2003 die Haltestelle **Shudehill**, wo im Januar 2006 ein Busbahnhof eröffnet wurde. Am **St. Peter's Square** ③④, neben dem Rathaus und der Zentralbibliothek, sind die ursprünglichen angerampten Bahnsteige noch erhalten. Der stufenfreie Einstieg ist dort nur an den mittleren Türen möglich.

*The largest part of **Piccadilly Gardens** ① was pedestrianised in recent years. The track in the foreground is for trams from Bury to Piccadilly.*

*The **Market Street** stop ② was rebuilt in 1998, with a single island platform replacing the former uni-directional profiled platforms on High Street and Market Street.*

*Between Victoria and Market Street a new stop was added in 2003 at **Shudehill**, where a bus terminal opened in January 2006.*

*At **St. Peter's Square** ③④, next to the Town Hall and Central Library, the original profiled platforms are still visible. Level access into the vehicles is only possible through the central doors.*

Einige der ursprünglichen Empfangsgebäude blieben zwar erhalten, als die Altrincham-Linie auf Metrolink-Betrieb umgestellt wurde, z.B. **Stretford** ①, **Sale** ② und **Brooklands** ③, die meisten werden aber nicht als solche genutzt.

Südlich vom Bahnhof **Timperley** ④ ist die Metrolink-Strecke bis **Navigation Road** eingleisig, da das zweite Gleis von den Diesel-

zügen nach Chester benutzt wird, die jetzt über Stockport zum Bahnhof Piccadilly fahren.

In **Altrincham** ⑤ benutzt die Metrolink die beiden westlichen Gleise, die zwei östlichen dienen den Regionalzügen zwischen Manchester und Chester.

Some of the original station buildings were preserved when the Altrincham line was converted to Metrolink operation, e.g. **Stretford** ①, **Sale** ② and **Brooklands** ③, although most are not used for this purpose.

South of **Timperley** station ④ the Metrolink route is single-track as far as **Navigation Road**, the other track being used by diesel services to Chester, which now run via Stockport to Piccadilly.

At **Altrincham** ⑤ the two western tracks are available for Metrolink trains, the two eastern ones being reserved for services between Manchester and Chester.

Der Ast nach Eccles wurde 1999-2000 in zwei Stufen eröffnet. Er erschließt das Sanierungsgebiet **Salford Quays** ①. Ein Abzweig zum Einkaufs- und Freizeitzentrum The Lowry ist geplant.
Weil der Abschnitt westlich von **Broadway** ② im Straßenraum liegt, haben die auf dieser Strecke eingesetzten Züge abgedeckte Kupplungen, um bei Unfällen die Auswirkungen zu verringern. Wie in **Langworthy** ③ wurden an allen Haltestellen von Anfang an Hochbahnsteige für doppelte Zugeinheiten gebaut. An der Endstation **Eccles** ④ ist am selben Bahnsteig das Umsteigen zu den Bussen möglich.

The branch to Eccles opened in two stages between 1999 and 2000. It serves the redevelopments along **Salford Quays** ①, with a short branch to The Lowry, an entertainment and shopping centre, being planned.
As the route west of **Broadway** ② is partly shared by motor vehicles, trains used on this line have their couplers covered to reduce impact in the case of an accident. Like at **Langworthy** ③ all stops were built with high platforms long enough for double units. At the **Eccles** terminus ④ interchange with buses is provided across the platform.

① Eine Stadtbahn nach Eccles überquert zwischen **Piccadilly** und **Piccadilly Gardens** auf der Aytoun Street den Rochdale-Kanal.
② Eine Stadtbahn nach Altrincham erreicht den Bahnhof **Sale**.
③ Eine Stadtbahn nach Bury verlässt die Haltestelle **Piccadilly Gardens**.

① *Eccles tram on Aytoun Street crossing the Rochdale Canal between* **Piccadilly** *and* **Piccadilly Gardens**.
② *Altrincham tram entering* **Sale** *station.*
③ *Bury tram leaving* **Piccadilly Gardens**.

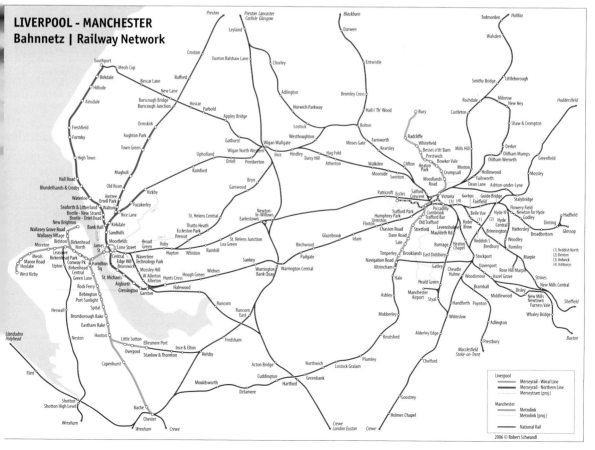

LIVERPOOL - MANCHESTER
Bahnnetz | Railway Network

2006 © Robert Schwandl

125

Mit 440.500 Einwohnern ist Liverpool das Zentrum des Großraums Merseyside, der sich im Nordwesten Englands auf beiden Seiten des Flusses Mersey erstreckt. In Merseyside leben etwa 1,36 Millionen Menschen; dazu gehören die Kommunen Liverpool, Wirral (Birkenhead), Sefton, St. Helens und Knowsley. Liverpool liegt ca. 55 km westlich von Manchester, beide Städte sind durch drei Eisenbahnstrecken verbunden. Die mittlere war 1830 eine der ersten Strecken der Welt mit Fahrgastbetrieb.

Das Bahnnetz von Merseyside, die **Merseyrail**, ist mit der Berliner S-Bahn vergleichbar, da sie als Vollbahn auf einem fast völlig unabhängigen Bahnnetz mit seitlicher Stromschiene betrieben wird und einen ganztägigen, dichten Verkehr anbietet. Im Stadtzentrum gibt es außerdem einige nur von der Merseyrail genutzte unterirdische Stationen. Wegen dieser besonderen Eigenschaften wurde das Netz, einst Teil der British Rail, nicht wie anderswo im Zuge der Privatisierung von der nationalen *Strategic Rail Authority* sondern von der lokalen *Merseyside Passenger Transport Executive* vergeben. Seit 2003 wird die Merseyrail von der *Merseyrail Electrics Ltd*, einem Konsortium aus Serco und NedRailways betrieben.

Die Merseyrail besteht aus zwei Liniengruppen, der Wirral Line und der Northern Line. Andere vom Hauptbahnhof Lime Street abfahrende, teils mit Diesel betriebene Strecken werden als City Line bezeichnet.

Neben dem heutigen Merseyrail-Netz hatte Liverpool einst eine wirkliche ‚Metro', nämlich die *Liverpool Overhead Railway* (LOR). Diese elektrifizierte Hochbahn fuhr ab 1893 auf einer 11,5 km langen Strecke am Hafen entlang. Der südliche Endpunkt Dingle, 1896 eröffnet, war unterirdisch und lag etwas landeinwärts. Am nördlichen Ende war die LOR mit den

Liverpool (444,500 inh.) is the centre of the (former) metropolitan county of Merseyside, which extends to both sides of the River Mersey in the northwest of England. Merseyside has a total population of 1.36 million, which includes the boroughs of Liverpool, Wirral (Birkenhead), Sefton, St. Helens and Knowsley. Liverpool lies some 55 km west of Manchester, both cities being linked by three railway routes. When it opened in 1830, the central route via Earlestown was among the world's first passenger railways.

*Merseyside's rail network, **Merseyrail**, is not a conventional underground or light rail network. It was included in this book because it has many features typical of urban rail systems:*

LIVERPOOL Merseyrail

118.5 km (~ 13 km unterird. | *underground*), 68 Bahnhöfe | *Stations*

Elektrischer Betrieb | *Electric service:*

03-05-1903	Liverpool Central – Birkenhead Park / Rock Ferry
22-03-1904	*Exchange Station* – Southport
07-12-1906	Sandhills – Aintree
01-10-1909	Aintree – Maghull
03-07-1911	Maghull – Town Green
12-07-1913	Town Green – Ormskirk
14-03-1938	Birkenhead Park – West Kirby / New Brighton
02-05-1977	Liverpool Central – Sandhills – Kirkby ('Link')
09-05-1977	'Loop' James Street – Central – James Street
31-10-1977	+ Lime Street
03-01-1978	Liverpool Central – Garston
08-05-1978	+ Moorfields (Loop station)
16-05-1983	Garston – Hunts Cross
30-09-1985	Rock Ferry – Hooton (+ Bromborough Rake)
04-10-1993	Hooton – Chester
29-05-1994	Hooton – Ellesmere Port
03-04-1995	+ Eastham Rake
09-03-1998	+ Brunswick
22-06-1998	+ Conway Park

Bahnen nach Southport und Aintree verbunden, welche bereits Anfang des 20. Jahrhunderts elektrifiziert wurden. Da Geld für eine Modernisierung fehlte, wurde die LOR schließlich 1956 stillgelegt und bald danach abgetragen.

Die **Wirral Line** gehört zu den ältesten unterirdischen Bahnen der Welt. Ähnlich wie die PATH-Linien, die New York und New Jersey unter dem Hudson-River verbinden, entstand die Wirral Line als Verbindung zwischen dem Liverpooler Stadtzentrum und Birkenhead auf der Halbinsel Wirral jenseits des Flusses Mersey. Die 2,7 km lange Tunnelstrecke, davon etwa 1,6 km unter dem Fluss, wurde 1886 zwischen James Street und Green Lane eröffnet. 1888 kam ein Abzweig bis Birkenhead Park dazu. Zwei kurze Verlängerungen bis Rock Ferry (1891) und Liverpool Central (1892) vervollständigten das ursprüngliche Netz der *Mersey Railway*. Ähnlich wie bei den ersten U-Bahn-Strecken in London war der anfängliche Betrieb mit Dampflokomotiven im Tunnel nicht sehr zufriedenstellend, so dass die *Mersey Railway* 1903 elektrifiziert wurde. Bis dahin waren die Züge von Liverpool kommend auf der *Wirral Railway* nach West Kirby und New Brighton durchgefahren. Für die folgenden 35 Jahre wurde die elektrische *Mersey Railway* getrennt betrieben und die Fahrgäste mussten an den Bahnhöfen Birkenhead Park und Rock Ferry umsteigen. Während die Äste nach West Kirby und New Brighton 1938 elektrifiziert wurden, wurde der elektrische Betrieb auf dem südlichen Ast erst während der letzten 20 Jahre in mehreren Stufen Richtung Chester und Ellesmere Port ausgedehnt. An Wochentagen verkehren die Züge der Wirral Line tagsüber auf allen Ästen alle 15 Minuten, wobei sie von Hooton abwechselnd nach Chester und Ellesmere Port weiterfahren.

Die **Northern Line** entstand 1977, als die nördlichen Strecken, die früher an der *Exchange Station* endeten, durch einen Tunnel mit einer Strecke im Süden verbunden wurden. Ein Abzweig sollte auch die östlichen Strecken von St. Helens, ab Edge Hill im Tunnel, anschließen. Während die Strecken nach Southport und Ormskirk bereits Anfang des 20. Jahrhunderts

it is almost entirely segregated from other rail traffic, it has third rail power supply (750 V dc), it offers a frequent service throughout the day and there are even several exclusive underground stations in the city centre. These special characteristics also explain the fact that Merseyrail is the only former British Rail franchise which is awarded by the Merseyside Passenger Transport Executive rather than the Strategic Rail Authority. Since 2003 Merseyrail has been operated by Merseyrail Electrics Ltd, a joint venture between Serco and NedRailways.

Merseyrail comprises two lines, the Wirral Line and the Northern Line. Other local rail services, some of which are diesel-operated, depart from Lime Street station and are referred to as the City Line.

Apart from the present Merseyrail system, Liverpool once had a proper 'metro', the 'Liverpool Overhead Railway' (LOR). This electrified elevated line opened in 1893 and ran along the riverside for 11.5 km, linking many of the once important docks. The southern terminus Dingle, opened in 1896, was underground and located further inland. At its northern end the LOR was linked to the rail lines to Southport and Aintree, which were electrified from the early 20th century. Due to a lack of funds for its modernisation the LOR was closed down in 1956 and demolished one year later.

The **Wirral Line** is among the oldest electric underground lines in the world. Similar to the PATH lines that link New York to New Jersey under the Hudson River, it was initially built to link the Liverpool city centre to Birkenhead

LIVERPOOL & BIRKENHEAD

Irish Sea

Southport
Ormskirk
Walton
Kirkby
Rice Lane
Bootle New Strand
Bootle Oriel Road
Northern Line
Kirkdale
Bank Hall
New Brighton
Wallasey Grove Road
Wallasey Village
Sandhills
Bidston
West Kirby
Liverpool Lime Street
Moorfields
Merseytram Line 1 proj.
Merseytram Line 2 proj.
James Street
Birkenhead North
Wirral Line
Liverpool Central
Edge Hill
Wigan Manchester Warrington London
Birkenhead Park
Conway Park
Hamilton Square
Northern Line
Upton
Birkenhead Central
Green Lane
Wirral Line
Brunswick
Dingle
Wrexham
Rock Ferry
St. Michaels
Ellesmere Port Chester
Mersey
Hunts Cross

2006 © Robert Schwandl

elektrifiziert worden waren, wurde die Kirkby-Strecke bis zur Inbetriebnahme des Innenstadttunnels 1977 mit Dieselfahrzeugen betrieben. Die 1972 geschlossene Linie nach Hunts Cross durch den Süden Liverpools wurde 1977 als Teil der Northern Line wiedereröffnet. Wie auf der Wirral Line verkehren die Züge der Northern Line auf allen Ästen wochentags tagsüber alle 15 Minuten. Der südliche Ast ist dabei direkt mit dem Southport-Ast verbunden, während die Züge der beiden anderen nördlichen Strecken am Bahnhof Liverpool Central wenden.

Das Herzstück der Merseyrail sind die in der siebziger Jahren gebauten unterirdischen Innenstadtstrecken: die 3,2 km lange und in 17-38 m Tiefe verlaufende eingleisige *Loop* (Schleife) für die Wirral Line, und die 2,6 km lange zweigleisige *Link* (Verbindung) für die Nord-Süd-Strecken. Der Großteil der Tunnelstrecken wurde mit sog. Roadheadern (mit Fräsköpfen) statt mit Schildvortrieb gebaut. Die Röhrentunnel wurden mit Betontübbings ausgekleidet.

Die Merseyrail wird mit 59 3-Wagen-Zügen der Baureihe 507 und 508, die 1978-80 in York gebaut wurden, betrieben. Alle Fahrzeuge sind in den letzten Jahren modernisiert worden. In den Hauptverkehrszeiten sind auch Doppeltraktionen zu sehen.

Derzeit ist in Merseyside ein Straßenbahnnetz mit drei Linien geplant (*Merseytram*), allerdings ist bislang von der Zentralregierung kein Geld dafür zur Verfügung gestellt worden. Die Linie 1 sollte 2008, wenn Liverpool europäische Kulturhauptstadt sein wird, fertig sein. Die Linie 3, die nicht auf dem Netzplan zu sehen ist, soll die südlichen Stadtteile und den John-Lennon-Airport auf einer noch nicht endgültig festgelegten Strecke anbinden.

on the Wirral peninsula on the other side of the River Mersey. The 2.7 km tunnel, of which approx. 1.6 km runs under the river, opened in 1886 to connect Green Lane to James Street. In 1888 a branch to Birkenhead Park was added, and in 1891 and 1892 two short extensions to Rock Ferry and Liverpool Central completed the original 'Mersey Railway'. As with the first underground routes in London, steam operation through the tunnels was rather dissatisfactory, so the 'Mersey Railway' was electrified in 1903. Up to then, cross-river trains had continued their journey on the 'Wirral Railway' to West Kirby and New Brighton. For the following 35 years, however, the electrified 'Mersey Railway' remained an isolated network, and passengers changed trains at Birkenhead Park and Rock Ferry. Whereas the West Kirby and New Brighton lines were electrified in 1938, the southern leg of the present Wirral Line was only equipped with a power rail in various stages over the last 20 years.

During daytime hours on weekdays, the Wirral Line now offers a train every 15 minutes on all branches, Chester and Ellesmere Port being served every 30 minutes.

The present **Northern Line** was created in 1977 when the northern branches, which prior to 1977 had terminated at Exchange Station, were connected underground to one line in the south (another planned branch incorporating the eastern lines from St. Helens via a tunnel curve from Edge Hill did not materialise). While the Southport and Ormskirk branches were electrified in the early 20th century, the present Kirby line remained diesel-operated until the central tunnel was completed in 1977. The Hunts Cross line through south Liverpool was closed in 1972 and reopened as part of the Northern Line in 1977. As on the Wirral Line, the Northern Line provides trains every 15 minutes on all branches during daytime hours on weekdays. The southern leg is linked to the Southport branch, the Ormskirk and Kirkby lines terminating at Liverpool Central.

The centrepiece of the present Merseyrail network is the so-called 'Loop and Link', built in the 1970s. This scheme included a 3.2 km single-track loop at a depth of 17-38 m for the Wirral Line, and a 2.6 km double-track link for the north-south lines. Most parts of the central underground sections were excavated with roadheaders instead of tunnel-boring machines. The tube-shaped tunnels were lined with precast concrete elements.

Merseyrail service is provided by a fleet of 59 three-car trains of class 507 and 508, built in York in 1978-80. All units have recently been refurbished. During busy hours double units can also be seen.

Over the past years Merseyside has developed plans for a 3-line tram network (Merseytram), but as of yet no funds have become available from the government. Line 1 was meant to be ready for 2008 when Liverpool will be the European Capital of Culture. Line 3, not shown on the map, would serve the southern suburbs and the John Lennon Airport on a route yet to be determined.

Im Liverpooler Stadtzentrum fährt die **Wirral Line** durch eine eingleisige Schleife und hält an vier unterirdischen Stationen, die alle einheitlich mit einer braunen Wandverkleidung aus Kunststoff gestaltet wurden. Die Bahnhöfe **Moorfields** ①, **Lime Street** und **Liverpool Central** sind eingleisig, da die Strecke nur im Uhrzeigersinn befahren wird. Bei Moorfields und Liverpool Central kann man zur Northern Line umsteigen. Am U-Bahnhof **James Street** halten die Züge stadteinwärts an einem separaten Bahnsteig, der gestalterisch den übrigen gleicht. Stadtauswärts hingegen wird der ursprüngliche Bahnsteig von 1866 benutzt. Der frühere stadteinwärtige Bahnsteig ② ist noch sichtbar, er wird aber nur bei Störungen auf der *Loop* benutzt.

Am U-Bahnhof **Hamilton Square** ③ wurde die ursprüngliche Bahnsteigebene an den Stil der neuen Bahnhöfe angepasst und etwas tiefer ein dritter Bahnsteig angelegt. Gleichzeitig wurde in den siebziger Jahren die niveaugleiche Kreuzung westlich des Bahnhofs umgebaut, so dass die Züge Richtung New Brighton und West Kirby nun unter den Gleisen Richtung Birkenhead Central durchfahren können. 1998 wurde entlang der unterirdischen Strecke durch Birkenhead der teils nach oben offene Bahnhof **Conway Park** ④ in Betrieb genommen.

*In the Liverpool city centre the **Wirral Line** runs in a single-track loop, serving four underground stations, all boasting an identical design with walls clad in chocolate-brown prefabricated panels made of glass-reinforced polyester. **Moorfields** ①, **Lime Street** and **Liverpool Central** are single-track, as trains only operate in a clockwise direction. Transfer to the Northern Line is possible at Moorfields and Central. At **James Street** inbound trains stop in a separate tube station (identical to the others), whereas outbound trains use the original station ② opened in 1866. The former inbound platform is visible in almost its original form from the opposite outbound platform, and can be used in the event of service disruptions on the loop. At **Hamilton Square** ③ the original station was redecorated in a style similar to the new loop stations, and a third platform located slightly deeper was added. The former flat junction west of Hamilton Square station was rebuilt in the 1970s so that trains to West Kirby and New Brighton could dive under the original tracks going to Birkenhead Central.*

*A new station was added at **Conway Park** ④ along the underground route through Birkenhead. It opened in 1998 and is partly covered.*

(Photo ④ Brian Hardy, 1999)

Im Westen verzweigt sich die Wirral Line westlich des Bahnhofs **Birkenhead North** ①, mit je einem Ast nach West Kirby (eröffnet bis Hoylake 1866 und bis West Kirby 1878) und nach **New Brighton** ② (1888). Am Bahnhof **Bidston** ③ halten die Dieselzüge der *Borderlands Line* nach Wrexham in Wales am selben Bahnsteig. Von 1888 bis 1903 fuhren die Dampfzüge von den westlichen Ästen auf der *Mersey Railway* weiter bis Liverpool. Die Strecken nach West Kirby und New Brighton wurden 1938 elektrifiziert, so dass der durchgehende Betrieb wieder aufgenommen werden konnte. **Hoylake** ④ wurde zu dieser Zeit umgebaut, am Endpunkt **West Kirby** ⑤⑥ kann man hingegen noch das Eingangsgebäude aus dem 19. Jahrhundert sehen.

The western branches of the Wirral Line diverge west of **Birkenhead North** ① and go to West Kirby (opened to Hoylake in 1866 and West Kirby in 1878) and **New Brighton** ② (opened in 1888). At **Bidston** ③, the diesel-operated 'Borderlands Line' to Wrexham in Wales shares the Merseyrail platform. From 1888 until 1903, steam trains operated between Liverpool and these lines, being linked to the 'Mersey Railway' at **Birkenhead Park**. The West Kirby and New Brighton routes were electrified in 1938 when through service under the river was resumed. **Hoylake** ④ was rebuilt at that time, whereas the terminus **West Kirby** ⑤⑥ preserves its original 19th century station building.

Der Tunnelmund der ursprünglichen *Mersey Railway* liegt direkt nördlich des Bahnhofs **Birkenhead Central** ①. Die Strecke endete damals am Bahnhof **Green Lane** ②③, einer teils nach oben offenen Station, bis sie dann fünf Jahre später bis **Rock Ferry** verlängert wurde. Dort mussten die Fahrgäste bis 1985 umsteigen, um ihre Fahrt auf der 1840 eröffneten *Chester & Birkenhead Railway* fortzusetzen.

Von **Hooton** ④ fahren die Züge abwechselnd alle 30 Minuten nach Chester bzw. nach **Ellesmere Port**. In **Chester** ⑤ wird der Bahnsteig 7b auch von anderen, jedoch mit Diesel betriebenen Zügen benutzt. Die Stationen südlich von Hooton liegen außerhalb von Merseyside und es gelten deshalb andere Tarife.

Die Wirral Line hat eine Gesamtlänge von 52,8 km, davon sind ca. 8 km in Liverpool und Birkenhead unterirdisch.

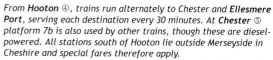

The tunnel portal of the original 'Mersey Railway' lies just north of **Birkenhead Central** ① *station. The line initially terminated at* **Green Lane** ②③, *a partly covered station in a cutting, but only five years later, in 1891, the line was extended to* **Rock Ferry**, *where, until 1985, passengers had to change trains and continue their journey on the 'Chester & Birkenhead Railway', which had opened in 1840.*

From **Hooton** ④, *trains run alternately to Chester and* **Ellesmere Port**, *serving each destination every 30 minutes. At* **Chester** ⑤ *platform 7b is also used by other trains, though these are diesel-powered. All stations south of Hooton lie outside Merseyside in Cheshire and special fares therefore apply.*

The Wirral Line has a total length of 52.8 km, of which approximately 8 km runs underground in Liverpool and Birkenhead.

Die **Northern Line** besteht aus einem südlichen und drei nördlichen Ästen. Die Strecke nach **Southport** ① wurde stufenweise zwischen 1848 und 1850 eröffnet und 1903 elektrifiziert. Ab 1905 fuhren auch die Züge der Liverpooler Hafenhochbahn Richtung Southport weiter. Wenige Jahre später wurde auch die 1847 erbaute Strecke nach **Ormskirk** ② elektrifiziert. Die Bahnhöfe hinter **Maghull** ③ liegen außerhalb von Merseyside in der Grafschaft Lancashire.

Die Endstationen **Ormskirk** sowie **Kirkby** ④ sind eingleisig, die weiterführenden Dieselzüge halten am hinteren Abschnitt desselben Bahnsteigs.

Die letzten 2 km der Kirbky-Strecke sind ebenfalls eingleisig. Südlich von **Kirkdale** ⑤ (und S. 133 ①) und **Bank Hall** laufen alle Strecken im Bahnhof **Sandhills** (S.133 ②) zusammen, bevor sie auf denselben Gleisen etwa 1,8 km weiter südlich den Innenstadttunnel erreichen.

*The Northern Line comprises one southern and three northern branches. The line to **Southport** ① was opened in stages between 1848 and 1850 and electrified in as early as 1903. Through-running on the Overhead Railway began in 1905. Electrification of the branch to **Ormskirk** ②, opened in 1847, followed soon after. The stations beyond **Maghull** ③ lie outside Merseyside in Lancashire.*

*The termini at **Ormskirk** and **Kirkby** ④ are only single-track, with connecting diesel services stopping further on along the same platform. The last 2 km on the Kirkby line is also single-track. South of **Kirkdale** ⑤ (and ① on page 133) and **Bank Hall**, all northern branches converge at **Sandhills** station (② p.133) before entering the north-south tunnel some 1.8 km further south.*

Die Northern Line kreuzt die Wirral Line an den U-Bahnhöfen **Moorfields** ③ und **Liverpool Central** ④. Bei letzterem handelt es sich um den ursprünglichen Endbahnhof der *Mersey Railway* von 1892. Die Wirral Line wurde 1977 in einen neuen Röhrenbahnhof eine Ebene tiefer verlegt.

Der südliche Abschnitt endet derzeit in **Hunts Cross** ⑤, obwohl die Strecke eigentlich Hough Green bzw. sogar Warrington erreichen sollte. Im Sommer 2006 werden die Bahnhöfe **Garsten** und Allerton durch eine neue Umsteigestation **Liverpool South Parkway** ersetzt.

Die Northern Line hat eine Gesamtlänge von 65,6 km, davon liegen etwa 5 km im Tunnel.

*The Northern Line intersects with the Wirral Line at **Moorfields** ③ and **Liverpool Central** ④. The latter is actually the original 'Liverpool Central Low Level' station opened for the 'Mersey Railway' in 1892. In 1977, the present Wirral Line was diverted into a new tube line and the station located at a deeper level.*

*The southern leg of the Northern Line terminates at **Hunts Cross** ⑤, although it was initially meant to run to Hough Green or even Warrington. At **Garston**/Allerton a new interchange station **Liverpool South Parkway** will open in summer 2006.*
The Northern Line has a total length of 65.6 km, with approximately 5 km in tunnel.

Blackpool (142.000 Einw., Grafschaft Lancashire) gehört zu den belieb-testen Badeorten Großbritanniens. Die erste elektrische Straßenbahn des Landes wurde hier im Jahr 1885 entlang der Promenade in Betrieb genommen, anfangs erfolgte die Stromversorgung über eine Strom-schiene, die in einer Rille im Boden angebracht war. 1899 wurde die Stromzufuhr auf konventionelle Oberleitung umgestellt.

Die heutige 18,4 km lange Linie von Fleetwood bis Starr Gate ist die einzige britische Straßenbahn der ersten Generation, die bis heute überlebt hat, weshalb ihr ein kurzes Kapitel in diesem Buch gewidmet werden soll. Die Strecke verläuft größtenteils auf eigenem Gleiskörper, bis auf einen kurzen Abschnitt nördlich des Talbot Squares sowie die letzten 900 m in Fleetwood.

Die Straßenbahn von Blackpool wird mit 75 Fahrzeugen betrieben, von denen die meisten aus den dreißiger Jahren stammen. Darunter gibt es viele offene Wagen, sowohl doppelstöckig als auch einstöckig. Der Betrieb findet das ganze Jahr statt, im Winter mit acht Fahrzeugen, im Sommer mit bis zu 65. Das derzeitige Netz soll modernisiert und erweitert werden.

Blackpool (142,000 inh., Lancashire) is one of Britain's most popular seaside resorts. The country's first electric tramway system opened along the Promenade in 1885, initially powered via a current rail fitted into an underground conduit between the rails. The power supply system was changed to conventional overhead wire in 1899. The present 18.4 km line from Fleetwood in the north to Starr Gate in southern Blackpool is the only surviving first-generation tramway in Britain and therefore deserves a special mention in this book. It runs mostly on reserved track, except for a short stretch north of Talbot Square and the final 900 m in Fleetwood.

The Blackpool Tramway is operated with a fleet of 75 cars, most of which date from the 1930s. Among them are many open cars, both single-deck and double-deck. Service is provided throughout the year, with 8 trams in use during winter and up to 65 during the summer season. There are plans to modernise and expand the present network.

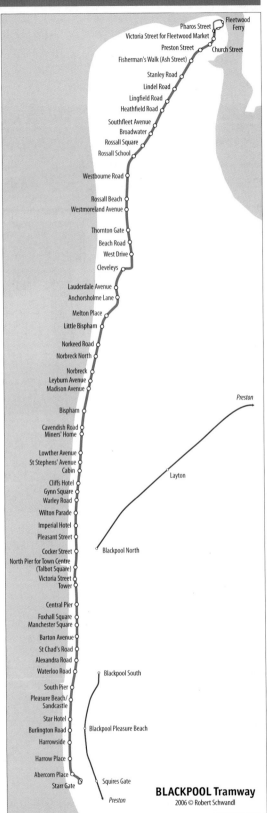

BLACKPOOL Tramway
2006 © Robert Schwandl

① Wagen Nr. 147 auf der südlichen Promenade am South Pier
② Wagen Nr. 602 (sog. ‚Boot') am Manchester Square
③ Wagen Nr. 600 von der Brücke in der Nähe des Towers gesehen
④ Wagen Nr. 5 (ex-Stockport) und ‚Baloon'-Wagen Nr. 726 am Central Pier
⑤ Wagen Nr. 701 wendet in Cleveleys, während der modernisierte Wagen Nr. 724 nach Fleetwood weiterfährt
⑥ Wagen Nr. 723 an der Endhaltestelle in Fleetwood

① Tram #147 on the southern Promenade near South Pier
② Tram #602 'boat' car at Manchester Square
③ Tram #600 seen from a footbridge next to the Tower
④ #5 (ex-Stockport) and Baloon car #726 at Central Pier
⑤ Tram #701 reversing at Cleveleys and modernised #724 continuing to Fleetwood
⑥ Tram #723 at the Fleetwood Ferry terminus

Newcastle-upon-Tyne (267.000 Einw.) ist eine der größten Städte im Nordosten Englands. Es gehört zum Großraum Tyne-and-Wear (ca. 1,1 Mill. Einw.), der die Kommunen Newcastle, Gateshead, North Tyneside, South Tyneside und Sunderland umfasst.

Obwohl die **Tyne-and-Wear-Metro** oft als ‚Light Rail' bzw. Stadtbahn bezeichnet wird, hat sie nicht viel mit anderen Stadtbahnen gemeinsam, da dieser Begriff heute meist für moderne Straßenbahnen, wenn auch meist auf eigenem Gleiskörper, verwendet wird. Die Tyne-and-Wear-Metro kann man zwischen S-Bahn und richtiger Metro einreihen. Sie verläuft durchgehend auf eigenem Gleiskörper, und bis auf wenige Bahnübergänge auf den äußeren Abschnitten ist sie völlig getrennt vom Straßenverkehr. Die Metro ist Eigentum von Nexus, der öffentlichen *Passenger Transport Executive for Tyne and Wear*, und wird auch von dieser betrieben.

Die Idee für die Tyne-and-Wear-Metro entstand in den späten sechziger Jahren, als sich die einst stark benutzten Vorortbahnen in einem sehr desolaten Zustand befanden und etwas getan werden musste. Nachdem mehrere Strecken stillgelegt worden waren, sollten die übrigen, nämlich der Küstenring und der Ast nach South Shields umgebaut und im Zentrum von Newcastle sowie Gateshead durch unterirdische Strecken miteinander verbunden werden. Der Küstenring war ursprünglich zwischen 1839 und 1882 in Betrieb genommen worden, der nördliche Ast endete bis 1909 in Newcastle an der New Bridge Street, bis ein kurzes Verbindungsstück zum Bahnhof Manors gebaut wurde, so dass die Züge im 1850 eröffneten Hauptbahnhof (Central) abfahren und enden konnten. 1879 wurde der Küstenring zwischen Manors und Percy Main durch eine Strecke am Fluss entlang ergänzt. Diese Nebenstrecke, die vor allem den Arbeitern der dortigen Schiffswerften diente, wurde 1973 stillgelegt. Der Küstenring und die Nebenstrecke wurden bereits 1904 mit 600 V Gleichstrom über seitliche Strom-

Newcastle upon Tyne (267,000 inh.) is among the largest cities in the northeast of England. It is part of the former metropolitan county of Tyne and Wear (approx. 1.1 mill. inh.), which included the districts of Newcastle, Gateshead, North Tyneside, South Tyneside and Sunderland.

Although often referred to as ‘light rail', the Tyne and Wear Metro does not have much in common with other light rail systems, as this term is nowadays mostly used for modern tramway systems. The Tyne and Wear Metro system can be described as a hybrid between a suburban railway and a proper metro. It runs entirely on its own right-of-way, totally segregated from road traffic, but with a few level crossings on outer branches. The Metro is owned and operated by the public company Nexus, the Passenger Transport Executive for Tyne and Wear.

The Tyne and Wear Metro was conceived in the late 1960s when

TYNE AND WEAR METRO

77.5 km (6.5 km unterirdisch | *underground*), 60 Bahnhöfe | *Stations*

Metro-Betrieb | *Metro service:*

11-08-1980	Haymarket – Tynemouth
10-05-1981	South Gosforth – Bank Foot
15-11-1981	Haymarket – Heworth
14-11-1982	St. James – Manors – Tynemouth
24-03-1984	Heworth – South Shields
15-09-1985	+ Kingston Park
16-09-1985	+ Pelaw
19-03-1986	+ Palmersville
17-11-1991	Bank Foot – Airport
31-03-2002	Pelaw – South Hylton
28-04-2002	+ Park Lane
11-12-2005	+ Northumberland Park

schiene elektrifiziert. 1967 wurden die in die Jahre gekommenen elektrischen Triebwagen durch Dieselzüge ersetzt.

Der heutige Ast zum Flughafen folgt der 1905 nach Ponteland eröffneten Bahnstrecke. Diese eingleisige Linie wurde jedoch nur bis 1929 für den Personenverkehr genutzt.

Auf der Südseite der Tyne wurden die Strecken, die heute von der Metro benutzt werden, zwischen 1835 und 1872 eröffnet. Die Linie nach South Shields wurde 1938 elektrifiziert, doch 1963 ersetzten Dieseltriebwagen die elektrischen Züge.

Der Bau der Metro wurde 1973 beschlossen, die Arbeiten dauerten 11 Jahre. Das Projekt umfasste die Elektrifizierung mit 1500 V Gleichstrom über Oberleitung, den Umbau oder eine Verschiebung einiger Stationen und ca. 10 km Neubaustrecken (davon 6,4 km im Tunnel, der Rest auf Geländeebene bzw. als Hochbahn). Zu den neuen Strecken gehörten die 350 m lange Queen-Elizabeth-II-Brücke über die Tyne und das 820 m lange Byker-Viadukt über das Ouseburn-Tal zwischen Byker und Manors. Die eingleisigen Tunnel durch Newcastle und Gateshead wurden im Schildvortrieb mit einem Durchmesser von jeweils 4,75 m gebaut.

Für den Betrieb der ersten Metro-Abschnitte wurden 88 zweiteilige Fahrzeuge (4003-4090) geliefert. Zwei Prototypen (4001+4002) waren vorher über einen längeren Zeitraum getestet worden. Ein Einzelwagen ist 27,8 m lang und 2,65 m breit; normalerweise verkehren die Fahrzeuge in Doppeltraktion. Die Fahrerkabine beansprucht nur die halbe Zugbreite, so dass die Fahrgäste den Ausblick auf die Strecke genießen können. Alle Züge und Bahnhöfe sind behindertengerecht zugänglich.

Nachdem das Grundnetz 1984 fertig gestellt worden war, wurde der nordwestliche Ast 1991 entlang der früheren Strecke nach Ponteland zum Flughafen verlängert.

the formerly busy suburban railway lines had reached a desolate state and some kind of action was needed. After several branches had been closed, the remaining routes, i.e. the coast loop and the South Shields line, were to be upgraded and linked by underground routes through the Newcastle and Gateshead city centres.

The coast loop was originally built between 1839 and 1882, although the northern leg terminated in Newcastle at New Bridge Street until 1909, when a short link to Manors station opened, enabling trains to depart and arrive at Central Station (opened in 1850). In 1879 the loop was complemented by the Riverside Branch, which until 1973 served the neighbourhoods and shipyards along the River Tyne between Manors and Percy Main. These routes were electrified at 600 V dc with a third rail in as early as 1904. In 1967 the aging EMUs were replaced by diesel trains.

The present Airport branch follows an alignment which was opened in 1905 to Ponteland. This single-track line, however, only carried passengers until 1929.

On the south side of the River Tyne, the routes now used by the Metro were opened between 1835 and 1872. The line to South Shields was electrified in 1938, but the electric trains were replaced by diesel units in 1963.

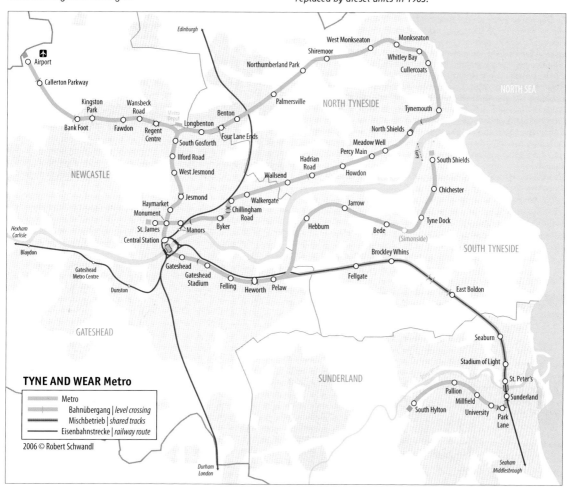

TYNE AND WEAR Metro

	Metro
Bahnübergang	level crossing
Mischbetrieb	shared tracks
Eisenbahnstrecke	railway route

2006 © Robert Schwandl

St. Peter's

In den neunziger Jahren stellte die Verlängerung nach Sunderland eines der größten Verkehrsprojekte Großbritanniens dar. Um die Kosten zu verringern, sollte die Metro zwischen Gateshead und Sunderland die vorhandenen Regionalbahngleise mitbenutzen. Die drei bestehenden Bahnhöfe auf dieser Strecke, Brockley Whins, East Boldon und Seaburn, wurden umgebaut und drei neue Bahnhöfe errichtet. In Sunderland konnte die Trasse der 1984 geschlossenen Bahn nach Durham zum Bau der neuen Strecke genutzt werden. 2002 wurde die Strecke nach South Hylton an die Yellow Line angeschlossen, womit das heutige Netz vollständig war. Im Dezember 2005, als der Bahnhof Northumberland Park eröffnet wurde, wurden die Linienläufe und Fahrpläne verändert. Von Newcastle Airport fährt derzeit alle 12 Minuten ein Zug nach Park Lane in Sunderland, jeder zweite fährt weiter bis South Hylton (Green Line). Eine Fahrt auf der gesamten Linie dauert 67 Minuten. Der Küstenring durch North Tyneside und der Ast nach South Shields bilden die Yellow Line, auf der die Züge zweimal den U-Bahnhof Monument bedienen. Eine Fahrt auf dem Küstenring dauert 54 Minuten, auf der ganzen Linie 82 Minuten. Die Yellow Line verkehrt tagsüber alle 12 Minuten, beide Linien fahren an Sonntagen sowie abends alle 15 Minuten. Auf dem gemeinsamen Abschnitt zwischen South Gosforth und Pelaw besteht tagsüber also ein 6-Minuten-Takt. Die Metro ist von ca. 5:30 bis 23:30 in Betrieb.

Obwohl die Tyne-and-Wear-Metro erst mit Eingangssperren ausgestattet wurde, ist sie heute ein offenes System mit gelegentlichen Fahrscheinkontrollen in den Zügen.

Nexus hat verschiedene Streckenverlängerungen untersucht, darunter auch einige auf der Straße verlaufende Abschnitte, die jedoch mittelfristig keine Chance auf Verwirklichung haben.

Ein Metro-Zug aus Sunderland nähert sich der Verzweigung bei Pelaw
Metro train from Sunderland approaching Pelaw junction

The Metro scheme was approved in 1973 and its realisation took 11 years. The project included electrification at 1500 V dc using overhead line equipment, upgrading or relocation of existing stations and, of course, the construction of approximately 10 km of new routes, of which some 6.4 km lies in tunnels, the rest being elevated or at grade, including the 350 m Queen Elizabeth II Bridge across the River Tyne and the 820 m Byker Viaduct across the Ouseburn Valley between Byker and Manors. The tunnels through Newcastle and Gateshead were excavated with tunnel-boring machines as single-track tubes with a diameter of 4.75 m.

For the opening of the Metro's first routes a total of 88 2-section vehicles (4003-4090) were delivered, two prototypes (4001+4002) having previously been tested for a lengthy period. A single unit is 27.8 m long and 2.65 m wide, and they are usually operated in pairs. The driver's cab only occupies about half of the train's width, so passengers enjoy a view out of the front window onto the railway route. Both trains and all stations allow level access. The initial network having been completed in 1984, the northwestern branch was extended to the Airport in 1991, still following the former railway to Ponteland.

During the 1990s the 'Sunderland extension' became one of Britain's major public transport projects. To reduce costs the existing railway line between Gateshead and Sunderland was to be shared with regional trains. The three stations along the route, Brockley Whins, East Boldon and Seaburn, were upgraded, and three new

Queen Elizabeth II Bridge

stations were built. In Sunderland, the still existing railway formation of the former Sunderland to Durham freight line, abandoned in 1984, was used to build a new route. In 2002 the 18.5 km stretch to South Hylton was linked to the Yellow Line, thus completing the present network.

In December 2005, when the Northumberland Park station opened, the routes and timetables were rearranged. Trains now leave Newcastle Airport every 12 minutes for Park Lane in central Sunderland, with every other train continuing to South Hylton (Green Line). A trip along the entire stretch takes 67 minutes. The North Tyneside loop and the South Shields branch form the Yellow Line, with trains running through Monument station twice. A trip around the loop takes 54 minutes and the entire journey to South Shields 82 minutes. The Yellow Line operates every 12 minutes during normal daytime service. Both lines run every 15 minutes on Sundays and in the evenings. On the shared section between South Gosforth and Pelaw there is a train every 6 minutes in each direction during daytime hours. The Metro is in service from about 05:30 to 23:30 .

Although initially designed with ticket barriers, the Tyne and Wear Metro is now an open system with ticket inspections on the trains.

Nexus has been examining several extensions to the network, including street-running sections, but no new lines are expected to open in the mid-term future.

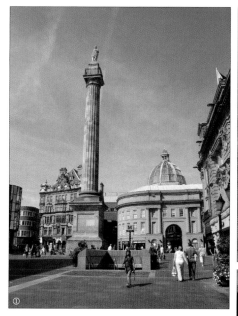

Am Bahnhof **Monument** ①-③ kreuzen sich die beiden Innenstadttunnel, wobei die Nord-Süd-Strecke auf der unteren Ebene liegt. Dieser Bahnhof gehört zu den wenigen weltweit, an denen dieselbe Linie zweimal hält. Der Bahnhof Monument liegt im Herzen von Newcastle und erschließt die zentralen Einkaufsstraßen der Stadt.

Der nächste Bahnhof Richtung Norden ist **Haymarket** ④⑤, von dem man den Einkaufsbereich sowie das Civic Centre (Bürgeramt) und zwei Universitäten bequem erreicht.

Der Nord-Süd-Tunnel durch das Zentrum von Newcastle besteht aus zwei jeweils 2 km langen, eingleisigen Tunnelröhren. Nördlich von **Jesmond** verlässt die Metro den Tunnel. Die ehemalige oberirdische Strecke steht heute als Betriebsgleis zum U-Bahnhof Manors auf der Ost-West-Strecke noch zur Verfügung.

At **Monument** ①-③, the two cross-city tunnels intersect, with the north-south route on the lower level. This is one of the few stations around the world which are served by the same line twice. Monument station lies in the heart of Newcastle, providing access to the main shopping area.

The next stop towards the north is **Haymarket** ④⑤, which serves the shopping area as well as the Civic Centre and two Universities. The north-south underground route through central Newcastle consists of two 2 km single-track tube tunnels. The Metro emerges from the tunnel just north of **Jesmond** station. The former surface alignment is still available as a single-track service link to Manors on the east-west route.

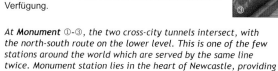

Von **Jesmond** folgt die Metro der 1864 in Betrieb genommenen Strecke. Der Bahnhof **West Jesmond** ①③ befindet sich noch weitgehend in seinem ursprünglichen Zustand, während die Station **Ilford Road** ② erst bei der Umrüstung auf Metrobetrieb eröffnet wurde. An diesem Bahnhof sind die Seitenbahnsteige nur von jeweils einer Seite erreichbar. Um auf den gegenüberliegenden Bahnsteig zu kommen, muss man eine weiter südlich gelegene Straßenbrücke benutzen. In **South Gosforth** ④ wurde das ehemalige Empfangsgebäude abgerissen, um Platz für die Leitzentrale der Metro zu schaffen. Die originale Fußgängerbrücke über die Gleise blieb jedoch erhalten. Nördlich dieser Station zweigt die Green Line Richtung Flughafen ab. Die erste Haltestelle auf diesem Abschnitt ist **Regent Centre** ⑤, wo über den Bahnsteigen ein Busbahnhof errichtet wurde.

From **Jesmond** the Metro follows the original route opened in 1864. The station at **West Jesmond** ①③ has been preserved in almost its original form, whereas the stop at **Ilford Road** ② was only established when the line was converted to Metro in 1980. Side platforms at this station are only accessible from one side, a nearby road bridge further south serving to get to the other side.

At **South Gosforth** ④ the former station building was demolished to make room for the Metro Control Centre. The original footbridge across the tracks was preserved. Just north of this stop the Green Line branches off left and west to the airport. The first stop along this route is **Regent Centre** ⑤. A bus interchange was built here on top of the station.

Wie auch einige andere Bahnhöfe scheint der Bahnhof **Regent Centre** ① unterirdisch zu liegen, weil der Bahnsteigbereich völlig abgedeckt wurde, um darüber einen Busbahnhof zu bauen. Die Linie zum Flughafen folgt der ehemaligen Strecke nach Ponteland, die bis 1929 in Betrieb war. Die neue Metro-Strecke verläuft meist im Geländeniveau und besitzt insgesamt vier Bahnübergänge, die alle an Bahnhöfen liegen. An den Bahnhöfen **Fawdon** und **Kingston Park** (die letztere wurde erst 1985 eröffnet) sind die Bahnsteige auf beiden Seiten des Bahnübergangs versetzt zueinander angeordnet. Der Bahnhof **Bank Foot** ②③ war von 1981 bis zum Jahre 1991, als die Linie zum Flughafen verlängert wurde, Endstation mit nur einer Bahnsteigkante. Der Bahnhof **Airport** ④⑤ ist durch Rampen mit dem Flughafenterminal verbunden. Der Ast zum Flughafen wird alle 12 Minuten von der Green Line bedient.

Like some other stations, **Regent Centre** ① appears to be underground, as the platform area is totally covered to provide space for a bus interchange above.
The route to the airport follows the route of a former single-track line to Ponteland, which ceased to carry passengers in 1929. The new Metro route is mostly at grade with a total of four level crossings, all located at stations. At **Fawdon** and **Kingston Park** (the latter added in 1985), platforms are staggered on either side of the level crossing.
Bank Foot ②③ was a single-track terminus from 1981 until 1991, when the line was extended to the airport.
Airport ④⑤ station is linked to the terminal building via a ramp. The Airport branch is served every 12 minutes by the Green Line.

Die Nordseite des Küstenrings wurde 1864 bis Monkseaton eröffnet. Der Bahnhof **Longbenton** wurde 1947 eröffnet und bedient den Hauptsitz der britischen Sozialversicherung. Die überbaute Station **Four Lane Ends** ① steht an der Stelle eines früheren Bahnhofs Long Benton und ist ein wichtiger Busumsteigepunkt. **Benton** ② ist der einzige Bahnhof auf diesem Abschnitt, der bis heute noch sein originales Eingangsgebäude besitzt. Nachdem die Stationen **Palmersville** (1986) und **Shiremoor** (1980) den ehemaligen Bahnhof Backworth ersetzt hatten, wurde im Dezember 2005 fast an der gleichen Stelle der Bahnhof **Northumberland Park** ③ eröffnet, um ein neues Wohngebiet zu erschließen. **Monkseaton** ④⑤ ist der erste von vier sehr gut erhaltenen Bahnhöfen am Küstenring. Die heutige Anlage stammt von 1915, als die Strecke neu trassiert wurde.

(Photo ③ Thomas Bowman)

The northern side of the loop opened in 1864 as far as Monkseaton. The stop **Longbenton** was established in 1947 to serve the large Social Security offices. **Four Lane Ends** ①, a covered station, was built at the site of a former Long Benton station, and is a major bus interchange. **Benton** ② is the only station on this section which preserves an original station building.

After **Palmersville** (1986) and **Shiremoor** (1980) replaced the former Backworth station, a new station **Northumberland Park** ③ opened in December 2005 at almost the same location to serve a new development. **Monkseaton** ④⑤ is the first of four well-preserved coastal stations, this one dating from 1915, when the route alignment was slightly modified.

Das Passagieraufkommen auf dem Küstenring stieg nach der Elektrifizierung 1903/1904 stark an. An den Stationen **Whitley Bay** (1910) ①②, **Cullercoats** (1882) ③ und **Tynemouth** ④⑤ sind wunderbare Bahnsteigdächer aus jener Zeit erhalten. Die breiten Bahnsteige sind Zeugnis für die einstige Beliebtheit dieser Badeorte, doch auch heute sind die Züge zur Küste an schönen Sommertagen gut ausgelastet. Am Bahnhof Tynemouth, der mit Vollendung des Küstenrings 1882 in Betrieb genommen wurde, findet an Wochenenden ein Flohmarkt statt.

The coastal route became especially busy after electrification in 1903/04. Whitley Bay (1910) ①②, Cullercoats (1882) ③ and Tynemouth ④⑤ preserve splendid awnings. The wide platforms reflect their former importance as seaside resorts, although even nowadays trains to the coast can still get very crowded on nice summer days. Tynemouth station, dating from when the loop was completed in 1882, now hosts a fleamarket on weekends.

Von Tynemouth fahren die Züge zurück in Richtung Newcastle. Der erste Abschnitt bis **North Shields** ① verläuft teilweise im Einschnitt und teilweise im Tunnel. **Meadow Well** ②③ (früher Smith's Park) wurde 1982 im Einheitsstil der Metro eröffnet, dann aber 1994 im Zuge der Modernisierung des umliegenden Wohngebiets erneuert. Am Bahnhof **Howdon** befindet sich der einzige Bahnübergang auf dem Küstenring, er liegt zwischen den beiden Bahnsteigen. Der Bahnhof **Wallsend** ④ liegt auf einem Damm, nahe der römischen Siedlung Segedunum am östlichen Ende des 'Hadrian's Wall'. Aus diesem Grund sind manche Schilder zweisprachig auf Englisch und Lateinisch ⑤ geschrieben.

*From Tynemouth trains head back towards Newcastle. The first section up to **North Shields** ① runs partly in a cutting and partly in tunnel. **Meadow Well** ②③ opened as a new standard Metro station in 1982 (originally called Smith's Park), but was refurbished in 1994 together with the surrounding area.*
*The only level crossing on the North Tyneside loop can be seen at **Howdon**, lying between staggered platforms.*
***Wallsend** ④ station lies on an embankment, close to the Roman settlement of Segedunum at the eastern end of Hadrian's Wall. Some signs are therefore displayed both in English and Latin ⑤.*

Platform 1
Suggestus I

No Smoking
Noli Fumare

Vom Bahnhof **Chillingham Road**, nahe des früheren Bahnhofs Heaton, verlässt die Metro die ursprüngliche Eisenbahn-strecke und wird zum Bahnhof **Byker** ① ② geführt, dessen östliches Bahnsteig-ende sich im Tunnel und das westliche im Einschnitt befindet. Vom Bahnhof Byker gelangt die Metro über das 820 m lange und 30 m hohe Byker-Viadukt zurück an die Fernbahntrasse, bevor sie in den Ost-West-Innenstadttunnel von Newcastle eintaucht. Der U-Bahnhof **Manors** ist heute durch eine Stadtautobahn vom Stadtzentrum abgeschnitten, so dass die meisten Fahrgäste den U-Bahnhof **Monument** ③ benutzen, wo der Ost-West-Tunnel auf der oberen Ebene liegt. Die Yellow Line endet am Bahnhof **St. James** ④⑤, direkt am Fußballstadion, von wo aus eine Verlängerung in die westlichen Vororte technisch zwar möglich, aber nicht sehr wahrscheinlich ist.

From **Chillingham Road** station, near the former Heaton station, the Metro leaves the original railway alignment and is diverted via the new **Byker** ①② station, which lies partly underground at its eastern end and partly in the open at the western side. From Byker, the 820 m long and 30 m high Byker Viaduct takes the Metro back to the mainline railway route, before disappearing into the east-west tunnel through central Newcastle.

Manors underground station is cut off from the city centre by an urban motorway, so most passenger traffic is concentrated at the central **Monument** ③ station, where east-west trains run on the upper level.
The Yellow Line terminates at **St. James** ④⑤, adjacent to the football stadium, from where an extension towards the western suburbs is technically possible but not very likely.

Wieder zurück auf der Nord-Süd-Linie bedient die Metro die 1850 eröffnete und gut erhaltene **Central Station** ①②, bevor sie 25 Meter über der Tyne die eigens für die Metro errichtete **Queen-Elizabeth-II-Brücke** ③ überquert. Die Metro-Brücke ist die dritte Eisenbahnbrücke in Newcastle: weiter östlich liegt die High-Level-Bridge (Hochbrücke) von 1849, auf der die Züge auf der oberen und die Autos auf der unteren Ebene fahren, und etwas westlich die King-Edward-Brücke von 1906. Die Metro quert das Zentrum von **Gateshead** ④-⑥, wo ein wichtiger Umsteigepunkt entstand, im Tunnel. Dieser U-Bahnhof wurde in offener Bauweise errichtet. Nach seiner Eröffnung wurde der frühere Bahnhof Gateshead in der Nähe der High-Level-Bridge geschlossen.

*Back on the north-south route the Metro serves **Central Station** ①② (opened in 1850 and well preserved) before leaving Newcastle via the purpose-built **Queen Elizabeth II Bridge** ③, 25 m above the River Tyne. The Metro bridge is the third railway bridge in Newcastle: to the east is High Level Bridge (1849), which accommodates trains on the upper deck and cars on the lower, and to the west King Edward Bridge (1906). Just after crossing the river, Metro trains return underground through central **Gateshead** ④-⑥, where a major interchange point was established. The new Metro station, built by cut-and-cover, made the former Gateshead station next to High Level Bridge redundant.*

Westlich des Bahnhofs **Gateshead Stadium** erreicht die Metro die alte Strecke von 1839 nach Pelaw. Die Metrostation **Heworth** ①② ist vollständig überbaut, während die 1979 errichteten Bahnsteige der von Northern Rail betriebenen Regionalbahn nebenan im Freien liegen. Der Bahnhof Heworth sollte den früheren, 1839 eröffneten Bahnhof Pelaw ersetzen und Endpunkt für manche Züge werden. Schließlich wurde auch in **Pelaw** ③ ein neuer Bahnhof gebaut, der 1985 eröffnet wurde. Östlich von Pelaw laufen die Gleise der Metro und der Regionalbahn in einer niveaufreien Kreuzung zusammen ④ (und S. 136). Die ältere Metrolinie zweigt hier nach Norden ab und fährt auf einer 1872 eröffneten Strecke Richtung **South Shields** ⑤. Die teilweise eingleisige Strecke soll demnächst zweigleisig ausgebaut werden. Der letzte Abschnitt ab **Tyne Dock** wurde für die Metro etwas umtrassiert, so dass eine neue Endstation direkt über der Haupteinkaufsstraße entstand.

West of **Gateshead Stadium** station, the Metro joins the original route from 1839 to Pelaw. The Metro station at **Heworth** ①② is totally covered, whereas the railway platforms, opened in 1979 and now served by Northern Rail trains, lie in the open. Heworth was planned to replace the former Pelaw station (1839) and function as a terminus for some trains. Eventually a new station was also built at **Pelaw** ③, which opened in 1985. East of Pelaw, Metro and mainline tracks converge at a grade-separated junction ④ (and p. 136).

The original Metro route diverges towards the north along a partly single-track route, opened in 1872 and soon to be doubled, to reach **South Shields** ⑤. The last section from **Tyne Dock** was slightly diverted for the Metro, with a new terminus located right above the main shopping street. (Photo ⑤ Thomas Bowman)

Die 2002 eröffnete Verlängerung nach Sunderland war die letzte Erweiterung des Metronetzes. Zwischen Pelaw und Sunderland verkehrt die Metro auf denselben Gleisen wie die im Stundentakt verkehrenden Dieselzüge der Northern Rail ②, die nur an den Bahnhöfen Heworth und Sunderland halten. Die Bahnhöfe **Fellgate** ①②, **Stadium of Light** und **St. Peter's** ③ wurden neu eröffnet und die vorhandenen Stationen wurden umgebaut. Im Bereich von **East Boldon** gibt es drei Bahnübergänge. Direkt südlich von St. Peter's überquert die Metro auf der denkmalgeschützten Monkwearmouth-Brücke ④ die Wear, um dahinter in den Sunderland-Tunnel einzufahren. Das Erscheinungsbild des schon vor dem Metrobau existierenden Bahnhofs **Sunderland** ⑤ steht in einem starken Kontrast zu den übrigen Metro-stationen, sowohl älteren als auch neuen. Für die Unterhaltung der 18,5 km langen Strecke von Pelaw nach South Hylton ist die nationale Infrastrukturgesellschaft Network Rail verantwortlich.

Opening in 2002, the Sunderland extension was the latest addition to the Metro network. Between Pelaw and Sunderland, tracks are shared with hourly Northern Rail diesel services ②, which call at Heworth only. Fellgate ①②, Stadium of Light and St. Peter's ③ stations were built for the Metro extension, and existing stations were upgraded. There are three level crossings in the East Boldon area.

Just south of St. Peter's the Metro crosses the River Wear on the listed Monkwearmouth Bridge ④ to enter the Sunderland tunnel. The appearance of the existing Sunderland underground station ⑤ is in stark contrast with the design of other Metro stations, both old and new.
The entire 18.5 km route from Pelaw to South Hylton is maintained by Network Rail.

Ab dem Bahnhof Sunderland folgt die Metro der Trasse der Mitte der achtziger Jahre geschlossenen und anschließend abgebauten Strecke nach Durham. Wie auf dem Abschnitt Pelaw - Sunderland unterscheiden sich die Stationen hier mehr voneinander als auf den älteren Metrostrecken. Der vollständig überdachte Bahnhof **Park Lane** ① liegt im Herzen von Sunderland in der Nähe des Civic Centres (Bürgeramt). An diesem wichtigen Umsteigepunkt endet nun jeder zweite Zug. Die Strecke verläuft im Einschnitt ② bis zum Bahnhof **University** [von Sunderland] ③. Weil an den Bahnhöfen **Millfield** ④, **Pallion** und **South Hylton** ⑤ nicht so viele Fahrgäste wie erwartet aus- und einsteigen, wurde im Dezember 2005 das Angebot auf diesem Abschnitt auf einen 24-Minuten-Takt reduziert. Die Verlängerung nach Sunderland war nur möglich geworden, weil man dafür keine neuen Fahrzeuge beschaffen musste.

*From Sunderland station the Metro route follows the alignment of the former railway to Durham, which was dismantled in the mid-1980s. As on the Pelaw - Sunderland stretch stations were built to a more individual design than on the original Metro network. The totally covered **Park Lane** station ①, now the terminus for every other train from Newcastle, is another major bus interchange, located in the heart of Sunderland next to the Civic Centre. The route continues in a cutting ② to the **University** [of Sunderland] stop ③. The following stations at **Millfield** ④, **Pallion** and **South Hylton** ⑤ have not delivered as many passengers as expected, so service has been reduced to a train only every 24 minutes since December 2005. The Sunderland extension was made possible as there was no need to acquire new rolling stock.*

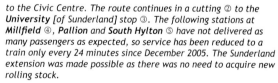

149

Bridge Street

With 580,000 inhabitants, Glasgow is the largest city in Scotland. The metropolitan area known as Greater Glasgow (including towns like Motherwell, Paisley and Clydebank) has a population of approximately 1.5 million.

The **Glasgow Subway**, opened in as early as 1896, is without doubt one of the world's most peculiar metro systems. The 'network' consists of only one circular route that has never been extended throughout its 110-year history.

The first proposals for an underground line were made in 1887 to link the city centre to the West End. One year later, the project became more ambitious with two river crossings and a route on the south bank of the River Clyde to form a full circle line with 15 stations. Two single-track tunnels were excavated through numerous different strata, ranging from various types of clay and sandstone to hard rock. The tunnels have a diameter of only 3.35 m, thus being slightly smaller than the London tube tunnels. About one third of the tunnels' length was lined with cast-iron rings, the rest being secured by brickwork. Two short sections on the south bank were built by the cut-and-cover method. All stations had a 3 m wide island platform, with exits only at one end. At 12 m below street level, Buchanan Street is the deepest station. The original subway trains were hauled by a cable, running between the rails, and the trains had to grip onto it except when stopping at stations. Track gauge was (and still is) 1219 mm (4 ft); there was no link between the two circular tracks, and neither were there any sidings.

In 1923, the Subway was handed over to the Municipal Corporation, which also ran an extensive tramway network. A need to modernise the Subway had become obvious, and eventually, in 1935, an electrification scheme (600 V dc, third rail) was completed. At the same time, the Subway was officially renamed the 'Underground' to give it a more modern image, although no new rolling stock had been acquired; instead, existing cars were retrofitted with current collector shoes and bogies were motored. Journey times, however, were reduced from 39 to 28 minutes for a full circuit.

Once the Greater Glasgow Passenger Transport Executive had been founded in 1973, a wide-ranging modernisation plan was approved. In 1975, the Subway was transferred to the new Strathclyde Regional Council. Modernisation began in earnest in 1977, when the entire system was closed for almost three years. New tracks were laid on a concrete bed and all stations were upgraded, although only the busiest were enlarged. New rolling stock was ordered from Metro-Cammell in Birmingham, with electrical equipment being supplied by GEC Traction (now Alstom). Major construction work was carried out at Govan, where a direct track link to the depot was built, the cars having been lifted from the tunnels by a crane for the previous 80 years.

Mit 580.000 Einwohnern ist Glasgow die größte Stadt Schottlands. Im Großraum Greater Glasgow, der Städte wie Motherwell, Paisley oder Clydebank einschließt, leben etwa 1,5 Millionen Menschen.

Die **Glasgow Subway**, die bereits 1896 eröffnet wurde, gehört ohne Zweifel zu den einzigartigsten Metros der Welt. Das ,Netz' besteht aus einer Ringlinie und wurde in seiner 110-jährigen Geschichte nie erweitert.

Die ersten Pläne für eine U-Bahn vom Stadtzentrum zum West End entstanden 1887. Ein Jahr später wurde das Projekt durch eine Strecke auf der Südseite des Flusses Clyde und zwei Unterwasserverbindungen erweitert, so dass daraus eine Ringlinie mit 15 Stationen wurde. Durch unterschiedliche Gesteinsschichten, von Ton und Sandstein bis hin zu hartem Felsgestein, wurden zwei eingleisige Röhren gegraben. Der Tunneldurchmesser beträgt nur 3,35 m und ist somit noch kleiner als bei der Londoner *Tube*. Etwa ein Drittel der Tunnelstrecken wurde mit Eisentübbings gesichert, der Rest mit Ziegelsteinen. Auf der Südseite des Flusses wurden zwei kurze Abschnitte in offener Bauweise errichtet. Alle Stationen hatten 3 m breite Bahnsteige mit nur einem Ausgang. Der U-Bahnhof Buchanan Street liegt in 12 m Tiefe und ist somit die tiefste Station der Ringlinie. Die Subway wurde von einem zwischen den Schienen laufenden Kabel gezogen. Die Züge mussten sich außer beim Halt in den Stationen an das Kabel anklemmen. Die Spurweite beträgt bis heute 1219 mm (4 Fuß). Bis 1980 gab es zwischen den beiden Streckentunneln keine Gleisverbindung, außerdem fehlten Abstellgleise.

1923 wurde die Subway an die städtische *Municipal Corporation* übergeben, die auch ein weitreichendes Straßenbahnnetz betrieb. Dass die Subway modernisiert werden musste, war zu diesem Zeitpunkt bereits klar. 1935 konnte schließlich die Elektrifizierung mit 600 V Gleichstrom über seitliche Stromschiene vollendet werden. Gleichzeitig wurde

GLASGOW Subway

10.4 km (völlig unterirdisch | totally underground), 15 Bahnhöfe | Stations

14-12-1896 Eröffnung der ges. Ringstrecke | opening of full circle line
31-03-1935 Inner Circle - elektrischer Betrieb | electric service
05-12-1935 Outer Circle - elektrischer Betrieb | electric service
21-05-1977 Schließung | closure
16-04-1980 Wiedereröffnung | reopening

die Subway offiziell in ‚Underground' umbenannt, was ein moderneres Erscheinungsbild vermitteln sollte, auch wenn für den elektrischen Betrieb keine neuen Fahrzeuge angeschafft worden waren. Stattdessen wurden die bestehenden Fahrzeuge mit Stromabnehmern ausgerüstet und Fahrmotoren an den Drehgestellen montiert. Die Fahrzeit auf dem Gesamtring konnte jedoch von 39 auf 28 Minuten reduziert werden.
Nach Gründung der *Greater Glasgow Passenger Transport Executive* im Jahr 1973 wurde das nächste Modernisierungsprogramm verabschiedet. 1975 ging die Subway in die Verantwortung des *Strathclyde Regional Council* über. Die Modernisierungsarbeiten begannen schließlich 1977, als der gesamte Ring für fast drei Jahre geschlossen wurde. Auf der gesamten Strecke wurden neue Gleise auf einem Betonunterbau gelegt, alle Stationen wurden umgebaut, allerdings nur die wichtigsten wurden erweitert. Neue Fahrzeuge wurden von Metro-Cammell in Birmingham gebaut, die elektrische Ausrüstung kam von GEC Traction (heute Alstom). Im Bereich Govan fanden umfangreiche Bauarbeiten statt, denn hier wurde eine Rampe von den beiden Tunneln zum Betriebshof errichtet. Die ersten 80 Jahre lang waren die Züge nämlich mit Hilfe eines Krans aus den Tunneln gehoben worden.

Inner Circle ↙		Outer Circle ↘	
West Street 🅿	Cowcaddens	Kinning Park	Partick 🚆
Bridge Street 🅿	St Georges Cross	Cessnock	Kelvinhall
St Enoch 🚆	Kelvinbridge 🅿	Ibrox	Hillhead
Buchanan Street 🚆		Govan 🚆	

The present fleet consists of 33 motor cars and eight trailers, with many remaining in an updated orange livery. Some have recently been repainted in the new SPT colours, first introduced in 2003. A 3-car train is 38 m long, 2.34 m wide and 2.65 m high; the floor height is 695 mm above rail and allows for level access. Trains are operated automatically, with drivers only needed to close the doors and put the trains in motion.
In 2003, the 'Underground' returned to its original name 'Subway', a designation it had never lost among the local population.

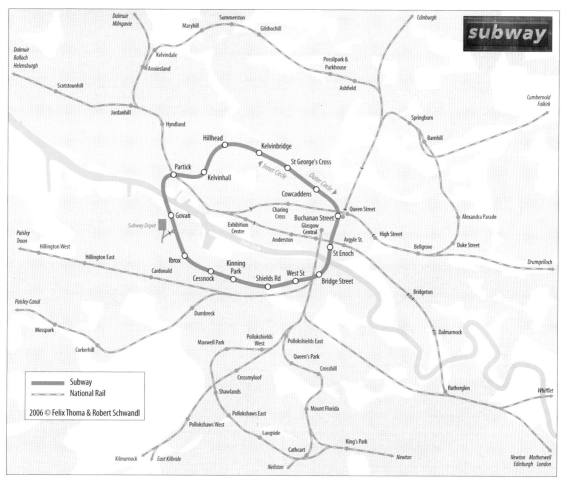

Subway
National Rail
2006 © Felix Thoma & Robert Schwandl

Bei der Subway sind derzeit 33 angetriebene Wagen und acht Beiwagen im Einsatz, manche in einem aufgefrischten orangefarbenen Anstrich, manche in den 2003 eingeführten Farben der SPT. Ein 3-Wagen-Zug ist 38 m lang, 2,34 m breit und 2.65 m hoch. Die Fußbodenhöhe beträgt 695 mm und ermöglicht stufenloses Einsteigen.

Die Züge fahren automatisch, wobei sich die Aufgaben des Fahrers darauf beschränken, die Türen zu schließen und den Zug in Bewegung zu setzen. 2003 bekam die Underground ihren alten Namen ,Subway' zurück, nachdem die lokale Bevölkerung nie aufgehört hatte, die kleine U-Bahn so zu nennen. Die Fahrtrichtungen sind mit ,Outer Circle' (Äußerer Ring - im Uhrzeigersinn) und ,Inner Circle' (Innerer Ring - gegen den Uhrzeigersinn) angegeben. Eine Rundfahrt dauert heute etwa 22 Minuten, im Fahrplan sind dafür 24 Minuten vorgesehen. Die Subway verkehrt montags bis samstags von 6:30 bis 23:30, sonntags nur von 11:00 bis 18:00. Während der Hauptverkehrszeiten fahren die Züge alle 4 Minuten, tagsüber sonst alle 6 Minuten und abends und sonntags alle 8 Minuten.

The Subway route is signposted as an 'Outer Circle' (clockwise) and an 'Inner Circle' (anti-clockwise). A trip around the full circle takes about 22 minutes, with 24 minutes being scheduled for a round trip. The Subway operates from 06:30 until 23:30 from Monday to Saturday; on Sundays, service is restricted to 11:00-18:00. During peak periods trains run every 4 minutes, during daytime hours every 6 minutes, and every 8 minutes after 19:00 and on Sundays.

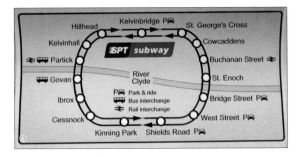

① Copland Road (> Ibrox) May 1977 (Photo Brian Hardy)
② Merkland Street Station – Glasgow Transport Museum
③ U-Logo 1980-2003 (Partick)
④ Netzplan im Zug | Network map inside trains
⑤ #122 im Anstrich zum 100-Jahr-Jubiläum | in 100th Anniversary Livery (1896-1996)
⑥ #41 – Buchanan Street (Ticket Hall)

Der U-Bahnhof **St. Enoch** ①-③ wurde während der Vollsperrung 1977-1980 völlig neu gebaut. Das alte Stationsgebäude blieb dabei erhalten und dient heute als Informationszentrum für den Nahverkehr. Der U-Bahnhof lag einst direkt vor dem gleichnamigen Fernbahnhof, auf dessen Areal jetzt ein Einkaufszentrum steht. Der Hauptbahnhof Glasgow Central liegt ein paar Häuserblocks weiter westlich. **Buchanan Street** ④⑤ ist die wichtigste Station im Stadtzentrum, weshalb hier ein zweiter Bahnsteig errichtet wurde. Seit 2005 schützt eine Glaswand die wartenden Fahrgäste auf dem alten Mittelbahnsteig. Der U-Bahnhof ist über einen Fußgängertunnel mit dem benachbarten Fern- und Vorortbahnhof Queen Street verbunden. **Cowcaddens** ⑥ liegt am nördlichen Rand der Innenstadt.

St. Enoch station ①-③ was totally rebuilt during the Subway's closure from 1977 to 1980. The emblematic station building was preserved and now functions as a travel information centre. St. Enoch Subway station once lay in front of the mainline station of the same name, since replaced by a huge shopping mall; Glasgow Central station is within walking distance, a few blocks further west. The busy *Buchanan Street* station ④⑤ serves Glasgow's main shopping street. An additional side platform was added here to separate passenger flows, and, in 2005, a dividing glass wall was installed on the island platform to protect waiting passengers from trains entering in the opposite direction. From the Subway station there is a covered passageway to the nearby Queen Street station. *Cowcaddens* ⑥ is a typical Subway station at the northern edge of the city centre.

Inner Circle

THIS STATION
Hillhead
Kelvinhall
Partick
Govan
Ibrox
Cessnock
Kinning Park

St. George's Cross ① lies north of the M8 motorway, which separates the city centre from the West End, at the eastern end of Great Western Road. The Subway follows this road up to the next station *Kelvinbridge* ②-④, located in the valley of Glasgow's second river. The station is linked to the high bridge via a pair of covered escalators. From Kelvinbridge, the route continues westwards beneath a hilly area, before

turning south into **Hillhead** station ⑥, the busiest in the West End due to the vicinity of the University of Glasgow. Like Buchanan Street, this station was enlarged with a separate side platform on the outer circle. Access to **Kelvinhall** station ⑤⑦ (formerly Partick Cross) is via a passage in a row of shops. The station features the standard design with vaulted melamine cladding. The Glasgow Transport Museum is located near this station.

St. George's Cross ① liegt jenseits der M8, der Autobahn, die das Stadtzentrum vom West End trennt. Die Subway führt weiter unter der Great Western Road bis zum U-Bahnhof **Kelvinbridge** ②-④, der im Tal von Glasgows zweitem Fluss liegt. Die Station ist mit der hohen Brücke über Rolltreppen verbunden. Von Kelvinbridge verläuft die Strecke unter einer Anhöhe und schwenkt dann vor dem Bahnhof **Hillhead** ⑥ nach Süden. Da es sich hier wegen der benachbarten Universität um die wichtigste Station im West End handelt, wurde auch hier ein zusätzlicher Bahnsteig für den äußeren Ring errichtet. Der U-Bahnhof **Kelvinhall** ⑤⑦ (früher Partick Cross) wurde wie die meisten Stationen mit weißen Melaminplatten verkleidet. In der Nähe befindet sich das Verkehrsmuseum.

Die heutige Station **Partick** ① ersetzte 1980 die frühere
Station Merkland Street, die 1977 geschlossen worden war.
Die neue Lage ermöglicht bequemes Umsteigen zu den
Vorortzügen, deren Bahnsteige auch verschoben wurden.
Südlich von Partick unterquert die Subway den Fluss Clyde.
Der U-Bahnhof **Govan** ② (früher Govan Cross), wo man zu
vielen Buslinien umsteigen kann, wurde völlig umgebaut.
Zwischen Govan und Ibrox zweigt ein Gleis zum Betriebshof
ab. Wegen der Lage neben dem Stadion der Glasgow Rangers
wurde auch in **Ibrox** ③④ (früher Copland Road) ein zusätzlicher Seitenbahnsteig eingebaut. Der U-Bahnhof **Cessnock**
⑤⑥ in der Paisley Road West hat einen schönen Eingang,
der in ein typisches Wohnhaus aus Sandstein integriert ist.

*The present **Partick** station ① replaced the original Merkland
Street station closed in 1977. The new location provides a
convenient interchange to the also resited elevated suburban
railway station, both of which share the same ticket hall. South
of Partick, the Subway runs under the River Clyde to **Govan** ②
(formerly Govan Cross), another totally rebuilt station with side
platforms and a major bus interchange. Between Govan and the
next station Ibrox, both circles are linked from each direction to
a track leading to the depot. **Ibrox** station ③④ (formerly Copland
Road) is similar to Hillhead and has an additional side platform;
with the Glasgow Rangers stadium nearby, this station gets very
busy on match days. **Cessnock** station ⑤⑥ on Paisley Road West
boasts a pleasant entrance incorporated into the basement of a
typical Glasgow sandstone tenement block.*

The entrance to the quiet **Kinning Park** station ① lies on the southern side of the park of that name, and can also be reached from the southern side of the M8 motorway via a footbridge. **Shields Road** ②③ and **West Street** stations ④ lie in an industrial area at the southern side of the M8. Before the Subway passes once more under the River Clyde to return to the city centre, it stops at **Bridge Street** ⑤⑥. As part of the modernisation efforts of the late 1970s, a brick-covered entrance building was erected at many stations. Several stations on the south bank have been refurbished in recent years, and now boast a more distinguishable colour scheme.

Der Eingang zur eher ruhigen Station **Kinning Park** ① befindet sich auf der Südseite dieses Parks und kann auch über eine Fußgängerbrücke von der Südseite der Autobahn M8 erreicht werden. Die U-Bahnhöfe **Shields Road** ②③ und **West Street** ④ liegen in einem Industriegebiet südlich der M8. Bevor die Subway nun ein zweites Mal den Fluss Clyde unterquert und in die Innenstadt zurückkehrt, hält sie noch am U-Bahnhof **Bridge Street** ⑤⑥. Während der Modernisierung der Subway in den späten siebziger Jahren wurde an vielen Bahnhöfen ein Eingangsgebäude aus Backstein errichtet. In den vergangenen Jahren wurden einige der U-Bahnhöfe auf der Südseite des Flusses renoviert, manche davon in einer leichter unterscheidbaren Farbe, wie z.B. West Street.

Neben der Subway wird in Glasgow eine *S-Bahn* mit zwei Tunnelstrecken durch das Stadtzentrum betrieben. Seit 1960 fahren elektrische Züge aus dem Nordwesten von **Partick** ① durch die nördliche Tunnelstrecke von 1886 über die unterirdischen Stationen **Charing Cross** und **Queen Street** ② nach Osten und erreichen an der **High Street** ③ wieder die Oberfläche. Seit 1979 steht auch die zweite Strecke von 1896 unter der Argyle Street mit den unterirdischen Bahnhöfen **Anderston**, **Glasgow Central** ④⑤ und **Argyle Street** ⑥ (welcher 1979 den früheren Bahnhof Glasgow Cross ersetzte) wieder zur Verfügung. Züge aus den südlichen Vororten enden in der Haupthalle am Bahnhof **Glasgow Central**. Von **Queen Street** (High Level) fahren nur Dieselzüge in die nördlichen Vororte.

Besides the Subway, Glasgow enjoys one of the best **suburban rail** networks in the U.K., with several lines running across the city centre through two tunnels. The northwestern routes, electrified in 1960, reach the inner city at **Partick** ①, where interchange to the Subway has been provided since 1980. The northern route runs through a tunnel, opened in 1886, via **Charing Cross** and **Queen Street (Low Level)** ②, before surfacing at **High Street** ③ at the eastern edge of the city centre. The second route runs through a tunnel built in 1896 beneath Argyle Street, serving **Anderston**, **Glasgow Central (Low Level)** ④⑤ and **Argyle Street** ⑥ (the latter only opened in 1979 to replace the former Glasgow Cross station). Lines serving the southern districts terminate at the upper level of **Glasgow Central** station, and diesel trains towards the north depart from **Queen Street (High Level)** station.

LONDON:

John R. Day, John Reed: **The Story of London's Underground**.
- 2005 (9th ed.), Capital Transport, ISBN 1854142895

Brian Hardy: **London Underground Rolling Stock**.
- 2002 (15th ed.), Capital Transport, ISBN 1854142631

John Glover: **Principles of London Underground Operations**.
- 2000, Ian Allan Publishing, ISBN 0711027390

Kenneth Powell: **The Jubilee Line Extension**.
- 2000, Laurence King Publishing, ISBN 1856691845

David Leboff: **The Underground Stations of Leslie Green**.
- 2002, Capital Transport, ISBN 1854142550

J.E. Connor: **London's Disused Underground Stations**.
- 2001, Capital Transport, ISBN 185414250X

Maxwell J. Roberts: **Underground Maps After Beck**. - 2005, Capital Transport, ISBN 1854142860

Docklands Light Railway - Official Handbook. - 2006 (3rd ed.), Capital Transport (in Vorbereitung/*in preparation*)

Michael Steward et al.: **Tramlink**. - 2000, Capital Transport

Eine umfassende Liste zu London finden Sie unter | *A more comprehensive list on London can be found at*
www.robert-schwandl.de/britain/booklist.htm

Brian Patten et al.: **Trams in Britain and Ireland**. - 2002, Capital Transport, ISBN 1854142585

BIRMINGHAM:
John Boynton: **Main Line to Metro**. Train and Tram on the Great Western Route Birmingham Snow Hill - Wolverhampton.
- 2001, Mid England Books, ISBN 0952224895

MANCHESTER:
David Holt: **Manchester Metrolink**. - (UK Light Rail Systems No. 1), 1992, Platform 5, ISBN 1872524362

LIVERPOOL:
T.B. Maund: **Merseyrail Electrics - The Inside Story**. - 2001, NBC Books, ISBN 0953189613

NEWCASTLE:
Alan Young: **Suburban Railways of Tyneside**. - 1999, Martin Bairstow, ISBN 1871944201

GLASGOW:
John Wright & Ian Maclean: **Circles under the Clyde**. A History of the Glasgow Underground. - 1997, Capital Transport, ISBN 1854141902

George Watson (Photogr.): **Glasgow Subway Album**. A Collection of photographs of the old Glasgow Subway taken before and during closure for modernisation. - 2000, Adam Gordon, ISBN 1874422311

Reihe 'Nahverkehr in Deutschland'
'Urban Transport in Germany' Series

Band 1 | Vol. 1
Robert Schwandl:

BERLIN U-BAHN ALBUM
Alle 192 Untergrund- und Hochbahnhöfe in Farbe
All 192 Underground & Elevated Stations in Colour

Jul 2002
ISBN 3 936573 01 8
144 Seiten | pages
17x24 cm
300 Farbfotos | colour photos
1 Netzplan | Network map
Text deutsch | English
14,50 EUR

Band 2 | Vol. 2

Robert Schwandl:

BERLIN S-BAHN ALBUM
Alle 170 S-Bahnhöfe in Farbe
All 170 S-Bahn Stations in Colour

April 2003, ISBN 3 936573 02 6
144 Seiten | pages, 17x24 cm
400 Farbfotos | colour photos
2 Netzpläne | Network maps
Text deutsch | English
14,50 EUR

Band 3 | Vol. 3
Robert Schwandl:

HAMBURG U-BAHN & S-BAHN ALBUM
Alle Schnellbahnhöfe der Hansestadt in Farbe
All Rapid Transit Stations in the Hanseatic City
in Colour

Nov 2004, ISBN 3 936573 05 0
144 Seiten | pages, 17x24 cm
400 Farbfotos | colour photos
2 Netzpläne | Network maps
Text deutsch | English
19,50 EUR

Band 4 | Vol. 4
Christoph Groneck, Paul Lohkemper, Robert Schwandl:

RHEIN-RUHR STADTBAHN ALBUM 1
Düsseldorf, Duisburg, Oberhausen, Mülheim & Essen
Light Rail Networks in the Rhine-Ruhr Area - Vol. 1

April 2005, ISBN 3 936573 06 9
144 Seiten | pages, 17x24 cm
400 Farbfotos | colour photos
4 Netzpläne | Network maps
Gleispläne | Track maps
Text deutsch | English
19,50 EUR

Band 5 | Vol. 5
Christoph Groneck, Paul Lohkemper, Robert Schwandl:

RHEIN-RUHR STADTBAHN ALBUM 2
Gelsenkirchen, Bochum, Herne, Dortmund
+ *Special* Bielefeld
Light Rail Networks in the Rhine-Ruhr Area - Vol. 2

Frühjahr | Spring 2006, ISBN 3 936573 08 5
144 Seiten | pages, 17x24 cm
400 Farbfotos | colour photos
4 Netzpläne | Network maps
Gleispläne | Track maps
Text deutsch | English
19,50 EUR

Band 6 | Vol. 6

Christoph Groneck:

KÖLN/BONN STADTBAHN ALBUM
The Cologne/Bonn Light Rail Network

Dez. 2005, ISBN 3 936573 07 7
144 Seiten | pages, 17x24 cm
350 Farbfotos | colour photos
3 Netzpläne | Network maps
Text deutsch | English
19,50 EUR

Band 7 | Vol. 7

Robert Schwandl:

HANNOVER STADTBAHN ALBUM
The Hanover Light Rail Network

Aug. 2005, ISBN 3 936573 10 7
144 Seiten | pages, 17x24 cm
400 Farbfotos | colour photos
3 Netzpläne | Network maps
Text deutsch | English
19,50 EUR

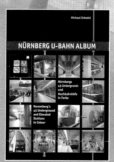

Band 8 | Vol. 8

Michael Schedel:

NÜRNBERG U-BAHN ALBUM
Nürnbergs 45 Untergrund- und Hochbahnhöfe in Farbe
Nuremberg's 45 Underground and Elevated Stations
in Colour

Herbst | Autumn 2006, ISBN 3 936573 11 5
96 Seiten | pages, 17x24 cm
300 Farbfotos | colour photos
2 Netzpläne | Network maps
Gleispläne | Track maps
Text deutsch | English
ca. 17,50 EUR

Weitere Informationen und Musterseiten finden Sie unter | *More details and sample pages are available at*

www.robert-schwandl.de

Unsere Bücher erhalten Sie in unserem Online-Shop | *Our books are available from our online shop*

www.schwandl.com

CREATING THE
THERAPEUTIC
RELATIONSHIP IN
COUNSELLING AND
PSYCHOTHERAPY

Other books in this series

What is Counselling & Psychotherapy?
by Norman Claringbull   ISBN 978 1 84445 361 0

Counselling and Psychotherapy in Organisational
Settings by Judy Moore and Ruth Roberts   ISBN 978 1 84445 614 7

Reflective Practice in Counselling and
Psychotherapy by Sofie Bager-Charleson   ISBN 978 1 84445 360 3

Books in the Mental Health in Practice series

Child and Adolescent Mental Health:
A Guide for Practice by Steven Walker   ISBN 978 0 85725 057 5

Cognitive Behavioural Interventions for
Mental Health Practitioners by Alec Grant   ISBN 978 1 84445 210 1

Mental Health Law in England and Wales
by Paul Barber, Robert Brown and Debbie Martin   ISBN 978 1 84445 195 1

To order, please contact our distributor: BEBC Distribution, Albion Close,
Parkstone, Poole, BH12 3LL. Telephone 0845 230 9000,
email: **learningmatters@bebc.co.uk**. You can also find more
information on each of these titles and our other learning resources at
www.learningmatters.co.uk

Want to write for the Counselling and Psychotherapy Practice series? Contact the
Commissioning Editor, Luke Block (luke@learningmatters.co.uk), with your ideas
and proposals.

CREATING THE THERAPEUTIC RELATIONSHIP IN COUNSELLING AND PSYCHOTHERAPY

JUDITH GREEN

Series editor: Norman Claringbull

LearningMatters

First published in 2010 by Learning Matters Ltd

British Library Cataloguing in Publication Data

A CIP record for this book is available from the British Library.

ISBN: 978 1 84445 463 1

This book is also available in the following ebook formats:

Adobe ebook	ISBN: 978 1 84445 771 7
EPUB ebook	ISBN: 978 1 84445 770 0
Kindle	ISBN: 978 0 85725 026 1

Cover design by Code 5 Design Associates
Project management by Diana Chambers
Typeset by Kelly Winter
Printed and bound in Great Britain by TJ International, Padstow, Cornwall

Learning Matters Ltd
33 Southernhay East
Exeter EX1 1NX
Tel: 01392 215560
info@learningmatters.co.uk
www.learningmatters .co.uk

FSC
Mixed Sources
Product group from well-managed
forests and other controlled sources
Cert no. SGS-COC-2482
www.fsc.org
© 1996 Forest Stewardship Council

Contents

Series Editor's Preface   vi
Acknowledgements   viii
About the author   ix

Introduction   1

Chapter 1   The therapeutic relationship   4

Chapter 2   First impressions   16

Chapter 3   Personal qualities   35

Chapter 4   Ethical practice   55

Chapter 5   Facing your nightmares or 'What on earth do
I do now?'   75

Chapter 6   Taking care of yourself   99

Chapter 7   Drawing the threads together   118

References   127
Index   130

Series Editor's Preface

Judith Green opens this book by noting that the counselling and psycho-therapy profession has moved beyond what she calls its 'tribal phase'. In using this term, Judith is referring to what some other texts in this series have called the 'single school' models or divisions of therapy. However, as Judith notes in this book, there is far more uniting counselling and psychotherapy's practitioners than there is dividing them.

Judith, in common with very many modern counsellors and psycho-therapists, believes that *we all develop a unique and individual way of working*. On the surface, it might seem almost that she is suggesting that the talking therapies have descended from some sort of professional anarchy. However, as Judith so clearly explains, anarchy is certainly not on her professional 'menu'. This is because, as she very powerfully tells us, *at the heart of any successful counselling encounter is the therapeutic relationship*; the working alliance formed between counsellor and client. This is where the therapies meet; this is where experienced practitioners focus their skills. It is the very bedrock of counselling and psychotherapy. Therefore, students of counselling and psychotherapy at any level must also be avid students of the therapeutic relationship. Not only that, but as is quite clear from this book's Introduction, and indeed throughout all its chapters, the study of the therapeutic relationship is a career-long task for all practitioners in the 'people business'.

This is very much a 'hands-on' book. It is a workaday book for workaday practitioners; it is a must-have reference source for therapy's students. All therapists will learn from this book, from the novice to the most advanced professional. Moreover, because establishing a productive client/practitioner relationship is essential for more or less anybody in any of the caring professions, this book's appeal extends far beyond the talking therapies and well into the other socially aware professions and services.

To start with, Judith tells us how to begin the delicate process of establishing a relationship with our clients and to set out to gain their trust. Noting that this process can cause our clients to become quite dependent on us, Judith goes on to carefully guide us through the potential pitfalls. She then encourages us to think about what many see as being the final stage of counselling, wherein clients gain more and more independence for themselves and, in doing so, gain ever increasing levels of personal autonomy.

Judith also explores the boundaries of the therapeutic relationship. Yes, both therapist independence and self-direction are essential but, as this book shows us, professional freedom is at its most productive when it is contained within some clearly defined therapeutic frameworks. Right now, some readers will be puzzled – surely framed or boundaried independence is a contradiction in terms? Well, a lot of learning about the therapeutic relationship is necessarily experiential. So put your caveats to one side for now and read on – *experience* this book. Judith will show how to find out about the therapeutic relationship for yourself and that is usually a great way to learn about anything.

Inside you'll find lots of case studies, activities and reflection points. These will help you to better your understanding of what the therapeutic relationship is all about. Always bear in mind, however, that Judith is not telling you *what* to think; she is showing you *how* to think. Yes, you will have to do some ground work if you want to really know more about the ways in which talking therapists and their clients interact with each other and how to make these interactions therapeutically productive – however, I can guarantee that any effort that you put into getting the best out of this book will be well rewarded.

Some of the best features in this book are the comments that Judith provides after each case study. They are all particularly rich and instructive. Like the whole of the Counselling and Psychotherapy Practice series, this is a practical, active learning book for students at any level; that is why most of the titles in this series are written by counselling and psychotherapy teachers. They understand the pressures students face – even more so in today's climate.

Judith is a very experienced practitioner and teacher, one who is well known and respected in the counselling world. Her professional reputation is enhanced by her earlier publications and by her current position as Director of the Counselling Programme at Cambridge University's Institute of Continuing Education. Judith practises counselling, she researches it, she teaches it and she supervises other practitioners. She is a committed educationalist and a great promoter of learning, especially adult learning, and it is these personal qualities that make this book such a worthwhile read. She is someone who has important things to tell us about counselling and psychotherapy, and in this book she tells them very well and to her readers' great advantage.

Dr Norman Claringbull – Series Editor
www.normanclaringbull.co.uk

Acknowledgements

I have had a great deal of help in writing this book. First, I would like to thank the team at Learning Matters for their guidance, encouragement and patience: specifically, Norman Claringbull, the Series Editor; Luke Block, the Commissioning Editor; and Lauren Simpson, the Development Editor.

The case studies in this book are mostly amalgams of different cases but in Chapter 1 there are two case studies written from the point of view of clients. The names and some of the circumstances of the people have been changed so they cannot be recognised but they are real people and I am extremely grateful to them both for allowing me to include their material, and to their two counsellors who also read the case studies and agreed to their inclusion in this book. I would also like to thank all my clients, supervisees and students from whom I have learned, and continue to learn, each day.

I am grateful to my university, Cambridge, which still has the wisdom and commitment to scholarship to allow its academics time to study, think and write, through its sabbatical system. I am aware that academic colleagues from other institutions of higher education are not so fortunate. I am very grateful to my colleagues, friends and comrades-in-arms, Maureen and Nick Papé. We have worked closely together for many years, during which time they have taught me a great deal and offered me unerring support. We have also had a great deal of fun!

On a personal level, I must thank my dear husband Pete for his patience, his kind words of encouragement and endless cups of coffee. Finally, I should acknowledge our two miscreant and overly enthusiastic border collies, Jack and Suki, who have tried every day to persuade me that my time is better spent walking on the common, unearthing muntjacs and rabbits, than writing books. I do so hope they are wrong!

This book is dedicated to all my lovely students, past and present.

About the author

Dr Judith Green is a counsellor and a Senior Accredited Practitioner with the British Association for Counselling and Psychotherapy (BACP). She is also a BACP accredited supervisor. Judith has worked in the field of counselling and psychotherapy for 25 years and for the past 12 years has been the Director of the Counselling Programme at the Institute of Continuing Education at the University of Cambridge. She has a small private practice in counselling and supervision, and is a consultant in the private, voluntary and public sectors. Her research interests have included counselling young people, emotional abuse, grief and bereavement, and counsellor education. Her passions include reading, singing, dog walking, football and being a grandmother.

Introduction

I love my job and I consider it a great blessing in life to get paid for doing something that brings me so much satisfaction. Twenty-five years in practice has not dulled my enthusiasm for counselling and I still get real pleasure from seeing a client move through the process and come out the other end having made some changes, gained new perspectives, or just learned to tolerate their own feelings. I must have seen thousands of clients and supervisees and each one of them has made an impression on me. Some, either because of the amount of time we have worked together, or because of the nature of the material, or our relationship, have impacted upon me very deeply. They have been among the most significant relationships in my life. Counsellors don't often say things like that because we don't want to be misunderstood. Of course, I am talking here about professional relationships, but can we really be in any meaningful relationship with another person, with all that that implies, without being in some way touched by it? I have never found it to be so.

I have also taught counselling for several years and have seen hundreds of students come and go. I have witnessed some start the training bright eyed and bushy tailed but who have fallen along the way, perhaps because of personal reasons or because they have very wisely decided that counselling is not for them. Sadly, I have seen a few who really wanted to do it but who just couldn't manage to make the grade. I have seen many bright and able students who have struggled and spluttered along the path but, as expected, have made it to the end. Then there is the group of students who have a special place in my heart. They are the ones who start at a bit of a disadvantage. Perhaps they haven't had much previous academic experience; maybe they lack confidence in themselves. Sometimes their lives have been very tough but they want to be counsellors so much, they work their socks off, get up again every time they are knocked down, take on board difficult feedback and use it constructively, keep going even when they are on their knees and get there in the end. How could you not admire and be inspired by such dedication and commitment? What joy to see them graduate!

Both my teaching career and research activity have made me reflect upon what makes a good counsellor. Although I do not underestimate the

importance of a highly developed skill base and a theoretical and philosophical understanding to inform the counsellor's thinking, I have come to
the conclusion that it is the 'person' of the counsellor, their own vulnerable
and flawed humanity, that is the crucial factor. It is not about what we do,
it is about who we are.

I like to think that as a profession we have moved into a post-tribal phase,
where we have learned that we have much more in common with one
another than that which divides us. Perhaps the assaults and challenges
which are coming to us from the outside are moving us forward in this way.
United we stand! My own experience has certainly taught me that there are
both brilliant and woefully inadequate counsellors within all the different
orientations. Experienced practitioners from different orientations do seem
to have more in common with one another than they have with newly
fledged colleagues from their own orientations. Whatever philosophy
underpins your approach, we all develop a unique and individual way of
working, which seems to me to reflect the kind of people we are just as
much as the orientation we espouse. There is so much wisdom within all
the different orientations, taking a fundamentalist approach to counselling
does seem, as in all things, to be a little small-minded.

As a veteran of the British Association for Counselling and Psychotherapy
(BACP), I have to admit to taking real pride in our *Ethical Framework for
Good Practice in Counselling and Psychotherapy*. I think the way in which it is
formulated and its content really do promote good practice. It puts us at the
forefront of ethical thinking. I appreciate the way it focuses on the personal
and moral qualities of the counsellor, encouraging us to look within
ourselves for the moral guidance required to carry out the important work
of counselling. Being part of a community of counsellors has always been
important to me in my practice. I can remember when I was new to the
profession, attending conferences and the like. As one of the 'young
pretenders' with a great deal more enthusiasm than wisdom, I viewed the
elders of our profession with awe. Their sometimes amused indulgence and
their wisdom allowed me to grow up within the profession and find my own
feet. It is a bit daunting to think, with the passage of so much time and
without my really noticing it happening, I am in danger of becoming one of
the elders myself.

Writing this book has given me the opportunity to tease out the important
factors in creating the therapeutic relationship that is undoubtedly at the
heart of successful counselling interaction and to focus also on ways in
which you, the counsellor, can sustain yourself and develop best practice, in
a profession that demands so much of you on a personal level. Chapter 1
focuses on the parameters of the relationship, the therapeutic frame. We will
also take a look at the therapeutic environment, the core conditions created
by the counsellor which facilitate the process of change. Chapter 2 explores

the establishment of the therapeutic agreement, the contract between counsellor and client, which underpins the work. We will also give some thought to first impressions, central to which are issues of difference and diversity.

Chapter 3 focuses on the personal and moral qualities of the counsellor, the ways of being to which all of us need to aspire to enable us to be as good as possible at the work of counselling. Building on this, Chapter 4 looks at the importance of ethical practice, the values and ethical principles that are central to the work and to the therapeutic relationship itself. Chapter 5 considers some of the issues that present the greatest challenges to counsellors, for example, the suicidal client and issues related to mental health. We will also look at what to do if the therapeutic relationship breaks down, a situation sometimes known as alliance rupture. Chapter 6 covers the ways in which you, as the counsellor, can look after yourself professionally, to ensure that you can offer the best possible service to your clients. In Chapter 7, we draw all these threads together and take a final look at the successful creation of the therapeutic relationship.

To create and maintain the therapeutic relationship you have to be willing to work not just with your head but, equally, with your heart. You have to learn to give of yourself freely without too much expectation of the other person. In this way, the counselling relationship is analogous with parenting a child; you set the boundaries and make the emotional investment, and the pay-off is in seeing the child develop and grow until he is independent and autonomous, and ready to leave home because he no longer needs you.

Is this a kind of love? I think at its best it is. The ancient Greeks divided love into different categories. One was 'erotic' love, which involves sexual love and is the kind of love we feel for our lovers and partners. Another was 'agape', which might be described as an unconditional, selfless, volitional and thoughtful love. When the therapeutic relationship is at its very best, I think what is being offered by the counsellor could be defined in this way. Perhaps that is the root of the magic and why so many people do seem to find counselling both helpful and restorative.

CHAPTER 1

The therapeutic relationship

INTRODUCTION

At the heart of any successful counselling encounter is the quality of the therapeutic relationship, which is the working alliance formed between you, the counsellor, and your client. Although the various theoretical orientations might describe the therapeutic relationship using different language, there is agreement about how important and fundamental it is to the success of counselling work. In this, the first chapter, we are going to be thinking about the concept of the therapeutic relationship. How does it differ from other kinds of helping relationships? What are the boundaries and parameters of it? How do you as the counsellor need to be within it, to facilitate the process for your client?

The theoretical orientations all have something to offer to the debate about how to create and maintain the therapeutic relationship. In this chapter, we are going to draw on psychodynamic ideas about the therapeutic frame and person-centred concepts about the conditions necessary for the therapeutic relationship.

REFLECTION POINT

- What do you think are the important elements of the therapeutic relationship? Draw on your experience of being a client yourself.

THE THERAPEUTIC FRAME

Counselling takes places within the therapeutic frame, which is first a real physical space, the physical setting where counselling takes places. Second, it is also a temporal space, the therapeutic hour in which it happens and which itself sits in the day and the week of both the client and counsellor – in other words, the time space in which they come together to carry out the activity. Third, it is an emotional space, in which the counsellor sets aside all their other concerns, to focus entirely on the client, the material they bring and the process between them.

Physical space

Therapeutic orientations do differ as to the significance they place on the physical environment in which counselling takes place, but all are agreed that it needs to be quiet, safe and can ensure the confidentiality of the counselling interview. There should be no telephones going off, no inter-ruptions and no distractions. In order to feel safe and secure within the therapeutic space clients need to become familiar with it and to know what to expect. It is not acceptable to be constantly changing rooms so that the client has no idea where they are going to be. Counselling rooms, although they should be comfortable, are best kept fairly neutral. Family pictures, for example, can intrude into the process. The room is a kind of metaphor for what will take place between you. You as the counsellor are going to be fully present, warm and available to the client but you are not going to bring other aspects of yourself, such as your family set-up or your religious beliefs into the equation.

Even small changes in the physical environment can sometimes throw a client. I once removed a cushion from my consulting room because I had spilled something on it. A client, who I had been seeing for some time, was uncomfortable at the start of the session. She asked in quite an angry voice where the cushion was. I enquired gently as to why the cushion was important to her. She told me that when she came into the room, to settle herself down and get ready for what was often painful and difficult work, she would go through a process of checking that everything was where she expected it to be in the room. That reassured her and reminded her that she had been there before and that everything was safe and familiar. This had never been the case for her when she was a child, as she had experienced both abuse and neglect. By removing the cushion, I had inadvertently tampered with an aspect of the therapeutic space that was very important to her sense of security.

Creating the right kind of physical environment is your responsibility as the counsellor and, sometimes, within institutions you have to be willing to fight for it. This is not just about looking professional or protecting your territory, it is much more important and significant than that and it will impact upon your work.

ACTIVITY 1.1

- Taking into account your theoretical orientation, plan your ideal consulting room. What would it be like? What would be in it?
- Now think about the physical environment in which you do practise. Given that it is probably not ideal, how might you improve it? Make a list.

Temporal space

We live in a very busy world where much is demanded of our time. The therapeutic hour (usually either the whole 60 minutes or 50 minutes with 10 minutes' reflection time for the counsellor) provides a space in time, during which the client and counsellor get together, in a quiet, private space, away from all the distractions and noise of the world, to give time to the client, to their concerns and the relationship. Usually a time slot is established on a weekly basis, although orientations do vary as to how flexibly this may be arranged. However, whatever your orientation may be, it is important to recognise the significance of the temporal space, as Spurling argues:

> *The time boundaries establish counselling as a continuous and developing process, as something which can only unfold over time. This process is about change and the rate or pattern of change cannot be predicted in advance as it is the outcome of the interchange between counsellor and client. The unpredictability of the counselling therefore needs predictability in the structure of the setting in order to be sustained.*
>
> (Spurling, 2004, p29)

Managing the time is an important skill for you to develop as a counsellor but it is crucial to ensure that your client is aware of time boundaries and I would advocate having a clock that is clearly visible to both parties. Sometimes, clients themselves become adept at working within the time frame. This may manifest in some interesting ways. For example, you may recognise the phenomenon that has become known in counselling parlance as the 'door handle' comment. This is when the client says something to you that you recognise to be possibly significant just as she is getting ready to leave, or indeed on her way out of the door. As with everything else in counselling, it is not a mistake. She didn't just forget to tell you that she had just left her husband and moved in with the man next door, until that point in the session. She could be testing the boundaries by holding out something to see if you will grab it, but more likely, she is flagging up something for the future that she wasn't quite ready to talk about today. The skilful counsellor will note it and return to it in future sessions.

Some therapists have argued very cogently for a more flexible approach to time. For example, counsellors working with children have expressed the notion that 60 minutes is too long a time for a child client to manage and 30 minutes might be more appropriate. Some counsellors working with severely traumatised clients have argued that 60 minutes is not long enough for the client who is gradually unearthing deeply painful experiences from their pasts (Woskett, 2008). However, there is agreement that any deviation from the therapeutic hour is both negotiated and agreed with clients and not just allowed to happen as a result of sloppy practice. Time boundaries, like all boundaries, are there to serve the work and not the other way around.

Another significant thing to think about with regard to the therapeutic relationship and time, relates back to the quotation from Spurling (2004) above. Counselling is a process which develops over time. It has a beginning, a middle and an end. Often, the time structure is imposed from the outside; you work for an agency that allows only six sessions, for example. Sometimes, as with open-ended work usually carried out within private practice, there are no such imposed time constraints, and so the counsellor has to develop the expertise to recognise which phase the client is in and work accordingly.

In the beginning stage, we have to establish the relationship and allow the client to develop trust. Depending on the client's previous experience and the manner and skill of the counsellor, this may take some time. In the middle stage, the client may become quite dependent on the counsellor and the counselling. The role of the counsellor here is to acknowledge and allow this dependency, while understanding it for what it is and not in any way exploiting it, being ever conscious of the vulnerability of the client during this stage. In the third and final stage of counselling, as you work towards ending with your client, you will become aware of the client's developing independence and strengthening autonomy.

In short-term or time-constrained work you need to be very responsible about how you manage the sessions and the focus. It would be highly inappropriate and even potentially dangerous to open up deeply painful and/or entrenched issues in your client, when you simply don't have the time to work through them properly and could end up having to abandon your client, in an extremely vulnerable state, because your six sessions are over. Better to acknowledge the existence of these issues and then help your client to access the kind of longer-term work that they need. Short-term work can be highly effective but it does need to be focused and the implications of time constraint must be acknowledged.

Emotional space

This is something that you, the counsellor, offer to your client and, just like time, it is quite a rare commodity these days. Providing the emotional space for your client means that you offer your undivided attention, having set aside all of your own concerns for the duration of the session. You are utterly available to your client but in an unobtrusive way (Leiper and Maltby, 2004). Winnicott (1965) called this phenomenon *holding*. Building on this holding, as the counsellor you make yourself available to your client: intellectually, through your thinking process; physically, through your presence, your stillness and your eye contact; and emotionally, through your willingness to listen to and receive what is often painful and difficult material, and to respond to it with empathy. Through this process, you detoxify the material and enable your client to tolerate the feelings it engenders. This process Bion (1970) described as *containment* and it is a vitally important part of the therapeutic relationship, whatever your orientation. Spurling (2004) speaks of the client's frightening and intolerable feelings being first held and transformed by the counsellor and then returned to them in a digestible form. Being able to contain, first yourself, and then your client and their material, is central to the role of the counsellor.

While you must bring your full attention to the interaction with the client, you don't interrupt the process or impose by bringing into this special relationship your own material or life experience. The really skilful counsellor has the ability to be fully emotionally present and experienced by the client as such, while always allowing the client to take centre stage. This makes the therapeutic relationship qualitatively different from other relationships, in that although two people are equally present in it, one has the benefit of being able to make therapeutic use of the emotional space, which the other one, you the counsellor, is facilitating.

Case study 1.1   Faith's story

Joe was actually my third counsellor. I wouldn't have gone back to counselling, which had never really worked for me up until that point, had I not been really desperate and in crisis. It started as my sister's crisis. She had made her third fairly serious suicide attempt and was having a stay in hospital. This time she told them all about what had gone on in our family, all the secrets and lies. I was furious with her because they were my secrets too and I didn't want it all coming out at that point in my life.

I had coped with things quite well, I thought. I had an excellent job, etc. and if you overlooked my private life and my drinking, you might think I was doing OK. I can admit now that I was very unhappy, but no one was going to know that except me.

Joe was recommended to me. Most people thought I should go to a woman counsellor, given what I needed to talk about, so I think I went to see Joe partly to show how tough I was. As a business woman I was quite impressed with how he set up the contract for the work. He seemed to manage to be quite business-like but also very warm. I still don't know much about him after seeing him for over a year, which is a bit odd, I think.

He never pushed me and however much I threw at him – anger, even taunts sometimes – he took it and I didn't seem able to damage him with it. I have damaged plenty of other people in the past, so again he surprised me with that. I ended up telling him everything, all the gory details. There was a sort of quiet kindness about him that let me do that. Sometimes I used to dread going, but I felt compelled to keep on with it. How I didn't crash my car on the way home sometimes I will never know because I was a mess. He was always the same, always there sort of holding me in it, which is a strange thing to say as he never touched me, except to shake hands when we first met. I can't really describe what it was about him but I did feel it. His room was like my sanctuary where I could be the mess that I really was, not the front that I put on to everyone else.

I ended up changing quite a lot of things, even my job which had meant so much to me. I cut down my drinking, and my sister and I had some really important conversations. I began to feel like I was ready to stop seeing Joe, although I was afraid to let go. I guess he sort of let me go, like he thought I was ready too. That made me feel a lot more confident. I do know he is still there, in that room seeing other people. I like to think of him still being there and maybe I will go back some time, but not just yet. I want to get on with living this new life now.

COMMENT

What Faith's story demonstrates is how the therapeutic relationship with Joe sustained her through her crisis and enabled her to make sense of her experience and find a different way of living her life.

REFLECTION POINT

- Do you think the three aspects of the therapeutic space were relevant to Faith's story and, if you do, then how?

A WAY OF BEING

We are now going to give some thought to the person of the counsellor and how their way of being within the therapeutic encounter helps to facilitate the development of the therapeutic relationship. The activity of counselling is very much about 'being' rather than 'doing'. If you think about the counselling encounter and ask yourself what does the counsellor actually physically do, then compared to other helping professions, the answer is they don't actually do very much. If you think of a visit to the GP, by way of comparison, the doctor is likely to ask a series of questions, take someone's temperature, refer to previous medical history, check in reference books or on the computer for the appropriate medication, etc. – all in all, quite a lot of 'doing'. Our work as counsellors is all about 'being'. Physically, we are quite passive, so it is reasonable to conclude that it is not about what you do that makes you an effective counsellor, it is about how you are, your way of being with another.

The term 'way of being' has come to be associated with Carl Rogers, the founder of the person-centred approach. He argued that, in counselling, it is the qualities exhibited by the counsellor and experienced by the client, within the therapeutic relationship, which form the building blocks of that relationship (Rogers, 1957, 1986, 1990). Rogers maintained that this relationship does not merely facilitate the process of therapy, it *is* the therapy.

Rogers (ibid.) stated that for successful therapy to take place there were six necessary conditions. Three of them, which he called the *core conditions*, related to the attitude and modus operandi of the therapist. They are:

- empathy;
- unconditional positive regard;
- congruence.

In his later writing there was evidence of the emergence of what Thorne (1992) has considered a fourth core condition, *therapeutic presence* (Rogers, 1980). Mearns (1994, 1997) has viewed this rather mystical and spiritual fourth characteristic as the successful blending together of the other three. This concept of therapeutic presence transcends the theoretical orientation divide. It is about bringing your whole self into the relationship with another, in the moment, without any self-centred purpose or goal.

Empathy, which is discussed in greater depth later in this book, is not an attitude or approach, but a process, through which you, the counsellor, attempt to see things through the eyes of the client, to inhabit their skin for that time. Lietaer (2002, p9) describes it as a *continuous endeavour throughout the therapy process,* stressing the moment-to-moment nature of this core condition. It requires intense and active attention to the feelings of your client and, when you are fully engaged in it, it is impossible to be diagnosing or working out solutions. You must immerse yourself in the world of your client. When empathy is present, there is a resonance between the two people, which Rogers (1986) maintained was healing in itself.

Hart (1999) suggests that deep empathy, in its connectedness to another human being, is not only helpful to the client and beneficial to the therapeutic process, but it also sustains you as the counsellor. Mearns and Thorne (2000, p93) go further in describing it as *a natural response for the person who experiences the essential worth of his or her own being.* They argue that it is vital for you to be empathically disposed towards yourself and you must address any lack of compassion, or regard towards yourself, to ensure the safety and appropriateness of your interaction with others. Watson et al. (1998, p38) argued that empathy *helps to gently and carefully deconstruct clients' world views so as to subject them to careful scrutiny and reflection.*

The second core condition is *unconditional positive regard*, which describes an attitude of acceptance, warmth, caring and interest towards the client and a willingness to acknowledge the separation between a person and their behaviour. It implies a non-judgemental approach and an acceptance of all of the constituent parts of an individual, without discrimination, with the view that through this experience of acceptance from another, the client will eventually be able to accept themselves (Barrett-Lennard, 1998). You can see here the connection with the psychodynamic concept of containment discussed earlier. It is based on a belief in the intrinsic value of every human being and their fundamental right to respect at all times. Mearns and Thorne have defined it as:

> the label given to the fundamental attitude of a person-centred counsellor towards her client. The counsellor who holds this attitude deeply values the humanity of her client and is not deflected in that valuing by any particular client behaviours. The attitude manifests itself in the counsellor's consistent acceptance of and enduring warmth towards her client.
>
> (1988, p59)

Bozarth (1998, p83) describes unconditional positive regard as the curative factor in counselling and growth promoting. Wilkins (2000) maintains that unconditional positive regard requires you to see each client as an individual with unique needs. This calls for an attitude of acceptance in you, the counsellor, which acknowledges the individuality and uniqueness of each person and accepts all the facets of a person, even those that are more difficult. Purton (1998) argues that in order to get over any conflicts in valuing the person, while disapproving of aspects of their behaviour, it is helpful to see this attitude as transcendent, focusing on the belief that people deserve respect and acceptance intrinsically. Mearns and Thorne challenge you to apply this condition to yourself, to engage in what they describe as the *struggle for self-acceptance* (2000, p90).

The third core condition, *congruence,* is a willingness on your part to be authentic within the relationship, to allow your external responses to the client to match as closely as possible to your internal process (Mearns and Thorne, 1988), but to do so in a sensitive manner appropriate to the relationship. Congruence on the part of the therapist engenders trust. Mearns and Thorne (2000) discuss the various debates within the person-centred community about the precise meaning of congruence, but they turn back to the counsellor's relationship with themself and raise the issue of openness to the self:

> There is then the further challenge of how to give expression to what is being thought, felt or physically experienced in such a way that the relationship is served and enhanced. What is at issue is the therapist's commitment to ensuring that he or she does not run away from thoughts, feelings or physical sensations which arouse confusion, excitement, anxiety or the fear of stumbling on unwelcome discoveries about one's way of being in the world.
>
> (2000, p96)

Thorne (1992) notes Rogers's confidence in the efficacy of the core conditions within the therapeutic relationship and Mearns (1994) suggests that, despite the almost mystical way in which Rogers describes them, he communicates his meaning well. Both are agreed that the core conditions have remained the lynchpin of person-centred practice as it has developed over three-quarters of a century. However, it is important to see the core conditions as something a practitioner is always working towards (Barrett-Lennard, 1998) and difficulty in creating or maintaining them with particular clients is the stuff of every counsellor's clinical supervision.

REFLECTION POINT

- Even if your orientation is other than person-centred, what do you think these ideas, and particularly the concept of applying the core conditions to yourself, have to offer you as a practitioner?

Case study 1.2   Wayne's story

For a lot of my life I don't think I was a very nice person. I learned a lot of bad things as I was growing up. I learned to throw my weight around and never ever to give someone a second chance. I met Gloria through the project I had to take part in as part of the terms of my probation. We were offered this counselling to 'help us to confront our offending behaviour'. For me in the beginning it was about playing the system in the hope that I would get out the other side that bit quicker. However, it wasn't that long before I began to enjoy seeing Gloria, or maybe not enjoy, but I found it helpful.

There was something about the way she was with me. Other people I had come across talk the talk and play at being respectful to you, but not her. She didn't spout a lot of jargon at me or put me down, she really did treat me as an equal, like what I said mattered to her. She was tough, mind you, and I couldn't get away with playing her. She was honest with me all the time, even when I made her angry, but she wasn't blaming. Even though she was a tiny little person and I am a big guy, she felt somehow bigger than me and she wasn't afraid, even of the bad bits of me. She always treated me like an intelligent person who could change if I really wanted to. It was like because she could see the good sides of me too, I began to see the good sides of myself and feel a bit better about the person I am.

I think the most important thing I learned from being with her is to say how I felt and say what I wanted without pushing it with the other person. I don't know if it was working with her or just getting a bit older and wiser but I did start thinking about important stuff, like what I want from my life, who I care about and where I want to be. That was all a bit new to me and it did feel exciting to be thinking about it. She didn't think it was weird when I told her I might like to do art at college. It was a big secret before I told her.

One thing I really hated at first was having to sit still for a whole hour. I had never done that before and at first I did pace about a bit, but Gloria, she just sat quietly and eventually I thought, 'Well, if I am going to talk to her I had better sit down too.' If she had tried telling me to sit down, that would have been a big mistake. Right from the start she was good at sussing me out like that. She just gave me the time to settle down for myself. That was how it was with us, she gave me time and then I came to doing the work for myself.

REFLECTION POINT

- What do you think it was about Gloria as a counsellor that enabled her to work successfully with this challenging client?

COMMENT

In thinking about this example of a successful therapeutic relationship we need to set aside Gloria's skilful handling of her work with Wayne and consider his part in it, because we are talking about a relationship between two people. Wayne originally came to counselling because he wanted to play the system. Sometimes, people come to counselling because their partners or their employers or someone else wants them to or puts pressure on them to come. Counselling cannot work unless the client, at some point, makes a choice to be there. In Wayne's case, he made the choice to stop pacing around and engage with Gloria. The client who has been 'sent', if given the space, may well choose to stay and participate in the relationship. If they do not make this free choice, then both of you will be wasting your time and there can be no therapeutic relationship.

Rogers (1957, 1984, 1990) recognised the role of the client by adding three other necessary conditions for therapeutic interaction to take place.

1. Psychological contact between therapist and client. In other words, there must be some real engagement between the two, on a psychological level.
2. The client must be experiencing some anxiety, vulnerability or incongruence. This means that the client must be willing and able to bring to the encounter some material on which they will work.
3. The client must receive or experience the conditions offered by the therapist. This does imply that the client needs to be mentally well enough and, on some level, open to receiving what is being offered by the counsellor.

Thus, you need to acknowledge that you cannot counsel someone who is not, on some level, open to it, or willing to engage with you in the therapeutic relationship. In other words, counselling is not something you do *to* someone, it is something you do *with* them, as partners in the enterprise.

CHAPTER SUMMARY

In this first chapter we have been giving some thought to what constitutes the therapeutic relationship and what it means in practice. We have considered how it is demarcated by the therapeutic frame. We have also thought about the counsellor's way of being and how this facilitates the work. Finally, we looked at the role of the client, who is the other partner in the therapeutic relationship. This chapter has included:

- the therapeutic frame – physical space, temporal space and emotional space;

- holding;
- containment;
- a 'way of being' – the core conditions for counselling;
- the role of the client in the therapeutic relationship.

SUGGESTED FURTHER READING

Mearns, D and Cooper, M (2005) *Working at Relational Depth in Counselling and Psychotherapy.* London: Sage.

Spurling, L (2004) *An Introduction to Psychodynamic Counselling.* Basingstoke: Palgrave Macmillan.

CHAPTER 2

First impressions

CORE KNOWLEDGE

- This chapter looks at how you can most successfully present yourself as a counsellor, from both personal and professional perspectives.

- You will learn how to establish the therapeutic agreement/contract and make an informed decision about what key elements need to be included.

- Working with diversity is an essential component to a counsellor's work. Here we examine the challenges inherent in working with difference and outline some ideas for approaching diversity.

INTRODUCTION

From our earliest childhood we are taught to assess other people when we first meet them. The way they look, the way they speak, their manner. All of these aspects of the other person will impact upon us. At its most basic level, this process of assessment is important for survival but it also has its roots in the socialisation process. Is this person like me? Is she different from me? How is she different? Do I like her difference or am I uncomfortable with it? Does she pose any kind of threat to me? However much you might prefer not to have all of this going on inside, it will be, and what is important is acknowledging it for what it is. Of course, it is an uncomfortable reality that the same process will be going on in reverse with the other person.

As a counsellor you need to give considerable thought to other people's perception of you and how it might impact upon the work of counselling. How do you present yourself and how might that presentation be received by others? This is not to say that all counsellors should dress alike or be alike – there is no right or wrong – but you cannot pretend that the way you present yourself doesn't matter. Let's consider some very stereotypical examples. If you are a middle-aged man working as a counsellor in a young people's counselling service and you turn up for a session in a three-piece business suit, what dynamics might that create? In another setting, say working in a GP's surgery, what if you turned up wearing a T-shirt espousing some extreme political views that you might hold? How might a client meeting you for the first time, whose opinions are radically different, be affected by that? What if you turned up to meet a client wearing a short skirt and a low-cut top? What might that do to the dynamics? What if you turned up looking unkempt, with greasy hair or in need of a shave? No one is saying that any of these forms of dress or presentation are inappropriate in the right context, but rather that as a counsellor you have to think carefully about how you present yourself because it will certainly impact upon the client.

This is a difficult issue and one which evokes quite strong reactions. In this particular context it is the client who should be the focus of attention and, as a counsellor, you need to be willing to give that therapeutic hour entirely to the client. Your role is to focus upon the client, give them your whole and undivided attention, attend to their narrative. In other words, it is not about you, and if you are not willing to give this emotional space, take a back seat in this way, then are you really able to work as a counsellor? If the way you present yourself distracts the client constantly, then it will be taking them away from where they need to be. Of course, it could be argued that such distractions are grist for the mill of counselling, but clients will project things on to you and fantasise about you and your life without any help from you. Having a fairly neutral presentation may well facilitate this process much better. Counselling requires many things from the practitioner and one of them is an absolute willingness to give the floor to the other person.

Case study 2.1   Jason

Jason is a 35-year-old builder who owns his small company, which employs three other men. He has a wife and a four-year-old son. Things have been going quite well for him but he worries all the time about his responsibilities and at times he finds himself getting very angry for no real reason. He likes a drink, which helps him to relax, and occasionally he uses a bit of cocaine for recreational reasons. The other day on his way to work he had to pull over and stop his van because he was feeling very strange, sort of in a panic, and then to his absolute horror he just started sobbing and he found it really hard to stop. This experience both shocked and frightened him. He felt as though he had really let himself down and that he was not behaving as a man should. When he told Julie, his wife, she was very worried too and suggested that he went to see their GP to get some tablets to help him. Dr Khan listened sympathetically to Jason but said that before he prescribed any anti-anxiety medication, he would like Jason to see the practice counsellor, which is why Jason has turned up at the surgery today. He is feeling really awful. That panic is quite near the surface again. As he sits in the waiting room he considers just getting up and leaving. What good is talking going to do? If he wanted to talk to someone he would talk to Julie, but he knows she really wants him to give this counselling thing a go, because she trusts Dr Khan's judgement.

Karen, the counsellor, is 48 years old and lives with her long-term partner Jenny. They met at university. Jenny is an accountant and they live very comfortably. Karen was in human resource management until a few years ago when she re-trained as a counsellor. This is her first paid counselling work and she has been at the surgery for four months now. Karen picked up the paperwork for Jason last week. She was a little apprehensive because she hasn't had much experience of working with younger male clients. Also, she is not having a particularly good day because she is anxious about Jenny who has a health scare at the moment. At the appointed time Karen goes out into the waiting room to collect Jason. He comes back with her to the counselling room and they both sit down.

COMMENT

Let us freeze-frame at this point. First, consider the diversity in front of you: there is a young, male, heterosexual, probably working-class client and an older, female, lesbian, middle-class and educated counsellor. You know nothing of their racial or ethnic backgrounds, which might throw up other points of diversity. The client is obviously anxious as he finds himself in this unfamiliar environment and the counsellor also is a little apprehensive and possibly preoccupied. What might their expectations of each other and what is going to happen between them be?

Jason has never seen a counsellor before so he has no benchmarks. He has, however, seen other professionals – his GP and hospital doctors, his accountant, his solicitor, and so on. All of these people have given him advice, looked at the problems with which he has presented them and come up with possible solutions or courses of action that he should take. It is, therefore, reasonable to surmise that Jason will expect the same of Karen. He will tell her his problems, what happened to him in the van, and she will tell him what he needs to do about it to avoid a reoccurrence. He expects he will have to describe in some detail all the events surrounding the panic attack. He is unlikely to be expecting that she will ask him about his childhood, his relationship with his wife, possibly his sex life, his alcohol and drug use, all of his emotional experience, how he feels, etc. He is expecting her to be some kind of expert, but expert on what exactly? Life, his life in particular, emotions, panic? He hasn't fully thought that through, but surely she is some kind of expert or specialist or why else has he been referred to her? Perhaps he will need to see her a couple of times before she is able to sort things out for him.

As Karen looks at the young man sitting in front of her, what does she expect from him? Well, he has come to counselling so presumably he is open to talking about himself. She assumes he will be willing to open up to her about many different facets of his life and his past, how he feels about things, his relationships, background, etc. This is likely to take several weeks, although the policy of the surgery is that she will be allowed a maximum of twelve sessions, six in the first instance, which probably won't be enough. She expects that together they will explore his issues and that hopefully this will give him some insight into what is happening for him, and make him more aware of his choices. This, in turn, might lessen his anxiety and the symptoms he is experiencing, although in the short term it could possibly make them worse. She hopes he will be able to make good use of the service she can offer him, but it will ultimately be up to him.

Although this is an imaginary scenario, it is not an untypical one. Given the differences between these two people and their expectations, how could the counselling relationship be established between them and how could it possibly be expected to work?

If Karen and Jason are to work together successfully, they need to arrive at some common understanding of what they are actually going to do together and establish an appropriate framework within which this activity can safely take place. They will need to arrive at a 'therapeutic agreement' or 'contract', although as Jenkins (2007) points out, the term 'contract' implies an exchange of money and may therefore be more applicable to counselling which takes place within a private practice setting.

THE THERAPEUTIC AGREEMENT/CONTRACT

The point at which a person becomes a client is most often at a time in their life when they are vulnerable, something is going wrong and the equilibrium in their life is disturbed. This is not always the case as some people do use therapy for personal growth and, not infrequently, people come into counselling because it is a requirement of a training course. However, because of the likelihood that the client is vulnerable, it is particularly important to put in place a framework which will ensure that no exploitation of the client will take place.

The client needs to understand, as far as possible, what counselling is, so that they can be said to have given informed consent before embarking on the work. Jenkins (2007) cites the British Medical Association Ethics

Department (BMAED) in explaining that for consent to be valid the patient must:

- *be able to understand in broad terms the nature and purpose of the procedure;*
- *be offered sufficient information to make informed choices;*
- *believe the information and be able to weigh it in the balance to arrive at a decision;*
- *be acting voluntarily and free from pressure;*
- *be aware that he/she can refuse.*

(BMAED, 2004, p72)

Of course, the issue of informed consent in counselling is not as straight-forward as it is in other contexts. If you were about to have an operation, for example, a doctor might reasonably be able to tell you the outcome they hope for and the risks involved. You can be informed as to exactly what the procedure involves, how long it will take and what the aftercare will be. You can then decide, taking into account the information you have been given, whether or not you wish to proceed with the surgery. Counselling is an interpersonal interaction between counsellor and client, and it isn't possible to predict outcomes with any degree of certainty. It would not be appropriate to start trying to explain to the client how your particular orientation works, for example long descriptions of working in the trans-ference or establishing the core conditions. The client's eyes would quickly glaze over and they would probably find the first opportunity to politely leave. What it is certainly possible to do, however, is to briefly make clear to the client what counselling is and isn't. All experienced counsellors have a well-rehearsed patter, which might go as follows.

Counselling isn't about advice giving and I certainly won't be telling you what you should or shouldn't do. It is about providing you with a safe and confidential place in which you can talk about and explore the things that are troubling you. I will be using my skills to help you to focus on the issues that are really important to you, to help you to understand and perhaps express how you are feeling and maybe look at your options, to see what you really want to do. Sometimes it can be a painful process and it can take time, but a lot of people do find it helpful.

ACTIVITY 2.1

- Think about the statement above and then write one that you would be comfortable presenting to a client.

Once you are clear that the client does want to embark on the process of counselling, then the therapeutic agreement/contract can be discussed. The *Ethical Framework for Good Practice in Counselling and Psychotherapy*, published by the British Association for Counselling & Psychotherapy (BACP), to which all counsellors, who are members of that organisation, work, states in clause 3:

> *Good practice involves clarifying and agreeing the rights and responsibilities of both the practitioner and client at appropriate points in their working relationship.*
>
> (BACP, 2010)

At the outset of the relationship this would involve developing a contract/therapeutic agreement.

Peter Jenkins (2007), who has done such excellent work on the legal aspects of counselling, suggests what might be included in such a contract. This model contract is applicable to fee-based therapy and a therapeutic agreement which didn't include fees might need to be modified accordingly. His list of what needs to be included is as follows:

- *costs of sessions;*
- *duration and frequency of sessions;*
- *arrangements and charges (if relevant) for cancellation or holiday periods;*
- *main characteristics of therapy provided;*
- *total number of sessions and arrangements for review;*
- *limits of confidentiality;*
- *arrangements for termination of therapy;*
- *cover or substitution of therapist in case of illness;*
- *date and signature of both parties.*

(Jenkins, 2007, p30)

Costs of sessions

If Karen in the above scenario is employed by the surgery, then she will be paid by them and will not be making a direct charge to Jason. However, if she had been working in other settings, for example within some parts of the voluntary sector, it may be part of her responsibility to explain to Jason about charges and means of payment. The point here is that there needs to be absolute clarity from the outset about the financial arrangements for the work, so that the client understands exactly what the costs are, when he or she is expected to pay them and how that payment will be made.

An important question to consider here is what if someone else other than the client is paying for the counselling? How does this impact on the therapeutic relationship and the contract/agreement? This is frequently an issue in counselling work with young people. If the parents are paying, for example, does that make them stakeholders in the work? Should they be kept informed about how the work is going? Should they have some knowledge of the content of the work? In the case of an adult, what if an employer is paying?

Whoever is paying, the client has the right to expect the same degree of autonomy and confidentiality as if they were paying themself. All of these issues need to be discussed and made clear to all parties during the contracting process.

Duration and frequency of sessions

Counselling is not an informal chat – it is a formal, boundaried interview and part of those boundaries comprise the time frame. Most counselling takes place within what is often referred to as the 'therapeutic hour', which is either the whole hour or a 50-minute session with ten minutes' reflection time at the end for the counsellor. It is part of the counsellor's work to manage this time appropriately and as they become more skilful they will be able to do this with greater effect. The client may not be aware of the time-limited character of the counselling interview and this will need to be explained sensitively, including the fact that if the client comes late the time frame of the session will not be shifted back. Although many a client has started the counselling process resenting the imposition of this framework, and some of the work in counselling may well include pushing against these boundaries, nevertheless, most clients come to an understanding, through their experience, of the therapeutic value of this formal time setting, which is very containing.

Clients will also need to know how often the counselling will take place, which is usually weekly and most often at the same time each week. Orientations do vary about how strictly they stick to the regular time slot, but the important point is that the client needs to be aware that they must set aside a regular time, prioritise and make a mental space in which the work may take place.

Arrangements and charges (if relevant) for cancellation or holiday periods

This element of the contract spans two important issues. First, the financial issue; obviously, the charges element applies only to counselling for which a client is paying fees. Most therapists in private practice will charge for missed appointments and cancellations at short notice, although arrangements for this do vary across the orientations. Psychoanalysts, for example, will usually charge for any missed appointments outside agreed holiday times, even if notice is given. Humanistic practitioners may be more flexible. Although the money is obviously important to people who earn their living through the work, it is not the only reason for making such charges. It is about being clear and open with the client about the level of commitment required for the counselling to work. It is not something a client can just pick up and put down on a whim.

The second important issue in this element of the contract relates to the psychological dependency on the counsellor and the counselling which a client is likely to develop (and which is a perfectly normal and appropriate part of the therapeutic relationship). As the therapy develops the client will build their autonomy and this dependency will lessen, but some clients do feel it very keenly and it is, therefore, important that they know what will happen if, for some unavoidable reason, the counsellor has to cancel a session. Even the most conscientious counsellor may be struck down by the flu or have the car break down. Every counsellor needs to have breaks and holidays and so the client must be apprised as to what happens in these eventualities.

Main characteristics of therapy provided

As mentioned above, this element of the contract does not provide an opportunity for the counsellor to launch into a lecture, however well informed, about her theoretical orientation. Rather, it is an opportunity to give some basic information that might be helpful about the way in which the work will take place. Clients may have read bits about therapy, seen things on the television and might have expectations based on this. For example, someone who had read about CBT and is expecting an interventionist model would be very disappointed to sit down with someone who was working psychodynamically and vice versa.

Total number of sessions and arrangements for review

Let's go back to Jason and Karen for a moment. Jason was expecting one or two sessions, Karen was concerned that 12 wouldn't be enough. Imagine what might happen if this was not discussed between them before they embarked on the work. Many agencies and counselling settings have a limit on the number of sessions available. Often the number is set at six. Some places may have an arrangement that in certain cases the number of sessions may be extended if the counsellor makes a good case for it. It is rare these days for a counsellor working in an agency to be able to enter into an open-ended contract with a client and, even if it was possible, imagine how daunting this could feel for that client who had never been in counselling before. Stating clearly how many sessions are available and how many the client will be expected to commit to, is essential. It is helpful here to explain to the client that counselling often takes time to work and that they will not necessarily feel better after the first session, although many clients who have been desperately needing someone to talk to or who are really ready to take their problems in hand by embarking on the work certainly do. For many, it takes time to establish the relationship and develop trust.

It is also helpful for the client to be made aware of the review process through which the way the counselling is going can be assessed by the client and the counsellor. In a six-week contract, for example, it would be useful to have a mini review in session three and a full review in session six. If further sessions are available, this would be the point at which the client could decide to commit to another set of sessions or, in the case of private practice, perhaps move on to an open-ended contract.

Limits of confidentiality

This is perhaps the most significant and the most problematic of all the elements of the contract. Here comes the punchline – within the counselling context, there is no such thing as absolute confidentiality. Clients may want it, which is completely understandable, but it would be an extremely unwise counsellor who offered it. The first and most obvious limitation to confidentiality is the reality of supervision. While the focus of supervision is on the counsellor's work, nevertheless, the case will be discussed and information about the client, albeit anonymously, will be imparted to the supervisor. If the counsellor is a student, the material may also be discussed in case discussion groups or supervision groups on the course. It may even provide the material for the dreaded case studies.

You should certainly refer to Jenkins (2007), who devotes a whole chapter to the subject of confidentiality. He gives examples of situations when it may be ethical and appropriate to break confidentiality or where the counsellor may find herself legally required so to do. Being a counsellor does not afford the privilege of being above the law. Bond (2010) also devotes a whole chapter to this important subject. He starts this chapter with the meaningful statement:

> Confidentiality is probably the single issue that raises most ethical and legal anxiety for counsellors. It is an issue over which practice has evolved from a total commitment to the client's privacy and confidentiality to something which requires active management by the counsellor and may involve making difficult judgements. These changes have taken place in response to a greater appreciation of the ethical complexities of providing counselling, but also have been driven by changes in the law.

> (p155)

Remaining ignorant of the debates and issues around confidentiality is not an option for a counsellor and would certainly not be considered as a valid excuse. The counsellor must also acquaint themself with the confidentiality policy of the agency for which they work and the constraints within it. They must then impart this to the client honestly and sensitively.

Cover or substitution of therapist in case of illness

This is unlikely to happen in private practice, or in voluntary agencies, unless the illness was long term. It is more likely to happen within NHS settings. However, whatever the situation is, the client needs to be apprised of it.

Date and signature of both parties

This does of course imply that the contract or therapeutic agreement is written. The purpose of signing is not to make this a legally binding agreement, but rather to provide evidence that the terms of the agreement have been read and understood by both parties. From a positive perspective this forms the basis of the therapeutic alliance; both parties know what they are entering into and do so freely. From a more cautious perspective, it might be helpful to both parties in the future, were there to be any dissatisfaction or complaint.

Important caveat

On occasions, clients come into their first counselling session absolutely bursting with emotion. They may have been waiting some time to be seen, be desperate to share what is going on for them with another person; they may be particularly anxious or upset. It is not that uncommon, for example, for a client to burst into tears within seconds of entering the counselling room. Your response needs to be empathic. It would be totally inappropriate and more than a little inhuman for you to launch into setting up your therapeutic agreement in such a situation. You would need to attend to your client and be respectful of the need to unburden. It would not be the end of the world if you did not establish the agreement until the second session.

REFLECTION POINT

- Having read about and considered this model contract, is there anything else that has been missed out?
- How might you change or develop this agreement for your own counselling practice?

WORKING WITH DIVERSITY

Let us go back to our example of Karen and Jason and the differences identified between them. We identified difference in gender, sexual orientation, age, class, educational level. Counsellor and client may also have difference in ethnicity, culture, religion, or difference in their level of physical or mental ability. Frequently, there will be a whole amalgam of difference and diversity.

Working with difference and diversity requires a degree of self-awareness and openness, and some specific skills. It requires attention to language and non-verbal communication and a sensitivity of approach. Training in working with difference and diversity should be an integral part of every substantial training course in counselling in the UK. Unfortunately, all too often it is tokenistic at best. As a counsellor you have responsibility to make up for any such shortfalls in your initial training through the process of continuing professional development (CPD), reading and research and, more importantly, by constantly increasing your awareness of your own assumptions and prejudices. There are a good many resources for you to draw on as much has been and continues to be written on this important subject. All we have space for in this section is to raise some of the issues involved, which will hopefully get you thinking about your own practice. While it is true to say that we learn from our clients, you absolutely cannot sit back and expect your clients to teach you about their world and their experience, and to put up with assumptions and mistakes that you make along the way. You have a responsibility to be much more proactive than that.

ACTIVITY 2.2

- Reflecting on your own training to date, which areas do you need to focus on to ensure that you can work well with a diverse client group?
- Make a list and identify ways in which you could rectify any shortcomings in your training. What research do you need to do? Prioritise and set yourself a timetable.

Sometimes, a person's life experience may set them apart. For example, they may be a refugee, an asylum seeker, someone who has been trafficked or who has experienced torture, or horrendous situations of conflict. It is stretching empathy to the limit for a person born in this country and brought up in relative affluence and social stability, with recourse to the law, the health and social services, etc., to really understand and appreciate such experience and trauma, and its impact on a person's psyche. We might appreciate it cognitively but allowing it in on an emotional level is quite another thing. Specialist supervision, from someone experienced in this kind of work, can be extremely helpful not only in extending the practitioner's understanding but also in providing the emotional support needed to work effectively with this client group.

Counselling, with its focus on the well-being of the individual, is fundamentally a Eurocentric activity. The theories and concepts informing it come historically either from Europe or more recently from the United States. Underlying it is a value system that asserts that individual happiness and well-being is important, and that we have a right to our aspirations and to fulfil what we ourselves perceive to be our own potential. In addition, counselling and psychotherapy hives off the mental and psychological aspects of a human being. We are not primarily focused on a person's physical state of health, as a doctor might be, or his spiritual well-being, as a priest might be, although there is obviously some cross-over (Tuckwell, 2006). Our work focuses on a person's individual psycho/social world. It is vital to appreciate that this is not the only way of understanding or addressing a person's distress. Other cultures do not separate the individual from the family or the community as we do and may not place the same value on individual happiness as opposed to the well-being of the community as a whole. The idea of going to a stranger to discuss your problems could be a complete anathema.

How counselling actually happens, in a room with just two people, may in itself prove to be problematic. In some cultures, for example, it would not be acceptable for a man and a woman who are not from the same family, to be in a room together alone, or indeed at all. As counsellors we are trained to hold eye contact with our clients and to encourage them to do the same. In some cultures this would not be acceptable, or very different meanings could be attributed to the behaviour. It might also be important to give some thought to the meaning a person might attribute to being on their own in a room with another.

Case study 2.2   Steve

Steve is working in a voluntary counselling service that serves his local community. Magdalena is his client. Steve is concerned because his client seems to be very uncomfortable in the room. She is clenching her fists, looking down all the time, seems unable to engage with him at all. By nature, Steve is quite a gentle person and he has never experienced anything like this before. He talks to his supervisor and he is affirmed in his thinking that he really isn't doing anything to cause this response in Magdalena.

He goes back and reads her referral again. All it tells him is that she is from South America, now resident in the UK and that she has been referred because of panic attacks. Steve decides the only thing he can do is try to raise this with Magdalena as gently as he can. When he does so she begins to cry. She tells him that she came to the UK seeking political asylum. Before escaping from her own country she had been arrested, beaten and tortured on several occasions and that this torture had included the use of sexual violence. It emerged that she was really afraid of being on her own in a room with a man and that doing so was bringing up all kinds of difficult and painful memories for her. Steve asked her why she had come, given her history, and to his amazement she said that she had been told to come and she was afraid to disobey. Steve assured her that being referred did not mean that she was obliged to come to counselling, it was just a suggestion and she really did have free choice. He also told her that he could arrange for her to see a woman counsellor, if she preferred, and that, with some planning over the times so that her confidentiality could be taken care of, she could have sessions with the door open and sit next to it. He told her that while counselling might be of some use to her, she would have to make a free choice to engage in it, that he and the whole service would respect her decision and that there would be no repercussions if she wished to stop. He suggested that she take some time to think about it and that she should ring the service if she wished to continue. He told her that he would, with her permission, explain her situation to the clinical lead at the service, in confidence, so that should she wish to return, her needs could be accommodated. Magdalena agreed to this and then they ended the session.

Some weeks later Magdalena did get in touch with the service again. She did want to have some sessions, but would like to work with a woman counsellor. She did, however, tell the clinical lead that this was no reflection on Steve – in fact, he had been really helpful and that her meeting with him had been very important to her. The service assigned her to work with their most experienced woman counsellor and arranged for this counsellor to have specialist supervision for this work.

SEXUAL DIVERSITY

The world of psychotherapy and more particularly psychoanalysis has something of a shameful past with regard to its understanding and treatment of people with sexual orientations other than heterosexuality. Classical psychoanalytical theory pathologised any orientation other than heterosexuality on the grounds that it (heterosexuality) was the only possible healthy outcome of the psychosexual development process and, specifically, the Oedipal conflict. While Freud, in the context of the time when he was developing and writing his theories, can be forgiven for arriving at such conclusions, it is perhaps harder to understand and excuse much more current theorists, psychoanalytical practitioners and training organisations who held to these beliefs, long after they had been abandoned by most thinking people. Mair poses an interesting question that might get to the root of the desire to cling to such outdated and damaging ideas: *If this aspect of the Oedipus complex is challenged may not other concepts of psychodynamic theory be open to question?* (Mair, 2006, p58). Thankfully, most psychodynamic counsellors no longer hold these beliefs.

One response to this oppressive and discriminatory approach has been the emergence of what is called 'gay affirmative therapy', which in the UK has become known as *Pink Therapy* (see the website www.pinktherapy. com). This movement seeks to provide information, education and resources to those who work therapeutically with people who are lesbian, gay, bisexual or transgendered, and to provide a list of associates who work in an affirmative manner with these sexual minorities. The key here is the concept of affirmation, which in this context means that the therapist is positive in their view of sexual minority lifestyles and choices, and that they do not view them as in any way sick or undesirable. Davies and Neal (2003) summarise the main requirements for a gay affirmative therapist as follows.

- *Gay affirmative therapists are those whose beliefs and values appreciate homosexuality and bisexuality as a valid and rich orientation in their own right and who perceive homophobia, not diverse sexuality, as pathological.*
- *Such therapists offer clients respect for their sexuality, personal integrity, culture and lifestyle.*
- *Therapists need (re) training to work with bi and homosexual client groups.*
- *Therapists need to remain alert to their own power and how they use this to reinforce negative authoritative messages, or to heal through self-affirming 'reparenting'.*
- *Therapists have a key role as educators.*

(p40)

The majority of pink therapists come from humanistic backgrounds. Current psychodynamic therapists would offer a different approach.

Psychodynamic counselling with gay clients may be very different from gay-affirmative counselling where the latter is understood to have a part to play in re-programming or educating clients about their situation and where there is an onus on the counsellor to assume responsibility for leading the client out of his or her restricted life experience. Psychodynamic counsellors will be concerned to facilitate a client to gain greater insight into processes that have previously been unconscious, whilst being careful to avoid communicating pressure to conform to a new therapist imposed 'norm'.

(Mair, 2006, p70)

Of course, people from sexual minorities do not always come into counselling to discuss their sexuality, any more than heterosexuals do. While a person's sexuality should not, in an ideal world, define them entirely, nevertheless, their experience of discrimination and prejudice is likely to have impacted significantly on them and may well make them reticent about being entirely open about their lifestyles, before they have built up trust with the counsellor.

Case study 2.3   Hazel

Hazel is an officer in the armed services whose role it is to support service men and women who have been seriously injured either physically or mentally in armed conflicts and help them to reintegrate into civilian life. She also occasionally supports families who have been bereaved. She has herself been in the armed services since she left university and she is nearing retirement. The army pays for her to have supervision and personal support for her work with Patricia, an experienced supervisor. Some of Hazel's work is extremely emotionally taxing and she can see that this supervision and support could be very useful to her, at least in theory.

Although Patricia feels that their work has got off to a good start, she is aware that whenever they talk about the impact her work has on Hazel personally and in terms of her personal life, Hazel is somewhat evasive. It is very subtle and quite skilfully done. Patricia certainly does not want to push at this stage in their relationship. Hazel and Patricia have a good deal in common; they are both white women, close in age and very experienced in their work, but Patricia senses that there is something stopping Hazel from being really open with her and she begins to wonder if it is related to Hazel's sexuality and her possible experience of oppression.

Patricia knows that it will take a time to earn Hazel's absolute trust. She makes sure that Hazel understands their contract of confidentiality properly and she is very careful and sensitive about her use of language. If she makes reference to someone's partner, for example, she always says 'he or she' to convey to Hazel that she does not see the world from an entirely heterosexual perspective. Gradually Hazel begins to respond to this sensitive approach and she begins to mention her own partner, though still not giving the name. When Patricia feels it is appropriate and that Hazel is open to it, she asks if they might use Hazel's partner's first name. There is a lovely moment where Hazel tells Patricia that her partner's name is Chris! She smiles and then says that it is Chris, short for Christine.

Hazel shares with Patricia that even though the regulations have changed in the armed services, to eliminate discrimination against gay and lesbian service people, nevertheless prejudice is still rife and she feels the need to be very careful and circumspect about being open about her sexuality and life choices. This interaction between Hazel and Patricia is pivotal in their relationship. From this point forward Hazel is able to share openly about how her work impacts upon her personal life and relationships, and Patricia is able to help her to work through this.

Hazel is very happy with her life choices, is accepting of her own sexuality and it is not the issue that she brought to the work. However, Patricia needs to understand and appreciate Hazel's personal circumstances and the effect that homophobia has had on both her professional and personal life, in order to be effective as her supervisor. Had Patricia forced this issue before Hazel was ready, she would have simply clammed up, as she was very experienced at doing and something very important would have been lost between them, in that Hazel would not have been able to bring her whole self to their meeting, in the confidence that she is accepted and respected for who she is and the choices that she has made.

THE BALANCE OF POWER

When thinking about issues of difference and diversity, it is worth noting that power, both formal and informal, political and personal, is a significant factor. Power engenders a sense of entitlement. A client I worked with, who was going through the process of gender reassignment, once told me that the hardest thing she was having to learn when living as a woman was to take up less space in the world. When I asked her to elaborate she said that, even though she had a high-flying, well-paid, responsible job, she was having to learn to say less at meetings, be less vocal and do things more quietly. She was a commuter and, when travelling as a woman, she had to take up less space, keep her bag on her knee, not spread her legs out into the aisles, etc. It seemed to me that her experience in doing these activities both as a male and now as a female enabled her to offer a unique insight and they provided a powerful metaphor for the way in which, in this case, gender impacts on the world.

Counsellors are sometimes uncomfortable in acknowledging the power balance within the therapeutic relationship. As the counsellor within that relationship you do hold power. Add to this these other dynamics, such as race, age and class, and it can be a heady mix. For this reason, it is vital for you, as the counsellor, to think these things through and bring them into your consciousness.

CLASS DIVERSITY

Perhaps the 'elephant in the room' when it comes to thinking about diversity in counselling is class. A great deal has been written about, for example, the dynamics of race, but class has not attracted much attention from researchers and writers. This is perhaps a little strange given that, according to the Child Poverty Action Group (2004), social class is the most significant determinant when it comes to a person's life chances (Isaac, 2006). It cannot be denied that counselling is predominantly a middle-class activity where middle-class values have hegemony and the majority of counsellors and clients themselves come from middle-class backgrounds. Perhaps part of the reason for this silence lies in our national embarrassment about issues of class. Outsiders view Britain as a class-bound society but we ourselves often try to deny its potency. It remains true, however, that put two British people in a room together for five minutes and they will almost certainly have worked out each other's social class and may well have made a set of assumptions based upon this classification. The truth of this was brought to my attention very vividly some years ago when I was interviewing potential diploma students with a colleague of mine who is American. We were discussing a woman who we had just interviewed. She had been a strong candidate and I expressed my pleasure that she would increase the diversity of the student group. My colleague looked puzzled and asked me how that would be so as she was a white woman, in her mid thirties like so many of the candidates. I was astonished as everything about this candidate – the way she spoke, the way she presented herself – indicated to me that, unlike most of our other candidates, she was from a working-class background. Even though my colleague had lived in Britain for many years and is a highly insightful and astute person, she had not been schooled from an early age into class consciousness as I clearly had been and so had not picked up on all these subtle and not so subtle class cues.

One really positive consequence of the proliferation of employee assistance programmes (EAPs), is that they do bring into counselling clients who are very unlikely to have arrived there under their own steam. The counselling is paid for by their employers. Many working people do not have the resources to pay for private counselling sessions – their priorities lie else-where – and even if they did have the money, counselling is not necessarily how they would choose to spend it. Sitting opposite a middle-class do-gooder, who hasn't the faintest idea what it is like to work the night shift in a factory, or deliver the mail on a rainy morning, or be a linesman hav-ing to deal with the aftermath of a suicide, does not always seem like an interesting prospect or something that might actually help. However, as counsellors, we can only hope and work towards the situation where the client's actual experience is different from what they might expect and provides an encounter that is respectful, helpful and affirming.

Mick Cooper in *Essential Research Findings in Counselling and Psychotherapy* (2008, pp85–90) summarises all of the research findings about working with difference and this is essential reading. Counsellors need to develop a sensitivity to the effect of diversity both on themselves and on their clients. As a counsellor you need to learn how to acknowledge diversity appropriately and work with it in a way that is empowering and respectful of the client and does not simply reinforce the power imbalance. Some would argue that in an ideal world there should be a match between every client and counsellor, but this is not an ideal world and you will certainly be faced with clients who are very different from you. You should, therefore, remember that, without in any way denying difference, human beings do all have the same emotions. We all feel anger, disappointment, shame, loss, joy, love, etc. and so there is a common ground. This, together with the ability to empathise and a willingness to acknowledge and confront our own assumptions and prejudices, does make it possible for us to work at some level with most clients.

CHAPTER SUMMARY

In this chapter we have looked in some depth at the first encounter with a client. We have drawn on the work of Peter Jenkins in thinking about the process of contract/therapeutic agreement making. You have been challenged to think about your personal presentation and how this might affect your work as a counsellor. We have also considered diversity and its impact upon the first encounter with a client. We have focused on some kinds of difference and diversity, sexuality and class, for example, and have not discussed others, such as differences in race, religion or ability, in any detail. I would, however, like to make some suggestions that hopefully will be a good guide for you in working with diversity of any kind.

- It is your responsibility to research and educate yourself about different cultures and lifestyles. You will learn from your client as the work proceeds, but it is absolutely not the role of the client to teach you. You have to do the work.
- You need to explore and challenge your own prejudices and preconceptions, your covert racism and hidden homophobia, etc. This is an ongoing and continuous process. As well as cognitively, you need to do it on an emotional level and experientially. Find a way not only of raising your consciousness but also your emotional availability.
- Abandon your assumptions, which say much more about you than about the person sitting opposite you in the counselling room.
- Acknowledge and accept responsibility for the formal and informal power you hold in the role of counsellor. Use it sensitively and wisely.
- Be willing to acknowledge and be sensitive to the pain and damage that oppression causes and the lasting impact it has on people's lives.
- Be sensitive to your client's responses and behaviour; you may not know all of the history.

- Commit yourself with both your mind and your heart to practising in an anti-discriminatory manner and use your supervision to help you with this commitment.

SUGGESTED FURTHER READING

Cooper, M (2008) *Essential Research Findings in Counselling and Psychotherapy.* London: Sage.

Chapter 5 makes an interesting read with regard to working with diversity.

Davies, D and **Neal, C** (2003) *Pink Therapy.* Buckingham: Open University Press.

Jenkins, P (2007) *Counselling and Psychotherapy and the Law,* 2nd edition. London: Sage.

This is an essential read for counsellors and would-be counsellors. For a discussion on the first encounter you should look at Chapters 2 and 4.

Lago, C (2006) *Race, Culture and Counselling,* 2nd edition. Maidenhead: Open University Press.

Wheeler, S (ed) (2006) *Difference and Diversity in Counselling. Contemporary Psychodynamic Perspectives.* Basingstoke: Palgrave Macmillan.

CHAPTER 3

Personal qualities

CORE KNOWLEDGE

- This chapter examines the personal and moral qualities that a counsellor must possess, as defined by the BACP in its *Ethical Framework*: empathy; sincerity; integrity; resilience; respect; humility; competence; fairness; wisdom, and courage.

- In addition we will look at some qualities that might be added to this list, such as: open-mindedness; a sense of humour; being genuinely caring; positivity; and patience.

- You will learn how to examine your own personal qualities and morals in order for you to better understand and develop your client relationships.

INTRODUCTION

In this chapter we will give some thought to the counsellor as a person. If you were to think of a time in your own life when you have been really distressed, angry or just generally emotional and then you bring to mind all of your acquaintances, it is most likely that you could fairly quickly identify those people who you might choose to go to for help, advice or a listening ear and those people who you would never want to speak to in such circumstances. What is it about the people in the first group that makes them approachable and facilitative? To be the kind of person that another human being is willing to open up to, and be vulnerable and emotional in front of, we need to demonstrate certain qualities, ways of being that create the right emotional environment for this to take place. We are not talking here of simply being a good or kind person. There are plenty of people around who would willingly help out by, for example, lending a friend £20, or their car, or indeed doing anything practically supportive but who would not be easy to talk to or cry in front of.

In the case of a counsellor, of course, we are not talking about an emotional exchange between friends, but between two people who have no relationship other than the therapeutic one. In this context, we are asking the client to open up to a stranger. In this chapter we are going to be teasing out the qualities and ways of being on the part of the counsellor that engender trust in the client and thus facilitate the process of therapy.

PERSONAL MORAL QUALITIES

The title for this section is taken directly from the BACP's *Ethical Framework for Good Practice in Counselling and Psychotherapy*. This important document recognises that it is not just the practitioner's training or modus operandi that makes them ethical and effective counsellors; it is something about the way they are as people.

> *The practitioner's personal and moral qualities are of the upmost importance to clients. Many of the personal qualities considered important in the provision of services have an ethical and moral component and are therefore considered as virtues or good personal qualities.*

> (BACP, 2010)

Great thought has been given by the counselling fraternity to define what sort of personal and moral qualities might be desirable in practitioners and the *Ethical Framework* does provide a list. However, it is important to acknowledge that you are only human and the list is something that you are encouraged to aspire to and strive towards rather than something you are expected to be on the first day of your training.

REFLECTION POINT

- When you read the subtitle for this section, did you have any internal response to it?
- Did you, for example, question how morality might come into this discussion?

Consider how a person develops personal and moral qualities.

- Are they genetic or the result of socialisation?
- If we don't have them, can we develop them as an act of will or through training?
- In other words, are there born counsellors and those who could never become capable of creating sustaining the therapeutic relationship?

Let's now have a look at the list of qualities compiled by the writers of the *Ethical Framework* and consider what each of them really means in practice.

Empathy – the ability to communicate understanding of another person's experience from that person's perspective

Empathy is not a skill, it is a process, an emotional resonance between two people. Although it is quite a complex concept cognitively, in reality we instinctively know if another person is empathic towards us because it fundamentally affects the quality of the interaction. Go back to the situation mentioned above when you have felt upset or angry about something and you have tried talking to someone else about it. If the person is empathic you will have felt heard, understood, as though the person was able to accurately recognise your emotional experience.

Empathy requires you, as the counsellor, to be willing to recognise in yourself the full gamut of emotional responses and to be accepting of yourself and these responses. So, for example, if the client is talking about rejection, you as the counsellor have to be willing to go to the place in yourself that knows what it is like to feel rejected. You have to touch that place, however uncomfortable it may be and then, with that recognition in hand, immediately come back to the client, using your own experience of the emotion to help you to fully take in and appreciate the experience of the client. This whole process takes place within milliseconds.

The great gift that empathy brings to a relationship is a real sense of equality. If you, as the counsellor, are willing, for example, to acknowledge your own sense of helplessness, or defeat or jealousy, you are not likely to stand in judgement of your clients, or to see them as poor, lesser beings who need your help to sort themselves out. Empathy is about our common humanity. You don't need to have exactly the same experience as someone else to understand the feelings involved. Your client may, for example, be describing a sense of loss at the death of a parent. You may not have lost your parents but you have experienced a painful separation from your partner. The circumstances of the losses may be quite different but both are on the same spectrum of emotion. All human beings experience the same emotions: loss, love, disappointment, anger, etc. The real key to the ability to empathise with another is the willingness to accept the whole range of your own emotions. So, for example, if you cannot accept and come to terms with your own anger, you are not likely to be able to empathise with the client who comes to you and needs to talk about their anger and aggression. Clients have a nasty habit of confronting you with the very parts of yourself that you would rather avoid, hence the need for supervision and the willingness on the part of the counsellor to go back into personal therapy when it is appropriate.

Empathy is sometimes described as the ability to step into another's shoes, but of course, even if you did that, your experience would not be identical. It is important to recognise that. Empathy gives you a felt sense of the other's emotional experience but it is still vital to be focused on listening to and really hearing and accepting the experience of the other and not assuming that empathy is all you need. Everyone knows how irritating and unhelpful it is when someone tells you that they know how you feel. You can imagine how someone else might feel, based on your own experience of the emotion, but you can never really know and so you need to listen without assumption.

It is doubtful that someone could be taught to empathise. It is true that people who are on the autistic spectrum and are high functioning, who do not appear to naturally feel empathy for others, can be trained to behave as if they were feeling empathic, for reasons of social inclusion. This is, however, different from actually teaching someone to empathise. The ability to empathise can be developed and improved, and this is a natural consequence of the personal development and increased self-awareness required of counselling students during their training and of practitioners through the process of CPD.

Whatever your orientation, a proper in-depth understanding of empathy is vital for your work as a counsellor. Rogers (1961), the founder of person-centred counselling, has written at length about it and his work is very accessible. A good place to start would be *On Becoming a Person: A Therapist's View of Therapy*. Dave Mearns and Brian Thorne (2000) in their book *Person-Centred Therapy Today* have argued that it is vital for the therapist to be empathically disposed towards themself and must address any lack of compassion or regard towards themself, to ensure the safety and appropriateness or their interaction with others. Their book challenges the therapist to think about the real meaning of empathy and is a very useful resource in this regard.

ACTIVITY 3.1

Think of two situations from your own life, one where someone has shown you sympathy and the other where someone has empathised with you.

- How did you respond to these two situations?
- How did you feel in each case about the response from the other person?

Based on these experiences, make some notes teasing out the difference between empathy and sympathy.

Sincerity – a personal commitment to consistency between what is professed and what is done

If you do not think through each of the qualities in depth and focus on what they mean in practice, it would be easy to dismiss them as somehow obvious. Sincerity, like mother's milk and apple pie, is generally considered to be a 'good thing', but what does it really mean for you in your practice as a counsellor? What is being required of you here and why has it been selected by the great and the good of the counselling world to be included in this list? Perhaps it has something to do with being genuine. During the process of contracting you will be laying out before the client what you are going to be doing within the therapeutic relationship, what the client can expect from you and what you expect from them. You will need to be open and transparent with the client about the limits to confidentiality, for example, and to be clear about such matters as payment. The client needs to be able to trust that you will do your very best to conscientiously carry out your side of the agreement, working in the way that you say you are going to in a trustworthy manner.

The client needs also to experience you as a real person, not someone hiding behind a role or a title. How you manifest this will to some extent depend on your orientation.

Integrity – commitment to being moral in dealing with others, personal straightforwardness, honesty and coherence

As a counsellor, you will not only be dealing with clients, but with other professionals and with your peers in the counselling world. You will most likely be engaged in financial arrangements, contracts, EAPs and other points at which your practice touches the world outside your counselling room. Not infrequently in the course of your career, you may find yourself being the ambassador for the counselling profession. It is not at all uncommon for a counsellor to be part of a team where you are the sole representative of the profession. When thinking about integrity it is important, therefore, to think not only about its ramifications within the therapeutic relationship but also within this wider context.

Case study 3.1   Marion

Marion is a counsellor at a doctor's surgery. At a staff meeting the receptionists and the practice manager begin to complain about a patient, Carl, who is one of Marion's clients. He is always in the surgery, making demands and taking up time. He is constantly bothering the doctors. All in all, they are really fed up with him. Marion remains silent. She does not join in or comment at all, despite several invitations to do so. Nor does she comment on what the receptionists are doing. When one of the GPs asks her directly if she is working with Carl and how he is doing, she replies that a referral has been made to her and she has responded to it. She makes no further comment. After the meeting, the GP who referred Carl to her comes to speak to her privately. Marion tells him that Carl has been given appointments, which he is keeping and that they are working well together. Marion notices that her referral rate goes up after the meeting, not just from the GP who sent her Carl, but from all the GPs. A day or so after the meeting, the practice manager approaches Marion in the coffee room and tells her that her son is very depressed after a divorce. Could Marion work with him in her private practice? Marion says that would not really be appropriate, as she is working in the same practice as his mother, but she would be happy to make a referral, to a colleague whose good work she knows.

Let us now consider what integrity means within the therapeutic relationship itself. The issue of the power imbalance between counsellor and client is significant here. One-to-one counselling is exactly that, two people sitting in a room together with no observers, no third party present, one of whom holds considerably more informal power than the other. It would be very easy in this circumstance for the relationship to slide into one that has become abusive. The responsibility for establishing and maintaining the contract and the boundaries lies firmly with the counsellor. Integrity is crucial here. It would be the counsellor's integrity that would have you running hot foot to your supervisor to work through issues such as your attraction to a client, or the client's obvious attraction to you. It would be this integrity that would absolutely prevent you from acting on this attraction and make you extremely vigilant about your behaviour towards this client. It would also encourage you to think carefully about how your own emotional and sexual needs are being met, so that you are not looking to clients to meet them for you.

It would be this integrity that would make you prioritise the well-being of your client over your own financial or other requirements so that, for example, the number of sessions a client has and the need to make endings are solely therapeutic considerations and not influenced by your need to make the mortgage payment or even to accumulate hours for the clinical placement or accreditation requirements.

Your integrity would ensure that you make proper use of your supervision to see that you are providing the best possible service to your client, that you bring your issues and difficulties to supervision. Your supervisor relies on your integrity for this. She can only work with what you bring her and if you are not honest and straightforward about your struggles, how can she help you to overcome them? Every supervisor worth her salt worries about the 'hidden client', the client that the supervisee for some reason doesn't want to present. Perhaps it is because you don't feel you are doing a good job with this client and you don't want your supervisor to pick up on this and see you in a negative light. Perhaps you think you are doing a really good job with this client and so you don't need supervision on this work. This is where the possibility of collusion and over-identification with the client must be thought about. Every client deserves to come under the scrutiny of the supervision process, honestly and openly, and it is the integrity of the counsellor that is called upon here. For supervision to be effective the counsellor needs to be honest, open and willing to take responsibility for herself and her work.

Integrity is also central to the maintenance of confidentiality. Maintaining confidentiality is a huge subject for counsellors and you need to inform yourself about this so that you are clear not only about your moral and ethical responsibilities but also about the law (see Jenkins, 2007; Bond, 2010; Bond and Mitchels, 2008). However, let's broaden our thinking even further. As a counsellor, you will hear many things which in another context might be thought of as salacious or even just very juicy gossip. It is very tempting perhaps when discussing work with peers, fellow students, etc. to share some of this, suitably anonymised. However, your integrity should make you question why you are doing this. Is it to deepen your understanding or help you to provide a better service to the client? Is it to contribute to a case discussion and facilitate the learning of your peers? You must question yourself about these kinds of disclosures using your integrity to really challenge yourself and your motives.

Your counsellor's integrity will also ensure that your counselling work is taken seriously by others. It will spur you on to stand up for proper standards for counselling work. For example, the counsellor in the GP's practice who refuses to work in a different room every week, or in the stock cupboard, because she knows this would impact upon the work and on the experience of the clients. She is willing to be seen as 'inflexible' or 'difficult' rather than allow the work to suffer, as she knows it will. Another example might be the counsellor in the college who will not discuss his work with a student with the tutor, without the client's permission, even when pressure is put upon him. Or the counsellor in the agency, who despite being fairly junior, questions the arrangements for keeping notes in an unlocked cabinet where security cannot be guaranteed. Or the counsellor who is willing to blow the whistle about the unethical practice of another, but do so with respect and compassion for all concerned.

Other professionals, if they experience you, the counsellor, as a person with integrity, will be more likely both to work co-operatively with you and to trust you and what you do, even if their agenda is different from yours.

Resilience – the capacity to work with the client's concerns without being personally diminished

Counselling work can be very emotionally taxing. Generally speaking, clients don't come into counselling to talk about what is going right in their lives. As a counsellor you have to be willing to hear, with compassion and empathy, some very difficult things. Counselling is not the only profession where the practitioner has to listen to difficult and painful stories, but whereas in some other contexts adopting a dispassionate and detached position might be the appropriate response, as a counsellor it would be a disaster. You have to listen with your heart as well as your ears and, while you have to maintain your objectivity, you cannot do this by not allowing yourself to feel and experience the emotional impact of what your client is saying. It is painful to listen to a person expressing intense emotions about a bereavement, or to witness the damage to someone's psychological well-being from the experience of childhood abuse or neglect. It is sometimes a little daunting to feel the impact of another person's anger in the room or their sense of hopelessness.

Through experience, training and proper professional support you will learn to cope with this, and counsellors do develop the capacity to be wholly emotionally present for someone during the therapeutic hour and then let it go as the person walks out of the room. However, even the most experienced counsellors will occasionally get caught and find themselves thinking or even worrying about a particular client while doing the garden, eating lunch or, worse still, lying in bed at night. This could be because the client's material resonates too closely with their own. So, for example, if the client is talking about the experience of being bullied and you yourself have unresolved issues of your own related to bullying, this might chip away at your ability to contain the work of this particular client. At first you may not even be conscious of what is going on for you and you will be using your supervision to help you to identify why you can't let go of this client between sessions. If the emotion scab that has been inadvertently knocked off is a big one, then it might be the business of personal therapy rather than supervision. It could also be that you are tired and run down and ready for a break. Sometimes, it is just simply the magnitude and depth of the client's problem and pain that is hard to let go of. However, as a rule, you do have to be able to contain your own emotional response to clients' material and their emotions, and you need to ensure that you have a support system and appropriate strategies for so doing. If the personal cost to you is too high, you would only damage and diminish yourself and this would make you ineffective as a practitioner.

Respect – showing appropriate esteem to others and their understanding of themselves

This quality requires the counsellor to view every person as having an intrinsic value, just by dint of being human, not because of the position they might hold in the world, or the way they might look or present, but just because they are another person. To offer respect of the kind required here, you would need to be able to make at least some separation between the person themself and their behaviour. We are all more than our behaviour. If you are honest with yourself, there are probably things that you do, or have done, about which you are not proud and by which you would not like to be defined.

You may well dislike or disapprove of a person's behaviour, but that is different from disrespecting the person themself. For example, if a client presented with a gambling problem and told you that they are spending most of their wages on gambling, which means that they are not paying the rent or giving their partner sufficient money to pay for necessities for themselves and their children, you might think this is a terrible way to behave. However, if you are incapable of respecting the client, as a person who is struggling with a problem and is coming to you in order to try to help themself, if you cannot see the vulnerable human being deserving of your respect underneath the behaviour, then you are unlikely to be of much use to them.

Respecting a client also means accepting where they are in terms of their development and self-awareness. This involves a willingness to work at the client's pace and to appreciate that they may or may not be able to make use of your intervention, however insightful or brilliant it may be. A person has to be ready for a new awareness before they can allow it in, or take advantage of it, and sometimes you have to be willing to try an intervention and then just let it go, if the client cannot make use of it. Perhaps you have sown a seed which might develop a little later.

Being respectful about and towards clients will manifest in the way you speak about them when discussing work with supervisors or peers, not blaming them automatically if the work is not going well. Sometimes, among groups of professionals, there develops a culture of speaking disrespectfully and even cynically about the client group. Perhaps this is a way of dealing with the tensions and stresses of a job, but this is something that a counsellor needs to think carefully about before engaging in. There may be times within the supervision process when it is quite appropriate and indeed necessary for the counsellor to explore negative feelings about a client, but this is quite different from the kind of disrespectful banter mentioned above.

Humility – the ability to accurately assess and acknowledge one's own strengths and weaknesses

It would be very easy as a counsellor to develop an inflated sense of your own importance and value. Because it is so rare in our society for people to be properly listened to, clients can be inordinately grateful and sometimes be full of praise. Being a counsellor is a very privileged position and it is one where you will experience relatively little scrutiny in terms of your actual counselling work, so keeping a level head and awareness of your own strengths and weaknesses is particularly important. In Western society we tend to value assertiveness, standing up for yourself and even being willing to blow your own trumpet, and it would be easy, from this perspective, to dismiss or undervalue the quality of humility. However, humility is not about doing yourself down or undervaluing yourself – it is about being realistic and honest about yourself, your experience and your capability.

An example of how this quality might come into play might be the thorny question about when it is appropriate for a counsellor to consider going into private practice. Is it really appropriate for a newly qualified counsellor, however talented, to set up in private practice without the safety net and structure afforded by an agency, where other more experienced practitioners are around to support the counsellor and assess clients? A little humility might well temper the enthusiasm here and remind the inexperienced counsellor that should they fall into the many pitfalls that surround private practice, it is likely to be the clients that suffer the most. There is, after all, no substitute for experience.

Humility will help you to identify the kind of clients with whom you are less likely to work well. You will be able to refer them on without judging either them or yourself. Knowing when to refer on is an important skill. Even very experienced counsellors will have some kinds of clients with whom they might struggle. For example, if your own private life has been blighted by the alcohol issues of another, then perhaps you would struggle to work with someone presenting this issue to you in counselling. Having the humility to accept your own struggle and referring the client on to another counsellor could be the best course of action.

Humility would also ensure that you were willing to bring struggles and issues to your supervisor, without wishing to maintain a professional front behind which to hide. Your supervisor can validate you for what you do well, but you can only really learn from what you have got wrong and talked through to see how you might have done things differently. Paradoxically, a great strength can be having the humility to admit to and confront your own weakness.

Competence – the effective deployment of the skills and knowledge needed to do what is required

It is interesting to see competence listed among the personal moral qualities required of a counsellor. It could be argued that competence itself is not a moral issue and perhaps what is meant here is acknowledgement of your own level of competence and a commitment to increasing your knowledge and skills base through training and supervision. Knowingly working beyond your competence could be judged as an immoral thing to do, because the possibility of actually harming the client is greatly increased. However, this is not as simple a question as it might initially seem. Imagine the situation where you, as the counsellor working in an agency, are given a client who at assessment presented with issues of self-esteem. This seems well within your level of competence and experience, but as you work with this client over the weeks you begin to suspect that they have quite serious and possibly undiagnosed mental health issues. While you might have sufficient knowledge and skills to recognise these issues, you do not have the training or competence to deal with them. What do you do? You have already established a good working relationship with this client and your concern is that if you now end the relationship they will feel rejected and that their trust has been abused. There is not an obvious or straightforward way out of this situation. You would need to take it to your supervision and back to your line manager at the agency, but you simply cannot ignore the issue of your own level of competence here. You may need to refer the client on to someone with the skills and experience needed to work with someone presenting with such mental health issues. Making appropriate referrals is an important part of the work of a counsellor and it is sometimes the most helpful and appropriate intervention you could make for the long-term well-being of the client.

As a counsellor you have the responsibility to keep your skills and knowledge up to date by CPD, reading and research. It is an absolute mistake to imagine that at the end of your training you are a fully formed finished product. In fact, the opposite is true – you are just beginning what will be a journey that carries on throughout your career. Competence is something we are always striving towards. This is also a good example of how these qualities interact with one another because honest assessment of your competence requires the application of both humility and integrity.

Fairness – the consistent application of appropriate criteria to inform decisions and actions

The inclusion of this quality in our list challenges you to think about such issues as access to services within the agency or service for which you work as a counsellor. It would be comforting to think that anyone needing the services of a counsellor would have free access to such a service, but of course this is not the case. People who have the means to pay for their own therapy can do so and can also have the luxury of choice as to what sort of counselling they receive and from whom. However, for many people, the only way they can receive counselling is through an agency or, if they are very lucky indeed, through the health service. They might also have access to an EAP through their place of work or, if they are a student, the counselling service at their college or university. However, even if they are successful in accessing one of these services, someone else will probably decide who they will see, what kind of therapy they will have and how many sessions they will be allowed. A commitment to fairness and anti-discriminatory practice is therefore particularly important and is the responsibility of every counsellor working within a service.

Case study 3.2   A moral challenge

You are working in a counselling agency as one of the few paid counsellors. Most of the clients are seen by counselling students on placement. There is fierce competition for these placements as your agency has a ready and consistent supply of clients. You notice that the placements are always given to students from one particular training establishment, which is well known and quite prestigious. Most of the students who come from this training do well in the agency because they are well trained and prepared for the work. There is another training agency in your area, which is much less prestigious and less expensive. They have students from a different socioeconomic group and more people from minorities. The clinical lead at the placement is reluctant to give these students a chance, because she is not so impressed with their training. She says she knows the course at the first training establishment because she trained there herself. She emphasises that the most important thing is the service to the clients, so she needs well-trained students who know what they are doing. You can appreciate this, but you are left feeling uncomfortable. Should you challenge this informal policy?

Wisdom – possession of sound judgement that informs practice

Wisdom is often associated with age and experience, but this is perhaps a misconception. Wisdom is an attribute which is quite hard to define. Is it some kind of combination of intelligence and common sense perhaps? But then wisdom is not just about the head, it is also about the heart. To be wise within a counselling context means that something beyond your training and theoretical understanding is informing what you do. It is about seeing the whole picture and the person in front of you in the context of their life as they live it. It is about fitting the theory to the person and not the other way around. Counselling can be quite a profound experience, not only for the client but also for the counsellor. Not only do you have to let the client be as they are in the moment, but you have to let yourself be. In doing so you will be able to draw on your instinctive responses to the other person, not necessarily acting out of them or even sharing them, but being conscious of them and allowing them to inform your responses (Mearns and Thorne, 2000; Mearns and Cooper, 2005).

Sound judgement also relates to the pacing of a session, knowing when to press forward with something and, more importantly, when to let something go. Wisdom will help you to know when to take a risk with a client and when what is needed is a much more tentative approach. Wisdom will also help you to accept the limitations of what you do. Counselling is not about making people better or taking away their pain; it is about helping people to tolerate their own feelings and enhance their understanding. Like any other kind of intervention, sometimes it works and sometimes it doesn't.

REFLECTION POINT

- How would you define wisdom in this context? Think of any occasions when you have witnessed it, perhaps from your own therapist.

Courage – the capacity to act in spite of known fears, risks and uncertainty

It is really heartening that courage is a quality included in the BACP's framework. To the lay person it might seem a little strange; counselling is, after all, just two people in a room talking to one another. How could you possibly need courage in that circumstance? In reality, there will be many occasions in the course of your career when you will be called upon to show courage. Imagine a situation where you are working with a client who is suicidal. You believe that this client could well take their own life; however, you do have a really sound therapeutic relationship and they do trust you, although it has taken many months to build that trust. They are at present in crisis and it is just at the time when a holiday break is coming up. You have discussed the possibility of speaking to their GP but they are adamantly against that, saying that if you break their confidence they will immediately end their counselling with you. You spend a good deal of time talking this through with your supervisor and you decide that, in this particular situation, the risk to the client is greater if you break confidence because you are the only person with whom they are sharing their suicidal ideation and if they end their relationship with you, they will be completely isolated. Should you talk to their GP there is nothing that can be done without the client's co-operation because they are certainly not mentally ill. You have discussed the up-coming break with the client and they have agreed not to attempt to end their life during this period and you have discussed how they might take care of themselves while you are away. So, you have thought the situation through carefully and weighed up the odds. In discussion with your supervisor you have decided on a course of action, which is not to talk to the client's GP, but it is a big risk. What if you are wrong and the client doesn't keep to the agreement with you not to attempt suicide? What if they do actually kill themself? In a situation like this you will need your courage, the courage to take a calculated risk and to live with the consequences of it. You will need the courage to stand by your decision, accepting the anxiety it may create in you.

In one sense, every intervention is a risk. If a client is going to move forward they will need to confront difficult feelings and you are going to be a part of that confrontation process. Challenging your client takes courage as well as confidence in what you are doing. It is sometimes much easier to collude. All counselling takes place on a continuum between challenge and support, and both are important aspects of the work. You can be cosy and supportive with your client but this will not help them without appropriate challenge, just as challenge is not helpful without support. Russell and Dexter make this point very clearly – *Not to challenge is to do the client a disservice; counselling cannot move forward without it* (2008, p94).

In thinking about risk taking we are not talking here of reckless behaviour decided upon as a whim. We are talking about informed decision making, but as the counsellor you will still sometimes need to trust your instinct and go with your gut – and that does take courage. In the counselling room you haven't got the time to refer to literature or even check things out with your supervisor. To a large extent you are on your own and without courage you will very likely miss important opportunities to really help your client move forward. Much, of course, will depend upon the skill and sensitivity with which you deliver your interventions involving a risk, but without having the courage to embrace uncertainty and take a risk it is quite likely that nothing very important is going to happen.

Case study 3.3   Eve

Eve is a fairly experienced counsellor working in private practice. A client, Anna, is referred to Eve by a GP. Anna is 18 and has left university after just one term. She has a history of anxiety and depression and she has also made three quite serious suicide attempts, the last one being before she left university. She has a good relationship with her GP who made the referral. Anna's parents will pay for the counselling. The contract is for long-term work. Anna is on anti-depressant medication, which is being monitored by the GP.

Although Anna is committed to the work, she is far from easy to work with. She finds it very difficult to talk about herself and is generally withdrawn. However, she never misses a session, always arrives on time and is obviously anxious when it comes to breaks in the work for holidays, etc. One problem Eve encounters quite early on is Anna's mother who telephones fairly regularly asking for updates and reassurance as to how the work is going. Eve does not give any information to the mother and does tell Anna when the mother has rung. Anna is concerned about confidentiality, although she is happy for Eve to liaise with her GP as long as she is party to any communication, but certainly not with her mother.

Some weeks Anna hardly speaks at all and Eve shares with her supervisor that on these occasions it is like 'pulling teeth'. Eve worries about her work with Anna, but is reassured both by Anna's obvious commitment to the work and by the GP who tells Eve that Anna has never managed to engage with any other therapist for this long before and that she believes this is progress in itself.

As the weeks go on Anna does open up a little more easily. She works on her relationship with her mother and on her self-image and self-destructive behaviour. Eve also supports Anna while she is gradually coming off the anti-depressants. Anna decides that she does want to go back to university, although to a different city and on a completely different course, this time one she has chosen herself. Together, they work on strategies for managing Anna's feelings and Anna asks Eve to write a referral letter to the counselling services at the university.

After nine months of work Anna leaves to continue her education. Eve thinks Anna is still vulnerable although she has made good progress in their work together. She has worries about Anna, which she shares with her supervisor. However, when Anna finally comes for her last session, she is really quite animated (unusual for her) about how much she has gained from her work with Eve and she thanks Eve for being there for her all of these months, allowing her space and not pushing her. It is a very positive ending.

ACTIVITY 3.2

- What qualities do you think Eve needs for her work with Anna to be successful?
- What qualities do you think Eve has displayed?

OTHER QUALITIES THAT COULD BE USEFUL TO THE COUNSELLOR

Although the *Ethical Framework* provides us with quite a comprehensive list, there are one or two other qualities that I think would be helpful to the counsellor.

Open-mindedness

One quality worth considering here is open-mindedness, which is a willingness to respectfully accept the way of thinking and being of others as well as their life choices and styles. This is quite crucial to the work of a counsellor. Cooper (2008), when discussing research relating to the personality of the counsellor and its relationship to outcomes, says that although clients tend to rate personality as one of the most important factors in the success of counselling, there is little research evidence to support this. He does, however, make an exception.

> *There is some evidence to suggest that therapists who have more dogmatic or controlling 'introjects' (i.e. unconscious attitudes or ideas) tend to have poorer client outcomes.*
>
> (Henry et al., 1990, cited in Cooper, M, 2008)

As a counsellor you will be called upon to work with many different kinds of people, with many different lifestyles, and a genuine openness to other ways of living seems to be helpful and facilitative. Clients quickly sense if you are censorious about lifestyles or if you have an agenda of your own. One issue where this may frequently come to light is abortion. If you are a person who holds a strong pro-life position, for example, and if for you this is a matter of conscience, then could you really be totally open to a client who wanted an abortion or who was undecided and needed the space to work through her options? As a counsellor you would need to be able to put aside your own position and be truly objective, without any hidden agenda, because clients are extremely sensitive to what is going on beneath the surface.

Many people in the counselling world feel anxious about what has become known as the Christian Counselling Movement. This is because of its pro-life stance and the homophobic position many of its number have adopted, seeing lesbian and gay lifestyles as sinful and unnatural or homosexuality as a condition from which people can, and should, be cured. Having such a fundamentalist mindset is not congruent with the ideals of mainstream counselling and is unlikely to be of any benefit to anyone, unless the client held identical values and beliefs, and even then it is questionable. In April 2010, the High Court upheld the sacking by Relate of the couple counsellor, Gary McFarland, and refused his application to appeal their ruling. He had refused to offer his services to gay couples seeking sex therapy. The court upheld the principle that someone offering a public service cannot unfairly discriminate on the grounds of sexual orientation, even if this conflicts with his religious beliefs. It is, however, important to make a distinction between this movement and people who think in this way, and the many excellent counselling services that are supported and staffed by counsellors who hold Christian beliefs themselves but have no desire to proselytise or to unfairly discriminate against anyone.

A sense of humour

This is perhaps a tricky one. On the one hand, psychodynamic thinking suggests that humour can be a defence mechanism, a way in which we can sidestep and deny our emotional reality. Obviously, the counselling room is not the place for stand-up comedy or joke telling and it would be completely inappropriate for you to collude with the client in laughing at themself or indeed making light of their own situation or emotions. In fact, you would probably want to challenge this behaviour in your client and bring to their attention what they are doing. However, there are occasions where humour and laughter do have a place. There may be a moment where a client is able to stand back from their own behaviour, perhaps see it in another light and recognise a funny side. It would be quite appropriate for the counsellor to share this moment and such an experience can be cathartic in itself.

A sense of humour and of the absurd also acts as a good counterbalance to any tendency you might have to see yourself in a grandiose manner, as the expert on human kind. Cultivating the ability to laugh with yourself, as opposed to at yourself, will enable you to cope with your own mistakes and inadequacies with gentleness. It is true that, just as some of the things you hear are very sad and tragic, some are also quite funny and even absurd, and every experienced counsellor will identify with having a little private smile to themselves on occasions about the contents of a session. Appropriateness is the key here, but your being po-faced and overly serious will not help your client.

Being genuinely caring

Mick Cooper (2008) in his book on counselling research, references John McLeod (2006) who has argued that clients particularly value a sense that their therapist genuinely cares about them. This seems like an important quality to include therefore. It is a quality that might encompass several of the others mentioned above, such as empathy and respect. It is the ability to convey to clients that their well-being really matters to the counsellor and it is likely to manifest as a kind of warmth. Caring in the context of the therapeutic relationship is qualitatively different from caring for a friend or a partner, for example, where you are likely to be invested in how they live their lives. Caring for a client is much more about your way of being during the sessions. This kind of caring does not conflict with objectivity. You are not going to express it physically or manifest it by remembering the client's birthday or commenting on her new haircut. However, you are not likely to be facilitative to your client if she experiences you as cold or bored or indifferent to her suffering. It is also about the consistency of caring. Many clients end up in therapy because they have never experienced consistent caring from another human being, caring that comes without expectations, reservations or conditions. It is not the job of the counsellor to provide either praise or blame.

Caring for clients does not conflict with the therapeutic framework and boundaries. In fact, maintaining the framework and boundaries is often the most caring thing to do, as long as they are serving the work and not the other way around. It is not dependent on orientation either. It is, for example, perfectly possible to be highly psychodynamic in your approach and still convey your caring to your client.

This caring, however, does come with a bit of a cost. If you talk to experi-enced counsellors they will tell you that something you have to learn to cope with is letting clients go. You have been seeing a client weekly for some time and you have genuinely cared about them. You have listened to their story, witnessed their emotions and seen them grow and develop, perhaps even heal as a result of their work with you and then, like a bird flying the nest, they are gone. You may never ever see them or hear of them again. You are left wondering how things have gone for them, how they are doing, and you have to learn to manage this in yourself. Part of this kind of caring is being able to let go when the time comes.

Positivity

In suggesting that you think about positivity as a useful quality no one is thinking that you need to be a raving optimist believing that 'all is for the best in the best of all possible worlds' in order to be a good counsellor. It is more that you need to believe that, given the right circumstances and support, people can come to terms with themselves, change and make their lives better. If you really believe that things are predestined, or fixed, then what would be the point of putting clients through what can be a painful and demanding process? If being a counsellor for any length of time teaches you anything, it is something about the ability of the human spirit to triumph over disaster and adversity. You will hear some terribly sad stories of people's lives, but you will also witness clients who have had a dreadful start in life, unloved, neglected and abused, who try really hard not to repeat patterns and to be loving partners and parents, and to make a contribution to society. You will witness extraordinary acts of forgiveness and courage. The ability to believe in another person and have confidence in them, even when they are struggling to have confidence in themself, can be very facilitative.

Patience

The final quality we are going to consider is patience because, in truth, as a counsellor you will often need a good deal of this quality. In the world of short-term counselling perhaps it is not so valuable, but when working longer term with some clients you are going to need to be able to go at the client's own pace, which may seem to you to be very slow. You have to wait for the client to be ready to take on and respond to your interventions, and they may be slow to gain awareness of what might seem blindingly obvious to you. However, pushing or hurrying a client is not only clumsy and unhelpful, it may even be harmful and bullying. We have our defences for very good reasons and we will let them down when we are ready. If, as the counsellor, you force the pace you may leave your client feeling exposed and vulnerable. The skilful counsellor needs patience and a willingness to wait until the moment is right.

ACTIVITY 3.3

- Are there any qualities that you would like to add to those outlined above? Make a list with your arguments for including them.

NATURE OR NURTURE?

At the start of this chapter we raised the question as to whether a counsellor is born or made; in other words, are there some people who, even if they were to undergo a very good and thorough training programme, could never quite make it because of personality or personal traits or qualities, or perhaps more importantly because of what they may lack as people? To a large extent, this is purely academic and you will come to your own conclusion. Tutors involved in the selection of students to train as counsellors often do spot innate potential in candidates, but it is also common for students who do not appear to have so much to offer at the outset, to make expediential progress and outshine their peers who seemed like the 'naturals'. You would probably not choose to be a counsellor if you weren't interested in people, and to get through the training with all the commitment and sacrifices it requires, you have to be both enthusiastic and tenacious. Being psychologically minded is a help, as is having a philosophical bent, being interested in the meaning people attribute to their experience. There are also people who tutors would instinctively feel would not make good candidates, but this is most often related to where the person is in their life at the time of application, rather than anything innate.

CHAPTER SUMMARY

In this chapter we have explored the personal qualities that a person needs to become and to work as a counsellor. We have looked at the list provided by the BACP in its *Ethical Framework* and we have looked at some other qualities that might be helpful in addition. Of course, these lists, though extensive, are not all encompassing and you may well have thought of additional qualities that you feel would be conducive to the work.

Although it is rather an old-fashioned thought, perhaps counselling is a vocation as much as a profession. It is certainly not a job people would take up if their aim was to get rich quick and so the satisfaction that is to be gained from it is more than pecuniary. Huge trust is placed in the counsellor by both the client and by the wider community, so it is very important that the counsellor behaves not just professionally but also in what might be described as in a decent and moral way. Just as we would expect high standards of a doctor or a lawyer, for example, so we should be able to trust the counsellor to behave appropriately, always with the well-being of the client uppermost in their mind. While none of us is perfect, thinking about how we are and how we behave and aspiring to these qualities can only be helpful.

We have discussed:

- the personal and moral qualities for counsellors as defined in the *Ethical Framework* of the BACP;
- practical applications for these qualities;
- some additional qualities that counsellors might find helpful;
- how these qualities are developed and enhanced;
- the nature/nurture debate with regard to personal qualities.

SUGGESTED FURTHER READING

Mearns, D and Cooper, M (2005) *Working at Relational Depth in Counselling and Psychotherapy*. London: Sage.

This is an excellent and insightful book about the therapeutic encounter between counsellor and client.

Russell, J and Dexter, G (2008) *Blank Minds and Sticky Moments in Counselling*, 2nd edition. London: Sage.

Chapter 4 on challenging is relevant here. The whole book is interesting and an easy read.

CHAPTER 4

Ethical practice

CORE KNOWLEDGE

- This chapter outlines the importance of ethics to the profession of counselling and examines the development of an ethical approach to counselling and psychotherapy work.
- You will gain an understanding of the core values of counselling and psychotherapy, as identified in the BACP's *Ethical Framework*, and what these mean in practice.

INTRODUCTION

In Chapter 3 we considered the personal and moral qualities which are required of you as a counsellor. These form one of the three pillars of the BACP's *Ethical Framework for Good Practice in Counselling and Psychotherapy*. In this chapter, we will be looking at the other two pillars on which the framework is built, which are the values of counselling and psychotherapy and the ethical principles. You will be thinking about the interplay between these three pillars and how together they combine to underpin good practice. In order to do this you will be asked to reflect upon three case studies based on ethical dilemmas and consider how you might apply the principles to come to a decision about what would constitute good practice in these cases.

AN ETHICAL APPROACH

All professions have a code of ethics or an ethical framework that serve several distinct purposes. The first is to guide and inform practitioners and to help them to approach their work in an ethical manner and the second is to provide a benchmark against which a practitioner's professional behaviour can be judged when it is called into question as a result of a complaint. Another is that the code or framework is a way in which the professional organisation sets out its stall to the public, this is who we are, these are our values, this is what you can expect from us, etc. It serves as a kind as banner behind which the troops can rally.

The *Ethical Framework for Good Practice in Counselling and Psychotherapy* was first published in late 2001 (most recently revised in February 2010), and it both replaced and amalgamated all the previous codes of practice of the BACP. Prior to the framework, the organisation had separate codes for different aspects of its members' work so, for example, there was a code for counsellors, one for supervisors, one for trainers, etc. All of these were incorporated into the one *Ethical Framework*, but its emergence signified something much more important than that: it signified a kind of professional 'coming of age'.

The difference that was so significant here between the previous codes and the framework was in the thinking that underpinned them and in what was expected of members adopting them. The adoption of the *Ethical Framework* has put counselling as a profession at the vanguard of ethical thinking because it was a moving away from a prescriptive approach – this is what you must do, this is what you may not do – to an approach which required every member of the BACP to engage with the framework and to work out their response to every ethical issue on a case by case basis. The framework requires you to think for yourself, martial your arguments, which are informed by and related to the framework, and then adopt your ethical position, which you must be able to defend before your peers. It allows for the possibility that two counsellors, when faced with an ethical dilemma, may well, after thought and deliberation, come to quite different con-clusions. There is rarely a straightforward and simple right or wrong response. The move to the *Ethical Framework* has taken away the safety and security of a 'ten commandments' approach. It requires you to engage with it, think for yourself and then, most importantly, accept responsibility for the actions you take, based on your conclusions. In other words, it requires you to be a professional grown-up! If you have a philosophical bent and you enjoy engaging on this level, with grey areas and uncertainties, you will value the framework and enjoy working with it. If, however, you prefer everything to be straightforward and clear cut, and you would rather inhabit a world full of black and white, it may prove to be more of a challenge for you.

Bond (2010) argues that the framework addresses several different audi-ences: first, the clients, whose interests it is meant to serve first and foremost; second, the membership of the professional body itself, in this case the BACP, whose members agree to observe it and be held accountable if they fail to do so; third, the professionals working alongside the counsellors in interdisciplinary teams; and fourth, what Bond describes as the gatekeepers, such as politicians, policy makers and commercial managers who determine which services attract funding. What unites these audiences, according to Bond, is:

> *a concern about the ethical integrity of the services being provided. A published statement of ethical commitment by a professional body on behalf of its membership provides evidence of a collective commitment to being ethical.*

(2010, p63)

THE VALUES OF COUNSELLING AND PSYCHOTHERAPY

If an ethical framework is to have any meaning for an organisation like the BACP, it has to be based on a set of values that we all hold in common. These values are a unifying factor; they are what bring us together as a community of professionals. Part of the obligation of membership of the BACP is a commitment to uphold these values. There are nine fundamental values, identified in the ethical framework, which we will now consider individually and to which, as a member of the BACP, you are required to be committed.

Respecting human rights and dignity

This will have implications in the way in which you, as the counsellor, deal with not only your clients but also your colleagues and indeed the general public. It is a commitment to a way of being with other people both on a micro and a macro level. It could be seen as a political position and many counsellors see their work as a political activity in the broader sense of the word.

Ensuring the integrity of the practitioner–client relationship

This value relates to the special and particular nature of the therapeutic relationship and the responsibility you hold as a counsellor to protect and sustain that relationship, both in terms of your work with the client and also in your interactions with other professionals and the outside world. This honours the trust the client places in you in making themselves vulnerable within your working relationship.

Enhancing the quality of professional knowledge and its application

There are two elements to this value. The first is a requirement to enhance your own individual knowledge and skills base continuously, by means of training, professional development, reading, research, supervision and contact with your peers, etc. Second, implicit in this value, there is the requirement that we work together as a profession, sharing and building on each other's knowledge and experience through such activities as engaging in and disseminating practitioner research. We are aiming as a profession to get better at what we do by continuously developing and assessing our work, always with the aim of providing an improved service to our clients. Perhaps this value also challenges you to think about your own contribution to this and ask if it is acceptable to simply sit back and let your colleagues take on this responsibility.

Alleviating personal distress and suffering

This value needs some thinking about if you are not to see yourself as the caped crusader, putting the world to rights. You are not a doctor who is going to go out there and do things to people to make them better. You are going to arm yourself with a set of skills and a knowledge base, which will enable you to help people to help themselves to tolerate their own feelings, make appropriate life choices, etc. Because you hold this value, you will be working behind the scenes in your clients' lives through a process of facilitation and enablement.

Fostering a sense of self that is meaningful to the person(s) concerned

The phrasing of this value acknowledges that a sense of self may be a cultural construction and not necessarily the Eurocentric individualistic concept we might first think of. However, whether it may be, for example, the need for me to know where you begin and I end, or the need to know how I, the individual, fit into and harmonise with my community, nevertheless a good sense of self seems to be helpful to people in living a meaningful and fulfilled life. It is, therefore, a value we hold as counsellors that we should work to promote in our clients.

Increasing personal effectiveness

Implicit in this value is the understanding that the process of counselling may well have wider implications than simply addressing whatever the presenting issue may be. Through the process, the client may actually acquire transferable skills, such as assertion, articulation of feelings and needs, and other forms of communication, which may be helpful outside the counselling room and may increase personal effectiveness. As counsellors we would see this as a valuable outcome.

Enhancing the quality of relationships between people

Working with people to help them improve their relationships with others is one of the most important areas of work for a counsellor. You will be doing this not only by helping them to explore their existing relationships and the issues and difficulties they may be having, or have had in the past in creating and maintaining relationships, but in your interactions with your clients you will be modelling a way of relating and a way of being within a relationship which will hopefully be helpful to your clients and will enhance the way they are able to relate to others themselves.

Appreciating the variety of human experience and culture

In committing to this value you, as the counsellor, assert that you recognise that clients may well come from cultures and lifestyles that are very different from your own and that you will approach these differences with both an open mind and an open heart. It requires you to value and respect other people's ways of living and of seeing the world, as they present themselves to you in your counselling room.

Striving for fair and adequate provision of counselling and psychotherapy services

This value underpins anti-discriminatory practice. It too has political undertones. It is why many experienced counsellors, in private practice, offer their services as senior counsellors or supervisors in voluntary agencies, or serve in some capacity on the various committees and working parties of the BACP. This is not a fair world and the provision of services is not based on need as we might all like it to be. This value drives the desire to do something about inequality within our own sphere of influence.

REFLECTION POINT

You will have your own value system, which may well be related both to your background and upbringing, and your personal philosophical, and possibly religious, standpoint.

- How do the values of the BACP, which we have been considering above, dovetail or clash with your own value system?

Thinking about your own values and also your willingness to commit to the values of the BACP is a really important exercise in terms of ethical practice because these two sets of values will underpin your work as a counsellor and will sustain you when times are hard, as sometimes they inevitably are in this work.

ETHICAL PRINCIPLES OF COUNSELLING AND PSYCHOTHERAPY

Ethical principles are the basis on which you will make and justify your decisions and actions as a counsellor. As such, they are extremely important. Some ethical issues are clear and straightforward, and in these situations the ethical principles laid out below complement and support one another. However, there are also occasions where the principles are impossible to reconcile and you will have to give one precedence over another. For this reason it is vital to familiarise yourself with the six principles as defined by the BACP, so that when you are faced with an ethical dilemma, which you certainly will be at some point in your career, you will already have the tools at hand with which to begin to tackle it.

Fidelity – honouring the trust placed in the practitioner

This principle is largely concerned with the issue of confidentiality, but it does include any situation where trust is an issue and would include, therefore, any occasion in which exploitation of the client is a possibility. Let us start by thinking about confidentiality in this context. The *Ethical Framework* states that in adhering to this principle:

> *Practitioners act in accordance with the trust placed in them; regard confidentiality as an obligation arising from the client's trust: restrict any disclosure of confidential information about clients to furthering the purposes for which it was originally disclosed.*
>
> (BACP, 2010)

Clients do make themselves extremely vulnerable in their relationships with their counsellors. We know many of the secrets of their lives, we see them stripped of their defences, emotional, uncertain, etc. and so it is vitally important that we do honour this trust, by keeping confidence and not exploiting them in any way for our own advantage.

Autonomy – respect for the client's right to be self-governing

This principle is particularly important given the power inequality which, if we are honest, we have to admit is inherent in the counselling relationship, in favour of the counsellor. It allows for the self-determination of the client and challenges the counsellor who seeks to pursue their own agenda in their work with clients. Bond states clearly:

Without a commitment to respect for client autonomy or self determination, counselling would be an ethically compromised and potentially self-diminishing activity for clients.

(2010, p79)

You may not always agree with the course of action your client is taking. On occasions you may see it as potentially disastrous and highly self-destructive, but just as you have the right to make your own choices, so does your client. It is your job simply to help them to explore their options and consider the possible consequences of them.

This principle requires you, as the counsellor, to acknowledge that your client may hold values that are very different from yours, may be less assertive or self-assured and may live their life very differently. Respect for autonomy moves beyond simply refraining from giving advice to your client; it is about making sure that you are not subtly coercing your client, perhaps by means of giving or withholding approval, into doing or being as you think they should do or be. It is all too easy for a counsellor who is not paying attention to this principle, to end up badgering and even bullying a client.

Case study 4.1   Eileen

Eileen came from a strict religious community and was experiencing domestic violence. She went to see Sue for counselling. Sue was very concerned about Eileen and felt that she needed to leave her husband as soon as possible. Sue herself had lived as a single parent and had managed fairly well to bring up her children. In the counselling Sue began to challenge Eileen and, as she perceived Eileen was resisting her challenges, she became stronger and stronger in them. Eileen, who had very low self-esteem, began to feel even worse about herself. Not only had she failed at everything else, now she was failing at counselling and letting Sue down, who was only trying to help her. Had Sue done her homework, she would have learned that if Eileen left her husband, it would have very serious consequences in her community. Unlike Sue, Eileen did not have a profession and would find it very difficult to support herself and her four children. She was at a particularly low ebb and was not feeling resourceful. The pressure that Sue was putting her under, however well intentioned, became yet another problem for Eileen and she dropped out of counselling.

Through supervision Sue began to see what she had done. She had not paid sufficient attention to the differences between herself and her situation, and Eileen and her life. Unintentionally, she had become another person who was bullying Eileen and sadly she had only made her feel worse about herself. Given time, Eileen may well have come to the decision to leave her abusive relationship, but Sue had failed to respect Eileen's autonomy and had begun working to her own agenda, so the chance to help Eileen had been lost.

To work within this principle of autonomy you must be sure that you have your client's informed consent before you begin your work (Jenkins, 2007, p10). This has implications for the way in which you advertise your service, the way you contract with your clients to ensure that they are absolutely clear of what you are offering and what will be expected of them, before they commit to the work. This can raise conflicts for counsellors working in certain settings where the client may not always have a free choice about coming for counselling. One example may be counselling in a school or college. However careful you as the counsellor might have been to make it clear to staff how you operate, it is very likely that an occasion will arise when a client is 'sent for counselling'. Perhaps they have been playing up in the classroom, or they are upset about something and the tutor isn't comfortable dealing with emotional issues and so sends them over to the counsellor without checking if this is what the young person wants to do. The wise counsellor, attending to the principle of autonomy, will acknowledge what has happened, that the client has not freely chosen to be there, explain what they can offer in terms of the service and then allow the young person to decide if they would like to make use of it. The unwise counsellor, ignoring the principle of autonomy and attempting to work without the client's freely given informed consent, is liable to have a very unproductive and frustrating time trying unsuccessfully to work with the 'captive client' who feels intruded upon and disrespected.

You also need to consider the client's autonomy with regard to how you use client material. I may have agreed to be your client, share personal information with you and allow you to take this material to your supervisor in order that you provide me with a better service. However, I have not agreed for you to use my case to illustrate an article you are writing, or for your dissertation, and you would certainly not be respecting my autonomy were you to do so without my informed consent.

The principle of autonomy is multifaceted and has wide implications for many aspects of your counselling practice. It requires much attention and reflection from the counsellor who wishes to ensure ethical practice.

Beneficence – a commitment to promoting a client's well-being

This principle requires you always to have in mind what you consider, in your professional opinion, is in the best interest of the client. A good place to start here is by thinking about yourself and if you are able to offer the service that the client might need. Is it within your level of competence or experience, or would the best interest of the client be served by your referring them on to someone with a specific expertise or greater experience than you currently have? Are you doing everything you can and should be to enhance your knowledge and skills base, through reading and research,

CPD, training, and adequate and appropriate supervision? Are you taking this particular client to your supervisor to ensure their well-being?

The *Ethical Framework* reminds us that when it comes to beneficence, we have a special responsibility towards clients whose *capacity for autonomy is diminished because of immaturity, lack of understanding, extreme distress, serious disturbance or other significant personal constraints* (BACP, 2010). This means that you will be required to make a judgement call, when it comes to clients who are particularly vulnerable because of these reasons, acknowledging at this specific time in their lives that they may not be able to make sound and considered decisions regarding their own welfare or well-being.

REFLECTION POINT

- Thinking about your own practice, could you identify situations where you might decide that a client's capacity for autonomy is diminished?
- How might this impact on your way of working with this client?

Non-maleficence – a commitment to avoiding harm to the client

It is this principle that seeks to avoid exploitation of clients, sexually, financially, emotionally or in any other form. It requires you, as the counsellor, to think about your own fitness to practise. If you are ill or are working through some emotional situation of your own, such as a close bereavement, or if you are overly tired, hung over or in any way intoxicated, then you are probably not in a fit state to see a client and to provide them with the degree of emotional holding that they have every right to expect from you as their counsellor. Just as you would not want a surgeon to operate on you when they are under par, it is inappropriate for you to try to carry out your work. If you are unsure about your own fitness, then the best thing to do is to ask for the help of your supervisor. Sometimes, when the problem is emotional, your own judgement may be impaired a little and it would be very helpful to seek the advice of a person who has both your clients' interests and yours at heart. It can come as a great relief at times of stress to draw on the opinion of another who understands and shares these ethical principles.

Non-maleficence as a principle should also make you think about maintaining appropriate boundaries with your clients. So much malpractice, through which clients get hurt and damaged, starts with boundary violations on the part of the counsellor, through which exploitation of the client emerges and subsequently grows. So, thinking about the importance of good boundaries, why we need them and what purpose they serve is really important for good ethical practice.

Being realistic about your own competence will also help you to avoid harming your clients or indeed yourself as a practitioner. The *Ethical Framework* also mentions the importance of holding appropriate insurance, so that if your practice does fall short of the required standard in any way, you may have at your disposal the means of making at least some form of restitution.

This principle also requires you to think beyond your own practice. As a counsellor you have an ethical responsibility to do something about the malpractice or incompetence of others in the field, if it should come to your attention. If you think the practice of another is either harmful to their clients and potential clients or likely to bring discredit to the profession, then you have an ethical responsibility, under this principle, to do something about it. No one is saying here that you should become a counselling vigilante, rushing around naming and shaming rogue counsellors. In fact, the *Ethical Framework* lays out clearly what your responsibilities are and how you should go about discharging them (see clauses 39–42) and what is clear is that the principle of non-maleficence means that what you absolutely cannot do is put your head in the sand and ignore malpractice. Many a counsellor has had sleepless nights trying to work out the best thing to do about a colleague's malpractice and many have also taken their courage in their hands and made the appropriate challenge, contributed to the investigation and have done everything they can to prevent any further harm being done.

Jenkins (2007) argues that the principle of non-maleficence also raises the question of whether the counsellor has a 'duty to warn' if she thinks her client poses a significant risk to others. It is an interesting debate and, like all ethical debates, quite complex. Under the British legal system there are very few circumstances in which 'the duty to warn' is enshrined in law, a notable exception being anti-terrorism legislation. Jenkins maintains that breaking client confidentiality for this reason would have to be strongly supported by it being 'in the public interest'. You would have to think long and hard about taking such a course of action.

Justice – the fair and impartial treatment of all clients and the provision of adequate services

The inclusion of justice among the ethical principles acknowledges the fact that counselling does not take place in a social vacuum. Issues of fairness and unfairness, anti-discriminatory practice, human rights and justice are central to the world of the ethical counsellor. This principle requires you to think about your legal requirements and obligations, and how ethical considerations may support or conflict with them. A conscientious and responsible counsellor has an ethical duty to familiarise themself with the law as it touches their practice, for example, with regard to confidentiality, data protection, child protection, etc. A good place to start is by checking with the agency which employs you and making sure you are familiar with policies and procedures relating to legal issues and your particular client group. In recent years there has been a plethora of publications on the subject and such writers as Peter Jenkins and Tim Bond have produced helpful and informative works on the subject, which could usefully grace the bookshelves of every sensible counsellor.

Justice also requires you to reflect upon the allocation of services to clients and between clients. Is there an equality of opportunity and has enough thought been given to issues and practices that might discourage inclusiveness?

> *Practitioners have a duty to strive to ensure a fair provision of counselling and psychotherapy services, accessible and appropriate to the needs of potential clients.*
>
> (BACP, 2010)

Self-respect – fostering the practitioner's self-knowledge and care for the self

This, the last of the principles, focuses on the way you as the counsellor take care of yourself. Given that in the counselling room the only tool you have with you is yourself, then it is not hard to see why this is so important. The ethical framework talks about applying all of the previous principles to yourself and this is a good starting place for thinking about this principle. Taking good care of yourself makes you a good model for your clients and the reverse is also true. If you turn up in the counselling room looking ill-kempt and tired, what sort of a model are you going to be?

Daines et al. point out that:

> *Counselling differs from virtually all other professions in the lack of acceptability of a substitute in the absence of the usual person.*
>
> (2007, p43)

They emphasise the importance of taking care of your own health and well-being and even go so far as to suggest that, although it may clash with current ideals about equal opportunities etc., if a person has a chronic medical condition that may require considerable time off work for treatment, or if they are susceptible to viruses, for example, then they may need to question if they are suitable to work in counselling. Harsh as this may be, this thinking prioritises the rights and needs of the clients, something we all need to be willing to do as counsellors.

Working within your competence, having good supervision that supports and sustains you professionally, using personal therapy to work through your own issues as they arise, keeping up to date with developments in the counselling world, and having appropriate and adequate insurance are all ways of caring for yourself professionally.

However, just as important is having a life outside counselling. Going dancing, walking the dog, following your football team, reading a trashy novel, watching an old movie on a wet Sunday afternoon, whatever it is that sustains you, is crucial to your well-being. Perhaps most important of all is the quality of the relationships you have outside your counselling room with friends, lovers and family, which fulfil you and prevent you from looking for nurture within the counselling room. As the professional, you are there to give counselling, not receive it and, being human, you will certainly need to get it from somewhere else. Counselling can take a lot out of you and, if you are to remain effective, you will need to make sure something is being put back. Taking care of your own spiritual needs, whatever they may be and as you define them, is also vital.

The principle of self-respect also challenges you to think about your own well-being with regard to the hours you work and the breaks you need. You are your own most precious resource and self-respect is telling you to make sure you don't squander it.

Now that you have had the opportunity to consider the six principles individually, it is time to think about how, when facing an ethical dilemma, you might find yourself in the situation where the principles conflict with one another and you will have to use your judgement to give one precedence. What follows are three case studies containing ethical dilemmas. Read them carefully and imagine that you are the counsellor in these cases. What ethical conclusions might you come to?

Case study 4.2   Ethical dilemma 1

Sophie, who is 38 years old, is the widow of an officer who died in the conflict in Afghanistan. She has two children, Matthew, who is eight, and Elise, who is four and who suffers from a variety of life-threatening allergies. After several hospitalisations, Elise was prescribed an EpiPen (a tool for giving an injection against anaphylactic shock) and Sophie was trained how to use it, should Elise go into anaphylactic shock. Nick, Sophie's husband, died almost two years ago. Sophie never really took to army life and though she is grateful for some of the support she receives – Nick's pension, for example, which means that she is has no financial worries – she can find being an army widow, with all that that entails, a bit claustrophobic. Sophie misses Nick dreadfully and feels full of rage about some aspects of how he died. They had had a good marriage, despite lots of separations because of his work. Ironically, this would have been his last tour of duty as he had decided to leave the army.

Sophie has been coming to you for counselling for over a year now and the work has gone very well. Together you have been working through her grief and anger and Sophie has come to trust you, which is not that easy for her as she does sometimes feel a bit suspicious of people and is a person who values her privacy and her independence. She was originally referred to your private practice by her GP.

Some weeks ago Sophie told you that she was a bit worried about her drinking. She said that the hardest time for her is after the children have gone to bed. She is a bit surprised about this because being on her own is something that she had got used to as an army wife. However, she says that it is at these times when she begins to brood and her anger comes to the surface. Occasionally when this happens, she will start to drink and she drinks until she passes out. You have discussed this with her and challenged her about her responsibility for her children, particularly Elise. Sophie feels terrible about what she is doing and assures you that it has only happened a few times. She is not going to do it again because she really loves her children and wouldn't want anything bad to happen to them.

Time has passed and all appeared to be going well until today's session. When Sophie arrived at your consulting room, you couldn't help noticing that she had a black eye and serious bruising on one side of her face. She breaks down and tells you that after a bad piece of news, relating to the enquiry into Nick's death, she had another binge-drinking session and this time she fell over in the kitchen, hitting her head on the work surface. She had taken herself to the hospital the next morning to be checked out and she is fine. She had told them that she had had a fall. That was the day before yesterday.

Here is your dilemma. You know that Sophie is drinking herself into a stupor when she is in sole charge of two children, one of whom has a serious medical condition. You also know that Sophie is a good and loving parent, and you believe her when she tells you that this happens only very occasionally and that she wants and intends to stop doing it. You know that Sophie is working hard to come to terms with the loss of her husband but that the issues surrounding his death and the daily coverage of Afghanistan in the media exacerbate her grief. You know that she is a very private person who does not find it that easy to accept help and support or to talk to people about her situation. Given that Sophie's children have been and could be at risk, what do you do?

ACTIVITY 4.1

Go back and look at the principles.

• Which one(s) do you think is most important in Sophie's situation?

Martial your argument carefully, as if you had to present it to your peers. Think also of the values discussed in this chapter and the qualities discussed in Chapter 3.

COMMENT

In examining Ethical dilemma 1, we are going to look at three different possible conclusions. Counsellor 1 might come down on the side of *fidelity* and *autonomy*. She does not feel that at this point she has sufficient reason to break Sophie's trust. Sophie has shown herself to be a loving and responsible parent in all matters other than this. Counsellor 1 thinks that if she can carry on working with Sophie, she can address these matters with her. Counsellor 1 has checked her legal position (*justice*) and she knows that under British law there is no duty to disclose except in very particular circumstances, which this case does not come under and, as she is in private practice, she is not bound by any policies or procedures other than her own. Counsellor 1 thinks that the best way she can support this family and minimise any risk to the children and to Sophie (*non-maleficence*) is to respect Sophie's autonomy. After discussing the situation and her concerns with her supervisor, Counsellor 1 is addressing the issue of the risk to her children from Sophie's binge-drinking episodes. She is helping Sophie to explore what else she might do in these moments of desperation, for example calling a friend or a member of her family, or even drawing on some of the support offered to her through the army. She has raised the option of going back to the GP, but Sophie is at present unwilling to do this, and anyway, she doesn't have a good relationship with the doctor. Counsellor 1 believes that if she were to break confidentiality at this point in the work, it would cause irreparable damage to the therapeutic relationship; in fact, she is convinced that Sophie would simply stop coming. So, although she acknowledges that she is taking a risk, drawing on her courage and in discussion with her supervisor, Counsellor 1 has decided to give precedence to the principles of *fidelity* and *autonomy*.

Counsellor 2 starts with the principle of *beneficence*. She thinks that Sophie's capacity for autonomy is diminished by the intensity of her grief reaction and that her binge drinking, even if it is only occasional, may cause serious harm to Sophie or, more significantly, the children. If Elise were to become seriously unwell when Sophie was intoxicated, she could actually die, which clearly is not in the best interests of any of them. It also puts massive responsibility on Matthew, long before he is old enough or mature enough to cope with it. Counsellor 2 feels that she would be acting in the best interest of Sophie and promoting her well-being if she were to raise the alarm about Sophie's drinking and that her decision is also supported by *non-maleficence*, in that failing to take action may cause harm to Sophie and her family. She is also aware that she has no duty to disclose (*justice*) under the law, but she thinks that she has a moral and ethical responsibility because these children may be at risk. Counsellor 2 does appreciate that making the decision to break confidentiality may well cause a serious rupture in the therapeutic relationship between herself and Sophie. She has tried to raise the option of Sophie going back to talk to the GP but Sophie is quite unwilling to do this. After discussion with her supervisor, Counsellor 2 has decided that, drawing on her courage and her integrity, she will tell Sophie at their next session that, with great regret, she must break confidentiality and contact Sophie's GP or possibly social services. Counsellor 2 also thinks that this course of action accords with the principle of *self-respect*, in that she is taking care of herself by sharing this knowledge with other appropriate professionals.

Counsellor 3 takes an ethical position that rests somewhere between the other two. She thinks *fidelity* is crucially important here. She has considered if, under *beneficence* it could be argued that Sophie's capacity for autonomy is diminished. Counsellor 3 considers that while this might be so when she is actually drinking, it is certainly not so when she is in her sessions and that the right approach is to support Sophie's autonomy by challenging her about her behaviour and thus encouraging her to take responsibility for the actual and possible consequences of her actions. Counsellor 3 thinks that to break confidentiality at this point would be going against the principle of *non-maleficence*, in that this course of action may actually be harmful to Sophie. Counsellor 3 is not convinced that the authorities (the GP or social services) would do anything other than speak to Sophie about the issue and that, at this point, this would be counter-productive. She believes that the last incident has so shocked Sophie that she may now be open to serious challenge and possible change. So, at this point, Counsellor 3 is willing to continue trying to work with Sophie. However, with the support of her supervisor, she has decided she must review this position after each session with Sophie and that if Sophie is unable or unwilling to stop binge drinking in this way, and putting her children at risk, then Counsellor 3 would have an ethical responsibility to break confidentiality, supported by the principles of *beneficence*, *non-maleficence* and *self-respect*. She has decided to give it a little more time.

Hopefully, you can see that all three of these counsellors have arrived at their ethical positions through careful reflection, using the supervision process to help them. If this situation had taken place within an agency, it would have been appropriate to talk also to the line manager or counselling co-ordinator, or whoever has overall clinical responsibility for the work. In this case the counsellor was in private practice, so this additional support was not available.

REFLECTION POINT

- What would you do? Think through the issues raised in Ethical dilemma 1 and make an argument for your own stance.

Case study 4.3   Ethical dilemma 2

You work at a women's resource centre and you also have a small private practice. You have been seeing Grace at the centre for several months. She has been working on her lack of self-esteem and assertiveness, and a big factor in that has been her relationship with John, her husband. He is a lecturer in a college and over the years he has had several affairs, a situation which has sapped away at Grace's self-confidence. Your work with Grace is going well and you have an open-ended contract with her for long-term work.

In your private practice you see a new client. Her name is Ruth and she works in Human Resources. She comes because she has been suffering from depression. One factor in her depression is the recent ending of a relationship, in which she had been deeply in love and the man concerned had left her. You have been seeing her for a couple of months and the work is going very well. Then one day she tells you something about her lover and you get a dreadful sinking feeling in your stomach because you strongly suspect that the person she is talking about is John, Grace's husband. You ask a couple of questions that confirm your suspicion. Ruth met John when she was taking a course at her local college and he was her lecturer.

ACTIVITY 4.2

- What would you do in this circumstance and why?
- Can you go on working with either or both of these women?
- Which principles would guide you and what personal qualities might you draw on to support you in your decision?

COMMENT

You already have a well-established relationship with Grace and, even though it is more recent, a good therapeutic alliance with Ruth too, so to end either of these relationships at this point in the work could be damaging. On the other hand, what if either of them were to discover that you were seeing the other one too? That could be really hurtful for either client and they might well feel betrayed or exploited. Grace does not know of Ruth's existence and Ruth in turn does not know that John is even married, so you have information about both of your clients' situations of which they themselves are not even aware.

If you first think about the principle of *fidelity* with regard to this dilemma and if you carry on working with both clients, are you really honouring the trust each has placed in you? *Autonomy* is certainly relevant here because the fact that you now have information about both of them that they don't know, means that it is questionable that you could be holding their informed consent for the work as they are actually not fully informed. Informed consent is not a one-off action; it is an ongoing process and either of them might withdraw their consent to work with you if they knew what you know. A conflict of interest has now arisen and the principle of autonomy implies that you must address such a conflict as soon as possible.

Beneficence tells you that you should act in the best interest of the client based on your professional assessment. It may be your assessment that each of these clients is working well with you and to disrupt the work may not be in either of their best interests. You could not tell either of them what you know without breaking the confidence of the other, so all you could say is that a conflict of interest has arisen. This is unlikely to be satisfactory to whichever one of them you decided to stop seeing. In fact, breaking the relationship with either of them might even be harmful and, taking into account *non-maleficence*, you may decide that you can't do it in this way. You may decide that it is so unlikely that either of them will find out that the best thing to do is to take this risk. But what if they do? Is it right for you to gamble with their well-being in this way?

Justice requires that you show impartiality between your clients, so how do you decide which one you would stop seeing? Do you decide to keep seeing Grace because she was your client first, or Ruth because she is at present very depressed and perhaps needs you more? *Self-respect* requires you to think about your own well-being here too. Attempting to manage such a situation may prove extremely stressful.

This is where the interplay between the principles and the personal qualities discussed in the last chapter would be really important. Your *integrity* might be crucial, being straightforward, honest and coherent. *Humility* would be very useful and would help you to realise that you need the help of others – your supervisor, your colleagues at the resource centre – to resolve this. It will also keep you in touch with the fact that you are not irreplaceable – with a careful and sensitive process of referral, either or both clients could be passed on to colleagues. *Courage,* on the other hand, might help you to take the risk of working with them both, if that is what you decide is the best course of action, and *resilience* would help you to work your way through this dilemma. Perhaps the most important of all would be *wisdom*, which would enable you to make the fine judgement call required.

REFLECTION POINT

- Taking into account all the factors in this case, what would you do and how would you support your decision?

Case study 4.4   Ethical dilemma 3

You are working in an agency where a more senior counsellor assesses the clients and decides what financial contribution they have to make for the service. You meet a new client, Chris, who has come to work on his relationship with his children. Chris tells you straightaway that he is unhappy about the amount he has to pay for the service. It is not that the amount is unreasonable – he thinks it is quite fair – but he is in debt and is worried about how he is going to pay it. He is desperate for the counselling and has waited quite a long time on the agency's list. You can see that he is very distressed and anxious about his presenting problem and you are keen to get going on the work.

Chris tells you that he runs his own business which involves going into people's homes to sort out their computer problems. You reply, almost in passing, that having experienced lots of problems with your computers at home, you can imagine there is a lot of call on his services. Chris immediately homes in on this. Could he do a deal with you? If you will see him now and tot up the fees, he will offer you a service for your home computers as and when you need it, to the value of the sessions he has with you.

ACTIVITY 4.3

- What do you do here and how do you support your actions with reference to the ethical principles?

COMMENT

Perhaps a good point for you to start here would be *justice*. Has the service really been fair to Chris in setting the rate as it did in the assessment? Did the assessor check on Chris's ability to pay, taking into account his debts? How does what Chris has been asked to pay compare with what is asked of other clients? You would need to think this through and to check it out.

If you agreed to Chris's suggestion, might you be going against *non-maleficence* in that you could lay yourself open to an allegation of financial exploitation? Even though Chris thinks this is a good solution for him, in his desperation to get on with the work, you know about the importance of boundaries to the therapeutic relationship. Would it be acceptable to have Chris in your house working on your computer? How would either of you manage this dual relationship? How might such a violation impact on the relationship? Even if you didn't call on Chris's services while he was your client, clause 18 of the *Ethical Framework* warns:

> *Practitioners should think carefully about, and exercise considerable caution before, entering into personal or business relationships with former clients and should expect to be professionally accountable if the relationship becomes detrimental to the client or the standing of the profession.*
>
> (BACP, 2010)

In fact, you would need to be a very courageous practitioner who has thought this through very carefully indeed, before agreeing to anything so potentially risky.

CHAPTER SUMMARY

By now you will appreciate that the *Ethical Framework* of the BACP exists primarily to enhance good practice rather than simply to prevent bad practice. It is an excellent tool for the mature and responsible practitioner and it is, therefore, really important that you familiarise yourself with it and make use of it routinely, when reflecting on your practice and when preparing for your supervision. Hopefully, you now have a sense of how the framework functions and of what is expected of you, the practitioner. The *Ethical Framework* is a working document and is constantly being reviewed and revised, to keep it up to date and responding to new issues in the world of counselling. The framework is devised to enhance your own professional autonomy and it leaves the responsibility for your actions and decisions quite firmly with you. You have to think and reflect carefully on what you are doing, take advice from your supervisor and come to your own ethical decisions, which you then have to stand by and be able to argue in front of your peers. Given the nature of the therapeutic relationship and what is expected of them, your clients should be able to expect nothing less of you. In this chapter we have discussed:

- the emergence of the *Ethical Framework for Good Practice in Counselling and Psychotherapy;*

- the values that underpin the framework;

- the ethical principles that form the third pillar of the framework;

- practical examples of ethical dilemmas.

SUGGESTED FURTHER READING

Bond, T (2010) *Standards and Ethics in Counselling,* 3rd edition. London: Sage.

Chapter 6 on client autonomy is an invaluable read.

Daines, B, Gask, L and Howe, A (2007) *Medical and Psychiatric Issues for Counsellors,* 2nd edition. London: Sage.

A useful text in general but in the context of this chapter, relevant to the debates about the principle of self-respect.

Jenkins, P (2007) *Counselling, Psychotherapy and the Law,* 2nd edition. London: Sage.

This is a seminal text for all issues relating to counselling and the law.

CHAPTER 5

Facing your nightmares or 'What on earth do I do now?'

CORE KNOWLEDGE

- This chapter will help you to identify strategies for working with difficult issues in counselling such as:
  - suicide;
  - romantic attachment between client and therapist;
  - the impact of mental health problems in the counselling relationship.
- It is important to know what to do when the client/therapist relationship breaks down – a situation known as an alliance rupture – and this chapter provides practical examples and coping mechanisms.

INTRODUCTION

In this chapter we are going to think about some of the situations that most new counsellors seem to dread. Anyone involved in training counsellors will tell you that whenever there is an opportunity for trainees to raise their anxieties about becoming a counsellor, the same old chestnuts emerge, such as: 'What do I do if my client is threatening to commit suicide?'; 'What do I do if my client says she is in love with me?'; 'What if I really don't like the client?'; 'What do I do if I think my client may be mentally ill?' Situations such as these can be unsettling for the most experienced counsellor and so it is not surprising that they strike fear and dread into the hearts of people new to the work. Unfortunately, you will not be given the answers to these questions in this chapter, because the truth is that there are no simple and straightforward answers. It really is a question of facing your fears and thinking about how you can best manage the situation. Perhaps your personal worst fear is something different and, if so, you should be able to transfer your learning from the situations discussed here and apply it to your very own worst nightmare.

THE SUICIDAL CLIENT

It is a sad fact that if a person is absolutely determined to take their own life, then it is really very difficult to stop them doing so (Durkheim, 1979). Fortunately, suicide is really not that common. In 2008, for example, according to the Office of National Statistics website, there were slightly fewer than 6,000 deaths of people aged 15 or over that were attributed to suicide. Obviously, these statistics are of scant comfort to the people whose lives any one of these suicides has touched, but it is important to realise that the vast majority of counsellors do get through their entire careers without ever losing a client in this way.

Counsellors, like any other sector of the population, are divided in their philosophical positions with regard to the issue of suicide (Bond, 2010). At one end of the spectrum would be those who believe in the absolute right of a person to take their own life if they so choose. People holding this position would argue for autonomy and the person's right to self-determination, even to the manner and timing of their own death. Those espousing this position would wish to claim this right to end their own lives for themselves also, if and when they think it is appropriate. Of course, suicide is no longer a crime under British law, although some of the terminology we use – committing suicide – harks back to those darker times when a person who had attempted suicide could be prosecuted for so doing. At the other end of the spectrum would be those who could never condone or accept the act of taking your own life. They believe in the absolute sanctity of human life and this is sometimes, though not always, connected to their religious convictions. If we think of this as a philosophical spectrum, there are innumerable points between the two diametrically opposed positions.

It is helpful if you have thought about this issue yourself and come to your own philosophical standpoint. Rather than thinking of it in concept, consider the case below and then decide what you think.

Case study 5.1   Emmy

Emmy is a woman, 42 years old, who is in sound physical health. However, since her mid-teens she has suffered several prolonged periods of acute clinical depression. Emmy has seen a whole variety of doctors and therapists, and has undergone some quite long periods in therapy. She has also taken many different types of medication. She has had several stints as an in-patient in psychiatric clinics and has even had a programme of electroconvulsive therapy more than once. Unfortunately, none of these treatment regimes, or any combination of

---

them, has had anything other than a short-term effect for Emmy. She is not, at present, depressed, although she feels that the quality of her life is extremely poor. The longest period of time between her bouts of depression has been two years. She is unable to work and has no family or friends with whom she has any relationship that is meaningful to her. She is not unhappy about the treatment she has received for her illness and feels that the professionals with whom she has come into contact have genuinely tried very hard to help her with her condition. Emmy is not religious and has no philosophical or moral objections to ending her own life, nor is she mentally ill at present. It is her fervent wish to end her own life now. This is not a 'knee-jerk' reaction, but is the result of reflection and consideration over many months.

REFLECTION POINT

- What do you think about Emmy's case? Does she have the right to take her own life?
- Do you think Emmy would be wrong to take her own life? Consider your position on suicide.

COMMENT

Emmy's case highlights the complexity of the whole issue of suicide. In her case, she has thought through her situation carefully and has arrived at what for her is a sensible and rational decision. This is qualitatively different from a person who makes an attempt at ending their own life in a moment of crisis, such as a newly convicted prisoner, or the person who has been deserted by their partner, or the newly bereaved person. This is different again from the parasuicide (Bond, 2010), the person who has made several unsuccessful suicide attempts as a means of drawing attention to their acute emotional distress. As in all aspects of counselling, a 'one size fits all' approach really will not do.

The first thing you need to do as a counsellor is to educate yourself about suicide, because the more you know about the subject – risk factors, prevention strategies, etc. – the more you are likely to be able to help. The internet is an excellent resource and it is worth looking for information about the Centre for Suicide Prevention at the University of Manchester; at MIND, the charity whose work focuses on the provision of services for those suffering from mental illness; and indeed at the National Suicide Prevention Strategy, from the Department of Health (see website addresses in Activity

5.1 below). Having background knowledge of the subject will increase your confidence and your awareness of significant indicators.

ACTIVITY 5.1

Visit the websites mentioned below and then answer the following questions:

- What groups of people are particularly at risk of taking their own lives?
- What strategies are being developed to address this issue?

www.mind.org.uk/information/factsheets/suicide
www.uk.sobs.org.uk (the website for survivors of bereavement by suicide)
www.suicide.com
www.dh.gov.uk (Department of Health publications on suicide prevention)
www.chooselife.net (Scottish suicide prevention strategies)
www.centre-suicide-prevention.man.ac.uk

Perhaps the most important advice anyone can give you as a counsellor about potentially suicidal clients is that it is vitally important that you make sure that your client knows it is something that they can talk about with you and that you will be able to contain both them and yourself in any such discussion (Daines et al., 2007). Furthermore, if your client starts implying that they are feeling suicidal – 'I don't think I can go on much longer'; 'Sometimes I feel as though I want to go to sleep and never wake up'; 'I just want to put an end to all of this' – then you need to sensitively clarify exactly what they mean. You might start the intervention by acknowledging their feelings: 'It sounds like all of this is very painful for you. Are you saying that you are thinking about taking your own life?' This is not an occasion on which you can pussyfoot around. You need to know if your client is experiencing suicidal ideation and, if so, how far down the line with it they are. In other words, is the thought that they want to take their own life just some vague fleeting idea that crosses their mind occasionally, or is it something that occupies their mind constantly and do they have a plan as to how and when they mean to attempt to take their life, or are they at some place in between these two points? This clarification is not only for your client's benefit, but also for your own, because it is not at all uncommon for people to sometimes think that they would like to take their own lives as a means of stopping the stress or emotional pain they are feeling at the moment. Obviously, you would prefer it if your clients never entertained such thoughts. However, the counsellor has much less need for concern than they would have in the case of a client who does actually and actively want to be dead, and has the means and a timetable for bringing this about. If this is the case you, as the counsellor, have a lot to concern you and serious decisions to make about what, if anything, you are going to do about the situation. However, suicidal ideation, if it is mentioned by a client, must be kept on the agenda for the sessions you have together and it is crucial that it doesn't become a taboo subject between you. Clients are extremely observant and are often very well attuned to their counsellors. If you panic or overreact at the very mention of suicide, your clients will pick this up and will not feel safe enough to talk freely with you.

So, let us suppose that you have a client who you think is seriously at risk of taking their own life. What should you do? The first thing to think about is getting some help and support for yourself so that you, in turn, can better take care of your client and the place to start is with your supervisor. When you are setting up your contract with your supervisor, it is very important to have an arrangement as to what you should do in an emergency; can you telephone, can you have an emergency session if it is required? Before you find yourself in such a situation, you need to have such a framework in place. If you are working in an agency or some kind of institution, you should be able to get support from the counselling coordinator, or senior counsellor or placement manager, whoever is the clinical lead. If you are still in training, you could have access to your tutors. Basically, you need to find an appropriate person, someone with experience, with whom you can talk through the situation in confidence and as soon as possible. There are ethical dilemmas to think through and you will need to decide what, if anything, needs to be done. Your own position on suicide will be significant here and will very likely impact upon your decision-making process.

Opinion is divided as to whether being actively suicidal constitutes being mentally ill (Daines et al., 2007, p109). This is significant here in that it may not be realistic to think that if you were to try to enlist the help of other professionals, anything very substantial would be available to your client, or to you. Furthermore, as stated earlier, taking one's own life is not against the law (Jenkins, 2007, p125). For these reasons, having the knowledge that someone is seriously suicidal can create tremendous pressure on the counsellor, which is why it is very important to draw on the help and support available to you.

Some counsellors would advocate trying to come to an agreement with the client that, during the period in which you are seeing them, the client does not try to take their own life. It has been reported that some clients have found this very helpful, because the counsellor's request for this agreement implies that they do care about what happens to the client at a time in their life when they feel of no value to anyone. However, it is of course no guarantee, and counsellors who have tried this strategy report waiting with bated breath for the client's knock on the consulting room door at the start of the next session. It is in your own interest to ensure that when a client is vulnerable in this way, you keep up-to-date and careful notes.

Case study 5.2   When the worst happens

Mike is a counsellor working in a drug and alcohol agency. He was the counsellor for Jack, a young man in his early twenties, who was a drug user and had a serious problem with alcohol. He had compound and complex family issues, and a background of both physical and emotional abuse. Mike saw him in the day service unit of the agency. Jack also attended groups at the unit. Mike and Jack had been working together for almost a year and had formed a good working relationship, despite Jack's chaotic lifestyle. Jack finally decided that he wanted to come off both the drugs and alcohol, and the agency helped him to arrange funding for, and a place, in rehab, although first he had to go into his local hospital psychiatric wing for detoxification. All of this suddenly began to fall into place at the time when Mike was about to go on leave and he was concerned about this, because he knew that Jack was extremely vulnerable. However, it was all arranged that Jack should do his week of detoxification and then go straight into rehab. Mike and Jack ended their counselling relationship for the present with a view to working together again when Jack had finished in rehab. Mike went off on holiday.

Unfortunately, things did not work out as planned. Jack went through detoxification, which was very gruelling for him, and he was due to go from the hospital, straight to the rehab clinic on the Friday. There was some last-minute problem with the funding and the rehab was unwilling to take him without the authorisation, which unfortunately could not be faxed to them until the Monday. The hospital, short of beds, released Jack into the community until the Monday when he would go to rehab. However, without the crutch of the drugs and drink, Jack fell into a crisis and on the Saturday evening he hanged himself.

Mike returned from holiday unaware of what had happened. Jack's funeral had already taken place. Mike was very upset indeed and also angry about what he saw as Jack being badly let down by the system. He felt terrible about having been away on holiday when all of this happened. There were also several important issues that he needed to work through and so he set up additional sessions with his supervisor.

Together, they discussed Mike's emotional response to Jack's death and Mike was able to express how he felt. Mike was able to share how much he had liked Jack but also how damaged and vulnerable he had perceived Jack to be. Working in a drug and alcohol unit for many years, Mike had experienced the death of many clients, from accidents, illness and acts of violence, but this was the first time he had experienced a death through suicide. Jack's behaviour had been so self-destructive and even reckless at times that Mike would not have been surprised if he had died at any time during their work together, but it was Jack actively taking his own life that Mike really struggled with. In a way, he was relieved that the funeral had taken place while he was on holiday, because that had saved Mike the dilemma of deciding whether or not to attend, but at the same time he felt robbed of the opportunity of saying a final goodbye to Jack.

Mike also needed to work out what he would do if he was summoned by the coroner to give evidence at the inquest. Mike felt very strongly that his contract of confidentiality with Jack was not broken by Jack's death. His supervisor encouraged Mike to seek legal advice, were he to be called to appear, to ask for a preliminary discussion with the coroner and also to have legal representation in the coroner's court. Together, they decided what Mike was willing to reveal and they went through Mike's notes. Fortunately, the coroner did not call Mike, as his counselling relationship with Jack had ended a couple of weeks before Jack's death (see Bond, 2010, pp117–18).

Gradually, Mike began to regain his equilibrium. He accepted that Jack's decision to end his life was an act of desperation in a moment of crisis, which was supported by the coroner's decision that it was suicide when 'the balance of his mind was disturbed'. On reflection, Mike could see that, even though Jack had chosen to kill himself, still their relationship had been important and something positive in a life that contained very little that was positive or good. Mike felt sure that Jack knew that he had cared for him. Mike also acknowledged that, given Jack's past and his present circumstances, Mike's care alone was not enough to sustain Jack, or to prevent him from taking the action that he did. Mike had to accept Jack's choice and to face up to the fact that services, however well intentioned, do fall short, make mistakes and let people down. To make a proper ending with Jack and to mark his existence in the world and his potential as a human being, Mike quietly had a tree planted in Jack's name, because Jack loved trees and birds, and that was something that they had had in common.

COMMENT

You need to notice that Mike survived this difficult and painful experience. He had made good use of the support available to him and had honoured his relationship with Jack throughout. He had thought through what he would need to do, had he been called to give evidence at the coroner's court, which fortunately he was spared (see Jenkins, 2007, Chapter 3 and Bond and Sandhu, 2005, Chapter 4). He had come to terms with Jack's death and had made sense of it for himself. When a person takes his own life, everyone who has contact with the deceased is affected in one way or another. The counselling relationship is close and intimate, even taking into account the boundaries inherent in it. Whenever we allow ourselves close contact with another human being, we open ourselves up to the possibility of being hurt when that person dies and, even more so, if the person has taken his own life.

'THAT FUNNY LITTLE THING CALLED LOVE'

Number two on the list of scary things for student counsellors is the idea of the client falling in love with the counsellor. A very wise and experienced practitioner, who would prefer to remain anonymous, once said:

> *I was never really that sure about the concept of erotic transference until one day I was sitting in my consultation room and opposite me was a very attractive and intelligent woman, twenty years my junior. She was looking at me in a really doting fashion, me, a middle-aged man, with a bald patch, a beer belly and a grizzly grey beard. I had a fashion bypass many years ago. In that moment I was absolutely convinced that something other than the obvious was going on.*

For a psychodynamic counsellor, a client experiencing erotic, or indeed romantic, feelings towards the counsellor would be understood as erotic transference (Freud, 1925), but whatever your orientation, it does sometimes happen that clients have these kinds of feelings towards you. Taking a step back can be helpful if this should happen to you. Remember that your client only sees and experiences a part of you. If you were to administer a truth serum to your nearest and dearest, they would probably tell you just how annoying you can be. Your knowledge of the team sheets for every cup match, your collection of dolls in national costumes, your annoying little hum and your habit of cutting your toe nails at the breakfast table has them plotting your imminent demise the moment your back is turned. However, your client sees and experiences none of this. What your client experiences is a person who listens to them and appears to understand, a person who shows them empathy, and gives them space and uninterrupted attention. Finally, they have met someone with whom they can be really vulnerable or someone who does not reject them when they make mistakes. Wouldn't it be surprising if the client did not begin to imagine that you might be the perfect partner, the lover they have been looking for all of their life?

There is nothing wrong in the client experiencing or even expressing feelings like this towards you. In fact, they could prove to be pivotal in the work, but before you get to that there are some things you need to consider. First, you need to think about your behaviour towards the client (Russell and Dexter, 2008, p48). Have you been acting in a flirtatious way and perhaps inadvertently encouraging this response in your client? Perhaps you are naturally a bit of a flirt, which can be perfectly appropriate in many social settings, but absolutely not in the counselling relationship. What has your body language and the way you present yourself in the counselling room been conveying to your client? Have you checked your own feelings about this client? Do you find yourself attracted to them? Sometimes, this is not immediately obvious and needs some thinking about. For example, a counsellor working with a man who had issues concerning his relationship found herself feeling highly critical of his wife. How could she behave in such a way to her husband? This was a bit unusual for this counsellor who wasn't given to being so judgemental. Examining these feelings with her supervisor, she discovered that she hadn't noticed just how attractive she found her client and, because she was not conscious of this in herself, she had started to collude with him against his wife, instead of remaining objective and challenging him about his behaviour within his relationship.

How should the counsellor respond?

Once you have checked out your part in this equation and that you are behaving responsibly and with consciousness, you can begin to think about what is going on for your client and how you need to respond. Once again, your first port of call will be your supervisor, who will help you to properly assess the situation. It is vital to work out a way of responding to your client that makes it clear that you will be holding the boundary absolutely, but in this you are not rejecting the client and are both open and available to discuss what the client is feeling. You need to be able to contain yourself and your client in this tricky work.

The BACP's *Ethical Framework* contains only a handful of prohibitions, but clause 18 states very clearly:

> *Sexual relations with clients are prohibited. 'Sexual relations' include intercourse, any other type of sexual activity or sexualised behaviour.*
>
> (BACP, 2010)

There is no wriggle room here or any doubt as to the meaning of this clause and it provides you with a good starting point for your response to a client who wishes to change the parameters of the relationship. The skill is in finding a way of conveying this to your client that will not leave them feeling rejected or humiliated. It is worth thinking about what this might be about for your client. Perhaps they have never had a relationship that is close or intimate and not sexual; perhaps they have never experienced being with someone who does not have expectations of, or make demands on, them. Holding the boundaries will give them a different experience and a massive opportunity for growth and development, and increasing self-worth. Sometimes, clients will initially be angry about what they perceive as rejection, but this again opens up the possibility of working with the client's feelings according to your own orientation.

Just a little word of caution: in the mishmash of emotions that clients often experience through the process of counselling, it is not that unusual for them to feel attracted to someone against the flow of their usual sexual orientations. As a counsellor, you will be aware that human sexuality is not generally a fixed thing and any of us can develop strong sexual attraction towards people, regardless of our, or indeed their, sexual orientation. A woman heterosexual client, for example, could feel attraction and longing for her counsellor who is a woman and, as far as the client knows, also heterosexual. Given that in counselling we are often dredging through the client's past and unearthing all kinds of emotions, rooted in both the past and present, none of this is really that surprising, although it may be very uncomfortable and unnerving for the client, and indeed the counsellor, when it happens.

The good news is that if you can keep your nerve, using your supervision and other support available to you, hold fast to the boundaries, avoid panicking and simply reject the client and allow time for them to work through these feelings, they will come to realise that unfortunately you are not the perfect combination of Marilyn Monroe and Mother Teresa, or the male equivalent, and both of you will be able to survive this realisation, none the worse for the experience.

Let us return to the question of what to do if the boot is on the other foot. What if you find yourself feeling very attracted to your client? You know that ethically you cannot change the parameters of the relationship. You will need to take this issue to your supervisor as soon as possible because the danger is that you will lose your objectivity and start to collude with the client, or you may inadvertently start to punish them for making you feel so uncomfortable. Bringing your feelings fully into consciousness is really important, taking responsibility for them and, most importantly, avoiding any client blaming. Taking a long hard look at your private life and seeing how well your own emotional and sexual needs are being met is crucial, because this is not something you should be getting from your client work.

REFLECTION POINT

- Do counsellors 'love' their clients?

Of course, it will depend upon how you define love. Kahn made a useful distinction between the kinds of love that might be applicable:

> Eros is characterised by the desire for something that will fulfil the lover. It includes the wish to possess the beloved object or person. Agape, by contrast,

is characterised by the desire to fulfil the beloved. It demands nothing in return and wants only the growth and fulfilment of the loved one. Agape is a strengthening love, a love that, by definition, does not burden or obligate the loved one.

(Kahn, 1997, p39)

- How does this idea sit with you in your role of counsellor?

HELP! I DON'T LIKE MY CLIENT

So, you don't like your client. Is this going to be a problem? Well, if by this you mean that you wouldn't choose this client for a friend or you wouldn't particularly like to have them in your life in any other context, then this in itself is not really an issue. In fact, it could be an advantage. If you really like a client and identify with them and their issues, it can sometimes be difficult to maintain objectivity and avoid collusion. The fact that you may not particularly like a client may affect your ability to empathise with them.

REFLECTION POINT

- What sort of clients do you think you might struggle with?
- Would it be their views and values that would be difficult for you? Would it be their behaviour?
- If you were faced with such a client, what do you think you would need to do?

Something that can be really difficult for a counsellor is to be faced with a client who expresses views or values that are fundamentally at odds with the counsellor's own values, to the point of being offensive. The fact that you are a counsellor does not strip you of your human rights and, in the unlikely event of a client being seriously abusive to you, for reasons of your gender, race, culture, sexual orientation, etc., or indeed for any other reason, you would be perfectly within your rights to refuse to see the client, or to terminate the session. The ethical principle of self-respect would support you, were you to decide to take such action, but in reality it is extremely unlikely that you would ever have to. What is much more common is the situation where, in the course of the client's work with you, the client begins to express views or values that really jar with you. How are you going to create and maintain the therapeutic relationship in these circumstances? Earlier in this book we discussed the importance of values to the counsellor. They are, in fact, what bring most of us into the work and it is not reasonable, or indeed possible, to expect you to hang them up with your coat when you come into your consulting room. It is also true, however, that the counselling room is not an appropriate forum for political correctness and it has to be possible for the client to express feelings and opinions, even those that are not palatable to the counsellor (Bond, 2010, p98). Optimists might even argue that the process of counselling itself is a medium through which a client might come to reassess their views and beliefs about others and have the opportunity for changing them. Whether you are an optimist or not, this situation is one which you need to approach with great skill, and after much reflection and consultation with your supervisor.

Case study 5.3   'Did he really say that?'

Asif, a middle-aged Asian man, comes to see Pete, who is white, because he has been the victim of violence and is suffering from post-traumatic stress. He is a taxi driver and late one night he picked up two black youths. They attacked him and robbed him at knife point. He was left with head injuries and a dislocated shoulder but, worst of all, as far as Asif is concerned, he has nightmares, flashbacks and other psychological difficulties. So far, in almost six months, he has not been able to return to his work. Asif is understandably angry about what has happened to him and at first Pete allowed free expression of his anger, although he did feel uncomfortable about some of Asif's language when he spoke of his attackers. However, in one session Pete could no longer put his discomfort to one side because the way Asif was speaking included the assumption that Pete was in agreement with him: 'You know what those boys are like. None of them has got a father. They are all on drugs and running the streets. They don't know how to behave because they are brought up by unmarried girls as mothers. They are just feral the lot of them. I don't see them when I pick up the students from the graduate ceremonies I can tell you, plenty of white kids and Asian kids, but not that lot. And you and me, all we do is pay for them and their benefits. My daughter hangs around with some of them at school and I have told her she had better not bring any of them back to our house.'

Pete had previously raised the issue with his supervisor and together they worked out how Pete might approach it with Asif. Pete was not willing to let this go because he didn't agree with Asif's generalisations and stereotyping, and he didn't feel he could collude with it by silence, which might imply that he concurred with Asif's prejudice. So he responded: 'Asif, I need to tell you that I feel uncomfortable with what you are saying and it is important that we are honest with each other. I can really understand and appreciate how angry you must be with the two young men who attacked you. I know all of this has been really tough for you, but I don't agree with the things you said about black people and young black people in particular. I think differently from you and, if we are being honest, then you need to be aware of that.'

Asif was initially defensive but Pete just held his position and eventually Asif began to talk about the incident again. It took a little while for their relationship to get back on track. Asif tempered some of his language and Pete felt that, although it had been difficult between them, he had acted with integrity and been true to his own values.

COMMENT

Pete raised a really important point in his response to Asif and that is the question of honesty and being real with the client. If Pete had simply ignored Asif's remarks, then he would have been acting dishonestly and something important in the therapeutic relationship would have been lost. It is quite possible that Asif, in the delicate and unspoken resonance between client and counsellor, would have picked up on this and have felt less trusting of Pete. If Pete had chosen not to say something, then he would have been keeping his disapproval of Asif's values covert, which Bond (2010, p99) argues has implications for both parties. As the counsellor, you must question if you can go on helping someone to live their life according to a set of values of which you actively disapprove, and the client in turn may have a moral objection to being counselled by someone who strongly disapproves of their values and yet keeps that secret from him.

Another consideration here is the issue of self-disclosure. If I challenge you about your values, then by definition, I am telling you something about mine. Different orientations approach the concept of self-disclosure in various ways, but generally speaking it is good practice to ensure that self-disclosure is for the benefit of the client and is therapeutic in its intent. Hill and Knox have defined self-disclosure as *therapist statements that reveal something personal about the therapist* (2002, p255). The kind of challenge that Pete made was certainly doing that and, in that his intent was to ensure the honesty and integrity of the counselling relationship, it was indeed therapeutic in its intent.

SELF-INVOLVING STATEMENTS

Self-disclosure of this kind, sometimes referred to as *self-involving statements* (Cooper, 2008, p114), can also prove to be a useful tool in dealing with something else that might initially impact negatively on the therapeutic relationship, namely the client's behaviour within the relationship. An example would be the client who persistently arrives late, so that you, the counsellor, are left twiddling your thumbs, wondering if they are going to arrive. There is always a reason: the traffic, the late arrival of the babysitter, the phone call just as they were about to leave, difficulty in finding a parking space, etc. You have held the boundary and ended on time, but over the weeks you notice that you are becoming irritated with them and that it is hard for you to concentrate for the first ten minutes they are actually with you because this unsettles you. Two things are happening at once. The therapist in you is wondering what it means for them. Why are they doing this? Is it that they don't value your time together? Is it hard to prioritise themself? The person in you, however, is thinking something else. Isn't it a bit rude to do this to me every week? What about the value of my time? Isn't it rather disrespectful to me? Why don't they get themself organised? I can get here, so why can't they?

Initially, the inexperienced counsellor might dismiss such 'personal' feelings, even be critical of themself for thinking such unkind and unprofessional things. However, if you can open yourself up to your own feelings, accept and validate them, you might find you are on to something useful for the client. First, might the feelings you are experiencing towards the client give you some indication of how they are experienced by others in the outside world? If you can find a skilful way of giving them this feedback, in the moment, wouldn't this be useful for them? Second, what about your commitment to an honest relationship with your client? You are feeling irritated with them and you can either pretend that this is not happening or you can address it. The skill, of course, is in how you do it, taking responsibility for your own feelings and putting them before the client in the spirit of exploration. Obviously, you would only make such a challenge to your client if you had already established a sound therapeutic alliance with them, in which they feel supported and therefore open to being challenged. Wosket explains the kind of interaction described here:

> I am inviting the client to see further into him or herself through what I am revealing of myself. When I use an immediate response effectively the client will momentarily switch attention to me and then it will bounce back in such a way that they are able to receive and hold it.
>
> (Wosket, 2008, p51)

Dealing with the here and now is an important way of creating and maintaining the therapeutic relationship and, if you and your client can work through what arises between the two of you, in the moment, your relationship will deepen and act as a model for your client's other relationships outside the counselling room.

So far, we have looked at an example of a client's behaviour within the relationship between client and counsellor, but what if you are confronted with behaviour on the part of the client, which they tell you about, that is unacceptable to you? Obviously, you are not there to sit in judgement over your client, but you are only human and you have your own values.

Counselling students, when invited to reflect on what kind of clients they might struggle to work with, invariably come up with 'the abuser'. The reality is that, unless you want to work with offenders, it is not very likely that you are going to end up with someone who has sexually abused children or been convicted of serious sexual offences sitting opposite you. This is highly specialist work, requiring specialist training and expertise, and certainly is not something that a counsellor would be involved with in the early stages of their career. It is crucial that you always work within the level of your own competence, which, as you know, is an ethical requirement. In the unlikely event that you are faced with such a client, you would need to make an appropriate referral, drawing on the expertise, of your supervisor and your line manager. Attempting to work with this kind of pathology when you are not appropriately trained and experienced would be both irresponsible and potentially dangerous. It would certainly not be in the best interest of your client.

What you are much more likely to be faced with is a person telling you about emotional or physical abuse, perhaps within a domestic context, and what can be very unsettling is when it becomes obvious that while you might see the person's behaviour as abusive, they might not be seeing it in this way.

Case study 5.4   Maggie

Maggie has issues about her relationship with Tony, her husband, and she tells you about a particular episode that had taken place the previous week: 'He had been driving me mad all day, just sitting in the chair staring at the telly. I had been asking him for hours to take the dog out and when I came downstairs from making the beds, the poor dog was in the kitchen and he was desperate to be let out. I went into the front room and I started shouting at Tony and he just ignored me, so I picked up the tray that he had had his lunch on and I threw it at him. The coffee cup hit his head and cut him, and then I just picked up anything I could get my hands on – books and ornaments – and just chucked them at him. He was just pathetic, cowering and begging me to stop. To get out of the room he would have to get past me and he daren't try that. So when I ran out of things to throw, I just grabbed my coat and the dog's lead, and me and the dog went out. When I got back he was out and he had gone to the hospital because he had to get a couple of stitches in his head.'

Maggie doesn't appear to have any sense of remorse or regret about what she has done. This is not the first time Maggie has described assaulting Tony, who doesn't try to defend himself or fight back.

COMMENT

The first thing that is in Maggie's favour is that she is coming to you wanting to work on her relationship. It is not unreasonable to assume, therefore, that even if she isn't saying it, on some level she is not comfortable with how things are. Hopefully, you would assert that, while Tony's indolence may be extremely irritating to Maggie, it is not acceptable for her to respond to it with violence. It is against Tony's human rights and indeed the law. Maggie could cause real harm to Tony and get herself into very serious trouble. Failure to challenge Maggie could lead her to assume that you think her behaviour towards Tony is acceptable or normal between partners, which may of course be her experience. On the other hand, if you don't handle the situation skilfully, Maggie may simply vote with her feet and stop coming.

You will need to be aware of your own responses to anger, which will undoubtedly be related to your own history. How would you cope if Maggie was to get angry in the session, or with you, were you to challenge her? You should consider your own safety, as you know that Maggie has a history of violence. Assaults against counsellors are very rare indeed, but they do occasionally happen and you have a responsibility to consider and take seriously your personal safety. Where and when are you seeing her? Are other people in the building at the time? Is someone aware of your timetable? These kinds of safeguards being in place will allow you to relax in the session and they are good practice in themselves. If you feel edgy in the session, your client will very likely pick up on it.

Like many of the situations we have already discussed, the issue is how to make a successful and constructive challenge. You know that such a challenge can only really come when the therapeutic relationship is properly and firmly established, so that your client feels supported within the relationship and therefore open to your challenge. Russell and Dexter (2008) have argued that the counsellor can usefully focus on the client's desired goals when constructing a challenge on a client's behaviour. In doing so, you can remain true to a non-judgemental position. In the case of Maggie, she says she wants to improve her relationship with Tony, communicate better with him, etc., so the questions are: Do her violent outbursts towards him help with this? What does she see as the likely outcome of them, with regard to her relationship with Tony?

Maggie's life experience may have taught her that violence is the way to sort out interpersonal disputes. Perhaps through the counselling she may learn that she has other, more constructive, options available to her.

This section has discussed situations where you might find it difficult to like your client and we started by saying that it is not really necessary to like your client, in the conventional sense, to create a good therapeutic relationship. However, as you work with a person, hear their story, observe their struggles and emotions, empathise with them, it is almost inevitable that you will develop a relationship with them that goes beyond mere liking and is much more meaningful. They may never be the person you would choose to be marooned with on a desert island, or to be the best man at your wedding, but you will have had an important encounter with them that will have changed both of you.

WHAT IF I THINK MY CLIENT HAS MENTAL HEALTH PROBLEMS?

At some point in your career it is most likely that you will be confronted by a client whose mental health is of concern to you. When you are in the apprentice phase of your career, as a student counsellor, or the journeyman phase, as a newly qualified and inexperienced practitioner, it is really important that you gain your clinical experience in an environment where someone more knowledgeable and experienced than you is assessing would-be clients for their suitability for counselling in general, and specifically their appropriateness to work with you at your level of experience and expertise. Many years ago, when counselling was emerging as a profession, there was much less emphasis on the importance of the assessment process, to the detriment of many a poor client and indeed counsellor. Experienced counsellors today often look on with concern and trepidation, when newly qualified counsellors set themselves up in private practice, apparently ignorant of the pitfalls and potential dangers of such a course of action, one of the most significant of which is the client with serious, but not immediately apparent to the untrained eye, mental health issues. There are some people who are too unwell, or have too poor a grasp of reality to enable them to engage in counselling safely and constructively. The vast majority of counsellors are not medically trained and cannot therefore diagnose mental illness per se, but the more experienced and well-trained counsellor is an educated and experienced lay person, who may well be able to recognise warning signs and indicators of serious mental illness and would screen out such a person at the assessment process, because other forms of treatment, such as medication or, in severe cases, sanctuary as an in-patient, are likely to be much more beneficial.

Counsellors can rarely retreat into the comfort of reality and the issue of mental health is no different from many others. The whole concept of mental health is constantly under challenge and writers like RD Laing (1967) and Thomas Szasz (1986) disagree profoundly with the medicalisation of mental health. They question the hegemony of one person's reality over another. These are important debates and ones about which you should certainly inform yourself, but this is essentially a practical book and we are thinking about practice. Russell and Dexter (2008) quote the definition of mental health used by the World Health Organisation, which is:

> *A state of well being in which the individual realises his or her own abilities, can cope with the normal stresses of life, can work productively and fruitfully and is able to make a contribution to his or her community.*
> (www.who.int/mediacentre/factsheet/fs220/en/)

They then suggest, perhaps tongue in cheek, that if we really think about it, perhaps the fact that a person is presenting for counselling could lead us to come to the conclusion that he or she is not in good mental health (2008, p112). However, there is a qualitative difference between a person whose emotional equilibrium is a little off kilter and a person who is seriously unwell.

REFLECTION POINT

- What kind of conditions do you think would render a person unable to benefit from counselling?

For practical purposes and purely as a rule of thumb, it is helpful to divide mental health issues into two categories: those that can be described as psychotic and those that can be described as neurotic, and then to think of each group as on a continuum. A person with a psychotic disorder, or someone experiencing a psychotic episode, does not have a good grasp of reality and will have little insight into what is happening to them. This state may be permanent or temporary, depending on the nature of their disorder and the treatment the patient is receiving. It is generally accepted that people in a psychotic state would not be helped by counselling because they do not have a grasp of reality and in fact the activity of counselling may even be harmful to them. It is considered possible to work with people suffering from psychotic disorders when they are well and appropriately medicated, but only if the counsellor has a good understanding of the condition, the medication, the person's mental health history and the likelihood of the reoccurrence of a psychotic episode, indicators, warning signs, etc.

An important issue to consider is the concept of team working to ensure the best quality of service. Someone with a psychotic illness is likely to have a history of involvement with mental health services. Historically, there has sometimes been a mutual suspicion between mental health workers, such as psychiatrists and community psychiatric nurses, and counsellors, perhaps even something of a turf war. However, the interests of such clients are probably better served by cooperation and a unified approach. Any counsellor working with clients with psychotic conditions would do well to establish networks in their local area with other mental health professionals so that, when appropriate and with the client's consent, they can draw on the expertise and support of others for this sometimes difficult and challenging work.

A client suffering from a neurotic condition has a good grasp of reality and has insight into their situation. All of us are neurotic in some way or another, but some neurotic illnesses, such as serious clinical depression and severe anxiety states, can be extremely debilitating and, given that they are often factors in suicidal behaviour, life threatening. Neurotic conditions are often what bring clients into counselling and can be successfully treated with 'talking therapies', although sometimes a combination of counselling and medical intervention, such as through the provision of medication, is the best course of action for the client.

As a counsellor who will be involved with clients' mental health, you need two things: a reasonable working knowledge of the gamut of mental health conditions, and a knowledge and understanding of psychotropic medication (drugs which work on the brain). This is to inform your thinking, rather than to encourage you to attempt diagnosis. In the case of the medication, it is so that you are aware of potential side effects and also because the medication that a client has been prescribed may be an indication of their condition.

While the assessment process will, to some extent, protect you as the counsellor from inappropriate referrals, it is the case that sometimes, during the counselling, the client, who appeared fairly stable in the beginning, starts to share things with you that cause you concern, perhaps suggesting that their grasp of reality is slipping or that their symptoms are becoming much more pronounced. You should immediately seek support and advice from your supervisor and from the clinical lead in your agency. Remember that, as a counsellor, while you are not responsible for your client, you do have a duty of care towards them and you also have an ethical responsibility to work within your level of competence. You may need to check with your client if other professionals, such as their GP, are aware of how things are and, with their permission, you might contact the GP to express your concern. On occasions, it may be that you need to refer the client on, to ensure that they will get the kind of help they need. This must be done sensitively, but it cannot be avoided safely.

Case study 5.5   Ben

Ben has been working with Gemma for some weeks. He has noticed during the last few sessions that Gemma seems very agitated. She wriggles around in her chair and, during the last session, got up and began pacing around. Also, she cuts off in the middle of her sentences and seems to lose her train of thought. Gemma's personal care seems to be declining. She looks ill-kempt and her hair is dirty. Gemma is saying strange things and at first Ben assumed they were metaphors, but his concern is mounting. Then in one session Gemma says: 'I know you are really trying to help, Ben. You have been keeping an eye on me between sessions, haven't you? I have heard you talking to me quietly through the television.'

Ben is alarmed, but he doesn't want to scare Gemma and knows it wouldn't be helpful to challenge her reality at this stage. He responds: 'You are right, Gemma, I do want to help you and I have been thinking that maybe we should consider my contacting your GP to see if we can get her on board as well. She may be able to help you too. What do you think?'

Gemma agrees, because she does trust Ben. After the session Ben immediately contacts his supervisor and she agrees that contact needs to be made with the GP. It turns out that Gemma has a history of psychotic episodes, which she had not shared with the person who assessed her. The GP takes it up from there and contacts the mental health team to whom Gemma is known. Ben is advised that he should not work with Gemma while she is so unwell, so, in consultation with his supervisor, he sends her the following letter.

Dear Gemma

After our session on Tuesday, I did as we agreed and contacted your GP. As I understand it, she in turn contacted Dr Woods at the Mental Health Team and I gather you are now being seen both by him and by the community psychiatric nurse. I am sure you did the right thing in agreeing to my making contact with your GP as it sounds like you are now going to get the help and support that you need at the moment.

Dr Woods contacted me today and we have agreed that while you are receiving treatment from his team, it would not be advisable or in your best interest for you to continue with your counselling work with me, as seeing so many different practitioners might be a little confusing or overwhelming for you. We will not therefore be meeting again next Tuesday or for the foreseeable future. I hope you will soon be feeling much better and once you are discharged by Dr Woods and, with his agreement, you can of course contact Spring Road Counselling Service, should you wish to begin counselling again.

Best wishes

Ben Wright

Senior Counsellor

WHAT DO I DO WHEN IT ALL GOES WRONG?

Counselling is an interaction between two flawed human beings and, as such, with the best will in the world, sometimes you are going to get it wrong. Even the most experienced and talented counsellor can read a situation wrongly and occasionally you will make an intervention which is so off the mark, so crass and inappropriate that you will long for the earth to open and swallow you up. Unfortunately, this is not going to happen and you will have to clear up the mess that you have created within the therapeutic relationship just as in any other kind of relationship. Sometimes, your mistake will be glaringly obvious; at other times, you will not initially notice and it will be your client who will bring it to your attention.

Current research, carried out by Safran and Muran, has studied the phenomena of what they have described as alliance ruptures – *a tension or breakdown in the collaborative relationship between patient and therapist* (Safran et al., 2002, p236 cited in Cooper, 2008). They have suggested that the breakdown will manifest itself in one of two ways, either through confrontation, where the client actively challenges the counsellor about the rupture, or through withdrawal, where the client fully or partially withdraws emotionally from the relationship. They argue that the repairing of the rupture is critical, not only to allow the therapeutic work to continue, but also because experiencing the process of rupture and then repair is very important to the development of the client. This seems to make sense, given the fact that many clients who struggle with anger and conflict do so because, while they may have plenty of experience of fighting and conflict in their childhood families, what they didn't see was those conflicts being worked through and resolved by the parties concerned in a constructive rather than a punitive way.

If your client tells you either directly or indirectly that you have made a mistake or got something wrong, try your best to receive this feedback openly and honestly, without being defensive, or worse still by attempting to push the blame on to your client. Allow the client not only to tell you what you have done, or failed to do, but allow them to express their emotional response to your mistake. Avoid rushing in to make apologies, which might stop your client from saying what they need to say and encourage them to start trying to make you feel better. Try to understand your client's feelings and, if necessary, ask for clarification. An honest acknowledgement, which validates your client's experience, is a good deal more therapeutic than a premature grovelling apology. You must be able to contain both yourself and your client through this potentially difficult exchange. You will need to draw on the personal qualities of both humility and courage.

It may be that your client is unable to make a direct challenge to you, either because this is too scary for them or because they are not really clear in their own mind about the issues. What you may experience is the client withdrawing, as described above. This is where you would use your skills to invite them to bring into consciousness what is happening and to help them to express their concerns and grievances. You will also need to pay attention to your own internal process with regard to this rupture and, where appropriate, make use of this within the dialogue, taking responsibility for yourself and absolutely avoiding slipping into client blaming.

Sadly, on some occasions, if you have made a mistake, or got things wrong, your client may just vote with their feet, cancel future appointments or simply fail to turn up. This can be very difficult for the counsellor because you are robbed of the opportunity of putting things right or, indeed, really understanding where it all went wrong. As a counsellor, you have to have broad shoulders and deal with it. Using your supervision, you can reflect on what has happened and do your best to learn from it. The more open you are with your supervisor, the greater the opportunity you will have. Your confidence may have taken a bit of a bashing, but this does provide you with the opportunity for growth and development, if you open yourself to it.

Clients do occasionally make complaints against their counsellors, either directly to the agency for which the counsellor is working or directly to the BACP or other professional bodies. The procedures for dealing with complaints is laid out in the *Ethical Framework* and it is a good idea to familiarise yourself with it, just in case. However, this is a final resort and, despite all attempts to make the process as painless as possible, it is emotionally taxing and time-consuming for all concerned. It is very much in everyone's interest to make every effort to sort matters out informally, perhaps using the mediation of a third party, before it gets to this.

Facing up to your mistakes and learning from them is important in another and very profound way because it says something about the equality that should exist between counsellor and client. Either you acknowledge that you are both flawed and vulnerable human beings or you retreat into the much more dangerous fantasy of damaged and needy client and perfectly evolved and sorted out therapist/expert, which is such a nonsense. In reality, most of us may be the counsellor at 10am but at 4pm we are in someone else's consulting room as the client. Baldwin quotes Rogers, who said in an interview:

The therapist needs to recognise very clearly that he or she is an imperfect person with flaws which make him vulnerable. I think it is only as the therapist views himself as imperfect and flawed that he can see himself as helping another person. Some people who call themselves therapists are not healers, because they are too busy defending themselves.

(Baldwin, 2000, p36)

CHAPTER SUMMARY

Whatever the nature of your worst nightmares, hopefully this chapter will have given you some pointers as to how you might go about dealing with them. The common denominators for facing your worst nightmares are:

- don't panic! – reflect and respond rather than simply reacting – take your time and think ethically about the issue;
- take advice – discuss the problem with your supervisor, the clinical lead in your agency, your tutors if you are still a student or your counselling peers, making sure that you are respecting confidentiality in the manner in which you do this;
- educate yourself, read around the issue, including current research;
- develop your skill of challenging your client appropriately;
- try to be open to and honest about your own process – this way you are likely to avoid 'client blaming';
- if an alliance rupture occurs, accept responsibility for your part in it and try to repair it;
- familiarise yourself with the complaints procedure, just in case.

SUGGESTED FURTHER READING

Bond, T (2010) *Standards and Ethics for Counselling in Action*, 3rd edition. London: Sage.

Chapter 7 on suicide is extremely informative and helpful.

Bond, T and Sandhu, A (2005) *Therapist in Court: Providing Evidence and Supporting Witnesses.* London: Sage.

Chapter 4 is very informative about appearing in coroners' courts.

Daines, B, Gask, L and Howe, A (2007) *Medical and Psychiatric Issues for Counsellors*, 2nd edition. London: Sage.

This is a useful reference book for counsellors on matters of mental health.

Parkes, CM and Wertheimer, A (2001) *A Special Scar: The Experience of People Bereaved by Suicide.* Hove: Routledge.

This is a really good read and offers great insight into this experience.

Russell, J and Dexter, G (2008) *Blank Minds and Sticky Moments in Counselling,* 2nd edition. London: Sage.

Chapter 6 on mental health issues is really accessible and user friendly.

Taking care of yourself

CORE KNOWLEDGE

- Counsellors, if they are to be effective, must take care of themselves both professionally and personally. This chapter encourages you to look regularly at your working practices and personal life to ensure that you maintain a balance between your needs and the needs of your clients.
- This chapter explores the following core strategies:
  - personal therapy;
  - supervision;
  - networking;
  - joining professional organisations;
  - continuing professional development (CPD);
  - work/life balance;
  - keeping good records.

INTRODUCTION

Earlier in this book, we discussed the ethical principles, which are one of the pillars of the *Ethical Framework*. In this chapter we are going to re-visit the last of these principles – self-respect – which puts counsellors under an ethical imperative to take proper care of themselves and to take their own emotional and physical well-being seriously. This is not primarily because they are a sharing, caring community of practitioners who want all of their number to be healthy and happy, however laudable that might be. It is because the collective wisdom is that counsellors who do take proper care of themselves both professionally and personally are going to be able to provide a better and safer service to clients whose interests are paramount.

One of the drawbacks of counselling as a career is that it is, by its very nature, a solitary pursuit. Because of the specific way in which we, as counsellors, understand the concept of client confidentiality, we are not free in the way that other professionals are to discuss our work with clients. We always see them on our own. In a multidisciplinary team, counsellors do often find themselves on the margins with their work, not always understood or appreciated by their colleagues. More experienced practitioners may work in private practice as a sole practitioner or maybe sharing premises with others, but not working together as such. While this kind of autonomy is attractive to many of us because counsellors do tend to be rather individualistic and autonomous by nature (managing a group of counsellors has been compared to herding cats!), it can also be quite isolating, particularly during times of personal or professional crisis. In the consulting room, you stand alone as the counsellor. You don't have colleagues with you, you don't have tools or books available to you during the session, you yourself are your only resource, so you owe it both to your client and to yourself to ensure that you are in a good place with yourself and are able to shoulder the responsibility inherent in the work without harming yourself. In this chapter we will consider the ways in which you can support and take care of yourself as a counsellor and the networks you could set up to support yourself in your work.

PERSONAL THERAPY

There is a long-running debate in the world of counselling as to whether or not a person who wishes to train as a counsellor should be required to have counselling themselves, as part of the training experience (Dryden and Feltham, 1994; Johns, 1996; Mearns and Cooper, 2005). Those in favour argue that in order to fully integrate the learning on a counselling course, the student needs to have the experience of counselling from the perspective of the client and that a counsellor cannot take a client somewhere they haven't been themselves. In addition, the experience of being a client wards against any tendency towards inequality, seeing the client as a troubled individual who will be cured by the expert practitioner. Enhanced self-awareness is clearly desirable in counselling students and the opportunity to process material stimulated by the training, in personal therapy, is seen as extremely valuable.

Those who argue against the requirement are not arguing against the value of personal therapy per se; their concern is more about making a student engage in it at a particular time. The danger is that it becomes a box-ticking exercise, motivated by the desire to meet the course requirements. It substantially adds to the cost of training and may indeed make it prohibitive to some. They would argue that it denies the student's autonomy and their right to decide when to go into therapy themself.

REFLECTION POINT

- What position do you take in this debate and why?

Whatever position you have taken on the above debate, it would seem a little nonsensical and even hypocritical to work as a counsellor without ever having experienced what it is like to be a client. Many experienced practitioners are in and out of personal therapy throughout their whole working lives and find it really helpful and supportive to them. It is a useful and constructive way of taking care of yourself. In your work as a counsellor, you will be trudging around in emotion and clients do have a nasty habit of confronting you with the very emotions and, indeed, situations that you would most like to avoid.

Case study 6.1 Cathy

Cathy is an experienced counsellor working with Phil, who is engaged in long-term work about his relationships with women. In the course of the work it emerges that Phil was adopted as a baby. Time and time again the work comes back to the issue of rejection. Phil will do almost anything to avoid feeling rejected, including breaking off relationships that had been going well, being unfaithful and avoiding intimacy. They make the connection between Phil's behaviour and his rejection by his birth mother. Phil had actually had quite a loving and supportive family and has good relationships with his adoptive parents, but this does not compensate for his deep-seated terror of rejection.

    Cathy finds herself in emotional turmoil. Phil's work is stimulating memories for her and opening old wounds. She herself had a baby when she was only 16 years old. Although she desperately wanted to keep him, she had no support from her family and was persuaded that it was in his best interests to give him up for adoption. She has worked on her feelings of devastation at having to give up her baby in her own therapy, but had always believed that she had done the best she could for her son, given her age and circumstances. Now Phil's work is making her feel troubled. She wonders what emotional damage was caused to her own little boy. She begins to feel a whole new level of guilt. She takes these feelings to supervision and, with her supervisor, she comes to the decision that she needs to go back into therapy because she knows she must be able to put her own issues and feelings to the side when she is working with Phil, so that she can be truly present for him. She is experienced enough to know that she cannot achieve this through attempting to suppress her feelings; she needs to face up to them and work through them. This is not the business of supervision. It belongs to personal therapy.

COMMENT

Cathy's case is a classic example of what can happen when working as a counsellor. Phil's work had peeled away another emotional layer for Cathy and had brought to the surface unresolved issues that Cathy has to address if she wants to be fully available to Phil in his work. If she doesn't do this, then she could find herself cutting off from Phil emotionally, which he would very likely experience as another crushing rejection. Cathy has to be able to separate her issues from Phil's work so she is able to put her own concerns on the 'back burner' during Phil's sessions and focus entirely on him. As Wosket argues:

> *My client will be helped to the extent that I can be fully available to him or her as my authentic and whole self. If I need to block, dodge, duck and dive when faced with certain aspects of the client's story in order to protect myself, I will certainly be preventing the client from doing the therapeutic work that they need to do.*
>
> (2008, p117)

A counsellor is not a finished product; you are work-in-progress and it is likely that you will have to return to personal therapy from time to time to clear up issues that your work with clients has stimulated.

The other important reason for using personal therapy to support your work as a counsellor relates to levels of self-awareness. The more you know about yourself and, more importantly, the more you are able to accept all aspects of yourself, the better your psychological well-being, and there does seem to be some correlation (although it is important to say quite a small one) between the therapist level of psychological well-being and functioning, and positive client outcomes (Cooper, 2008, p83). Cooper summarises the research relating to the value of personal therapy for counsellors. He tells us that there is a small but significant number of studies that show that personal therapy is positively related to therapists' levels of warmth, empathy and genuineness, as well as their awareness of countertransference. He also tells us that therapists themselves identify personal therapy as a really important and significant developmental experience. This does seem to suggest that personal therapy is a helpful way for therapists to take good care of themselves.

ACTIVITY 6.1

- If you have had personal therapy yourself, make a list of the ways in which it has been helpful to you in your therapeutic work and in your personal life.

SUPERVISION

I am sure you will have noticed that throughout this book, I am constantly suggesting that you should consult your supervisor. This is because of a firm belief that the most important support any counsellor has is a good and experienced supervisor. Your supervisor is the one person with whom you can freely discuss your work as a therapist, the client's material, your process, the interactions and dynamic between the two of you, the issues raised, your emotional responses and any problems or difficulties. A good supervisor is worth their weight in gold. The BACP recognises the important function that supervision serves by requiring that all counsellors in practice have a minimum of 1.5 hours of supervision each month. The requirement for students on accredited courses is greater as they are required to have supervision on a fortnightly basis.

One way in which you, as a counsellor, can take good care of yourself is by choosing a supervisor who is really going to meet your needs and there is a lot to think about in this choice. If you are at the apprentice or journeyman stage of your counselling career, as a student or an inexperienced practitioner, you will want a supervisor who has much more experience and expertise than you have at present. As an analogy, imagine you are a tennis player. When you first take up the sport and are looking to build and develop your skills, learn how to read the game, develop strength and fitness specific to the sport, etc., there would not be much point in choosing as your coach someone who has only been playing a year longer than you. You would want the club pro, someone who has much to teach you and whose experience you can draw on.

You need a supervisor who understands the supervision process. It is probably wise to choose someone who has been trained in supervision, although there are still some very experienced supervisors out there, probably nearing the end of their careers, who began supervising before there were any such courses. The BACP has a supervisor accreditation process, but it has never been as popular as the counsellor accreditation process, and many trained and experienced supervisors have never sought accreditation for their supervision work. Particularly at the early stages of your counselling career, there is a strong argument for seeking a supervisor who has the same theoretical orientation as you. In fact, many training courses require it as it helps you to integrate your learning because your supervisor will be speaking the same theoretical language as you. Imagine how confusing and unhelpful it could be, for example, if your supervisor, coming from a CBT perspective, is banging on about core beliefs and cognitions, while you, coming from a psychodynamic perspective, are desperately trying to get your head around unconscious process and defences. At the early stages, it could feel as if one of you is speaking French and the other German, both beautiful and expressive languages no doubt.

Do I have the right supervisor?

Once you have identified that someone has training, sufficient expertise and experience, and is of an appropriate orientation, how do you actually decide if they are the right person for you? Well, to some extent, it will be a matter of matching your two personalities because it is going to be extremely helpful to you if your supervisor is someone with whom you can identify and get along. They have to be approachable and you have to feel that they are someone to whom you can bring your difficulties and struggles as well as your good work and triumphs. However, they also have to be someone who will challenge you and be on your case if necessary. So, going for someone who seems really passive and gentle may not be in your best interest, even if it seems quite attractive. A good supervisor will sometimes act as the advocate of the client and will take you to task on ethical issues as and when it is appropriate. This is their responsibility (Wheeler and King, 2001).

What should a supervisor be doing?

A supervisor has many jobs to do with you, the supervisee, and a good supervisor is able to slip effortlessly from one job or role to another. The first role is educative, where your supervisor acts as a teacher, helping you to work towards best practice, perhaps making connections with theory and helping you to develop your thinking and awareness. The second is the managerial or monitoring role, which focuses on the quality of your work, ethical practice, anti-discriminatory practice, etc. The third is the supportive role, where the supervisor helps you to discharge your emotional responses to the work of counselling and look after yourself appropriately. Owen (2008) describes a fourth mode, the transformative mode, which brings about real in-depth learning for the supervisee, combining the other three modes but also set in the context of a really creative, open and honest relationship between the supervisee and her supervisor. It moves supervision beyond the mechanical to something much more nurturing and creative.

As you become more experienced and your expertise develops, it is likely that the style of supervision you will require will change. The more experienced you become professionally, the harder it becomes to find a person who is more experienced than you, within reasonable travelling distance, unless you live in the middle of one of the big cities. However, it is not such a problem because, if we go back to our tennis analogy, you are now yourself on the pro circuit and what you need to help you keep on top of your game is another experienced pro to play with. Together, you will be able to identify the weaknesses and strengths of your game and focus your practice accordingly. In supervision terms, we refer to this as consultative or collegial supervision. This is when an experienced practitioner provides supervision for a peer. The focus is a little different, in that the teaching function of supervision recedes somewhat, although we can always learn from one another. Hawkins and Shohet (1990) argue that at this level it is not about acquiring more knowledge but rather allowing it to deepen and integrate until it becomes wisdom. Consultative supervision should still be both challenging and supportive.

Group supervision is also an option, but must complement and not replace individual supervision. Creatively conducted by an experienced supervisor, group supervision provides the opportunity for learning not just from your supervisor but also from the work of other group members.

REFLECTION POINT

- What do you think you personally really need from your supervisor to help you to work as well as possible?

There are one or two important indicators for when it might be the right time to move on and find yourself a new supervisor. Do you feel as though you are getting what you really need from the sessions? Do you get both challenged and supported? Are you able to be really open and honest with your supervisor, particularly about what you may be getting wrong or what they have got wrong with you? Has it all got a bit too chatty and comfortable? Can you predict what your supervisor is going to say or can they still surprise you? Do you collude with one another? Do you look forward to going to your supervision and come away thinking that it has been time and money well spent?

The relationship with your supervisor is absolutely crucial to your well-being and development as a counsellor, and so is a vital part of taking care of yourself. If it is not working for you, you have an obligation to change it, either by raising it with your supervisor and attempting to renegotiate a way of working that would be more beneficial to you or, if that doesn't work, then perhaps you need to change your supervisor. Changing supervisors every few years is something that many practitioners do as a matter of course, to get a fresh perspective on their work.

NETWORKING

Even the word networking makes some of us go cold as it conjures up images of men in sharp suits, handing out their beautifully crafted business cards over their freshly squeezed orange juice at breakfast meetings.

However, if we start with the premise that counselling can be a lonely business for the counsellor and that isolation is without doubt one of the negative aspects of the work, then the importance of creating networks, by which I mean identifying other like-minded practitioners and making connections with them, becomes more obvious.

Informal networks serve many purposes. They are an excellent source of personal and professional support. Imagine, for example, that you have finished your training and have no further contact with your peers or tutors. Something happens with a client, or at your agency, that you are troubled by. You would immediately take it to your supervisor but unfortunately she has just gone off on a three-week trip to Outer Mongolia. What do you do? Issues of confidentiality would prevent you from talking it over with your partner or a friend you meet in the pub. Having a network of colleagues whose values are the same as yours, who are likely to understand the issues and complexities with which you are struggling, would be invaluable. You could set up an impromptu peer supervision, with an appropriate contract of confidentiality. If you are able to extract the issue from the context, you could have a confidential discussion or you could ask for the support and help you need to tide you over until your supervisor returns.

Having a group of peers who understand your work context also enables you to engage safely in that good old activity of moaning. Moaning can be divided into two distinct sorts. The first sort is the negative kind, which we often find in work places where people form moaning clubs. They sit around, perhaps over a cup of tea, and engage in the game of 'ain't it awful?', which only serves to reinforce each other's dissatisfaction and to discharge sufficient emotional energy to enable the participants to carry on in the situation that is so awful to them. Nothing ever changes from this kind of negativity. There is, however, another kind of moaning, which allows the moaner to let off a bit of steam but at the same time strengthens his or her resolve to take some action to change things. This kind of moaning is constructive and part of the change process.

Case study 6.2   Greta

Greta works as a counsellor in a GP's surgery. For some time she has been feeling fed up because she thinks her colleagues at the surgery do not take her work seriously. The practice manager is always altering the room she allocates to Greta and Greta has had several arguments with her about it. Also, she is sometimes excluded from meetings she thinks she should be a part of. Sometimes the doctors send her referrals that are really unsuitable for counselling. She goes to the monthly get-together she has with a group of counselling colleagues from her area after a particularly difficult week at the surgery. They give her space to let off steam about her work situation and listen to her with empathy. Once she has finished what she needed to get off her chest, they begin to think about what she might do to improve the situation. Someone suggests that she might put together a paper to present to the next practice meeting explaining clearly what she can offer the practice but also what she needs from them to support her work. Colleagues offer to read her paper, if she emails it to them, so they can help her refine it. One colleague knows another GP's practice counsellor in a different area. This counsellor is integrated into the practice very well. Her colleague offers to make contact with this person and see if he is willing to talk to Greta, so he can help her to think about best practice. They come up with lots of resources that Greta can draw on. She leaves this meeting feeling much better and highly motivated to try to bring about positive change in her work situation.

Peers in the field can also prove to be very useful if you need to make a referral. They may either be able to take the case themselves or they may know someone with exactly the kind of expertise and experience you are looking for to work with the person you wish to refer. You can bounce ideas around, discuss theory and developments in the world of counselling, swap books, etc. Peers can support you through your accreditation process. If you eventually choose to go into private practice, they become even more important to you, because the threat of professional isolation is even greater in this kind of work.

Perhaps because of the rather peculiar work we do, and because we are constantly striving to be as real and open as possible in our interactions with one another, it seems to be the case that colleagues from our training and peers from our practice days have the habit of morphing into lifelong friends.

JOINING A PROFESSIONAL ORGANISATION

Most professions have some kind of professional body, for example, the Law Society or the Royal College of Nursing. Some of those that haven't, such as social workers, are at present debating whether or not it would be to their advantage to set one up as a means of getting themselves taken more seriously as a profession and to create an august body that speaks for the profession as a whole. For counsellors and therapists, the two biggest and most influential professional bodies are the British Association for Counselling and Psychotherapy (BACP) and the United Kingdom Council for Psychotherapy (UKCP). (The BACP has a sister organisation in Scotland, which is Counselling and Psychotherapy in Scotland (COSCA).) At the time of writing, the largest of these organisations, the BACP, has around 30,000 individual members. Its aims and objectives can be found on its website (www.bacp.co.uk), but they are, broadly speaking, to promote the education and training of practitioners; to raise standards, primarily for the benefit of clients; to educate the public about counselling; and to serve the community.

As with every other issue related to counselling, there is a long-running debate as to whether or not it is a good idea for counsellors to have such professional bodies. A minority of practitioners believe that the whole professionalisation of counselling strikes at the very heart of the therapeutic relationship and diminishes autonomy and creativity. They are also fiercely against what they see as the medicalisation of therapy. This debate has been brought to a head by current developments in counselling, particularly the imminence of statutory regulation. Claringbull (2010) has summarised these debates very succinctly in his book (which is part of this series) *What is Counselling & Psychotherapy?*

ACTIVITY 6.2

- Visit BACP's website and follow the threads relating to statutory regulation. Next, go to the website of the Alliance for Counselling and Psychotherapy Against State Regulation (www.allianceforcandp.org). To help you to understand this debate, and others relating to the future of counselling, you should refer to Chapter 10 of Claringbull's book mentioned above.

This chapter is about taking care of yourself as a practitioner, so that you can provide the best possible service to your clients. There is a strong argument for saying that being part of a community of 30,000 colleagues whose work is underpinned by the same set of values, who all accept the *Ethical Framework* as their benchmark against which they hold themselves accountable, having access to all the shared resources, research and accumulated wisdom, and whose officers work on a daily basis to promote the best interests of the profession, is a good way of doing this. Like any organisation made up of flawed individuals, it doesn't always get it right. It can be overly bureaucratic, elitist, etc., but it has been and is an important factor in the development of counselling in this country.

Particularly in the early stages of your career, when you have not yet had the time to build up your individual credibility or reputation as a practitioner, being a member of BACP may prove helpful to you in obtaining placements or even work. Many agencies are themselves organisational members of BACP and governed by its *Ethical Framework*. Accountability is a crucial issue and, while at present BACP does not have the power to prevent someone from practising as a counsellor (in the way that a doctor or solicitor can be struck off their professional register and are therefore unable to continue in practice), having your membership of BACP withdrawn would be a serious blow to a practitioner's credibility. Given that we live in a technological age and that the internet is the starting point for many people seeking a service, it could have a serious effect on your income too.

CONTINUING PROFESSIONAL DEVELOPMENT (CPD)

Counselling does not take place in a vacuum. It takes place in a social context and one which is constantly changing and evolving. New scientific discoveries are being made, new research is being carried out, technology is developing, new social issues and political situations are emerging, life unerringly moves on.

When I began practising as a counsellor more than 25 years ago, the internet and mobile phones did not exist, and the Cold War was still dragging on. We hadn't experienced the full impact of Thatcherism and no one had heard of New Labour. The idea that the West would find itself locked into an ideological and military struggle with the forces of radicalised Islam would have seemed faintly ridiculous to the general public. Society was more overtly racist, homophobic, etc. In short, it was another world entirely. The point is that the context in which my training was set was radically different from the present social and political context. Counselling and counsellors have to evolve and develop new skills, new knowledge and understanding, and we have to refine our responses to the context in which we work, hence the need for CPD. Bond (2010) points out that there is also a perpetual need for updating with regard to legal obligations and professional accountability.

CPD can include several activities, such as attending courses and conferences, which offer excellent opportunities for meeting new colleagues and catching up with those you already know. It is sensible to give proper thought, on an annual basis, to identifying your existing training needs and how you can best meet them, while also leaving yourself open to training and development opportunities that catch your interest as you go along. In addition to courses, keeping up with your reading is vital and here I make a particular plea for getting yourself into the habit of accessing and reading current research papers. Train yourself to approach them with discernment, as Cooper argues:

> *Research findings can be like good friends: something that can encourage, advise, stimulate and help us, but also something we are not afraid to challenge and argue against.*

(2008, p1)

Once you have found your feet as a counsellor of individuals, perhaps you might like to extend your expertise and repertoire by training in another specialism, such as couples work, or working with children, or supervision. Others may wish to continue with their academic study of counselling to masters or doctoral level. All of these activities will help you to keep on growing and developing as a practitioner. Engaging in practitioner research is an increasingly popular area of CPD (McLeod, 2003).

Focusing on personal development, through therapy groups, for example, can be really helpful and productive for counsellors in their professional work. Wosket argues that such activity is:

> *A prerequisite for those counsellors who aspire to draw on their own life experience and personal attributes to any significant degree in their work with clients.*

> (2008, p115)

Think creatively when you consider what you might include personally under the heading of CPD. Bringing a baby into the world and raising it through the toddler stage could provide you with substantial learning, if you are reflecting upon your experience. So is helping someone close to you through a mental illness or caring for a person with dementia – indeed, anything that gets you thinking about your subject and reflecting on your practice. It is a shame to write off CPD as something that you have to do, instead of something that will be both stimulating and improving, and is an excellent way of taking care of yourself professionally.

REFLECTION POINT

- Thinking ahead to the next three years, what are the areas that you need or would particularly like to focus on for your CPD? List and prioritise them.

WORK/LIFE BALANCE

Due to both the nature and the context of counselling work, if you are trying to take care of yourself professionally, then paying attention to your work/life balance is particularly important.

One reason why so many of us really enjoy the work we do is because the work of counselling comprises real and meaningful interactions with other people, i.e. our clients. If you think for a moment about the nature of most everyday interactions with other people, much of the content is a little banal. No one is really speaking about things that are important to them or expressing their feelings. Counselling by comparison is often very intimate and emotionally charged. When counselling is really working and at its best, we are engaging at what Mearns and Cooper (2005) have referred to as relational depth. Engaging at this level is a profound and meaningful experience not just for the client, but also for the therapist. Mearns and Cooper have described it as:

> *A feeling of profound contact and engagement with a client, in which one simultaneously experiences high and consistent levels of empathy and acceptance towards that Other, and relates to them in a highly transparent way.*
>
> (2005, p36)

Herein lies the rub – sometimes counsellors fall into the trap of relying on this intimacy, this highly emotionally charged personal contact, to fulfil their own need for closeness and human contact, instead of ensuring that their emotional needs are being met elsewhere, in their family lives and with their friends. When this happens a subtle but damaging shift can take place within the dynamic between counsellor and client. The counsellor begins to piggyback on the client's life and live vicariously through the client (Miller, 1997).

Wosket (2008) pulls no punches when she says somewhat bluntly:

> *Counsellors who find themselves immersed in their clients' world to the exclusion of extratherapeutic interests and relationships would do well, in colloquial parlance, to 'get a life', for as Guggenbuhl-Craig (1979,*

*p57) asserts, it is only the therapist 'who is passionately engaged in his
own life (who) can help his patients to find theirs'.*

(2008, p203)

Case study 6.3   Alan

Alan is a middle-aged counsellor who does not have a very good relationship with
his wife. His son and daughter have left home. Alan works as a counsellor in a
college. It doesn't happen with all of his clients, but he notices that some of his
clients are becoming very important to him. He thinks of them often between
sessions. He gets quite annoyed if they don't turn up for sessions and sometimes
tries to discourage them from ending their counselling with him. Alan really likes
it when they give him positive feedback about his work with them. He likes it
when he sees them about the college, maybe in the refectory when he is having
his lunch. He likes to feel that he is playing an important role in their lives, making
a difference, maybe understanding them in a way that other people, like their
tutors or their parents, don't seem to do. In the staff room, he often finds himself
speaking up for young people and one of his colleagues actually accused him of
being grandiose, fancying himself as the student's hero. He is not so good as he
used to be at keeping boundaries, he stays late at work and will always fit in the
extra client who turns up at his door. If he is honest, he doesn't always take these
'special' clients to supervision. There is no need, he is doing fine with them. He is
not impressed with other counsellors who do not appear to have the same level
of commitment as him. It's just a job to them, he thinks, whereas for Alan it is a
vocation, a calling even.

REFLECTION POINT

- What do you think of Alan and his situation?
- Would you have any concerns about him and, if so, what are they?

So, what other than therapy passionately interests you? What makes you
feel really alive? Who are the people that matter to you and how much
quality time do you spend with them? How do you take care of spiritual
needs? What stimulates your mind? These questions are not academic. As
a counsellor you have a duty to think about them and to take action. So,
whether it is dancing alone on a beautiful beach at sunset or jumping up
and down in the terraces of some football stadium with a bunch of mates,
then go and do it with gusto.

KEEPING GOOD RECORDS

Finally, we are going to consider the process of keeping good and appropriate records as a way of taking care of yourself as a practitioner. The keeping of records is contentious in itself and there are counsellors who do not keep records at all. However, the argument for keeping records is growing in strength as the context of counselling develops. In the early part of your career, when you are working for an institution or agency, you are unlikely to have any choice in the matter and will almost certainly be required to keep records. The arguments for and against keeping records are well rehearsed elsewhere (see Bond, 2010, Chapter 13) and information about how to write records, what should be included, etc., is to be found both in that chapter and in Bond and Mitchels' *Confidentiality and Record Keeping in Counselling and Psychotherapy* (2008).

Here we are going to focus on how the process of keeping records might be a good way of taking care of yourself, but before we do that we need to give some attention to the practicalities of keeping records. The most significant issue here is obviously confidentiality. The agency for which you are working will hopefully have a policy about record security and is quite likely to insist that you do not take records out of the building, either physically or electronically. However, if you are moving records around you obviously have to think carefully about their security.

Once you get the records home, you should keep them in a locked drawer or cabinet and, if they are electronic, they need to be password protected. You should also make arrangements with someone, like a colleague or supervisor, as to what should happen to them, should you fall under a bus, or be abducted by aliens.

To support your practice, your records should be something you use to help you to reflect on your work, keep track of developments over the weeks and prepare for your supervision, so that you can use the time effectively. The process of writing up a session gives you the opportunity to really think about your interventions and the flow of the work. It will also help you to develop your 'internal supervisor' and the ability to focus on the important aspects of the content and process of the session. This is of crucial importance developmentally for you as a practitioner. On occasions, when you are feeling disheartened about the work, a trawl through your records will remind you just how far your client has come.

Should any issues arise, or should you need to make a referral, etc., your notes will provide you with an aide-memoire. They will also enhance your professional credibility with other colleagues, particularly if your coun-selling work is under challenge or scrutiny. Very occasionally, counsellors become embroiled in legal proceedings, such as inquests, or because the client is looking to the counsellor for support in an application made to the court for custody of children, for example. Such a situation can be something of a minefield for a counsellor and, for this reason, one important way of taking care of yourself is to make sure you are informed about your ethical and legal responsibilities with regard to the keeping of records. You should learn about the Data Protection Act 1998 and its implications for your work and you should familiarise yourself with such issues as access to records by the police and the courts. It is much better and safer for you to do this as a matter of course, rather than in a time of crisis, when you may already have compromised your position. Jenkins (2007) covers all these issues in great depth and, given that society has become so litigious, it would be foolish to ignore them.

ACTIVITY 6.4

With reference to Jenkins, answer the following questions:

- What rights does a client have under the Data Protection Act 1998, to have access to records kept about them?
- Are hand-written records treated the same as records kept on computer?
- If the police or the courts were to request access to your confidential records about a client, what should you do?

COPING WITH BURN-OUT OR 'PHYSICIAN, HEAL THYSELF'

What exactly does this term 'burn-out' mean? We hear it often in the conversations of those who work in the helping professions. As a working definition perhaps we could think of it as a situation where the counsellor has become exhausted – physically, emotionally, or both – to the point that they are temporarily unable to provide the level of care and service required by their client work because they don't have the necessary emotional resilience. I will attempt to illustrate this with an example from my own life.

Many years ago, when my own family were still quite young, I helped to nurse a good friend of mine who was dying of cancer. Each day was taken up by juggling all my responsibilities: looking after my family and home; seeing my clients; teaching my courses; then in any other time I had, rushing off to my friend's house to do my share of the rota we had established. This went on for a period of about four months until she died. I took a week off and then returned to work. As often happens when people are extremely stressed, and despite the fact that I had written my master's thesis on the grieving process, I was paying no attention at all to my own emotional state; in fact, if I was conscious of any feelings at all, it was a numbness. Several weeks after my friend's death, I was at my supervision. My supervisor commented that I seemed to be rather irritated with all my clients. I had to confess that I was, which really surprised and disturbed me. I had lost my ability to empathise with them and, to my shame, was feeling that they all just needed to pull themselves together and stop whinging, and the same was true of my wretched students! My supervisor, very skilfully and by using humour, encouraged me to really pay attention to what I was doing, thinking and feeling. She sowed the seed in me and then left it to germinate. It was going around in my head for the rest of the day. That evening, I was putting on my boots to take my dogs out and one of the laces snapped. To my amazement, I began to cry uncontrollably. The poor old dogs had to wait while I howled, then they got an extra long walk, during which I was able to acknowledge my own emotional and physical exhaustion and make the decision that I needed to take a few weeks off, because I was completely burnt out.

Painful and difficult as this experience was, it did teach me a good deal about the nature of burn-out. First, you don't always see it coming. It is like the juggernaut, hurtling towards you at great speed, but around the bend in the road. Paradoxically, just when you need your wits and senses about you to help you to notice your own condition, they can desert you while you rush on like the proverbial headless chicken.

Of course, like any other human condition, the way we experience burn-out will be different, depending on our circumstances and personality types. For some it comes as a sense of hopelessness and of being totally overwhelmed and unable to cope any more; for others it may be a sense of impotence, an inability to relax or settle to anything. It is, however, almost always a frightening and disconcerting experience, which saps your confidence, and so it makes great sense to think it through carefully and develop strategies for avoiding it.

In thinking about burn-out, it is perhaps useful to divide it into two sorts – work-related burn-out and burn-out that relates to your private life, while at the same time acknowledging the interplay between the two. An important factor in work-related burn-out is obviously case load, not only the number of clients you have and particularly the number you see each day, but also the nature of your client work. For example, if you are working with clients who have complex and compound issues, or issues that are highly emotionally charged, such as recent bereavement or abuse, or if you are working with very damaged clients, then the emotional toll this is going to take from you is likely to be greater than if you were, for example, working with an EAP client who wanted to look at their assertiveness skills. If you are going to be truly emotionally available to your clients, then their work will impact on you and it is therefore important that you negotiate a work load that is manageable for you. Your personal life circumstances will be relevant here, as will your level of experience in the work.

Experienced counsellors dealing with emotionally demanding work develop strategies for discharging the emotions they are left with after a client has gone, such as popping out for a quick walk, listening to music, playing with the dog, whatever helps you to get rid of one lot of emotional detritus, before making yourself available to the next person. One counsellor reported that after working with a client who had been severely sexually abused, she got into the habit of taking a shower, so that through the ritual of the running water and washing herself, she could let go of the visceral experience of being with her client and hearing the details of the dreadful abuse the client had suffered.

Taking breaks and holidays away from client work, away from shop-talk can be a good way of looking after yourself and avoiding burn-out. Obviously, such breaks have to be appropriately clinically managed, so you should think ahead and get them in the diary. The period between the Christmas break and summer holidays can be a long slog, particularly with the dark evenings and rainy days, and having something ahead to look forward to is a sensible idea. Even a weekend, doing something completely different and unrelated to your counselling work, can be enormously restorative.

The best way of avoiding burn-out is, without a doubt, thinking about yourself and your own responses to stress and exhaustion. What happens to you when you are in this state? What are the physical, the emotional, the cognitive and the social signs that you are under stress? For example, does your eating or your sex drive change? Do you lose your concentration or become overly focused on tasks? Are you snappy or withdrawn? It could be useful to discuss this with someone who knows you really well and who you think is insightful. Ask them about how you have appeared in the past when you have been under stress. With their assistance, draw up your own stress profile. What you will have then is a set of indicators, red flags to warn you that you are getting close to burn-out. Your red flags could, for example, be that you drink more, you are not sleeping well, you become withdrawn, it is harder for you to concentrate so you skip from task to task, you forget things, etc. The trick is that once you notice no more than two of these red flags, you do something about it. You take it to your supervisor and your manager to see what could be done. You start looking after yourself better and with consciousness. You take action to stop the process before it becomes really serious for you.

Finally, it is worth acknowledging that life itself can sometimes deal you a very difficult hand. People we love get sick and die. Relationships break up. Caring responsibilities can become really heavy and difficult. Financial problems come along. We get ill. Being a counsellor does not make you immune to any of those things. Sometimes, counselling, like any other work, can be a welcome distraction from what is going on in your personal life and you are able to put your own concerns on the back burner and be fully present with your client. However, occasionally that is not possible. Then you simply have to take time out. The only ethical thing you can do is, with the support of your supervisor and manager, stop working until your equilibrium is restored and you are able to give your clients the quality of attention that they deserve and should be able to expect.

CHAPTER SUMMARY

In this chapter we have:

- given thought to how you, as the counsellor, can take care of yourself, so that you can offer the best and safest service to your clients;
- discussed ways of supporting yourself and the kind of networks that are going to prevent isolation and promote your well-being and development as a practitioner;
- looked at the kinds of activities that are developmental and which keep you alive and learning as a counsellor;
- considered strategies for avoiding burn-out and for ensuring that your counselling work fits into and complements the rest of your life, rather than taking it over.

SUGGESTED FURTHER READING

Bond, T (2010) *Standards and Ethics in Counselling in Action*, 3rd edition. London: Sage.

This is an excellent resource for many of the issues raised in this chapter.

Jenkins, P (2007) *Counselling, Psychotherapy and the Law*, 2nd edition. London: Sage.

This really is an essential read to ensure that you understand your legal responsibilities as a counsellor.

CHAPTER 7

Drawing the threads together

CORE KNOWLEDGE

- This chapter consolidates the previous six chapters and reiterates the key elements of the therapeutic relationship.

- Awareness of the relevance of core psychodynamic concepts such as holding and containment, and the application of the core conditions is reiterated.

- You are encouraged to develop a deeper understanding of the role of the therapist's own person in the relationship.

INTRODUCTION

In this, the final chapter, we bring together all of the various threads that have run through this book. In order to help do so we are going to consider a case study that looks at the different stages of the work between counsellor and client: from a client coming to counselling for the first time; to the middle part of the work where the relationship has shifted to a much deeper level; and then the third part of the work, which involves moving towards an ending. We will be thinking about how the ideas and concepts we have considered throughout this book might relate to this case. The main focus of our attention will be on the relationship between the two players in this drama: the counsellor and the client. We will be focusing on the therapeutic relationship.

Case study 7.1   Part 1

Graham is a 39-year-old graphic artist. He is doing well in his business, which he owns with a business partner. He has a wife, Cheryl, who he has been with for 16 years and they have two children. He would have said that they had quite a

---

solid relationship. However, a close friend tells him that Cheryl is having an affair with his business partner, Andy. Graham is absolutely devastated. He feels he has nowhere to go. He doesn't want to be at home with his wife and he doesn't want to go into work to be in the same office as his business partner. He is staying in the spare room of another friend. This friend recommends counselling and Graham contacts Bill, who agrees to see him.

Bill is 52 and has been a counsellor for several years. He works in private practice. When he receives the call from Graham, it is obvious that Graham is very upset. Bill gives Graham the first appointment that he has available. When Graham turns up he looks dreadful. Although he is neatly dressed and well-presented, he looks exhausted. Graham also seems very anxious about starting counselling. Bill takes his time and allows Graham to start the session. He very quickly spills out the situation in which he finds himself. Graham is quite surprised at how he is able to do this as he has never met Bill before. He even sheds a few tears. Bill just listens very respectfully. Although he is not saying much, it does seem that he is really listening, which Graham finds helpful and comforting. About half way through the first session, Graham has collected himself a little and comes to a natural pause. Bill then explains to Graham about counselling and about how they are going to work together. He explains about confidentiality, session times and regularity, payment, etc. He answers any questions that Graham has quite succinctly and then he asks Graham if he thinks he wants to proceed on that basis. Graham says he does, so they fix some appointments and Bill gives Graham a copy of the agreement they have made to take away with him.

In the first few sessions with Graham, the work goes slowly. Bill and Graham are establishing their relationship. Graham keeps asking Bill to tell him what to do. Bill resists telling him. Graham is under real pressure because he has some decisions to make. He can't stay at his friend's indefinitely and he is missing his children but at the same time he doesn't want to be with his wife at the moment. He is finding the situation at his office almost impossible. He wants Bill to help him by telling him what he should do. He feels he needs some advice and he feels quite angry with Bill for not giving him any. He doesn't have all the time in the world. As the weeks go by he is becoming quite discontented with the counselling because it doesn't seem to be getting him anywhere. He contemplates giving up. They are now three months into their relationship.

REFLECTION POINT

- How well do you think they are doing?
- Have they established the therapeutic relationship?
- What about Graham's discomfort?

COMMENT

This is the beginning of what turned out to be quite a long working relationship. Bill made a good start and, quite early on, conveyed to Graham that he is listening empathically. This has enabled the client to express his emotion somewhat, by crying. He also defined the therapeutic agreement/contract and made sure that Graham understood it and agreed to it. Bill is holding true to his ethical principle of autonomy by not telling Graham what to do, but Graham is finding this frustrating and is thinking of leaving, so what about beneficence (BACP's *Ethical Framework*)? Should we view this as a problem or is this just the therapy working? Graham is in the therapy because he has very pressing and immediate problems and he needs to take some action to sort them out. Is Bill addressing the value of increasing personal effectiveness here? Graham does seem to be very stuck both in his therapy and in his life. Something needs to happen to break the deadlock before they get to the point of alliance rupture.

Case study 7.1   Part 2

Graham comes to his session and, after giving him a few minutes to start the session, which he doesn't take, Bill decides to take the initiative himself, so he asks Graham how he is feeling about being here at his counselling today. Graham is rather unresponsive at first and then says he is wondering if there is any point in his coming as he is not getting out of it what he hoped for. Bill responds as follows:

> Graham, I can see that you are getting quite frustrated with me. You keep asking me to tell you what to do about your situation and I am not doing that for you. I do appreciate things are really tough for you right now and it seems as though you are feeling that the counselling is a waste of time too, but I do wonder if it would really be helpful for me to tell you what you should do in your life.

This intervention seems to break through something for Graham and he starts to express his anger with Bill openly. Bill receives it without either justifying himself or attempting to stop Graham in his flow. Eventually, Graham acknowledges that Bill can't tell him what he needs to do. He calms down. He tells Bill that he doesn't want to end his counselling, he just wants things in his life to change and it doesn't seem to be happening for him. Bill responds:

> I notice that when you were feeling angry and disappointed with me, your first thought was that you should leave here and that would have been one way to deal with it. But you have done it differently this time. You have told

me how you felt and I have heard what you have said and that you were angry and now we can move forward, but what about outside of here? What about your anger with Cheryl and Andy?

This proves to be quite an important intervention and Graham begins to share his difficulty in expressing anger and where that came from in his childhood. Their work moves on to another level. Over the next few months they work on several of Graham's issues, including his passivity and indirect aggression. He begins to understand what had happened in his relationship with Cheryl and is able to meet her and to discuss the arrangements for the children. He begins to understand how his policy of 'anything for an easy life' and his difficulty with confrontation has allowed Andy to manipulate him in their business together. He instigates the proceedings for winding up their business and begins thinking about the direction he wants to go in for himself. He is pleasantly surprised by the positive response he receives from clients and work colleagues alike.

During this period, despite the positive developments, Graham is often extremely low. His counselling is like an anchor for him in a stormy sea. Whatever is going on in his life outside, he knows that Bill will be there. He doesn't always find Bill's challenges easy, however. In fact, Bill could be quite tough, but he has learned that he can tell Bill how he feels even when these feelings were difficult and Bill would both hear and respond to him.

ACTIVITY 7.1

- From the standpoint of your own theoretical orientation, how do you think Bill is doing at building and maintaining the therapeutic relationship? Make a few notes and don't forget to reflect upon the *Ethical Framework* and the concepts therein.

COMMENT

So, progress appears to be being made. By fielding Graham's anger in the way that he did, Bill got the counselling relationship back on track. He showed Graham that he could survive Graham's anger and provide containment (Bion, 1970). Through his experience of his relationship with Bill, Graham was able to look at relationships both in the present and most importantly his part in where they were going wrong. He was also able to make meaningful connections with his past, the root of his present difficulties. This new awareness informed his behaviour and he was able to act differently with his wife, developing an important working relationship with her that enabled them to look after the best interests of their children.

Bill, by the provision of the core conditions (Rogers, 1957, 1986, 1990), and by his willingness to take risks with Graham and challenge him when it was appropriate, had facilitated Graham's breakthrough very effectively. Through Graham's dark times, Bill has provided the holding (Winnicott, 1965) that he needed, being a constant in Graham's life, thus enabling him to tolerate his own feelings, even when they are very difficult. Bill has demonstrated the moral qualities of empathy, resilience, competence and, indeed, courage in his approach to the work with Graham. His respect and his belief in Graham's autonomy do seem to be paying off.

Case study 7.1   Part 3

Months have now passed since Graham and Bill first began to work together and Graham has been very committed to the work. The initial shock of his wife's affair has diminished and he is gradually accepting his new life. He has his own house now, which although small, allows him to have the children to stay and he sees them frequently. His partnership with Andy is almost dissolved and he is successfully building his own business, focusing on aspects of the work that are particularly interesting to him. He finds he enjoys his own company on the evenings when he doesn't see his children. There are even times when he feels quite content. Although he is afraid to let go of his relationship with Bill, he feels that perhaps he could now go down to seeing Bill once a fortnight or even once a month. When he raises this with Bill, Graham is quite surprised that Bill does not agree. Once again he challenges Graham. Bill suggests that they work towards an ending. Graham looks at why he wants to hold on to Bill and gradually he has to admit it is just fear. He has noticed that in recent sessions they have not been working on such a deep level and the previous week, to his amazement, he had almost forgotten his appointment. Graham has to admit he no longer needs Bill. Over several weeks they bring their work to a close and there is a great warmth in their final handshake. Graham goes away to get on with the rest of his life.

REFLECTION POINT

- Has Bill handled this ending successfully?
- Should he have allowed Graham to go to once a fortnight or once a month?

COMMENT

Bill held to the principle of respecting the client's autonomy, even by being unwilling to go along with Graham's suggestion of fortnightly or monthly sessions. Bill's experience told him that Graham was ready to go and was now perfectly capable of managing on his own. To carry on seeing Graham only because Graham was afraid to let go would have been to exploit him. Graham had done the work he came to do and for which he and Bill had contracted. This is not to deny that there may well be whole layers of work yet to do, which at some point Graham might want to return to, but he has his new life to develop. By demonstrating his confidence in Graham, Bill is encouraging Graham to be confident in himself. Thinking back to the values that underpin counselling – alleviating personal distress and suffering, fostering a sense of self that is meaningful and increasing personal effectiveness – they would all be relevant here (BACP's *Ethical Framework*).

One thing that Bill does appear to be manifesting is therapeutic presence. There is something about the way Bill is with Graham that is tangible, but quite difficult to define – it is more than the sum of its parts. Graham's experience of being with Bill enables him to grow and develop as a person. Their relationship provides him with the model of how relationships can be: honest, lively, sometimes difficult but always constant and always dynamic. Bill seems able to bring the best out of Graham, enabling him to be more of the kind of person he wants to be and can be. Bill doesn't rescue Graham, doesn't make it all better. He doesn't get him his wife back or mend his relationship with Andy, but he does enable Graham to think about his options and choices, to make the best for himself out of the circumstances. Most importantly, Graham has learned that he can tolerate and survive his own feelings.

'TO THINE OWN SELF BE TRUE'

There is a story about Carl Rogers, which I have heard repeated many times, although it may well be apocryphal. It relates to the naming of the therapeutic approach he pioneered as client-centred/person-centred in the UK. Some of his followers wanted it to be called Rogerian therapy, in the mode of Freudian or Jungian therapy. Rogers is reported to have said that that would make its dissemination and practice very limited as only he himself and any other therapists who happened to share his surname could rightfully describe themselves as Rogerian therapists. I like to think the story is true, because the point it makes is crucial, which is that, whatever orientation you begin with, ultimately you will develop your own unique and particular way of approaching the role of therapist. I say this, of course, from an entirely Greenian perspective!

One of the great lessons I have learned from my years of experience as a supervisor is that, in almost all cases, there are many possible ways of approaching the work of any client. It is like finding yourself in the middle of a dark wood and trying to make your way out. There may be several different paths; some are much more easy and straightforward, some may land you in the thicket, or take you round in circles, but there are several possible ways of getting out of the wood and into the sunshine.

When working with a supervisee, listening to them describe their work with a client, I am sometimes amazed at something that appears obvious to me that they have missed, only to find that if I bide my time, before jumping in with my doubtlessly brilliant observation, there is something really obvious to my supervisee that I have completely missed. They haven't gone down the path that I would have chosen, but they are undoubtedly finding their way through the wood. I find this idea really fascinating, that within the context of the client's material, counselling could go in any number of ways, depending on the personality of the counsellor and what in the material of the client seems important and pertinent to them. It is the relationship and the resonance between the two players in the therapeutic alliance that is crucial.

Students in training will usually try very hard to immerse themselves in whatever particular theory they are learning, do things by the book, apply those particular skills, use the language of the orientation and view the aetiology of the client's distress through that particular lens. Sometimes, to the amusement of their tutors, they can become quite anxious and cross if they are presented with another possible perspective. It is as if they are hanging on to their orientation like a life raft in a stormy sea. They experience tutors putting forward other possible perspectives as somehow shaking them loose from that raft and setting them adrift. There is nothing wrong with this at that point in a counsellor's development. I think it is very important to have a solid grounding in a particular orientation and to develop a philosophy that informs your thinking as a counsellor. However, this is just the starting point and it would be a great shame if you did not expand and allow in new ideas and concepts, though you do so with discernment. Theory is not the received word of God, it is just a set of ideas.

Boundaries are there to serve the work and they do so really effectively. They have been developed out of collective wisdom and out of counsellors' bitter experience. However, sometimes, for sound therapeutic reasons, you need to take a risk and break or at least stretch them somewhat. I am not giving licence for a flagrant abandonment of this important aspect of the therapeutic relationship and I think it is crucial to talk through any such decisions with your supervisor; it is just an acknowledgement that sometimes a human response is more appropriate than slavish adherence to a set of rules. Of course, you take any such risks in the knowledge that you may be called to account for them.

Case study 7.2   Walking with counsellors

Some years ago I had a young client in her mid-teens who came to therapy with me because she had witnessed the violent death of her father. She had completely clammed up about her experience, which had utterly traumatised her. She was functioning reasonably well on a practical level, but emotionally she was absolutely frozen. I had some experience of working with such trauma and also in counselling young people, so the referrer thought I might be able to help this client.

The sessions did not initially go well; in fact, the process could have been described as analogous with pulling teeth. It was not doing either of us any good, particularly her, although she didn't seem to mind coming and we had struck up some kind of a relationship. On one occasion, just as she was leaving, one of my dogs escaped from the kitchen and ran down the hall to greet her. She responded to him with more enthusiasm and energy than I had ever seen from her, and she fussed and cuddled him. The next time she came for her appointment, after about ten minutes of the 'tooth pulling' I could take no more. I had something of a brainstorm and found myself suggesting that she might like to come with me on a dog walk. We began to do this each time she came, even when it was raining. Somehow, freed from the confines of the counselling room and walking beside me rather than sitting opposite me, she began to talk about her dreadful experience. On one occasion, we ended up sitting on a park bench, oblivious to people passing by, with her really crying and she was able to take comfort from my old dog, a third partner in our therapeutic relationship, who was leaning against her legs with his head on her knee. She did remark that she felt sure he could be trusted not to break confidentiality. After some weeks of these walks, we did manage to get back into the counselling room and the work continued in a more conventional manner. My willingness to take this risky course of action and follow my instinct did pay off on this occasion, though some may have judged it to be inadvisable.

REFLECTION POINT

- What do you think of my decision here? What could have gone wrong?
- Can you identify occasions in your own counselling work where you have gone with your instinct and perhaps come up against a boundary?
- What have you learned from this experience?

Becoming an adequate, competent counsellor requires a great deal of work, dedication, training and commitment to ethical practice and a healthy dose of experience. To become a really good, or even an inspiring practitioner requires much more. It is about knowing yourself, your weaknesses and strengths, being true to yourself and allowing the client to really experience you because you are open and available to be experienced. I think our clients get to know us on a very deep level, if we allow it. They may not know what kind of music we like or how many brothers and sisters we have or any of the other biographical details and information about us, but if the therapeutic relationship is really working, they know us on a heart level. They know they can trust us and that we will honour them in their vulnerability. Such is the depth and breadth of the therapeutic relationship.

Coming from an arts background myself, I do acknowledge my bias, but I am convinced that counselling is an art. You can teach all the techniques, provide all the theory, but just as you can't make someone into a Shakespeare, Mozart or Van Gogh, neither can you create a brilliant counsellor. It is about their own talent and how they internalise and work with what they have learned to create something beautiful and unique. It is something about the person's spirit that shines through to which the other person in the therapeutic relationship, the client, is able to connect. It is this deep and profound connection that facilitates the work of counselling and it is this that we describe as the therapeutic relationship.

CHAPTER SUMMARY

In this final chapter we have used a three-stage case study – beginning, middle and end – to integrate many of the aspects of the therapeutic relationship described in this book. In particular we have focused on:

- therapeutic presence and how this enables the work of the client;
- how the elements of the ethical framework underpin the therapeutic relationship;
- developing your own style of counselling;
- counselling as an art.

SUGGESTED FURTHER READING

Rowan, J and Jacobs, M (2007) *The Therapist's Use of Self*. Buckingham: Open University Press.

Wosket, V (2003) *The Therapeutic Use of Self*. Hove: Routledge.

References

Baldwin, M (2000) *The Use of Self in Therapy* (2nd edition). New York: Haworth Press.

Barrett-Lennard, GT (1998) *Carl Rogers' Helping System: Journey and Substance.* Sage: London.

Beauchamp, TL and Childress, JF (1979) *Principles of Biomedical Ethics.* Oxford: Oxford University Press.

Bion, WR (1970) *Attention and Interpretation.* London: Tavistock.

Bion, WR (1990) *Brazilian Lectures.* London: Karnac.

Bloomfield, I (1989) Through therapy to self, in Dryden, W and Spurling, L (eds) *On Becoming a Psychotherapist.* London: Routledge.

Bond, T (2010) *Standards and Ethics for Counselling in Action* (3rd edition). London: Sage.

Bond, T and Mitchels, B (2008) *Confidentiality and Record Keeping in Counselling and Psychotherapy.* London: Sage.

Bond, T and Sandhu, A (2005) *Therapist in Court: Providing Evidence and Supporting Witnesses.* London: Sage.

Bozarth, JD (1998) *Person-Centred Therapy: A Revolutionary Paradigm.* Ross-on-Wye: PCCS Books.

British Association for Counselling and Psychotherapy (BACP) (2010) *Ethical Framework for Good Practice in Counselling and Psychotherapy* (revised edition). Lutterworth: BACP.

British Medical Association Ethics Department (BMAED) (2004) *Medical Ethics Today: The BMA Handbook of Ethics and the Law.* London: BMA.

Chaplin, J (1989) Rhythm and blues, in Dryden, W and Spurling, L (eds) (1989) *On Becoming a Psychotherapist.* London: Routledge.

Child Poverty Action Group (CPAG) (2004) *Health and Poverty.* London: CPAG.

Claringbull, N (2010) *What is Counselling & Psychotherapy?* Exeter: Learning Matters.

Cooper, M (2008) *Essential Research Findings in Counselling and Psychotherapy.* London: Sage.

Craig, PE (1986) Sanctuary and presence: An existential view of the therapist's contribution. *The Humanistic Psychologist,* 14: 22–8.

Daines, B, Gask, L and Howe, A (2007) *Medical and Psychiatric Issues for Counsellors* (2nd edition). London: Sage.

Davies, D and Neal, C (2003) *Pink Therapy.* Buckingham: Open University Press.

Dryden, W, Horton, I and Mearns, D (1995) *Issues in Professional Counsellor Training.* London: Cassell.

Durkheim, E (1979) *Suicide: A Study in Sociology.* New York: Free Press.

Guggenbuhl-Craig, A (1971) *Power in the Helping Professions.* Dallas, TX: Spring Publications.

Hart, T (1999) The refinement of empathy. *Journal of Humanistic Psychology.* 39(4): 111–25.

Hawkins, P and Shohet, R (1990) *Supervision in the Helping Professions.* Buckingham: Open University Press.

Henry, WP, Schacht, TE and Strupp, HH (1990) Patient and therapist introject, interpersonal process and differential psychotherapy outcomes. *Journal of Consulting and Clinical Psychology,* 58(6): 768–74.

Hill, CE and Knox, BJ (2002) Self-disclosure, in Norcross, JC (ed) *Psychotherapy Relationships that Work: Therapists' Contributions and Responsiveness to Patients.* New York: Oxford University Press.

Isaac, M (2006) Psychodynamic counselling in class, in Wheeler, S (ed) (2006) *Difference and Diversity in Counselling: Contemporary Psychodynamic Perspectives.* Basingstoke: Palgrave Macmillan.

Jacobs, M (2004) *Psychodynamic Counselling in Action* (3rd edition). London: Sage.

Jenkins, P (2007) *Counselling and Psychotherapy and the Law* (2nd edition). London: Sage.

Johns, H (1996) *Personal Development in Counsellor Training.* London: Cassell.

Kahn, M (1997) *Between Therapist and Client: The New Relationship.* New York: Freeman.

Lago, C (2006) *Race, Culture and Counselling* (2nd edition). Maidenhead: Open University Press.

Leiper, R and Maltby, M (2004) *The Psychodynamic Approach to Therapeutic Change.* London: Sage.

Lietaer, G (2002) The united colours of person-centred and experiential psychotherapies. *Person-Centred and Experiential Psychotherapies,* 1(1&2): 4–13.

Mair, D (2006) Psychodynamic counselling and sexual orientation, in Wheeler, S (ed) (2006) *Difference and Diversity in Counselling: Contemporary Psychodynamic Perspectives.* Basingstoke: Palgrave Macmillan.

McLeod, J (2003) *An Introduction to Counselling* (3rd edition). Buckingham: Open University Press.

McLeod, J (2006) Relational depth from the point of view of the client. Working at Relational Depth Conference, Glasgow, University of Strathclyde.

McLoughlin, B (2005) *Developing Psychodynamic Counselling.* London: Sage.

Mearns D (1994) *Developing Person-Centred Counselling.* London: Sage.

Mearns, D (1996) Working at relational depth in person-centred therapy. *Counselling* 7(4): 306–11.

Mearns, D (1997) *Person-Centred Training.* London: Sage.

Mearns, D and Cooper, M (2005) *Working at Relational Depth in Counselling and Psychotherapy.* London: Sage.

Mearns, D and Thorne, B (1988) *Person-Centred Counselling in Action.* London: Sage.

Mearns, D and Thorne, B (2000) *Person-Centred Therapy Today.* London: Sage.

Parkes, CM and Wertheimer, A (2001) *A Special Scar: The Experience of People Bereaved by Suicide.* Hove: Routledge.

Purton, C (1998) Unconditional positive regard and its spiritual implications, in Thorne, B and Lambers, E (eds) (1998) *Person-Centred Therapy: A European Perspective.* London: Sage.

Rippere, V and Williams, R (eds) *(1985) Wounded Healers: Mental Health Workers' Experiences of Depression.* New York: Wiley.

Rogers, CR (1957) The necessary and sufficient conditions of therapeutic personality change. *Journal of Consulting Psychology,* 21(2): 95–103.

Rogers, CR (1961) *On Becoming a Person: A Therapist's View of Psychotherapy.* Boston: Houghton Mifflin.

Rogers, CR (1980) *A Way of Being.* Boston: Houghton Mifflin.

Rogers, CR (1986) Client centered therapy, in Kutash, IL and Wolf, A (eds) *Psychotherapist's Casebook: Therapy and Technique in Practice,* pp197–208. San Fransisco, CA: Jossey-Bass.

Rogers, CR (1990) *Client Centered Therapy.* London: Constable.

Rowan, J and Jacobs, M (2007) *The Therapist's Use of Self.* Buckingham: Open University Press.

Russell, J and Dexter, G (2008) *Blank Minds and Sticky Moments in Counselling* (2nd edition). London: Sage.

Shohet, R (2008) *Passionate Supervision.* London: Jessica Kingsley.

Spurling, L (2004) *An Introduction to Psychodynamic Counselling.* Basingstoke: Palgrave Macmillan.

Thorne, B (1992) *Carl Rogers.* London: Sage.

Tuckwell, G (2006) Psychodynamic counselling: Race and culture, in Wheeler, S (ed) (2006) *Difference and Diversity in Counselling.* Basingstoke: Palgrave Macmillan.

Watson, JC, Goldman, R and Vanaerschot, G (1998) Empathic: A post modern way of being?, in Greenberg, LS, Watson, JC and Lietaer, G (eds) (1998) *Handbook of Experiential Psychotherapy.* New York: Guilford Press.

Wheeler, S (1999) Can counselling be a profession? A historic perspective for understanding counselling in the new millennium. *Counselling,* 10(5): 381–6.

Wheeler, S and King, D (2001) *Supervising Counsellors: Issues of Responsibility.* London: Sage.

Wilkins, P (2000) Unconditional positive regard reconsidered. *British Journal of Guidance and Counselling,* 28(1): 23–36.

Winnicott, DW (1965) *The Maturation Process and the Facilitating Environment: Studies in the Theory of Emotional Development.* London: Hogarth Press.

Worsley, R (2002) *Process Work in Person Centred Therapy: Phenomenological and Existential Perspectives.* Basingstoke: Palgrave.

Wosket, V (2008) *The Therapeutic Use of Self.* London: Routledge.

Index

A
abusers 89–91
acceptance of clients 11–12
agape 84–5
agreements *see* therapeutic
     agreements/contracts
alliance ruptures 95–7
appointments, missed 22–3
autonomy 60–2

B
BACP *see* British Association for
     Counselling and Psychotherapy
being, way of 10–14
beneficence 62–3
Bion, Wilfred 8
Bond, Tim 24, 60–1
boundaries 124–5
British Association for Counselling and
     Psychotherapy (BACP) 2, 21, 36, 56–7,
     83, 107–9
British Medical Association Ethics
     Department (BMAED) 20–1
burn-out 114–17

C
cancellations 22–3
caring 51–2
charges 21–2, 22–3
Christian Counselling Movement 50
class differences 31–2
clients
     acceptance of 11–12
     dependency 23
     perceptions of 16–19
     role of 14
     see also clients, problems with; diversity,
         clients
clients, problems with
     alliance ruptures 95–7
     disliking clients 85–91
     erotic transference 82–5
     mental health issues 91–5
     suicidal clients 47–8, 76–82
competence 45, 63–4
complaints 96
     reporting malpractice 64
confidentiality 24–5, 41, 60
     duty to warn 64
     records 113
congruence 10, 12

consent 19–20, 62
consultative supervision 104–5
containment 8, 11
continuing professional development
     (CPD) 109–10
contracts *see* therapeutic
     agreements/contracts
Cooper, Mick 32–3, 102, 109, 111
core conditions, therapy 10
     congruence 12
     empathy 10–11, 37–8, 85
     unconditional positive regard
         11–12
costs of sessions 21–2, 22–3
counselling rooms 5–6
courage 47–9
CPD *see* continuing professional
     development
cultural diversity 27, 59

D
Daines, Brian 65
Data Protection Act (1998) 114
Davies, Dominic 29
dependency 23
Dexter, Graham 48
diversity, clients 26–8, 32–3, 59
     class 31–2
     and power balance 31
     sexual 28–31, 50
'door handle' comments 6–7
duty to warn 64

E
emotional space 8–9
emotions, dealing with 42, 116
empathy 10–11, 37–8, 85
employee assistance programmes
     (EAPs) 32
equality, access to services 45–6, 59,
     64–5
erotic transference 82–5
*Ethical Framework for Good Practice
     in Counselling and Psychotherapy*,
     BACP 2, 21, 36, 56–7, 83
ethical principles
     autonomy 60–2
     beneficence 62–3
     dilemmas concerning 66–73
     fidelity 60
     justice 64–5

non-maleficence 63–4
   self-respect 65–6
ethics and values 55–7
   common values 57–60
   disliking clients 85–91

F
fairness 45–6, 59
   justice 64–5
fidelity 60
fitness to practise 63–4

G
gay affirmative therapy 29
gender orientation 28–31, 50
group supervision 105

H
heterosexuality 28–9
holding 8
homosexuality 29–31, 50
humility 44
humour 51

I
inequality, access to services 45–6, 59,
   64–5
integrity 39–42

J
Jenkins, Peter 21, 24
justice 64–5

L
love *see* erotic transference

M
Mair, David 29
malpractice 63–4
McFarland, Gary 50
McLeod, John 51
Mearns, Dave 11, 12, 38, 111
mental health issues 91–5
'moaning' 106–7
morals *see* personal qualities,
   counsellors
Muran, Chris 95

N
Neal, Charles 29
networking 105–7
neurotic clients 93
non-maleficence 63–4

O
open-mindedness 50
organisations, professional 107–9

P
patience 52–3
peer support 105–7
perceptions, client/counsellor 16–19

person-centred approach 10–14
personal qualities, counsellors 35–6,
   49–53, 71–2
   competence 45, 63–4
   empathy 10–11, 37–8, 85
   fairness and wisdom 45–7
   resilience and courage 42, 47–9
   respect and humility 43–4
   sincerity and integrity 39–42
   see also ethical principles; ethics and
     values
personal therapy 100–2
physical space 5–6
Pink Therapy 29
positivity 52
power balance, client/counsellor 40
   and autonomy 60–2
   and diversity 31
prejudices *see* diversity, clients
professional organisations 107–9
psychotic clients 92–3

R
record keeping 113–14
regulation, statutory 108
relational depth 111
resilience 42
respect 43
risk, managing 47–9
Rogers, Carl 10–12, 38, 96–7, 123
Russell, Janice 48

S
Safran, Jeremy 95
self-acceptance 12
self-awareness 102
self-care 99–100
   burn-out 114–17
   CPD 109–10
   networking 105–7
   personal therapy 100–2
   professional organisations 107–9
   record keeping 113–14
   supervision 103–5
   work/life balance 110–12
self-determination 60–2
self-involving statements 87–91
self-respect 65–6
sense of self 58
sessions
   costs 21–2, 22–3
   duration/frequency 6–8, 22, 23–4
settings 5–6
sexual attraction, client/counsellor 82–5
sexual diversity 28–31, 50
sincerity 39
social class differences 31–2
Spurling, Laurence 6, 8
statutory regulation 108
stress, dealing with 116
suicidal clients 47–8, 76–82
supervision 24, 41, 103–5, 123–4

T
team working, mental health 92–3
temporal space 6–8
theory 124
therapeutic agreements/contracts 19–21,
    25
  confidentiality 24–5
  session costs/duration/frequency
    21–4
therapeutic frame 5–9
therapeutic presence 10, 123
therapeutic relationship 4, 118–26
  core conditions 10–14
  emotional space 8–9
  physical space 5–6
  role of the client 14
  temporal space 6–8
Thorne, Brian 11, 12, 38

time constraints, sessions 6–8, 22
transference, erotic 82–5
trust 60

U
unconditional positive regard 10, 11–12

V
values *see* ethics and values
violence 89–91

W
way of being 10–14
Winnicott, Donald 8
wisdom 46–7
work/life balance 110–12
World Health Organisation (WHO) 92
Wosket, Val 88, 102, 110, 111–12